D0313463

THE ROUGH GUIDE TO

The Cotswolds

This second edition written and researched by

Matthew Teller

C333769774

Contents

Introduction to
The Cotswolds

The Cotswold hills are special. Thatched cottages, dry-stone walls and, above all, the mellow, honey-coloured stone used in the area's buildings lend a unique warmth and unity of character to towns, villages and countryside. Sheep graze in the shadow of country churches, backwater hamlets slumber in the sunshine – catch the Cotswolds in the right place, at the right time, and you could almost imagine nothing's changed here in hundreds of years.

Except, of course, it has. Despite the appearance of natural tranquillity, this landscape, tilted gently from Oxfordshire's low-lying meadows up to the dramatic "**Cotswold Edge**", an escarpment overlooking the Severn and Vale of Evesham, has been intensively managed for centuries. Caught in the heartland of southern England, forming a rough quadrilateral between Oxford, Stratford-upon-Avon, Cheltenham and Bath, the Cotswolds first grew wealthy on the back of the **wool** trade: the local breed of sheep, sporting a distinctive shaggy mane, is known as the "**Cotswold Lion**".

By the early seventeenth century textile money was rolling in, and the Cotswolds were benefiting from the attentions of wealthy merchants. The landscape is still characterized by the grand "**wool churches**" they funded and the manor houses and almshouses they put up in the **Jacobean** style of the day – high gables, mullioned windows, tall chimney clusters and all, everything built using that rich-toned **yellow Cotswold limestone**.

COT'S WOLDS?

"**Wolds**" – an Old English word referring to rolling uplands – are not unique to the Cotswolds: both Lincolnshire and Yorkshire have their own. The origin of "**cot**" is trickier to pin down. Some say it has to do with a Saxon farmer named Cot or Cod, who settled near the source of the River Windrush. An alternative derivation is from the Old English term "cot", cognate with "cottage", meaning a simple rural dwelling: perhaps the Cotswolds were named for the stone shelters built on the wolds by Anglo-Saxon farmers for themselves and/or their sheep? Nobody really knows.

ABOVE DAYLESFORD ORGANIC FARM; ST MARY'S CHURCH, FAIRFORD **OPPOSITE** OXFORD CANAL

The second phase of prosperity has come in our own time. Twentieth-century **tourism** – alongside an equally significant rise in **property prices**, as wealthy outsiders seek to buy into the Cotswolds' cliché of rural timelessness – has changed everything. Victorian designer William Morris was perhaps the first, taking country ways as the inspiration for his **Arts and Crafts** ideals. Today, of the 120,000 people living within the protected Cotswolds **Area of Outstanding Natural Beauty**, 73 percent commute to jobs outside. For the first time, it has become uneconomic for many to farm. The **heritage industry** has taken over, ruthlessly marketing the region with an over-reliance on twee imagery and funnelling visitors onto a tired old circuit of stately homes and gardens, tearooms and "visitor attractions".

As a consequence there's a fair amount of **money** sloshing around the Cotswolds' economy, feeding a burgeoning **service sector** but also helping to keep **traditional skills** such as thatching and dry-stone walling alive.

This is a touristy destination, but there is a very definite beaten track and it's not hard to steer clear of the crowds. Construct a visit not just around stately homes, but also around **farmers' markets**. Rather than towns, resolve to stay in **villages**: some of the Cotswolds' loveliest places to stay – and best restaurants – are out in the countryside. Tour by car if you like, but options exist for slower, more interesting ways to travel: by **bus**, **bike** and **on foot**. That's what this book is all about – an attempt to dodge the predictable and help visitors reshape their experience of this most distinctive of rural regions.

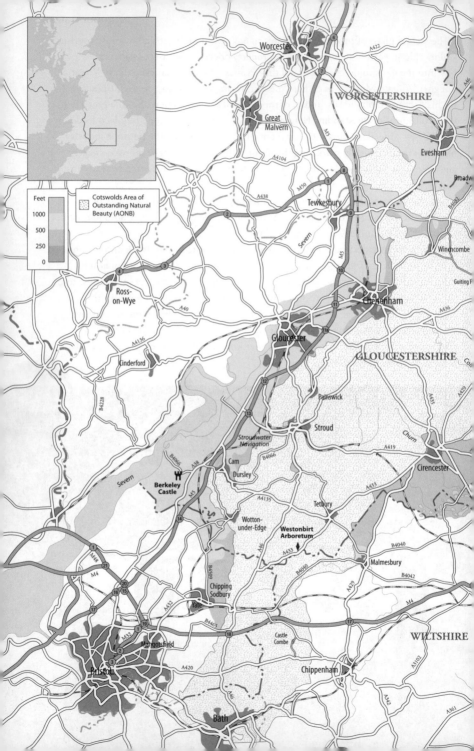

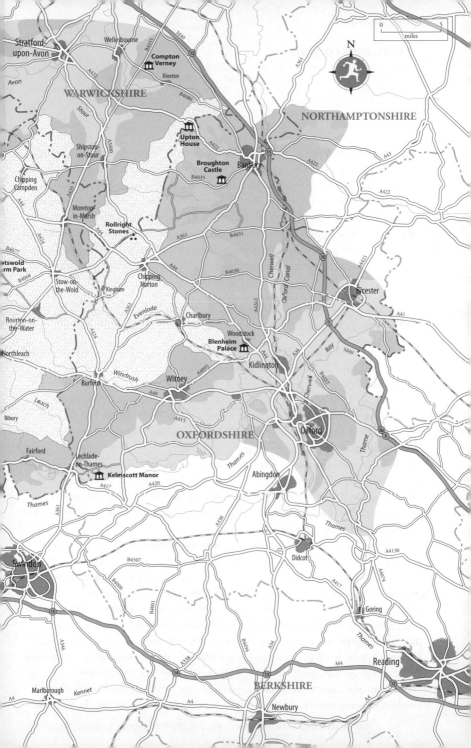

CELEB-FREE COTSWOLDS

From Damien Hirst to Jeremy Clarkson, Liz Hurley to Laurence Llewelyn-Bowen, Kate Winslet to Lily Allen – to name just six – celebrities galore call the Cotswolds home (or second, third or fourth home). Elton John pops by, Dom Joly lives here, Kate Moss has a mansion – and then of course there's Prince Charles at Highgrove and Princess Anne at Gatcombe… we could go on. But we don't. That's the last you'll hear of them.

Seasonality is key, expressed strongly in **food**. From the Stroud-Tetbury-Cirencester triangle all the way over to Woodstock, the last few years have seen an axis of excellence developing across the Cotswolds in terms of restaurants, food producers and markets. Raising the bar benefits consumers, through innovative cooking and exemplary standards in service and design, but also creates chances for home-grown talent both in and out of the kitchen to gain high-level experience locally. Producers fuel the increased demand with high-quality seasonal ingredients, from lamb to wild boar and beer to asparagus – often also sold direct on market squares region-wide. Food is making the Cotswolds famous all over again.

Where to go

Where the Cotswolds start and end is a matter of personal opinion: there are no formally agreed boundaries. This book sets its own limits. We include **Oxford** – with an extraordinary history and atmosphere, it's worth a few days of anyone's time. With minor exceptions, we do not venture further east than Oxford, nor further west than the cathedral city of **Gloucester**. In the south we stick to the River Thames and then dip down to the M4, stopping short of **Bath**. The northern limit is Shakespeare's home town of **Stratford-upon-Avon**.

In the heart of the Cotswolds, three of the most visited destinations lie within twenty miles of each other: **Burford** has a classically attractive sloping main street of old stone houses, **Bourton-on-the-Water** is a picturesque riverside village and **Broadway** forms a photogenic cluster of ex-coaching inns. All are pretty, but none is wholly satisfying – not least because everybody goes there.

The region's single most attractive town is **Chipping Campden**, a beguiling mix of golden Jacobean facades, fascinating history and thriving community spirit. Classic Cotswold landscapes abound in the villages nearby, including **Ebrington**, **Blockley** and **Stanton**, along with superb gardens at **Hidcote**, **Kiftsgate** and **Batsford**, great walking on the **Cotswold Way** and excursions to stately homes including **Snowshill** and **Stanway**.

Just to the east, past **Moreton-in-Marsh** and **Stow-on-the-Wold**, stretch the gentle **Oxfordshire Cotswolds**, anchored by the royal town of **Woodstock** (alongside splendid **Blenheim Palace**) but best experienced in the villages – notably **Kingham** and **Charlbury**.

To the west, the Cotswolds have turned Gloucestershire into "Poshtershire": **Cheltenham** and **Cirencester** are pleasant enough, but perhaps a touch over-reliant on well-heeled locals; **Tetbury**, though similar, is smaller and better-looking. Instead, seek

NAMES TO CONJURE WITH

Although the region covered by this book takes in villages such as Pancakehill, Knockdown, Little Rollright and Old Sodbury, that isn't the half of it. On our travels in (and just beyond) this compact bit of countryside, we've put together a dozen **place names** to conjure with, all no doubt with eminently meaningful derivations – but all, still, truly outlandish. Savour each one with pride: this is England.

- Marsh Gibbon
- Slad
- Goosey
- Toot Baldon
- Broughton Poggs
- Wyre Piddle
- Cold Aston
- Kingston Bagpuize
- Waterley Bottom
- Lower Slaughter
- Poffley End
- Bishop's Itchington

out lesser-known rural spots: evocative **Painswick** is on the beaten track – but **Minchinhampton**, **Nailsworth** and other hideaways in the deep **Stroud** valleys aren't. **Winchcombe** is a lovely spot, high on the hills for great walks and also on the doorstep of magnificent **Sudeley Castle**.

Wherever you go, don't think towns and A-roads – think villages and B-roads. The best of the Cotswolds fills the gaps on the map.

When to go

It's no surprise that **summer** is the busiest time in the Cotswolds – and a lovely time of year to visit – but visiting out of peak season can offer great rewards. **Autumn** encompasses the grandeur of leaf-fall colours: the Cotswolds' two big arboretums, at Westonbirt and Batsford, are obvious draws, but following footpaths or back roads through wooded dells is free-of-charge.

Winter is a wonderful time to explore – and not only because hotels and B&Bs drop their prices. If you thought all that Cotswold stone looked good in summer sun, wait till you see what it looks like on a clear winter's afternoon, with low, golden light pouring from blue skies, frost on the trees and your breath in the air. When you know there's a blazing log fire waiting for you at "home" – not to mention at just about every pub along the way – togging up to roam in the chill becomes an adventure. And from late January or so, **snowdrops** in their thousands adorn gardens all over the Cotswolds.

Thanks to the topography, you can even skip between seasons. Autumn can come a month early to gardens located up on the Cotswold Edge, compared with places down below: drift among late-summer flowers in Cheltenham, then shuffle through fallen leaves in Misarden, six miles away as the crow flies, but almost a thousand feet up.

Author picks

Over more than ten years living, working and travelling in and around this beautiful region, our Cotswolds author Matthew Teller has built up a welter of favourite places. He shares some here:

Captivating villages There are dozens: in the west try Painswick (p.55), in the south Castle Combe (p.75) and Bibury (p.90), in the east aim for Burford (p.156) or Great Tew (p.172), but the top dog is in the north: for all-round beauty and atmosphere, don't miss Chipping Campden (p.112).

Stately homes Blenheim Palace (p.177) is the grandest of them all – or you could take in the astonishing time-warp qualities of Chastleton House (p.172), highly idiosyncratic Snowshill (p.125) or gloriously photogenic Broughton Castle (p.194).

The Arts & Crafts Movement Cheltenham's Wilson gallery (p.45), the Gordon Russell Museum in Broadway (p.120) and Court Barn Museum in Chipping Campden (p.113) all have splendid collections, while Kelmscott Manor wonderfully evokes the life of the great William Morris and his circle (p.161).

Country churches Plenty of scope for making your own discoveries, but seek out in particular the bedazzling complete set of medieval stained glass at Fairford (p.88) and the ancient Duntisbourne Rouse (p.85), standing in entrancing isolation.

Quirky museums Two that stand out for sheer eccentricity are the Pitt Rivers Museum in Oxford (p.230) – all totem poles and shrunken heads – and the rather newer kinetic sculptures of the aptly named MAD Museum in Stratford-upon-Avon (p.141).

Formal gardens The Cotswolds is chock-full of gardens – and also chock-full of people enjoying them. For the space to breathe, explore Kiftsgate Court (p.119) and the grounds of unsung Rousham House (p.197).

Farmers' markets As much about atmosphere as commerce, with Stroud (p.60) on an impressive scale, Cirencester (p.78) unswervingly posh, and Stratford-upon-Avon (p.136) supremely down-to-earth.

> Our author recommendations don't end here. We've flagged up our favourite places – a perfectly sited hotel, an atmospheric café, a special restaurant – throughout the guide, highlighted with the ★ symbol.

16

things not to miss

It's not possible to see everything that the Cotswolds have to offer in one trip – and we don't suggest you try. What follows is a selective and subjective taste of the region's highlights: places to visit, top attractions and hidden gems. They're arranged in five colour-coded categories to help you find the very best things to see, do and experience. All entries have a page reference to take you straight into the guide, where you can find out more. Coloured numbers refer to chapters in the Guide section.

1

1 BLENHEIM PALACE
Page 177
Simply one of Britain's greatest stately homes, offering a memorable day out exploring the interiors and then roaming the park-like grounds.

2 KELMSCOTT MANOR
Page 161
This superbly preserved country house by the Thames was the home of William Morris, founder of the nineteenth-century Arts and Crafts movement.

3 LOWER SLAUGHTER
Page 97
One of the Cotswolds' most pleasing villages – popular, but not as relentlessly commercial as some of its neighbours.

4 CHELTENHAM
Page 42
The gateway town for the western Cotswolds, Cheltenham combines Georgian architecture with design hotels and buzzing lounge bars.

5 TETBURY
Page 65

Often claimed as the Cotswolds' most royal village – with the estates of Prince Charles and Princess Anne on the doorstep – Tetbury is dominated by the spire of St Mary's, with its breathtaking Georgian Gothic interior.

6 STROUD FARMERS' MARKET
Page 60

Farmers' markets dot the Cotswolds but the oldest – and still one of the best – is the weekly event at Stroud.

7 STRATFORD-UPON-AVON
Page 136

Shakespeare's home town – but dodge the heritage hype in favour of a good meal and some world-class theatre.

8 GLOUCESTER CATHEDRAL
Page 51

Rambling, absorbing old cathedral with perhaps England's finest cloisters.

9 WESTONBIRT ARBORETUM
Page 68

Sensational gardens near Tetbury filled with colour at any season – but especially vibrant in autumn, when the colours and rural atmosphere never fail to wow.

10 OXFORD
Page 202

Packed with atmosphere, amid stunning medieval architecture, Oxford entices with history and a cheerful student atmosphere.

5

6

7

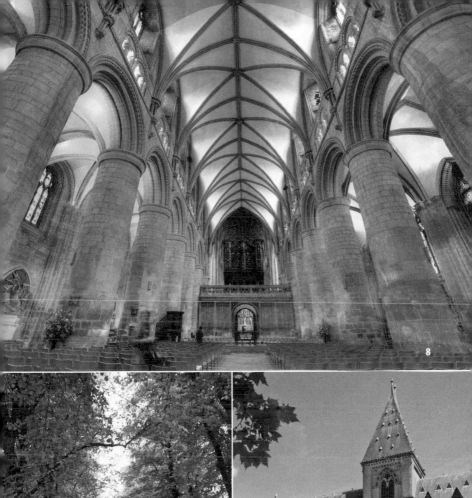

8

9

10

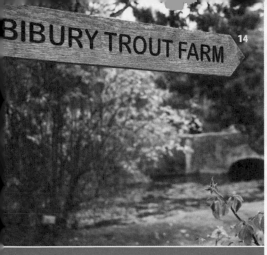

14

15

16

Itineraries

The Cotswolds isn't only about touring: many people choose one or other of the villages and then base themselves there to explore locally. But if you fancy mixing things up – and if you have your own transport: train and bus links aren't great – there's nothing to stop you taking in the whole region at a single bite.

CASTLES & COUNTRY HOUSES

❶ Berkeley Castle Craggy medieval castle near the River Severn, full of history and ghosts. See p.71

❷ Sudeley Castle Royal palace that is especially famed for its sixteenth-century associations with Henry VIII and Katherine Parr. See p.130

❸ Stanway House Jacobean mansion, in buttery Cotswold stone, that boasts the world's tallest gravity fountain. See p.126

❹ Broadway Tower This eye-catching folly tops one of the highest of the Cotswolds' hills, offering spectacular views. See p.124

❺ Sezincote House Unusual country house near Moreton-in-Marsh that sports a unique Indian-style exterior, complete with onion dome. See p.105

❻ Chastleton House Charming Jacobean pile that has been left largely untouched inside, still with original sooty fireplaces and dusty ladders. See p.172

❼ Blenheim Palace One of England's most palatial stately homes, birthplace of Winston Churchill, crammed with historical and artistic treasures. See p.177

❽ Oxford Castle Take a tour of the stone towers that survived the Civil War, as costumed jailers tell stories of hauntings. See p.228

❾ Sulgrave Manor An intriguing find, in the Banbury countryside – this well-presented country house was built by the ancestors of George Washington, first president of the United States. See p.192

❿ Broughton Castle Bewitchingly romantic country house that has starred in numerous costume dramas over the years, from *Shakespeare in Love* to Morecambe and Wise. See p.194

FOODIE HIGHLIGHTS

❶ Cheltenham Foodie hub for the Cotswolds, with markets and some of the region's leading restaurants. See p.42

❷ Stroud This small town impresses for the range and quality of its organic local produce, showcased weekly in one of England's top farmers' markets. See p.60

❸ Nailsworth A small, hard-to-reach village that takes local food seriously: cafés and restaurants abound. See p.64

❹ Tetbury One of the Cotswolds' poshest villages, with a range and quality of food – in delis and restaurants alike – that far outstrips expectation. See p.65

❺ Cirencester A key centre for Cotswolds food, with a great market and dozens of places to eat in the old lanes off the market square. See p.78

ABOVE BLENHEIM PALACE; DISPLAYS AT BROUGHTON CASTLE

❻ Lower Slaughter For rural dining amid the luscious Cotswolds countryside, this tiny village obliges with a fistful of upmarket country-house hotels and restaurants. **See p.97**

❼ Kingham Titchy backwater on the Oxfordshire-Gloucestershire border with world-class food at a handful of famous-name gastropubs and farm shops. **See p.169**

❽ Hook Norton This thirst-quenching stop offers England's finest surviving example of a Victorian tower brewery – and pubs galore at which to sample the village-brewed beers. **See p.195**

❾ Woodstock Picture-perfect Oxfordshire village that clusters an array of notable restaurants and gastropubs around a photogenic three-street historic core. **See p.173**

❿ Oxford Covered Market Atmospheric, aromatic hideaway in the city centre, with old-fashioned butchers, bakers and cheesemongers setting out their wares each morning. **See p.222**

SECRET COTSWOLDS

❶ Minchinhampton Tiny, breezy village high up above Stroud, perfect for windblown walking. **See p.63**

❷ Sheepscombe Traditional village down in the Stroud valleys, rewarding to explore and with a fine pub to boot. **See p.57**

❸ Duntisbourne Rouse Search hard to find this almost completely hidden medieval church near Cirencester. **See p.85**

❹ Chedworth Roman Villa The ruins of this large, late-Roman country house hide in the woods near Northleach. **See p.92**

❺ Coberley It takes perseverance to find the silent church in this hidden village – but your reward is a superb fourteenth-century knight's tomb. **See p.50**

❻ Belas Knap A Neolithic "long barrow" burial mound, which occupies one of the highest and wildest points in the Cotswolds. **See p.131**

❼ Hailes Abbey Seek out the ruins of this great Cistercian monastery near Winchcombe. **See p.126**

❽ Compton Verney This splendid Warwickshire country house now holds a captivating rural art gallery. **See p.148**

❾ Rollright Stones A scattering of megalithic monuments in the silent fields outside Chipping Norton. **See p.173**

❿ Minster Lovell Hugely evocative ruins of a medieval country house, hidden away in this hard-to-spot village by the River Windrush. **See p.164**

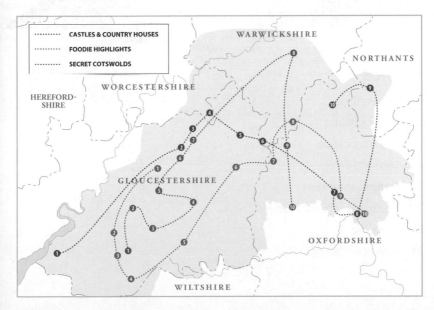

GLOUCESTERSHIRE WARWICKSHIRE STEAM RAILWAY

Basics

Getting there

The Cotswolds lie midway between London, Bristol and Birmingham. Internationally, it's easy to fly into Heathrow or Birmingham airport and pick up direct transfers by road or rail. Domestic rail and motorway links are excellent.

From around the UK

By **car**, the **M4** skirts the southern edge of the Cotswolds – junction 17 is useful for Tetbury, junction 15 for Lechlade and Cirencester. If you're approaching from the west/southwest, come off the **M5** at junction 13 for Stroud, junction 11 for Cheltenham and Northleach, or junction 9 to pick up routes to Chipping Campden and Stow-on-the-Wold.

Otherwise, aim for the **M40**. The Oxford exits (junction 8 from the south, junction 9 from the north) both serve the A40 heading west to Witney, and the A44 heading northwest to Chipping Norton and Moreton-in-Marsh. For Oxford itself, use the city's park-and-ride scheme (see p.232). Further north on the M40, leave at junction 11 for Banbury and junction 15 for Stratford-upon-Avon.

If you're coming from the south coast, avoid London by aiming for Winchester: from there (M3 junction 9), join the quick and convenient **A34** dual carriageway (signed Newbury) which cuts north directly to Oxford.

From the north, choose the **M6/M5** for Cheltenham and the western Cotswolds, or the **M6/M42** for Stratford and the northern Cotswolds. Alternatively, stay on the **M1** down to junction 15A (Northampton) to pick up the fast, easy **A43** dual carriageway towards Oxford.

By train

From London the main operator is First Great Western (FGW). Trains from Paddington go to Oxford (55min), with some continuing towards Worcester on the Cotswold Line, serving village stations including Charlbury, Kingham and Moreton-in-Marsh. Other FGW trains from Paddington go to Cheltenham Spa (2hr 15min), stopping midway at Kemble (for Cirencester and Tetbury) and Stroud. Otherwise, consider Chiltern Railways trains from London Marylebone to Oxford, Banbury (55min) and Stratford-upon-Avon (2hr).

From southern England Cross Country has trains to Oxford from Bournemouth, Southampton, Winchester and Basingstoke. Each of those has links from around Surrey and Sussex, or you could aim instead to join Cross Country or FGW trains at Reading – which has connections from Redhill, Guildford and Clapham Junction. **From the southwest** a separate Cross Country route runs from Plymouth and Exeter to Cheltenham.

From the north, opt for Cross Country trains from Manchester, Stoke, Derby, Sheffield, Leeds, York, Newcastle and Edinburgh direct to Banbury, Oxford or Cheltenham. They're slower than mainline Virgin services, but you can sit tight all the way without having to change at Birmingham New Street.

For information on routes, timetables and fares contact **National Rail Enquiries** (☎0845 748 4950, ⓦnationalrail.co.uk).

By coach

There are two specific routes where **coaches** beat the train. The first is to Oxford **from Central London** (1hr 40min) – the UK's highest-frequency service, with more than 150 coaches a day in each direction: Oxford Tube (☎01865 772250, ⓦoxford tube.com) and #X90 (☎01865 785400, ⓦX90 .oxfordbus.co.uk) operate day and night from Victoria, Marble Arch and elsewhere, with departures every ten minutes at peak times. Both offer luxury seating, free wi-fi and other commuter perks. An open return (valid 3 months) costs £20.

The other is the **east-west route** to Oxford, notoriously difficult to do by train (until the East-West line opens in 2017/18). The #X5 coach (☎01604 676060, ⓦwww.stagecoachX5.com) runs half-hourly to Oxford from Cambridge (3hr 35min), Bedford (2hr 15min) and Milton Keynes railway station (1hr 20min). An open return from Cambridge (valid 3 months) is £20.

Otherwise coaches are much slower than trains. **National Express** (☎0871 781 8178, ⓦnational express.com) has direct links to Oxford, Gloucester, Cheltenham, Banbury and Stratford – as well as, usefully, Cirencester, which has no train service – from, for example, central London, the south coast (Torquay, Portsmouth and others), and the north (Glasgow, Newcastle, Liverpool, Leeds and others). Their sole attraction is price: booking ahead could net you a "FunFare" on certain routes from around £5.

Megabus (☎0900 160 0900, ⓦmegabus.com) has even cheaper fares. If you can accept their restrictions about only boarding specific coaches at specific points, and always booking in advance, you could pay as little as £1.50 from London to Cheltenham; London, the south coast, Leeds, Manchester or Newcastle to Oxford; or on the #X5.

INTERNATIONAL ARRIVALS: AIRPORT LINKS

London Heathrow (LHR) ⓦ heathrowairport.com.
London Gatwick (LGW) ⓦ gatwickairport.com.
London Stansted (STN) ⓦ stanstedairport.com.
London Luton (LTN) ⓦ www.london-luton.co.uk.
Birmingham (BHX) ⓦ bhx.co.uk.
Bristol (BRS) ⓦ bristolairport.co.uk.
East Midlands (EMA) ⓦ eastmidlandsairport.com.
Oxford (OXF) ⓦ oxfordairport.co.uk.

FROM LONDON HEATHROW

From Heathrow you don't need to head into London: the best connections are by **bus** (or, to use the more common term for long-distance bus services, "**coach**"). Oxford Bus runs frequent Airline coaches (ⓦ theairline.info) from Heathrow nonstop to Oxford (1hr 20min) for £29 return. National Express (ⓦ nationalexpress.com) has coaches from Heathrow direct to Banbury (1hr 10min), Cirencester (1hr 25min) and Cheltenham (1hr 55min). The Witney Shuttle minibus (☎ 0800 043 4633, ⓦ witneyshuttle.com) runs several times a day from Heathrow to Witney, Stow-on-the-Wold, Bourton-on-the-Water and nearby villages; advance booking essential. Otherwise, there's a choice of trains from Heathrow to London Paddington: Heathrow Express (ⓦ heathrowexpress.com) is fast but very expensive (£34 return), Heathrow Connect (ⓦ heathrowconnect.com) is slightly slower (£20 return). Change at Paddington for trains to Cheltenham, Oxford or Cotswold villages.

FROM LONDON GATWICK

From Gatwick, the "Airline" **coach** (ⓦ theairline.info) heads nonstop to Oxford (2hr 30min) for £37 return, or book ahead for the Witney Shuttle minibus (☎ 0800 043 4633, ⓦ witneyshuttle.com). By **train** go from Gatwick to Reading (1hr 15min) and change there for Oxford, Banbury, Cotswold villages, Kemble, Stroud or Cheltenham.

FROM OTHER AIRPORTS

From **Birmingham airport** station (known as Birmingham International) Cross Country trains go direct to Banbury (40min) and Oxford (1hr), or take any train to Birmingham New Street (10min) and change there for Cross Country trains to Cheltenham (40min). From **Stansted airport** take a National Express coach to Oxford (3hr 5min); from **Luton airport** do the same (1hr 45min). From **Bristol airport** take the "Flyer" bus (£7; 30min) – either to Bristol bus station for a National Express coach to Cheltenham (1hr) and Stratford-upon-Avon (2hr 35min), or to Bristol Temple Meads station for a train to Cheltenham (40min). From **East Midlands airport** take the "Skylink" bus to Derby station (£4.20; 35min), from where Cross Country trains serve Banbury (1hr 25min), Oxford (1hr 45min) and Cheltenham (1hr 25min). **Oxford airport** is covered separately (see p.231).

From the US and Canada

From the US take your pick of dozens of scheduled and charter flights into London from New York, Washington DC, Boston, Chicago, Atlanta, Miami, Las Vegas, San Francisco, Los Angeles, and other cities. Return fares from New York start around US$500–700, from Los Angeles around US$700–900.

From Canada, look for nonstop routings from mainly Toronto, Montréal, Calgary and Vancouver, with return fares roughly covering the range C$600–900.

As well as checking for deals on the usual airlines, look for low fares on unusual carriers. Norwegian, for instance, flies between Oakland and London at bargain rates, as does Kuwait Airways out of Kennedy.

From Australia & NZ

Routes **from Australia and New Zealand** to London are highly competitive, with return fares out of Sydney, Melbourne or Perth usually A$1500–2500, or NZ$2000–3000 out of Auckland. Check out the obvious carriers first, such as Qantas, British Airways and Air NZ – but then explore options on, for instance, Emirates, Etihad or Qatar via the Gulf, or take a low-cost hop on a budget airline to, say, Bangkok or Singapore from where you can pick up super-cheap deals on scheduled carriers to London.

From Europe

For **flights** the best advice is to check the website of your preferred arrival airport, to find out who flies there from your country.

Trains serve London St Pancras from Lille (1hr 20min), Paris (2hr 15min) and Brussels (2hr). Eurostar (W eurostar.com) sells tickets for journeys from certain stations in western Europe (see website for list) to any UK station; otherwise consult a rail agent in your country.

By **ferry** Portsmouth is the Cotswolds' nearest Channel port, 86 miles from Oxford – served from ports in France and Spain by DFDS (W dfdsseaways .com) and Brittany Ferries (W brittanyferries.com).

Getting around

Although trains and buses are fine for moving between towns, and for accessing specific points in the country- side, public transport in the Cotswolds just isn't good enough to do any serious touring. To cover decent ground you'll need your own wheels – four or, perhaps, two. Back roads are invariably quiet and beautifully scenic, but main roads in summer can get busy with holiday traffic. Visitors from outside the UK should be prepared for high rental and fuel costs.

For public transport, two information sources are key. For trains, **National Rail Enquiries** (T 0845 748 4950, W nationalrail.co.uk) is the fount of all knowledge, if not wisdom, while the impartial official service **Traveline** (T 0871 200 2233, W traveline.info) has full details and timetable information for every bus, train, coach and ferry route in the UK.

Much more convenient is the **timetable booklet** *Explore the Cotswolds by Public Transport*, published by the Cotswolds Area of Outstanding Natural Beauty (W escapetothecotswolds.org.uk), covering trains and buses across the region. It is available free at tourist offices, and downloadable from the website.

By train

Train lines mostly skirt the edges of the Cotswolds, serving larger towns such as Oxford, Banbury, Stratford, Gloucester and Cheltenham.

The **Cotswold Line** – part of the London– Worcester main line, run by First Great Western – has approximately hourly trains serving a string of villages between Oxford and Evesham including

Charlbury, Kingham and Moreton-in-Marsh. This is supplemented by the Cotswold Line Railbus service (W railbus.co.uk), which has buses coordinated to meet arriving trains at Charlbury and Kingham to shuttle passengers to/from nearby rural areas. Most routes are for commuters, operating in peak hours only and/or requiring advance booking, but the handy #X8 bus to Chipping Norton runs all day from Kingham station, with through-ticketing possible. The website has details.

First Great Western trains from London to Cheltenham cut across country after Swindon, following the **Golden Valley Line** to Kemble – well placed for Cirencester and Tetbury – and Stroud. FGW also runs a few stopping trains on the **Oxford Canal Line** between Oxford and Banbury, accessing canalside scenery and country walks around Tackley, Heyford and King's Sutton villages.

For bridging the last few miles from the station to your final destination check **Traintaxi** (W traintaxi .co.uk), a useful database of local cab numbers for every railway station in the country.

RAIL CONTACTS IN THE UK

Chiltern Railways T 0845 600 5165, W chilternrailways.co.uk. Banbury, Oxford and Stratford-upon-Avon to London.

Cross Country T 0844 811 0124, W crosscountrytrains.co.uk Cheltenham, Oxford and Banbury to Birmingham, Bristol and Reading.

First Great Western T 0345 700 0125, W firstgreatwestern .co.uk. Cheltenham, Stroud, Kemble, Moreton-in-Marsh, Kingham and Oxford to London.

National Rail Enquiries T 0845 748 4950, W nationalrail.co.uk. The official source for UK train information, with timetables, maps, links for purchasing and more.

Seat 61 W seat61.com. Top resource for all rail travel, including a detailed section on travelling around Britain, with plenty of information, tips and links.

RAIL CONTACTS WORLDWIDE

BritRail US & Canada T 1 866 938 RAIL, W britrail.net.

Rail Europe US T 1 800 622 8600, Canada T 1 800 361 RAIL; W raileurope.com.

Rail Plus Australia T 03 9642 8644, W railplus.com.au; New Zealand T 09 377 5415, W railplus.co.nz.

By bus

Public transport in the Cotswolds mostly means **buses**. Services are run by dozens of companies, some national enterprises, others tiny local firms. You don't really need to know which is which – we've identified bus numbers, routes and options at each relevant point throughout this book. For **timetable** info check Traveline (T 0871 200 2233,

TRANSPORT PASSES

COTSWOLD DISCOVERER

The **Cotswold Discoverer** (one day £10/three days £25) brings unlimited travel by bus and train on a host of routes – check the restrictions carefully online (ⓦescapetothecotswolds.org .uk/discoverer) or on the widely available leaflet: it doesn't cover journeys to Woodstock or Banbury, for instance.

RAIL PASSES

Check ⓦrailcard.co.uk for details of the **16-25 Railcard**, **Senior Railcard**, **Two Together Railcard** and **Family & Friends Railcard**, which bring good discounts on train travel nationwide. Many other options exist to cut the cost of rail travel. If you're in a group of three or four adults, ask about **GroupSave**, whereby you can travel together off-peak for the price of two adults (with up to four children paying only £1 each).

First Great Western offer the **Cotswold Line Railcard** (£7.50), giving discounts for a year's off-peak travel between Oxford and Worcester, and the **Oxfordshire Day Ranger** (£15.50), giving unlimited off-peak travel between Reading, Oxford, Banbury and Moreton-in-Marsh. Chiltern Railways have the **Shakespeare Explorer** (one day £35/four days £50), valid from London for trips to and around Stratford-upon-Avon.

BUS PASSES

Each bus operator issues its own **tickets and passes**, which makes for a horribly confusing patchwork of options. The soundest advice is to have a chat with tourist office staff: they'll know what's best for your particular travel plans. Apart from local one-day tickets, worthwhile passes covering larger areas include the **Stagecoach West** MegaRider Gold (£20/week) for bus travel around Oxford, Cirencester, Cheltenham, Stroud and Gloucester. **Stagecoach Oxfordshire** offer a MegaRider Gold (£25/week), valid across their network, and a MegaRider Country (£16/week), which covers Oxfordshire villages excluding Oxford and Banbury. **Stagecoach Warwickshire** also has its own MegaRider Gold (£23/week), valid on buses between Oxford, Chipping Norton, Banbury and Stratford, plus local villages. Full details are at ⓦstagecoachbus.com.

PLUSBUS

Plusbus (ⓦplusbus.info) is a discounted bus pass which you buy at the same time as a train ticket. It allows unlimited bus travel for one day, seven days or longer in and around selected rail hub towns, including Cheltenham, Gloucester, Stroud, Banbury and Oxford. Prices are invariably lower than an equivalent bus pass bought on the spot from local operators. Children under 16 and railcard holders get further discounts.

ⓦtraveline.info) or the booklet published by the Cotswolds Area of Outstanding Natural Beauty (described above).

Beware: many villages, including relatively well-known places such as Broadway or Winchcombe, have very limited bus service – perhaps only two or three a day, often with none on Sundays,– while others have no buses at all. Some prominent attractions, such as the Cotswold Farm Park, are inaccessible on public transport.

By car or motorbike

The easiest and, for most people, best way to tour the Cotswolds is by **car**. Scenic drives abound: tourist offices like to tout specific routes but, in truth, just about any road between Cheltenham, Stratford and Oxford sooner or later offers up picturesque honeystone villages and gentle views over rolling fields. Some of the loveliest driving can be on ordinary back routes between untouristed villages.

Traffic on some main roads such as the A40 and A429 can be heavy over the summer – especially bad at weekends – and cars are being firmly given the squeeze in the town centres across the region, most notably central Oxford. That said, back roads are invariably quiet.

Parking in villages is rarely a problem, but in towns and popular tourist spots it can be limited – and often expensive. If you're driving to Oxford, Stratford, Gloucester, Cheltenham or Bath for the day (or longer), you'd do best with **park-and-ride** (ⓦparkandride.net), whereby you park at signposted car parks on the outskirts and take

ACCOMMODATION **BASICS** | 25

a cheap bus to the centre. Expect to pay roughly £2–5, depending on the location – there are often discounts for families and groups of two or more adults – and you rarely have to wait longer than ten minutes for a bus.

Car rental is usually cheaper arranged in advance through one of the global chains. If you rent locally, expect to pay around £30 per day, £50 for a weekend or from £120 per week. Book well in advance for the cheapest rates. Few companies will rent to drivers with less than one year's experience and most will only rent to people between 21 and 75 years of age. Cotswold Campers (☎01386 423009, ⓦcotswoldcampers.co.uk) and Comfy Campers (☎01242 681199, ⓦcomfycampers.co.uk) rent well-equipped retro VW **campervans** sleeping up to four people for self-drive adventures, for about £400–£700 a week, with cheaper weekend-only deals. Just Go (☎01582 842888, ⓦwww.justgo.uk.com) rents modern **motorhomes** for up to seven people for £300–1000 per week.

Cycling

Although the Cotswolds is renowned for its rolling hills, don't let that put you off **cycling** as a viable method of getting about. The A-roads can be a bit busy, but the quieter B-roads and country lanes see little traffic, and are boosted by a network of rural cycleways (see p.33). Specialist tour operators also offer cycling holidays (see p.33).

Accommodation

Accommodation in the Cotswolds ranges from roadside lodges to old-fashioned country retreats, and from budget guesthouses to chic boutique hotels. Well-turned out properties in towns and villages alike offer heaps of historic atmosphere.

Nearly all tourist offices will **book rooms** for you on request (by email, phone or in person), generally charging a booking fee of about £3–5, as well as taking a non-refundable deposit – usually ten percent – that is later deducted from your final bill. Official tourism websites ⓦcotswolds.com and ⓦwww.oxfordshirecotswolds.org offer online booking, and are often the best places to start a search, whether you're looking for a hotel, B&B, cottage or campsite. Other good sites to explore include ⓦcotswoldsconcierge.co.uk and ⓦcotswolds.info.

SECRET COTSWOLDS

Are there any secrets left in the Cotswolds? This is perhaps one of England's most visited rural regions: summer weekends see the classic Cotswold destinations – Chipping Campden, Bibury, the Slaughters, Castle Combe – and the three Bs in particular (Burford, Broadway and Bourton-on-the-Water) crammed with holidaymakers. But it's also a big place, and there are plenty of hideaways. The best of the Cotswolds is often to be found in the unvisited villages and on the nameless back roads.

5 SECRET VILLAGES

Ebrington Thatched cottages, a lovely pub – and Chipping Campden on the doorstep. See p.118.
Minchinhampton Quiet, handsome village up on the wild slopes above Stroud. See p.63.
Minster Lovell Cotswold charm aplenty in this romantic hideaway. See p.164.
Sheepscombe Beautiful walks and a great pub, hidden in a steep-sided valley. See p.57.
Stanton A historic village sporting classic good looks. See p.126.

5 SECRET B-ROADS

B4014 Tetbury to Nailsworth: scenic initially, then narrowing for a hairpin journey through deep, dark forest.
B4022 Witney to Charlbury: a beautiful drive over the tops from the Windrush to the Evenlode.
B4035 Banbury to Chipping Campden: airy views, interesting villages and a lovely climb to Campden.
B4066 Stroud to Uley: memorably scenic ridge-top drive with views to the Severn.
B4632 Broadway to Cheltenham: a gentle canter beneath forested slopes, then climbing through hilly Winchcombe.

Two bodies inspect accommodation nationwide and award star ratings: Quality in Tourism, acting for VisitEngland (**ⓦ**visitengland.com), and the AA (Automobile Association; **ⓦ**theaa.com). They both use the same criteria to grade properties from one to five stars. Rated properties will have a sticker or signboard displaying the star rating – either a blue sign with VisitEngland's red rose logo or a yellow and black sign with the AA logo.

However, the star-ratings are only a guide: bear in mind that there is no absolute correlation between rating and price – and official listings of rated accommodation may exclude otherwise excellent places which have either been left unrated, or which are awaiting inspection.

Hotels

Hotel prices in the Cotswolds start at around £50 per night for a simple double/twin room, breakfast included. Two- and three-star hotels can cost £90–110 a night, while four-and five-star properties may start at £150–180 or more. Character comes in spades: places at all budgets may occupy historic properties, often in Cotswold honey-coloured limestone, bedecked with ivy and/or sporting floral window boxes, offering classic views of village or countryside scenes.

Despite the Cotswolds' conservative reputation, don't imagine that chintzy drapes and fusty interiors prevail: lots of competition and a constant flow of visitors keep standards high, and you can expect good attention to detail across the board on interior styling, bathroom accessories and high-tech features such as flat-screen TVs and wi-fi. At the top end, besides the traditional country estates you might expect, the Cotswolds can also offer world-class boutique hotels, replete with contemporary styling and a sense of artful chic.

BUDGET HOTEL CHAINS

All the following budget chains have hotels in the region covered by this book, generally located on the outskirts of larger towns and/or beside main roads. They're fairly characterless places – but special advance offers can bring en-suite room rates down to an unbeatable £20–30.

Holiday Inn Express ⓦhiexpress.com
Ibis ⓦibishotel.com
Premier Inn ⓦpremierinn.com
Travelodge ⓦtravelodge.co.uk

Cotswolds Finest Hotels (ⓦcotswoldsfinest hotels.com) is a grouping that includes some of the region's best luxury properties. **Cotswold Inns and Hotels** (ⓦcotswold-inns-hotels.co.uk) draws together a handful of attractive but less stratospherically priced options.

B&Bs and guest houses

At its most basic, a **B&B** (bed-and-breakfast) is an ordinary private house with a couple of bedrooms set aside for paying guests. Larger establishments with more rooms may style themselves **guest-houses**, but they are pretty much the same thing. Either way, these can be a great option for travellers looking for charm and a local experience: the best – with fresh, house-proud rooms, hearty home-cooked food and a wealth of local knowledge – can match or beat a hotel stay at any price.

In countryside locations some of the best accommodation is found in farmhouses, while many village **pubs** (termed "**inns**" in listings) offer B&B. You may also come across the self-explanatory concept of a "**restaurant with rooms**".

Single travellers should be aware that many B&Bs and guest houses don't have single rooms, and sole occupancy of a double/twin room may be charged at seventy or eighty percent of the standard rate.

Tourist offices across the region list B&Bs, inns and the rest as part of their accommodation listings, and offer a booking service as described above. Nationwide schemes also cover properties within the Cotswolds area, including the following:

Distinctly Different ☎ 01225 866842, **ⓦ** distinctlydifferent .co.uk. Unusual buildings converted into accommodation, including an Oxfordshire dovecote and an old windmill near Bath.

Farm Stay UK ☎ 024 7669 6909, **ⓦ** farmstay.co.uk. The UK's largest network of farm-based accommodation.

Sawdays UK ☎ 0117 204 7810, **ⓦ** sawdays.co.uk. A wide range of B&B and self-catering accommodation across the Cotswolds.

Wolsey Lodges ☎ 01473 822058, **ⓦ** wolseylodges.com. Superior B&B in inspected properties, from Elizabethan manor houses to Victorian rectories.

Self-catering

Cotswold **self-catering** accommodation runs the gamut from purpose-designed new builds to historic, converted barns or **cottages**. The minimum rental period is usually a week: depending on the season, expect to pay around £250 a week for a small cottage in an out-of-the-way location, maybe three or four times that for a larger property in a popular spot. We've listed some agencies below; tourist boards also keep full details of self-catering rentals in their area.

ACCOMMODATION PRICES IN THIS GUIDE

Throughout this guide, hotel and B&B accommodation prices have been quoted based on the lowest price you would expect to pay per night in that establishment for a **double room in high season**, but not absolute peak rates (such as at certain bank holidays). For backpacker hostels we've listed the cheapest price of a **dorm bed**, plus the price for any double or twin rooms. **Campsite** prices are generally listed per pitch based on two people in one tent. **Single occupancy** rates vary widely. Though typically around three-quarters of the price of a double, some places charge almost the full double rate and others charge only a little over half that.

Almost everywhere will offer **discounts** for multiple-night stays and many places drop their rates considerably (or offer special deals) outside the late May to early September summer season.

Broadway Manor Cottages ☎ 01386 852913, ⓦ broadway manor.co.uk. Highly rated enterprise in Broadway, with a fistful of awards, that offers several good options.

Campden Cottages ☎ 01386 852462, ⓦ campdencottages.co.uk. Local agency in Chipping Campden with a good choice of properties.

Cottage in the Country ☎ 01608 646833, ⓦ cottageinthecountry .co.uk. Another local firm, based in Chipping Norton, offering cottages and holiday self-catering throughout the Cotswolds.

Cottages Direct ☎ 0845 260 0947, ⓦ cottagesdirect.com. Massive choice of properties, offering direct booking.

Cottages4You ☎ 0845 268 0760, ⓦ cottages4you.co.uk. Wide range of graded properties all over the Cotswolds.

Country Accom ⓦ countryaccom.co.uk. A grouping of local self-catering (and B&B) properties, dubbing themselves "Oxfordshire and Cotswolds Farm and Country House Accommodation".

HomeAway ☎ 020 8827 1971, ⓦ homeaway.co.uk. Hundreds of Cotswold properties, from luxury apartments in central Oxford to thatched countryside cottages.

Landmark Trust ☎ 01628 825925, ⓦ landmarktrust.org.uk. A preservation charity handling historic properties converted into holiday accommodation, including Jacobean banqueting halls in Chipping Campden.

Manor Cottages ☎ 01993 824252, ⓦ manorcottages.co.uk. Based in Burford, offering a broad choice of holiday cottages and houses across the Cotswolds.

National Trust ☎ 0844 335 1287, ⓦ nationaltrustcottages.co.uk. The NT owns more than 350 cottages, houses and farmhouses, most set in their own gardens or grounds.

Rural Retreats ☎ 01386 701177, ⓦ ruralretreats.co.uk. Upmarket accommodation, often in restored historic buildings. Especially strong on the Cotswolds.

Sawdays UK ☎ 0117 204 7810, ⓦ sawdays.co.uk. A wide range of both B&B and self-catering accommodation across the Cotswolds.

Sykes Cottages ☎ 01244 356666, ⓦ sykescottages.co.uk. Dozens of options throughout the Cotswolds.

Hostels and student halls

The **Youth Hostel Association** (YHA; ☎ 01629 592700, ⓦ yha.org.uk) has four properties in the area covered by this book, in Oxford, Stratford, Slimbridge and Stow-on-the-Wold; the last is the only hostel within the Cotswolds proper. Depending on the season, expect to pay around £15–25 for a bed, with some private twin/double and family rooms available. Meals – breakfast, packed lunch or dinner – are good value (around £5). The YHA is affiliated to the global Hostelling International network (ⓦ hihostels.com).

In Oxford, two **independent backpacker hostels** add a bit of choice and **student halls** can offer great value, generally in single rooms or self-catering apartments over the summer (July–Sept), plus at Easter and Christmas.

Camping

Campsites vary from rustic, family-run places to large sites with laundries, shops and sports facilities: charges can be from about £5 per adult up to around £20 per tent. Many sites also offer accommodation in permanent **caravans**, mostly large, fully equipped units. Check ⓦ campingandcaravanningclub.co.uk – and take a look at ⓦ ukcampsite.co.uk and ⓦ theaa.com for listings and reviews. **Farmers** and friendly **pub owners** may offer pitches for a nominal fee, but setting up a tent without asking first will not be well received.

Food and drink

The Cotswolds is foodie heaven. Changing tastes have transformed England's food and drink over the last decade, and few regions of the country have embraced this food revolution with more enthusiasm. Wherever you go, you'll find restaurants serving fresh, seasonal, locally sourced food that is also often organic or ethically produced, along with farm shops, farmers' markets, independent specialist delis and food shops galore. At a time when the old rural ways have changed forever, food has become the clearest, most resonant way to celebrate Cotswolds culture.

There's little doubt that the area's proximity to London has had an impact: second-home-owners, who bring big-city expectations with them, are one factor – but transport links are also key. Urban foodies can finish work, take the train from Paddington for fine dining in the sticks at (for instance) the critically acclaimed *Kingham Plough* – and still be back in central London before midnight. Critical mass is another issue: there are now enough Cotswold restaurants seeking high-quality ingredients that it has become viable for – to take one example – Cornish suppliers to make frequent, even daily, deliveries of fresh-caught fish and seafood, thereby fuelling a spiral of supply and demand which raises standards across the board.

Memorable, often award-winning, food is just as common nowadays in Cotswold village pubs as in the poshest of Oxford's or Cheltenham's formal restaurants. Sourcing quality products from local farmers, showcasing seasonal cooking – often with creative takes on traditional recipes – and taking pride in presentation and service have become articles of faith wherever you go.

FOOD AND DRINK FESTIVALS

BITE (Chipping Campden) February ⓦ www.thebite.co.

British Asparagus Festival (Evesham) April–June ⓦ british asparagusfestival.org.

Fairford & Lechlade Food & Drink Festival May ⓦ fairfordlechladefoodanddrink.co.uk.

Stratford Food Festival May ⓦ stratfordfoodfestival.co.uk.

Cheltenham Food & Drink Festival June ⓦ garden-events.com.

Foodies Festival (Oxford) August ⓦ foodiesfestival.com.

The Big Feastival (Kingham) August ⓦ jamieoliver.com /thebigfeastival.

Stroud Food & Drink Festival September ⓦ soglos.com.

Tetbury Food & Drink Festival September ⓦ tetburyfooddrink festival.com.

Useful websites

One way to keep pace with local foodie news is to follow chef James Benson's blog **The Cotswold Food Year** (ⓦ www.thecotswoldfoodyear.com): Benson's company was formerly based in Broadway, and his site is packed with anecdotes and local knowledge as well as recipe ideas.

For unique insight into local food culture, make contact with Rob Rees, "**The Cotswold Chef**" (ⓦ thecotswoldchef.com), who offers bespoke, upmarket food tours and runs a Food Centre in Cirencester, hosting cooking courses and showcasing the work of local producers. Many of the region's most acclaimed restaurants feature at

Cotswolds Finest Hotels (ⓦ cotswoldsfinesthotels .com). Foodie events sites, such as **BITE** (ⓦ thebite .co) and **The Cotswold Table** (ⓦ thecotswoldtable .co.uk), often include handy lists of local partners and food producers.

Markets and farm shops

Many towns around the region have a **market** at least once a week – often a commercialized affair for bric-a-brac and cheap bananas (ⓦ country -markets.co.uk has nationwide listings) – though lots of places also host weekly, fortnightly or monthly **farmers' markets**, where local food producers sell home-grown goods direct to the public: see ⓦ localfoods.org.uk for details. We've highlighted farmers' markets at relevant points throughout this book: they are often worth making a special journey for, and the best (such as Stroud, Deddington or Stratford) define their communities. Oxford's Covered Market – a permanent feature, open daily – is another draw, hosting butchers, bakers, fishmongers, cheese sellers and more.

You'll find similarly authentic local items in **farm shops**, often marked with a rudimentary sign propped by the side of rural roads. Don't be shy of turning off and following a bumpy track onto what may look like private farm property – the best of these farm shops are a revelation, selling country essentials and hard-to-find specialist products to those in the know. Take a look, for instance, at ⓦ thebuttsfarmshop.com, a highly regarded farm shop near Cirencester, or contrast sophisticated Daylesford (ⓦ daylesford.com/kingham) near Kingham with down-to-earth Wykham Park (ⓦ wykhampark.co.uk) outside Banbury. There are dozens more; we've highlighted special ones throughout this book, and ⓦ localfoods.org.uk pinpoints those that are members of the industry association FARMA.

Cotswolds specialities

Predominantly an agricultural area, the Cotswolds is crammed with local culinary specialities. Farms across the region produce **organic** fruit, veg and herbs, as well as **ethically farmed meat**, including the likes of Cotswold Beef (ⓦ cotswoldbeef.com), Love My Cow (ⓦ lovemycow.com) and Macaroni Farm (ⓦ macaronifarm.co.uk). Old Spot is a traditional Gloucestershire breed of pig which makes its way onto many menus, and the Real Boar Company (ⓦ therealboar.co.uk) is one of England's few producers of charcuterie, making home-reared and home-produced salami and chorizo from boar ethically farmed on the Cotswold fringes. Bibury, near Cirencester, and Donnington, near Stow, both host trout farms, while Upton Smokery (Ⓦupton smokery.co.uk), outside Burford, produces a range of smoked fish and game, most of it local: they also sell fresh seasonal game. Birdlip's Potted Game Company (Ⓦwww.pottedgame.com) does what it says on the tin. R-Oil (Ⓦr-oil.co.uk) and Cotswold Gold (Ⓦcotswoldgold.co.uk) produce cold-pressed extra virgin rapeseed oil as an alternative to imported olive oil.

Cheese

The Cotswolds excels in cheese – more than a hundred varieties are produced across the region, often on small family farms. Crudges, near Kingham, is one acclaimed artisan producer, sourcing their milk from a local Jersey herd; for others, see Ⓦspecialistcheesemakers.co.uk and keep an eye on Ⓦthecheeseweb.com, run by Oxfordshire-based expert Juliet Harbutt. Crudges also works with their Kingham neighbour Alex James (Ⓦalexjames presents.co.uk), a celebrity cheesemaker and former rock musician known for his mild Blue Monday and soft goat's cheese Farleigh Wallop.

The area's most famous cheese is double Gloucester, now produced nationwide. Its crumblier cousin single Gloucester is much rarer, made only from Gloucester cattle milked in Gloucestershire; the few producers include Ⓦsmartsgloucestercheese .com and Ⓦgodsellscheese.com. A variety of double Gloucester with chives and onion is known as Cotswold cheese.

Among many others, Gorsehill Abbey (Ⓦgorsehill abbey.co.uk) is an artisan producer near Broadway known for their Camembert-like St Eadburgha, while Simon Weaver near Lower Slaughter (Ⓦsimon weaver.net) makes a tasty organic Cotswold Brie. The Windrush Valley dairy outside Burford and Cerney Cheese (Ⓦcerneycheese.com) in North Cerney produce outstanding goat's cheese.

Creamy Oxford blue is made – oddly – at a Stilton dairy in Derbyshire but matured and distributed only by the Oxford Cheese Company (Ⓦoxfordfine food.com). For a wholly local endeavour plump for their aromatic, mead-washed Oxford Isis instead.

Beer

Artisan brewing has become hugely popular: Britain now has more breweries than at any time since World War II, and the Cotswolds hosts dozens.

Donnington Brewery (Ⓦdonnington-brewery .com), a family firm based in Donnington, near Stow-on-the-Wold, produces amber "BB" and malty "SBA" bitters for its seventeen pubs around the Cotswolds. The same family also runs Arkell's Brewery in Swindon (Ⓦarkells.com), a bigger concern with more than a hundred pubs, including many around the Cotswolds.

Oxfordshire's Hook Norton (Ⓦhooky.co.uk) produces a range of ales, available in their own 40-odd pubs as well as many others around the region – malted Hooky, fruity Old Hooky, golden Lion and others – supplemented by a welter of seasonal and special-edition beers, including the summer favourites Hooky Gold and Haymaker.

The Cotswold Brewing Company (Ⓦcotswold brewing.com) breaks the mould: it brews one ale, Cotswold Cask, but focuses mainly on producing a range of European-style lagers from its base near Bourton-on-the-Water, sold in pubs and restaurants around the area (and in London).

Witney's Wychwood Brewery (Ⓦwychwood co.uk), which produces the flavourful Hobgoblin, alongside speciality beers such as Bah Humbug and The Dog's Bollocks, is now controlled by Marston's, a huge national company – as is Brakspear (Ⓦbrakspear-beers.co.uk), a long-standing Oxfordshire brewery which went bust in 2002 and was revived at Wychwood's Witney site, where it continues to produce Brakspear Bitter and Oxford Gold.

Other local independent breweries include: Battledown (Ⓦwww.battledownbrewery.com), Cotswold Lion (Ⓦcotswoldlionbrewery.co.uk), Cotswold Spring (Ⓦspringbrewery.co.uk), Goffs Brewery (Ⓦgoffsbrewery.com), Halfpenny Brewery (Ⓦhalfpennybrewery.co.uk), Nailsworth Brewery (Ⓦvillageinn-nailsworth.co.uk), North Cotswold Brewery (Ⓦnorthcotswoldbrewery.co.uk), Oxfordshire Ales (Ⓦoxfordshireales.com), Patriot Brewery (Ⓦthe patriotbrewery.co.uk), Purity Brewing (Ⓦpurity brewing.com), Shotover Brewing (Ⓦshotoverbrewing .com), Stanway Brewery (Ⓦstanwaybrewery.com), Stroud Brewery (Ⓦstroudbrewery.co.uk), Uley Brewery (Ⓦuleybrewery.com) and Wickwar Brewing (Ⓦwickwarbrewing.co.uk).

BEER FESTIVALS

Banbury Beer Festival May Ⓦbanburybeerfest.org.uk.
Cirencester Cricket & Beer Festival May Ⓦcotswolds.com.
Ale & Steam Festivals (Winchcombe) May & August Ⓦnorth cotswoldcamra.org.uk.
Witney Beer Festival May Ⓦwitneybeerfestival.com.
Chadlington Beer Festival June Ⓦwww.chadlingtonbeer festival.com.
Charlbury Beer Festival June Ⓦcharlburybeerfestival.org.

Stratford Beer Festival June ⓦ stratfordbeerfestival.org.uk.
Cotswold Beer Festival (Winchcombe) July ⓦ gloucestershirecamra
.org.uk.
South Cotswold Beer Festival (Chipping Sodbury) July ⓦ bs37
.com/beer.
Hook Norton Festival of Fine Ales July ⓦ hookybeerfest.co.uk.
Frocester Beer Festival (near Stroud) August ⓦ www.frocester
beerfestival.com.
Gloucester Beer Festival September ⓦ gloucesterbeerfestival
.co.uk.

Sweet treats

The Cotswolds has loads of cake-makers and even chocolatiers – Lick The Spoon (ⓦ lickthespoon .co.uk) is a Cirencester favourite – while the Cotswold Pudding Company (ⓦ cotswoldpudding company.co.uk) is famed for sticky toffee puddings in multiple varieties. Winstones (ⓦ winstones icecream.co.uk) and Spot Loggins (ⓦ spotloggins .com) make delicious Cotswold ice cream.

Don't miss the fragrant Moroccan pastries made by the M'Hencha Company (ⓦ www.themhencha company.co.uk) in Bourton-on-the-Water. Banbury cakes – flat, currant-filled pastries, similar to Eccles cakes – have been baked and sold in Banbury for at least five hundred years (ⓦ www.banburycakes .co.uk), though deliciously dark and bittersweet Oxford marmalade has, regrettably, not been manufactured in Oxford for many decades.

Festivals and events

With its location in the middle of England, and its proximity to the innovation-loving urbanites of London, Bristol and Birmingham, the Cotswolds hosts an epic quantity of annual festivals and events. Some are out-and-out touristy, others are more authentic expressions of local life – and a fair few are plain daft, rollicking remnants of a less self-conscious age.

What follows is only a selection of events; for detailed local listings contact tourist offices or search ⓦ cotswolds.com, ⓦ www.oxfordshirecotswolds.org, ⓦ visitcheltenham.com, ⓦ visitoxfordandoxfordshire .com and ⓦ oxfordinspires.org.

JANUARY TO MAY

Cheltenham Gold Cup (March; ⓦ cheltenham.co.uk). Centrepiece of England's top steeplechase (fence-jumping) horse race meeting.

Oxford Literary Festival (March; ⓦ oxfordliteraryfestival.org). World-class book festival, featuring ten days of lectures, events and talks.
St George's Day (April 23; ⓦ stgeorgesholiday.com). England's patron saint is feted with traditional music and Morris dancing on village greens around the region. The same day, by happy chance, is also the birthday of William Shakespeare: expect parades, folk dancing and special events at Stratford-upon-Avon (ⓦ shakespearesbirthday.org.uk).
Stratford Literary Festival (April; ⓦ stratfordliteraryfestival .co.uk). Renowned event, with talks, readings and workshops.
Stroud International Textiles Select (May; ⓦ sitselect.org). Celebration of contemporary textile design, centred around exhibitions and talks.
Oxfordshire Artweeks (May; ⓦ artweeks.org). Artists and craftspeople open their homes and studios to the public.
Gypsy Horse Fair (May; ⓦ travellerstimes.org.uk). A week of travellers' stalls and horse-trading, held in fields near Stow-on-the-Wold.
Levellers' Day (May; ⓦ levellersday.wordpress.com). Burford hosts a day of debates, music and entertainment, linked to the seventeenth-century Levellers movement.
Eights Week (May; ⓦ ourcs.org.uk). Raucous rowing competitions on the Thames in Oxford.
Nailsworth Festival (May; ⓦ nailsworthfestival.org.uk). Varied choice of poetry, music and theatre.
Cheese Rolling (May; ⓦ cheese-rolling.co.uk). Mass pursuit of a cheese wheel down Cooper's Hill in Gloucestershire.
Tetbury Woolsack Races (May; ⓦ tetburywoolsack.co.uk). Men and women race up and down a steep hill carrying a giant sack of wool, while the town celebrates with a street fair.

JUNE, JULY AND AUGUST

Cotswold Olimpick Games (June; ⓦ www.olimpickgames.com). Traditional sporting endeavour on Dover's Hill near Chipping Campden dating back to 1612, celebrated with bands, cannon fire and shin-kicking. The day after sees the crowning of the Scuttlebrook Queen, followed by dancing round the maypole.
Banbury Old Town Party (June; ⓦ banburyoldtown.co.uk). A one-day knees-up in Banbury's lanes, with stilt-walkers, hog roasts, cask ales flowing and costume parades.
Ramsden Fete (June; ⓦ ramsdenvillage.co.uk). Village fete at Ramsden, near Witney, featuring tug o' war, egg-throwing, jousting, strong man competitions and more.
Deddington Festival (June; ⓦ deddingtonfestival.org.uk). Two weeks of community fun at Deddington, north of Oxford, featuring music, poetry competitions, willow-weaving and guided walks.
Fresh Air (June; ⓦ freshairsculpture.com). Open-air contemporary sculpture event at Quenington near Cirencester, held every two years: 2015, 2017, 2019.
Cowley Road Carnival (July; ⓦ cowleyroadcarnival.co.uk). Oxford's buzzing, multicultural Cowley Road district gets costumed up for parades, music and dancing in the streets.
Eynsham Carnival (July; ⓦ eynshamcarnival.com). Family-oriented shindig in Eynsham village, near Witney, featuring a craft fair, Morris dancing, pram-racing and more.

MUSIC FESTIVALS

England has gone **music festival** crazy, with every weekend from June to September now seeing some kind of musical happening. Here are some Cotswold events to choose from; check ⓦefestivals.co.uk for details of many more.

Cheltenham Folk Festival (Feb; ⓦcheltenhamtownhall.org.uk). A weekend of folk music to banish the winter chill.

Folk Weekend Oxford (April; ⓦfolkweekendoxford.co.uk). Three days of gigs at venues across the city.

Cheltenham Jazz Festival (April; ⓦcheltenhamfestivals.com). High-profile week, including free events and big-name stars.

Wood (May; ⓦwoodfestival.com). Small, rootsy festival outside Oxford with lots of folk and acoustic music.

Wychwood Festival (June; ⓦwychwoodfestival.com). Family-friendly weekend of music, comedy and cabaret, held at Cheltenham racecourse.

Cornbury (July; ⓦwww.cornburyfestival.com). Cheerful, easy-going music festival near Charlbury, supplemented by folk performers, craft stalls and more.

Truck (July; ⓦtruckfestival.com). Much-loved independent festival held on a farm south of Oxford.

Riverside (July; ⓦriversidefestival.charlbury.com). Independent free music festival in Charlbury.

WOMAD (July; ⓦwomad.co.uk). Massive world music weekend at Charlton Park, outside Malmesbury.

Global Gathering (July; ⓦglobalgathering.com). A weekend of electronic dance music at Long Marston Airfield near Stratford.

Wilderness (Aug; ⓦwildernessfestival.com). The Cornbury Park estate plays host to music, food, debates and performances.

Fairport's Cropredy Convention (Aug; ⓦfairportconvention.com). Genial weekend for a crusty crowd at Cropredy, near Banbury, always headlined by 1970s supergroup Fairport Convention.

The Big Feastival (Aug; ⓦjamieoliver.com/thebigfeastival) An upmarket weekend of music and foodie happenings in Kingham staged by Jamie Oliver and Alex James.

Banbury Folk Festival (Oct; ⓦbanburyfolkfestival.co.uk). Lively folk weekend which takes over Banbury's pubs and small venues.

CLASSICAL MUSIC FESTIVALS

Oxford May Music (May; ⓦoxfordmaymusic.co.uk). Concerts and lectures in central Oxford.

Spring Sounds (May; ⓦspringsounds.co.uk). Old favourites and premieres of new works at venues in and around Stratford-upon-Avon.

Chipping Campden Music Festival (May; ⓦcampdenmusicfestival.co.uk). Prestigious cycle of evening and lunchtime concerts.

English Music Festival (May; ⓦenglishmusicfestival.org.uk). Celebration of English music from Tallis to Britten, mostly staged in Dorchester Abbey, south of Oxford.

Bledington Music Festival (June; ⓦbledingtonmusicfestival.co.uk). Three nights of concerts and recitals.

Dean & Chadlington Festival (June; ⓦchadlingtonfestival.org.uk). High-quality recitals and concerts at venues near Chipping Norton.

Longborough Festival Opera (June & July; ⓦlfo.org.uk). Small-scale productions at this mansion near Moreton-in-Marsh.

Cheltenham Music Festival (July; ⓦcheltenhamfestivals.com). Major classical event, concentrating on chamber and orchestral music.

Bampton Opera (July; ⓦbamptonopera.org). Charming summer opera productions in an Oxfordshire garden, with some events in venues further afield.

Guiting Festival (July; ⓦguitingfestival.org). A week of classical music (with a spot of jazz) in Guiting Power, near the Slaughters.

Tetbury Music Festival (Sept; ⓦtetburymusicfestival.org.uk). Small festival that draws world-renowned soloists and performers.

Stratford Music Festival (Oct; ⓦwww.stratfordmusicfestival.com). Week-long showcase of classical and jazz.

Hobby Horse Festival (July; Ⓦ banbury.gov.uk). Quirky event in Banbury subsumed into "Town Mayor's Sunday", with folk dancing and lots of hobby horses.

Cotswold Show (July; Ⓦ cotswoldshow.co.uk). Cirencester hosts a weekend of child-friendly parades and events, from sky-diving to horse-whispering, along with a food market and fairground rides.

Royal International Air Tattoo (July; Ⓦ airtattoo.com). The world's largest military air show, held at RAF Fairford in Gloucestershire.

Football in the River (Aug). Two teams play a half-hour football game in the River Windrush at Bourton-on-the-Water, in a nutty hundred-year-old tradition.

SEPTEMBER TO DECEMBER

Moreton-in-Marsh Show (Sept; Ⓦ moretonshow.co.uk). Gloucestershire's largest agricultural show, with livestock competitions and country events.

Blenheim Palace Literary Festival (Sept; Ⓦ blenheimpalaceliteraryfestival.com). Woodstock hosts leading writers, academics and journalists.

Charlbury Street Fair (Sept; Ⓦ charlburystreetfair.org). Town fair and knees-up to raise funds for Charlbury's historic buildings.

Clypping Ceremony (Sept). St Mary's Church in Painswick is "clypped", or embraced, by local parishioners, who join hands to encircle the building in a ceremony dating back to 1321.

Heritage Open Days (Sept; Ⓦ heritageopendays.org.uk). A once-a-year opportunity to peek inside hundreds of historic buildings which don't normally open their doors to the public.

Cheltenham Literature Festival (Oct; Ⓦ cheltenhamfestivals.com). Prestigious event drawing world-renowned authors, with talks, readings, workshops and more.

Gypsy Horse Fair (Oct; Ⓦ travellerstimes.org.uk). Fun and horse-trading in fields outside Stow-on-the-Wold.

Halloween (Oct 31). All Hallows' Eve – and Samhain, last day of the Celtic calendar. Now swamped by commercialized US-style trick-or-treating, although druidic ceremonies survive at a few sites, such as the Rollright Stones near Chipping Norton (Ⓦ rollrightstones.co.uk).

Bonfire Night (Nov 5). Fireworks and bonfires held in village and town communities nationwide to commemorate the foiling of the Gunpowder Plot in 1605.

New Year's Eve (Dec 31). Expect plenty of jollity in town and village pubs alike.

Sports and outdoor activities

With its rolling landscape, bucolic scenery and networks of paths and country trails, the Cotswolds is classic walking country – but there are also many other ways to enjoy the great outdoors, from cycling to canal trips to horseriding.

Walking

Two of England's long-distance **National Trails** (Ⓦ nationaltrail.co.uk) pass through the region. The best known – and, many say, the best – is the **Cotswold Way** (Ⓦ nationaltrail.co.uk/cotswold), which leads for 102 miles along the highest points of the Cotswold escarpment from Chipping Campden in the north to Bath in the south, giving panoramic views over the Severn Vale much of the way. Walking the whole route takes, on average, seven days – but it's easy to tackle shorter stretches, and the website gives details of a dozen half-day circular walks at various points. We highlight the best of them throughout this book – as do the Cotswolds Area of Outstanding Natural Beauty on their excellent website Ⓦ **escapetothecotswolds .org.uk**, which is packed with ideas and route descriptions. A tougher test combines the Cotswold Way with an 86-mile stretch of the **Macmillan Way** (Ⓦ macmillanway.org) between Banbury and Bath, known as the "Cross-Cotswold Pathway", to form the epic 217-mile **Cotswold Round** circular route.

Then there's the **Thames Path** (Ⓦ nationaltrail .co.uk/thamespath), which stretches 184 miles from the source of the river near Kemble, outside Cirencester, to end at Woolwich in southeast London; some of its prettiest sections are around Lechlade and Oxford, again highlighted in this book – and at the excellent Canal & River Trust website (Ⓦ canalrivertrust.org.uk).

Hundreds of miles of other footpaths crisscross the area: we've noted the best of the shorter walks at relevant points. Ones to look out for include the **Windrush Way** and **Warden's Way**, sister trails connecting Bourton-on-the-Water with Winchcombe – the former a hill route, the latter passing between villages; the **Gloucestershire Way**, which includes a looping section between Stow-on-the-Wold and Gloucester; the **Glyme Valley Way**, a riverside path between Chipping Norton and Woodstock; numerous pretty walks along the **Oxford Canal** between Kidlington and Cropredy; and a host of others.

Winchcombe in particular has set itself up as "walking capital of the Cotswolds": its website **Winchcombe Welcomes Walkers** (Ⓦ winchcombe welcomeswalkers.com) has loads of tips and links, as does the **Long Distance Walkers Association** (Ⓦ ldwa.org.uk) and the tourist office sites Ⓦ cotswolds.com and Ⓦ www.oxfordshirecotswolds .org. Trail **maps** are widely available online, as are Ordnance Survey maps (see p.36).

Cycling

Several sections of the **National Cycle Network** (see Ⓦsustrans.org.uk) pass through the Cotswolds, including Route 45 (Gloucester to Stroud, Nailsworth and Cirencester), Route 41 (Gloucester to Cheltenham, Evesham and Stratford) and Route 5 (Oxford to Woodstock, Banbury, Chipping Campden and Stratford). As with walking, there are countless other trails to follow, gentle ones for leisure cyclists and tougher routes alike. We've picked out the best throughout this book.

You can take a bike free of charge on most **trains**, apart from certain peak-hour weekday services. From a starting-point at, say, Banbury or Stratford stations you could be cycling in open countryside within a few minutes, while trains on the Cotswold Line or Oxford Canal Line or to Kemble (see p.23) deposit you directly into countryside. Of circular routes with easy rail access, the **Cherwell Valley Ride** is a loop from Tackley station, north of Oxford, which passes through Woodstock; the **Kingham Route** covers ten easy miles from and to Kingham station; and one of the six Cotswold Cycling Routes, developed by Cotswold District Council and the Gloucestershire Rural Transport Partnership, includes a section from the station at **Moreton-in-Marsh** to Chipping Campden and back. All these – and others – are downloadable, with trail maps and descriptions, at Ⓦcotswolds.com and Ⓦwww.oxfordshirecotswolds.org, with extra info at Ⓦescapetothecotswolds.org.uk and Ⓦcanalrivertrust.org.uk.

Serious cyclists should take a look at Ⓦctc.org.uk for more ideas and/or consider entering the **Cotswold Spring Classic** (Ⓦcotswoldspringclassic.co.uk). If you're around in August, look out for the **Blenheim Palace Sportive** and charity family cycle day (Ⓦblenheimpalace.com), the only occasion when cyclists are permitted to ride through the Blenheim grounds.

ACTIVITY HOLIDAY OPERATORS

Blakes Holiday Boating ☎0844 856 7060, Ⓦblakes.co.uk. All kinds of boating holidays, including narrowboats on the Oxford Canal.
Carter Company ☎01296 631671, Ⓦthe-carter-company.com. Gentle self-guided cycling tours in the Cotswolds, in B&B or hotel accommodation.
Celtic Trails ☎01291 689774, Ⓦceltrail.com. Tailor-made walks along the Cotswold Way.
Compass Holidays ☎01242 250642, Ⓦcompass-holidays.com. A quality firm offering walking and cycling short breaks and longer holidays throughout the region.
Contours ☎01629 821900, Ⓦcontours.co.uk. Major operator with short breaks or longer walking holidays and self-guided hikes around the region.
Cotswold Country Cycles ☎01386 438706, Ⓦcotswoldcountrycycles.com. Cycle tours, advice, accommodation bookings and luggage transfer.
Cotswold Walking Company ☎01242 604190, Ⓦthecotswoldwalkingcompany.com. A small firm offering guidance, advice and walking holidays.
Cotswold Walking Holidays ☎01386 833799, Ⓦcotswoldwalks.com. Good selection of guided and self-guided walks – some featuring unique itineraries – with tailor-made options available.
Cotswolds Riding ☎01386 584250, Ⓦcotswoldsriding.co.uk. Horse-riding lessons, as well as guided and private "hacking" in the countryside, at this rural B&B near Broadway.
Discovery Travel ☎01904 632226, Ⓦdiscoverytravel.co.uk. Wide range of self-guided walking and cycling itineraries.
Footpath Holidays ☎01985 840049, Ⓦfootpath-holidays.com. Excellent selection of guided, self-guided and tailor-made itineraries.
HF Holidays ☎0345 470 8558, Ⓦhfholidays.co.uk. Co-operative-run company offering a wide range of guided and self-guided walking and cycling trips, including specialist themes such as medieval architecture or gardens.

COTSWOLD CANALS

Eighteenth-century canal engineers exerted monumental efforts to link the River Severn and the River Thames. First came the **Stroudwater Navigation** from Framilode to Stroud, followed in 1789 by the **Thames and Severn Canal**, linking Stroud to Lechlade – the highest navigable point on the Thames – via Sapperton Tunnel, once England's longest canal tunnel and still flanked by great pubs (see p.62).

After its 1840s heyday, the 36-mile link fell into disrepair; today, the **Cotswold Canals Trust** (Ⓦcotswoldcanals.com) is dredging and renovating to reconnect Stroud – and, eventually, the entire canal – to the national waterways network.

In the meantime you can still explore the **Oxford Canal**, which links Oxford with Coventry – either on a narrowboat, rentable at Lower Heyford (see p.197) and Thrupp (see p.198), on towpath walks nearby, or at the fine museum connected to the eighteenth-century boatyard in Banbury (see p.187).

Oxfordshire Narrowboats ☎ 01869 340348, ⓦ oxfordshire
-narrowboats.co.uk. Based at Lower Heyford wharf on the Oxford Canal,
offering day rental, short breaks and complete holidays afloat.

Ramblers Holidays ☎ 01707 331133, ⓦ ramblersholidays.co.uk.
Sociable guided walking tours: scenic, themed or special interest.

Rob Ireland Activity Days ☎ 01386 701683, ⓦ robireland.co.uk.
One-off special day events, such as quad-biking, tractor-driving,
helicopter treasure hunts, shooting, archery and more.

Saddle Skedaddle ☎ 0191 265 1110, ⓦ skedaddle.co.uk. Biking
adventures nationwide, including leisurely Cotswold tours.

Secret Cottage ☎ 01608 674700, ⓦ cotswoldtourismtours.co.uk.
One-woman company offering private full-day guided tours of Cotswold
villages, plus tea and cakes in the owner's cottage in Moreton.

Sherpa Van Project ☎ 01748 826917, ⓦ sherpavan.com. Luggage
transfer service for independent walkers and cyclists along the Cotswold
Way. Accommodation booking also available.

Talking Walks ☎ 01608 641839, ⓦ www.talkingwalks.co.uk.
Expert-led thematic walks through the north Cotswold countryside, part
of Gloucestershire University's public outreach programme. Scheduled
walks run once or twice a month year-round – with tailor-made options
and local B&B accommodation available.

Walking Holiday Company ☎ 01600 713008, ⓦ thewalkingholiday
company.co.uk. Tailor-made, self-guided walks along the Cotswold Way.

Walk the Landscape ☎ 01295 811003, ⓦ walkthelandscape
.co.uk. Family-run business near Banbury offering acclaimed guided,
self-guided and tailor-made walks, many with a historical and/or
botanical angle. Also affiliated to Talking Walks (see above).

Xplore Britain ☎ 01325 313609, ⓦ xplorebritain.com. Escorted
and independent walking and cycling holidays.

Shopping

**Shopping in many areas of the Cotswolds
can offer a refreshing change from the
chain-store monotony of some high
streets, with sleepy rural villages
sometimes coming up trumps for local
products in particular.**

Antiques are the "traditional" stock-in-trade of
Cotswold retailers – in some places, it seems that
almost every shop is selling furniture, ceramics and/
or craft items from a bygone age – but you'll also
find that the Cotswolds nurtures a surprisingly
healthy independent, often locally owned, retail
sector. Specialist **food** outlets are a favourite, from
cheesemongers and bakers to urban-style delis
and coffee shops. This region is also where the
nineteenth-century Arts and Crafts movement
flourished (see p.160) and there's no shortage of
potteries turning out local styles, upmarket **home
furnishing** outlets for locally designed textiles and
homeware, wood-turners, glassmakers, jewellers
and more. You may, in more popular locations, have

to wade through a proliferation of twee trinkets
and scented candles to find anything truly original
– but there's some good stuff out there. It's heart-
ening to remember, too, that even in this most
touristy of areas, many **independent retailers** have
little direct reliance on tourist trade – not least the
family-run butchers, shoeshops, florists and greengrocers that survive across Cotswold towns.

Travel essentials

Costs

Once you move away from the most heavily
touristed towns, the Cotswolds represents fairly
decent value for money. Nonetheless, even if you're
camping or hostelling, using public transport,
buying picnic lunches and eating in pubs and cafés
your minimum expenditure is likely to be around
£40/€45/US$65 per person per day. Couples staying
in B&Bs, eating at unpretentious restaurants and
visiting some attractions should expect roughly
£70/€85/US$115 per person, while if you're renting
a car, staying in hotels and eating well, budget for
£120/€145/US$200 each. Double that figure if you
choose to stay in stylish boutique hotels or grand
country houses.

Many of England's **historic attractions** – from
castles to stately homes – are owned and/or
operated by either the **National Trust** (☎ 0844 800
1895, ⓦ nationaltrust.org.uk) or **English Heritage**
(☎ 0870 333 1181, ⓦ english-heritage.org.uk). Both
usually charge entry fees (roughly £5–10), though
some properties are free. You can join online or in
person at any staffed attraction: annual member-
ship is around £30–40 and entitles you to free entry
to their properties.

Throughout this book, admission prices quoted
are the **full adult rate**, unless otherwise stated.
Concessionary rates – generally half-price – for
senior citizens (over 60), under-26s and **children**
(aged 5–17) apply almost everywhere, from tourist
attractions to public transport; you'll need official
ID as proof of age. Full-time students are often
entitled to discounts too. Children under 5 are
rarely charged.

Students can benefit from an ISIC (International
Student Identity Card), people under 26 can get an
IYTC (International Youth Travel Card) and full-time
teachers qualify for the ITIC (International Teacher
Identity Card). Each costs around £10/€12/US$16
and is valid for special air, rail and bus fares and
discounts at attractions; see ⓦ isic.org for details.

Crime and personal safety

Inspector Morse and *Midsomer Murders* are, of course, fiction: in the real world, Cotswold villages don't see body counts on a par with Detroit. Oxford does have some tough estates where **crime** flourishes, but as a holidaymaker you won't be visiting them. Village life remains placid: the worst trouble you're likely to see is a bit of late-night drunkenness at weekends in town centres. If you're the victim of any sort of crime, report it straight away to the police in person or by phoning ☎112 or ☎999: your insurance company will require a crime report number.

Electricity

The current is 240v AC. North American appliances may need a transformer and adaptor, those from Europe only an adaptor.

Entry requirements

EU citizens can travel to – and settle in – the UK with just a passport or identity card. US, Canadian, South African, Australian and New Zealand citizens can stay for up to six months without a visa, provided they have a valid passport. Many other nationalities require a visa, obtainable from the British consular office where you live. Check with the UK Border Agency (🌐 ukvisas.gov.uk) for up-to-date information.

Health

No vaccinations are required for entry into Britain. Citizens of all EU and EEA countries are entitled to free medical treatment within the UK's National Health Service (NHS), on production of their **European Health Insurance Card (EHIC)**. The same applies to Commonwealth countries with reciprocal arrangements – for example Australia and New Zealand. Everyone else will be charged: definitely take out health insurance before you travel.

MAIN HOSPITALS WITH 24-HOUR A&E

Banbury Horton Hospital, Oxford Road ☎01295 275500.
Cheltenham General Hospital, Sandford Rd ☎0300 422 2222.
Gloucester Royal Hospital, Great Western Rd ☎0300 422 2222.
Oxford John Radcliffe Hospital, Headley Way ☎01865 741166.
Warwick Warwick Hospital, Lakin Rd ☎01926 495321.
Worcester Royal Hospital, Hastings Way ☎01905 763333.

Pharmacies (also known as **chemists**) can dispense some drugs without a doctor's prescription. Most are open standard shop hours; check signs in the window for which local chemists are due to be staying open late and/or at the weekend. The website 🌐 nhs.uk is packed with useful health information, and also has directories of doctors' surgeries and walk-in centres nationwide.

Otherwise, minor issues can be dealt with at the surgery of any local **doctor**, also known as a **GP** (General Practitioner); get directions from the NHS website or your hotel. For serious injuries, go to the "**A&E**" (accident and emergency) department of the nearest hospital.

If you can't get to A&E, or if you're feeling ill and need medical advice, call ☎111 (free; 24hrs).

In a life-or-death emergency, call ☎112 or ☎999 (free; 24hrs) and ask for an ambulance.

Insurance

If you are visiting from overseas, always take out an insurance policy before travelling to cover against theft, loss and illness or injury. A typical policy will provide cover for loss of baggage, tickets and – up to a certain limit – cash or travellers' cheques, as well as cancellation or curtailment of your journey.

ROUGH GUIDES TRAVEL INSURANCE

Rough Guides has teamed up with WorldNomads.com to offer great travel insurance deals. Policies are available to residents of over 150 countries, with cover for a wide range of adventure sports, 24hr emergency assistance, high levels of medical and evacuation cover and a stream of travel safety information. Roughguides.com users can take advantage of their policies online 24/7, from anywhere in the world – even if you're already travelling. And since plans often change when you're on the road, you can extend your policy and even claim online. Roughguides.com users who buy travel insurance with WorldNomads.com can also leave a positive footprint and donate to a community development project. For more information, go to 🌐 roughguides.com/shop.

COUNTY NAMES

Berks = Berkshire
Bucks = Buckinghamshire
Glos = Gloucestershire
Northants = Northamptonshire
Oxon = Oxfordshire
Warks = Warwickshire
Wilts = Wiltshire
Worcs = Worcestershire

Medical cover is strongly advised. Keep receipts for medicines and medical treatment, and in the event you have anything stolen you must obtain an official statement from the police.

Mail

Post offices (Ⓦpostoffice.co.uk) open Monday to Friday 9am to 5.30pm, Saturdays 9am to 12.30pm. Main offices in larger towns stay open all day Saturday, while small branches sometimes close on Wednesday afternoons. In villages you may find that postal services are provided at a branded counter within a shop. Note that you can also buy **stamps** at a wide variety of ordinary shops, supermarkets and filling stations. Check Ⓦroyalmail.com for postal rates worldwide.

Maps

Some of the clearest road maps are produced by Geographers' A–Z (Ⓦaz.co.uk): their 1:150,000 *Cotswolds & Chilterns Visitors' Map* is perfect for most needs. If you're intending to explore minor roads and byways, opt for county atlases produced by A–Z, Philips (Ⓦphilips-maps.co.uk) and others at scales either side of 1:20,000. The most detailed maps are produced by Ordnance Survey (OS; Ⓦordnancesurvey.co.uk): their Landranger series (1:50,000) is fine for most walkers and cyclists, while their Explorer series (1:25,000) has detail down to individual farm buildings and field boundaries. Both have several sheets covering the Cotswolds. The OS website lets you buy paper maps, download digital maps to a smartphone and even create your own map, centred on any point in Britain. **Stanfords** (Ⓦstanfords.co.uk), the UK's premier map and travel bookshop, can order any product and will ship worldwide.

Money

UK currency is the **pound sterling** (£), divided into 100 pence (p). Coins come in denominations of 1p,

2p, 5p, 10p, 20p, 50p, £1 and £2. Notes are in denominations of £5, £10, £20 and £50.

Every sizeable town and village has a branch of one or other of the retail, or "high street", **banks**, along with smaller "building societies" (which operate in roughly the same way). The easiest way to get cash is to use your **debit card** in a "cash machine" (ATM); check in advance with your home bank whether you will be subject to a daily withdrawal limit. **ATMs** are widespread, but beware that a charge of £1.50–£2 may be levied on cash withdrawals at stand-alone ATMs in out-of-the-way places: the screen will notify you if so and give you an option to cancel.

Outside banking hours, you can change travellers' cheques or cash at post offices and **bureaux de change** – the latter tend to be open longer hours and are found in most town centres, airports and railway stations. Avoid changing in hotels, where the rates are normally poor.

Credit and debit cards are widely accepted – MasterCard and Visa are almost universal – **charge cards** such as American Express and Diners Club less so. A few smaller establishments may accept cash only. Paying by plastic involves inserting your card into a "**chip-and-pin**" terminal, then keying in your secret PIN. At supermarkets and some other shops, you may be asked at the checkout if you want "**cash back**": they let you pay (by card) for up to £50 more than the cost of your goods and give you the change in cash – very handy.

Opening hours and public holidays

Opening hours for most businesses, shops and offices are Monday to Saturday 9am to 5.30 or 6pm, with many shops also open on Sundays, generally 10.30am to 4.30pm. Big supermarkets have longer

ENGLAND'S PUBLIC HOLIDAYS

New Year's Day (Jan 1)
Good Friday
Easter Monday
Early May Bank Holiday (1st Mon in May)
Spring Bank Holiday (Last Mon in May)
Summer Bank Holiday (Last Mon in Aug)
Christmas Day (Dec 25)
Boxing Day (Dec 26)
If Jan 1, Dec 25 or Dec 26 fall on a Saturday or Sunday, the next weekday becomes a public holiday.

hours. Some towns have an **early-closing day** (usually Wednesday) when most shops close at 1pm. **Banks** are usually open Monday to Friday 9am to 4.30pm or 5pm, and Saturday 9am to 12.30pm or so.

We've quoted full opening hours for specific museums, galleries and other attractions throughout this book.

Phones

British **phone numbers** are a mess. Most have eleven digits, including a prefix beginning ☎01, ☎02 or ☎03 which denotes a fixed landline, or ☎07 which usually denotes a mobile phone/cellphone. However those eleven digits can be sliced numerous ways: some have three-digit area codes with eight-digit numbers, many have four-digit codes with seven-digit numbers, most are split five and six, and a few are split six and five. Some are only ten digits long, split five and five.

Numbers beginning ☎0800 and ☎0808 are free to call if you're using a landline, but usually expensive if you're calling from a mobile; ☎0844 and ☎0845 can be cheap or expensive depending on your phone provider; ☎0870 and ☎0871 are pricey whatever you do. "Premium rate" ☎09 numbers, common for pre-recorded information services (used by some tourist authorities), can cost anything up to £1.50 a minute.

Few public **pay phones** (or "phone boxes") survive – most accept coins (minimum charge 60p) and credit cards, but some are card-only. You can make international calls from any phone box, though it's cheaper to buy a **phonecard**, available from many newsagents.

Mobile phone coverage is universal in towns and cities, but rural areas often have blind spots.

UK **directory enquiries** on the phone is expensive; instead look online at ⓦbt.com. Business and service numbers are also searchable at ⓦyell.com.

Time

From the last Sunday in March until the last Sunday in October, the UK is on GMT+1, known as "British Summer Time" **(BST)**. For the rest of the year, it follows **GMT** ("Greenwich Mean Time", or Coordinated Universal Time, UTC). England is always one hour behind most of Europe and, apart from short periods around the changeovers, five hours ahead of New York. Full details at ⓦtimeanddate.com.

Tipping

Although there are no fixed rules for tipping, a 10–15 percent tip is anticipated by restaurant waiters. Tipping taxi drivers is purely optional. Some restaurants levy a "discretionary" or "optional" service charge of 10 or 12.5 percent, which must be clearly stated on the menu and on the bill. You are not obliged to pay it, and certainly not if the food or service wasn't what you expected. You don't usually tip in a pub; if you want to, you could offer the bar person a drink – and then give them enough money to cover it. In fancy hotels, porters and bell boys expect (and usually get) a pound or two.

Tourist information

The body promoting inbound tourism to the UK is **VisitBritain** (ⓦvisitbritain.com) – it has a

---

USEFUL NUMBERS

In emergency: police/fire/ambulance ☎112 or ☎999.
Police (non-emergency) ☎101.
Medical advice (non-emergency) ☎111.
Domestic operator ☎100.
International operator ☎155.

CALLING ENGLAND FROM HOME

Dial your international access code, then **44** for the UK, then the area code (excluding the zero), then the number.

CALLING HOME FROM ENGLAND

Australia 0061 + area code (excluding the zero) + number.
New Zealand 0064 + area code (excluding the zero) + number.
US and Canada 001 + area code + number.
Republic of Ireland 00353 + area code (excluding the zero) + number.
South Africa 0027 + area code (excluding the zero) + number.

TOURIST INFORMATION WEBSITES

ENGLISH REGIONS

Heart of England ⓦvisitheartofengland.com.
Southeast England ⓦvisitsoutheastengland.com.
Southwest England ⓦvisitsouthwest.co.uk.

THE COTSWOLDS

Cotswolds Tourism ⓦcotswolds.com. Official promotional body, based in Cheltenham. Its annual visitor guide is encyclopedic – and is also promoted by Cotswold District Council (for Cirencester and nearby villages; ⓦcotswold.gov.uk), Stroud (ⓦwww.visitthecotswolds.org.uk) and others. It also runs ⓦthe-cotswolds.org for Japanese visitors.
Oxfordshire Cotswolds ⓦwww.oxfordshirecotswolds.org. Brand name for the tourism promotion division of West Oxfordshire District Council, based in Witney – an excellent source of information for the area between Woodstock, Burford and Chipping Norton.
Escape to the Cotswolds ⓦescapetothecotswolds.org.uk. Encyclopedic site for outdoors tourism, run by the Cotswolds Conservation Board, the Northleach-based body overseeing the Cotswolds "Area of Outstanding Natural Beauty" (ⓦcotswoldsaonb.org.uk).

OTHER TOURISM BODIES

Discover Stratford ⓦdiscover-stratford.com.
Visit Cheltenham ⓦvisitcheltenham.com.
Visit North Oxfordshire ⓦvisitnorthoxfordshire.com. Includes Banbury.
Visit Oxford and Oxfordshire ⓦvisitoxfordandoxfordshire.com.
Visit Wiltshire ⓦvisitwiltshire.co.uk. Includes Castle Combe and Malmesbury.
Visit Worcestershire ⓦvisitworcestershire.org. Includes Broadway and Evesham.
Within Warwickshire ⓦwithinwarwickshire.com. Includes Stratford-upon-Avon and villages around Shipston-on-Stour.

comprehensive website, packed with useful tips and ideas. Its partner agency **VisitEngland** (ⓦvisitengland.com) is another excellent source of information. Within England, responsibility for promoting particular areas is in the hands of regional tourism boards (see box above) and smaller local bodies.

The Cotswolds straddles administrative boundaries: Oxfordshire counts as part of **Southeast England**, but Gloucestershire and Wiltshire are **Southwest England** and – to make matters worse – Warwickshire and Worcestershire are the Midlands (which, for tourism purposes, is retitled "**Heart of England**"). Responsibility for promotion is split across several bodies, public and private.

Many towns (and some villages) have a **tourist office**, called a Tourist Information Centre ("**TIC**") or Visitor Information Centre ("**VIC**"). They tend to follow standard shop hours (Mon–Sat 9am–5.30pm), sometimes also open on Sundays. Hours are curtailed in winter (Nov–Easter). Staff will nearly always be able to book accommodation, reserve space on guided tours, and sell guidebooks, maps and walk leaflets. They can also provide lists of local cafés, restaurants and pubs, and though they aren't supposed to recommend particular places you'll often be able to get a feel for the best local places to eat.

Travellers with disabilities

Aside from the obvious difficulties with hilly terrain and historic buildings (gravel drives, uneven footpaths and the like), the Cotswolds generally caters well for travellers with disabilities. All new public buildings – including museums and galleries – must provide wheelchair access, public transport is fully accessible and dropped kerbs and signalled crossings are widespread. The number of accessible hotels and restaurants is also growing, and reserved parking bays are available almost everywhere. If you have specific requirements, it's always best to talk first to your travel agent, chosen hotel or tour operator.

Access-Able ⓦ access-able.com. US-based resource for travellers with disabilities.

Disability Rights UK ⓦ disabilityrightsuk.org. Campaigning organization with links and advice.

Door-to-Door ⓦ dptac.independent.gov.uk/door-to-door. Travel website offering information and advice.

Tourism for All ☎ 0845 124 9971, ⓦ www.tourismforall.org.uk. Excellent resource, with advice, listings and useful information.

TEN IDEAS FOR FAMILIES

Alice Day Whimsical fun in Oxford. See p.227.
Berkeley Castle Storm the ramparts and admire the armoury. See p.72.
Blenheim Palace Tons of family-friendly activities. See p.177.
Cotswold Farm Park Rare breeds on a proper working farm. See p.98.
Cotswold Wildlife Park Penguins, rhinos, giraffes and more. See p.159.
Giffords Circus Ⓦ giffordscircus.com. Traditional local touring circus.
Gloucestershire & Warwickshire Railway Ride on a real-life steam train. See p.127.
Harry Potter film locations. Famously in Oxford (see p.226) and Gloucester (see p.52).
Natural History Museum, Oxford Full-size dinosaur skeletons. See p.230.
Walks on Wheels Ⓦ escapetothecotswolds.org.uk. Downloadable PDFs describing fifteen short country walks suitable for parents pushing buggies.

Travelling with children

If you're travelling with children, facilities in England are comparable with those in most other European countries. Breastfeeding is legal in all public places, including restaurants, cafés and public transport, and baby-changing rooms are available widely, including in malls and railway stations. Under-5s aren't charged on public transport or at attractions; 5–16-year-olds usually get a fifty-percent discount. Children aren't allowed in certain licensed (that is, alcohol-serving) premises – though this doesn't apply to restaurants, and many pubs have family rooms or beer gardens where children are welcome. Check Ⓦ netmums.com and Ⓦ babygoes2.com for tips and ideas.

Cheltenham and the south Cotswolds

BUTCHER'S SHOP IN CASTLE COMBE

1

Cheltenham and the south Cotswolds

Defined by the great escarpment of the Cotswold Edge, which rolls from one end of this chapter more or less to the other, the area we've dubbed the south Cotswolds encompasses some of the region's most dramatic scenery. From almost any point atop the Edge, panoramic views gaze westwards – perhaps out over Tewkesbury towards the Malverns, or across the Severn Vale and Forest of Dean into Wales. The gently bucolic Cotswolds scenery of imagination is here replaced by a tougher landscape, a tougher climate and a tougher history: the steep valleys around Stroud in particular experienced widespread industrialization during the eighteenth and nineteenth centuries, with hundreds of textile mills and ambitious canal projects.

Down below Cleeve Hill, the Cotswolds' highest point, flanking the M5 motorway and serving as a focus for road and rail, lie **Cheltenham**, famed for its horse-racing and its Regency architecture, and **Gloucester**, dominated by its breathtaking medieval **cathedral**. Villages along the Severn near Gloucester offer diversions – notably the **Slimbridge** wetland reserve and a fairytale castle at **Berkeley** – or otherwise you could head up again into the nearby hills for some of the loveliest of the Cotswolds' hideaways. **Painswick** is a popular draw, though nearby villages such as **Sheepscombe** remain quiet, and the valley countryside is as gloriously evocative today as when *Cider with Rosie* author Laurie Lee walked out one midsummer morning in 1934 from his home village of **Slad** to seek his fortune.

Unsentimental **Stroud** lies at a conjunction of valleys, with corrugated landscapes dominating the view: climb to the high commons at **Minchinhampton** to blow the cobwebs away, or aim for scenic drives around **Nailsworth** or along the towering Cotswold Edge near **Uley**, site of more prehistoric burial mounds. **Tetbury**, over towards the Wiltshire border, is another perfect anchor-point, with a range of high-quality hotels, some outstanding restaurants and attractions nearby which include nature walks within the extraordinary **Westonbirt Arboretum**.

The character of the southernmost tip of the Cotswolds, beyond the likes of Westonbirt and down-to-earth **Wotton-under-Edge**, is markedly different from that further north. Landscapes are flatter, grasses coarser, stonework greyer. Stop in at the market town of **Chipping Sodbury**, or brave the promenading crowds within the photogenic one-street village of **Castle Combe** – but, in truth, by the time you reach the M4, the best of the Cotswolds lies behind you.

Cheltenham

Until the eighteenth century **CHELTENHAM** was a modest Cotswold town like any other, but the discovery of a spring in 1716 transformed it into Britain's most popular **spa**. During Cheltenham's heyday, a century or so later, royalty and

PAINSWICK ROCOCO GARDEN

Highlights

❶ Cheltenham Engaging spa town with an artistic bent, a great museum and an instinct for poshness in hotels and restaurants. **See p.42**

❷ Gloucester Cathedral One of England's greatest cathedrals: visit in order to stroll around the superbly atmospheric cloisters. **See p.52**

❸ Painswick Delightful village of charm and taste, set in hilly Cotswold scenery. **See p.55**

❹ Slad Writer Laurie Lee's home village is in gorgeous countryside – perfect for long, lonely walks. **See p.58**

❺ Tetbury Top choice as a base for the south Cotswolds, offering good shopping, a fine church and great food. **See p.65**

❻ Westonbirt Arboretum Lose yourself in the natural splendour of these vast woods, not least when the autumn colours turn. **See p.68**

❼ Castle Combe Perfectly preserved old weavers' village on the Cotswolds' southernmost fringes. **See p.75**

HIGHLIGHTS ARE MARKED ON THE MAP ON P.44

1

nobility descended in droves to take the waters, which were said to cure anything from constipation to worms. The super-rich have since moved onto sunnier climes, but the town has maintained a lively, still rather posh atmosphere, holds lots of good restaurants and shows off some of England's best-preserved Regency architecture.

Having said that, there's not actually a great deal to do. Taking in the grand facades is pleasant, as is dipping in and out of the shops or holing up in one of the

CHELTENHAM AND SOUTH COTSWOLDS

HIGHLIGHTS

1. Cheltenham
2. Gloucester Cathedral
3. Painswick
4. Slad
5. Tetbury
6. Westonbirt Arboretum
7. Castle Combe

Cotswolds Area of Outstanding Natural Beauty (AONB)

0   5
miles

FARMERS' MARKETS

Dates may change around Christmas and New Year. See also ⓦlocalfoods.org.uk.

Cheltenham 2nd & last Fri of month 9am–2pm ⓦcheltenham.gov.uk.
Chipping Sodbury 2nd & 4th Sat of month 9am–1pm ⓦsodburytowncouncil.gov.uk.
Dursley March–Dec 2nd Sat of month 8.30am–1pm ⓦwww.stroud.gov.uk.
Gloucester Every Fri 9am–3pm ⓦthecityofgloucester.co.uk.
Malmesbury 2nd & 4th Sat of month 9am–1pm ⓦwiltshirefarmersmarkets.co.uk.
Nailsworth 4th Sat of month 9am–1pm ⓦnailsworthmarket.org.uk.
Stroud Every Sat 9am–2pm ⓦfresh-n-local.co.uk.
Wotton-under-Edge Feb–Dec 1st Sat of month 9am–1pm ⓦwww.stroud.gov.uk.

luxury spa hotels, but otherwise most visitors head off into the Cotswolds countryside fairly smartish. The exception is if you're here for the **racing** or for one of Cheltenham's excellent **arts festivals** (ⓦcheltenhamfestivals.com) – **jazz** (April), **science** (June), **classical music** (July) or **literature** (Oct), or the separately run **folk** festival (Feb; ⓦcheltenhamtownhall.org.uk) – when a stay in the town musters fresh interest.

The Promenade

Cheltenham is a town of two halves. Start on the broad **Promenade**, focus of the town centre, which sweeps majestically south from the High Street and is lined with some of Cheltenham's grandest houses and smartest shops (in among a welter of familiar high-street brands). Streets to either side effortlessly keep up appearances and, in a similar vein, the Ladies' College is a step away.

The Wilson (Cheltenham Art Gallery and Museum)

Clarence St • Daily 9.30am–5.15pm • Free • ☎01242 237431, ⓦthewilson.org.uk

Just off the Promenade stands **The Wilson**, formerly known as the **Cheltenham Art Gallery and Museum**. The building reopened in 2013 after extensive renovation, now housing the tourist office, a shop selling beautiful work by the Gloucestershire Guild of Craftsmen (ⓦguildcrafts.org.uk) and exhibitions spread across four airy floors. The rebranding is to honour Edward Wilson, a Cheltonian who was one of the explorers on Scott's ill-fated Antarctic expedition of 1912; watercolours he painted, photographs and some of his Antarctic gear – crampons, ice axe, tin mug – form part of the museum's collection. There are also displays on local history, archaeology and fine art – look out for Stanley Spencer's bucolic *Village Life, Gloucestershire* (1940) in the Summerfield galleries – but the main reason to visit is to take in the outstanding Arts and Crafts collection, ranging from superb furniture by Charles Ashbee and Charles Voysey to ceramics, jewellery, pottery and exquisitely hand-illustrated books and manuscripts in the museum's Emery Walker Library.

Holst Birthplace Museum

4 Clarence Rd • June–Sept Tues–Sat 10am–5pm, Sun 1.30–5pm; rest of year Tues–Sat 10am–4pm; closed Jan • £5 • ☎01242 524846, ⓦholstmuseum.org.uk

Housed in a refined Regency terrace house a short walk north of the town centre, the **Holst Birthplace Museum** was where the composer of *The Planets* was born in 1874. Its intimate rooms hold plenty of Holst memorabilia – including his piano in the ground-floor music room – and give a good insight into Victorian family life,

1

with a working kitchen and laundry downstairs and tasteful drawing-rooms and a nursery upstairs.

Pittville Pump Room

Pittville Park • Daily 10am–4pm • ☎ 01242 523852, ⓦ pittvillepumproom.org.uk

About ten minutes' walk north along handsome Evesham Road from the town centre brings you into the **Pittville** district, where local chancer Joseph Pitt began work on a grand spa in the 1820s, soon afterwards running out of cash. Most of the area is now parkland, though Pitt did manage to complete the domed **Pump Room** before he hit the skids. A lovely Classical structure with an imposing colonnaded facade, it is now used mainly as a concert hall, but you can still sample the **spa waters** from the marble fountain in the main auditorium for free. Very pungent they are too.

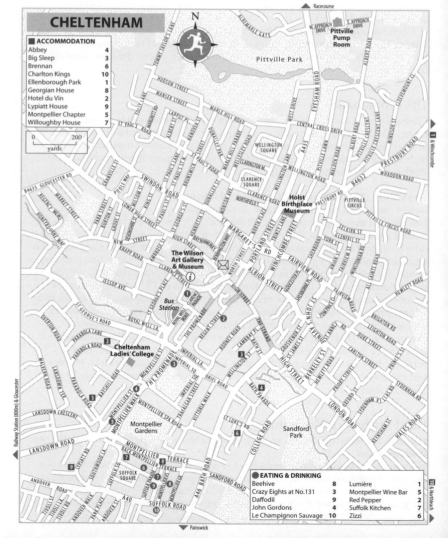

CHELTENHAM

ACCOMMODATION

Abbey	4
Big Sleep	3
Brennan	6
Charlton Kings	10
Ellenborough Park	1
Georgian House	8
Hotel du Vin	2
Lypiatt House	9
Montpellier Chapter	5
Willoughby House	7

EATING & DRINKING

Beehive	8	Lumière	1
Crazy Eights at No.131	3	Montpellier Wine Bar	5
Daffodil	9	Red Pepper	2
John Gordons	4	Suffolk Kitchen	7
Le Champignon Sauvage	10	Zizzi	6

1

CHELTENHAM RACES

Cheltenham racecourse (☎01242 513014, ⓦcheltenham.co.uk), on the north side of town, a ten-minute walk from Pittville Park at the foot of Cleeve Hill, is Britain's main venue for National Hunt racing, also known as "steeplechase" – that is, in which the horses must jump over hurdles or fences. The principal events are the four-day **Festival** in March, which attracts sixty thousand people each day, culminating in the famous **Cheltenham Gold Cup**, and the three-day **Open** in November, but there are smaller meetings throughout the season, which runs from late October to early May. For what many say is the best view, with the best atmosphere, book ahead for entry to the pen opposite the main stand, known as Best Mate Enclosure (about £10–50, depending on the event).

Montpellier and the Suffolks

The best of Cheltenham lies south of the centre. From the Promenade, wander past **Imperial Square**, laid out in 1818, whose greenery is surrounded by proud Regency terraces, into the **Montpellier** district. **Montpellier Walk** features a parade of shops sporting Classical-style caryatids – supporting columns carved as female figures – designed in the 1840s, or you could duck one street west onto **Montpellier Street**, a handsome and harmonious row of upscale bars, cafés, beauty parlours and independent boutiques.

Press on south, over the busy main road and into "**the Suffolks**", a pleasant residential district of terraces with a buzzy, engaging ambience. It's centred on the large, rather unkempt **Suffolk Square** but also takes in a powwow of interesting shops and restaurants along adjacent **Suffolk Parade**. Even if you're not hungry, be sure to pop into two architectural highlights: the Regency Gothic **church of St James** on Suffolk Square, transformed inside into a restaurant, and the superb Art Deco **Daffodil** restaurant on Suffolk Parade, occupying what was a cinema, complete with all its glorious 1920s fittings.

ARRIVAL AND GETTING AROUND   CHELTENHAM

BY TRAIN

Trains from all round the UK come into Cheltenham Spa, a surprisingly small two-platform station. The main entrance is on Queen's Rd, about three-quarters of a mile west of the town centre, from where the most frequent transport into town is Stagecoach bus #D (Mon–Sat every 10min 6am–6pm, then every 30min until 10.45pm, Sun every 30min 8.45am–6.45pm), which drops off on Clarence St in the centre. A taxi is about £5 – or it's a twenty-minute walk.
Destinations Birmingham New St (2–3 hourly; 40min); Bristol (every 30min; 40min); London Paddington (hourly, some change at Swindon; 2hr 15min), Stroud (hourly; 25min).

BY BUS

Long-distance National Express coaches from London and Heathrow Airport arrive at the bus station on Royal Well Rd, just behind the town centre: these are also a useful way to get to or from Cirencester on a Sunday, when local buses don't run.
Local Some buses arrive at the Royal Well bus station, but many drop off nearby on the main street, Promenade.
Destinations Bourton-on-the-Water (Mon–Sat hourly; June–Sept also 2 on Sun; 50min); Broadway (Mon–Sat 2–3 daily; 45min); Burford (Mon–Sat 3 daily, 1 on Sun; 45min); Chipping Campden (1 on Thurs; 1hr 40min); Cirencester

(Mon–Sat hourly; 40min); Gloucester (every 10min; 35min); Lower Slaughter (Mon–Sat hourly; June–Sept also 2 on Sun; 55min); Moreton-in-Marsh (Mon–Sat hourly; June–Sept also 2 on Sun; 1hr 15min); Nailsworth (hourly; 1hr); Northleach (Mon–Sat every 1–2hrs, 1 on Sun; 30min); Oxford (Mon–Sat 3 daily, 1 on Sun; 1hr 30min); Painswick (hourly; 30min); Stow-on-the-Wold (Mon–Sat hourly; June–Sept also 2 on Sun; 1hr); Stroud (hourly; 40min); Winchcombe (Mon–Sat approx hourly; 20min).

BY CAR

Park and ride Take advantage of Cheltenham's two park and ride facilities (ⓦgloucestershire.gov.uk/parkandride). Arle Court is on the western edge of town by the A40/B4063 roundabout, signposted from M5 junction 11; parking is free and bus #511 runs into the centre (Mon–Sat every 12min 7.15am–7pm; £3 return, additional passengers £1 each). Cheltenham Race Course car park is signposted on the northern edge of town; parking is free and bus #D runs into the centre (Mon–Sat every 10min 7.30am–6.15pm; £3.20 return; park and ride suspended during big race meetings).

BY TAXI

Try Andycars (☎01242 262611, ⓦandycarstaxis.co.uk) or Starline (☎01242 250250, ⓦtextbookings.co.uk).

1

INFORMATION AND TOURS

Tourist office Cheltenham's helpful tourist office is in The Wilson gallery on Clarence St (daily 9.30am–5.15pm; ☎ 01242 237431, ⓦ visitcheltenham.com & ⓦ cotswolds .com.

Tours The tourist office takes bookings for guided walking tours of Regency Cheltenham (April–Oct Sat 11am, July & Aug also Sun 11am; 1hr 30mins; £5) as well as coach tours

all round the Cotswolds and details of "The Romantic Road", a pair of self-guided countryside driving tours which start and end in Cheltenham. The first (70 miles) describes a route through Winchcombe, Broadway, Chipping Campden, Stow and the Slaughters; the other (90 miles) visits Northleach, Burford, Bibury, Cirencester and Painswick.

ACCOMMODATION

Hotels and guest houses abound across the town, many of them in fine Regency houses, and rooms are easy to come by – except during the races and festivals, when you should book weeks in advance. The tourist office offers a free booking service. Notable hotels in the vicinity include *Cowley Manor* (see p.50), a remarkable design hotel in rural surroundings five miles south of Cheltenham.

HOTELS

Big Sleep Wellington St ☎ 01242 696999, ⓦ thebig sleephotel.com. Excellent contemporary budget hotel in the centre, with 59 rooms including family rooms and suites, all with a retro designer feel and hi-tech gadgetry but no frills – and, more important, exceptionally low prices. **£55**
★**Charlton Kings** London Rd ☎ 01242 231061, ⓦ charltonkingshotel.co.uk. Informal, well-run three-star hotel two miles east of the centre on the A40 – a decent option if you want to leave your car and get a bus into town. Rooms are fresh and spotlessly presented, the food is good and the hands-on owners are charming. Great value. **£63**
Ellenborough Park Southam Rd ☎ 01242 807308, ⓦ ellenboroughpark.com. Top dog in town, one of the Cotswolds' leading country house hotels – indeed, regularly voted one of England's top spa hotels to boot. The style is very traditional – dark wood panelling, classic armchairs, portraits over the fireplace – updated with contemporary bathrooms and access to the spa. No expense spared. **£200**
Hotel du Vin Parabola Rd ☎ 01242 588450, ⓦ hotel duvin.com. Swanky boutique-style hotel in the sought-after Montpellier district, with 49 stylish rooms and suites and an excellent reputation for facilities, service and cuisine. **£105**
Montpellier Chapter Bayshill Rd ☎ 01242 527788, ⓦ themontpellierchapterhotel.com. Gloriously grand villa hotel in the classy Montpellier neighbourhood, proud of its air of sophistication. The restaurant is super-stylish, with its open kitchen and glassed terrace, and the same

contemporary flair extends to the rooms, with their monsoon showers, feature walls, hi-tech gadgetry and some with in-room bathtubs and/or balconies. **£125**
Willoughby House 1 Suffolk Sq ☎ 01242 522798, ⓦ willoughbyhousehotel.co.uk. A handsome Regency building south of the centre turned into a small, friendly hotel featuring classic traditional styling. All nine rooms retain a comforting sense of old-fashioned charm and opulence. **£120**

B&BS

Abbey 14 Bath Parade ☎ 01242 516053, ⓦ www .abbeyhotel-cheltenham.com. The thirteen rooms at this centrally located four-star B&B are attractively and individually furnished, with wholesome breakfasts taken overlooking the garden. Friendly service. **£87**
Brennan 21 St Luke's Rd ☎ 01242 525904, ⓦ brennan guesthouse.co.uk. Small, simple B&B in a Regency building on a quiet square, with six rooms, none ensuite. Not the most welcoming in town, but one of the most competitively priced. No credit cards. **£50**
Georgian House 77 Montpellier Terrace ☎ 01242 515577, ⓦ georgianhouse.net. Three fancy en-suite bedrooms – including one four-poster – in a fine old Montpellier house dating from 1807: quiet, spotless and full of period charm. **£90**
Lypiatt House Lypiatt Rd ☎ 01242 224994, ⓦ lypiatt .co.uk. Splendid, four-square Victorian villa set in its own grounds a short walk from the centre, with spacious rooms, open fires and a conservatory with a small bar. **£98**

EATING AND DRINKING

Cheltenham caters for all tastes and pockets, its restaurants, bars and pubs drawing in a mix of students and townies as well as better-heeled types from the villages nearby. You'll have no difficulty finding somewhere congenial – though if you're planning to be in town during any of the festivals or big race meetings, you'd do well to book a table in advance.

RESTAURANTS AND CAFÉS

★**Daffodil** 18–20 Suffolk Parade ☎ 01242 700055, ⓦ thedaffodil.com. Eat in the circle bar or auditorium of

this breathtakingly designed 1920s Art Deco ex-cinema in the lively Suffolks district, where the screen has been replaced with a hubbub of chefs. Great atmosphere and first-class British cuisine (mains £14–22), as well as cocktails and a swish of style. Live jazz Sat lunchtime & Mon night. Mon–Sat noon–11pm.

Le Champignon Sauvage 24 Suffolk Rd ☎01242 573449, ⓦlechampignonsauvage.co.uk. Cheltenham's highest-rated restaurant, its sensitively updated classic French cuisine awarded two Michelin stars among a welter of other awards and critical acclaim. The ambience is chic and intimate, the presentation immaculately artistic. The full menu is £48 (two courses) or £59 (three courses), or opt for the smaller set menu at £26 (two courses). Book well ahead. Tues–Sat 12.30–1.15pm & 7.30–8.30pm.

Lumière Clarence Parade ☎01242 222200, ⓦwww.lumiere.cc. Acclaimed restaurant showcasing upscale, contemporary, seasonal British food in a genial ambience of informality. Cornish scallops or sexed-up corned beef prelude mains such as Gloucester Old Spot pork done two ways, partridge or local venison. Three-course menus are £55 (or £28 at lunch). Tues 7–9pm, Wed–Sat noon–1.30pm & 7–9pm.

Red Pepper 13 Regent St ☎01242 253900, ⓦred peppercheltenham.co.uk. Family-run deli, coffee lounge and bistro in the centre of town, with a friendly, informal vibe and a wide range of dishes, from pie and mash or fishcake and salad for a light lunch (£7–9) through to rack of lamb, gnocchi or seabass in the evenings (mains £11–15). Downstairs coffee lounge daily 9am–6pm. Upstairs bistro Tues–Fri 6–9.30pm, Sat noon–3pm & 6–9.30pm, Sun noon–3pm.

Suffolk Kitchen 8 Suffolk Parade ☎01242 237057, ⓦthesuffolkkitchen.co.uk. Friendly upmarket restaurant in the posh Suffolks district, where hearty British cooking – braised pork belly with apple and thyme purée, steak and skin-on chips, pan-fried calves' liver with bacon – is offset with quirky contemporary design decor and a great, adventurous wine list. Mains £14–20, or two-course set menu £15 (lunch and early dinner). Tues–Fri noon–2.30pm & 6–10pm, Sat 9.30am–2.30pm & 6–10pm, Sun 9.30am–3pm.

Zizzi St James' Church, Suffolk Sq ☎01242 252493, ⓦzizzi.co.uk. Chain Italian restaurant, housed spectacularly within a converted Regency Gothic church, complete with stained glass and a soaring interior. The chancel now houses the spotlit open kitchen. The pizzas aren't bad (£7–13), but come to crick your neck at the architecture. Daily noon–10pm.

PUBS AND BARS

Beehive 1–3 Montpellier Villas ☎01242 702270, ⓦthebeehivemontpellier.com. Popular, easy-going pub in Montpellier, under new management in 2014, with good beer, a friendly ambience and decent pub grub in the atmospheric restaurant upstairs. Mon–Sat 11am–11pm, Sun noon–10pm.

Crazy Eights at No.131 131 Promenade ☎01242 822939, ⓦno131.com. Super swanky lounge bar attached to an equally swanky restaurant (and even swankier hotel) – leather sofas, dark wood and chandeliers – with the selling-point of tapas-style "Small Plates" to accompany cocktails and bottled beers: tuna sashimi, devilled crab on toast, lamb meatballs, poached egg on focaccia, and so on (£5–12). Daily 11am–11pm.

★**John Gordons** 11 Montpellier Arcade ☎01242 245985, ⓦjohngordons.co.uk. This lovely little independent wine bar, hidden off Montpellier's fanciest street, is a breath of fresh air among the more or less generically posh watering holes hereabouts. Drop in ostensibly to pick the brains of the knowledgeable staff about buying wines and whiskies. But then take a seat in the shop or outside in the old Victorian covered arcade to watch the world go by while sampling a glass or two of wine, alongside a plate of charcuterie, cheeses and/or antipasti (£6–14). Every town should have one. Mon–Wed 9.30am–11pm, Thurs–Sat 9.30am–midnight, Sun 11am–10pm.

Montpellier Wine Bar Bayshill Lodge, Montpellier St ☎01242 527774, ⓦmontpellierwinebar.co.uk. Stylish wine bar and restaurant with lovely bow-fronted windows on a busy little corner. Hang out at the bar with glass of something smooth, or drop in mid-morning for brunch. Mon–Thurs 10am–3pm & 6–9.30pm, Fri–Sun 10am–9.30pm.

DIRECTORY

Hospital Cheltenham General, Sandford Rd ☎0300 422 2222, ⓦwww.gloshospitals.nhs.uk.

Markets For farmers' markets, see p.45.

Pharmacy Boots, 197 High St ☎01242 527084, ⓦboots.com (Mon–Sat 8am–6pm, Sun 11am–5pm).

Police station Lansdown Rd ☎101, ⓦgloucestershire.police.uk (Mon–Thurs 8am–10pm, Fri & Sat 8am–midnight, Sun 8am–8pm).

Post office 192 High St (Mon–Sat 9am–5.30pm, Sun 10.30am–2.30pm).

Seven Springs and around

South of Cheltenham, the A46 heads to Prinknash (see p.57) and Painswick (see p.55), while the A435 forms the most direct route to Cirencester. A couple of miles beyond Cheltenham's suburbs, it rises to the junction with the east–west A436 at the resonantly

1

named **SEVEN SPRINGS**, where the source of the River Churn – or, some say, the true source of the Thames (see p.86) – is marked by a chain pub and a busy roundabout.

From the pub, the "Leckhampton Loop" **circular walk** (4.5 miles; 3hr) climbs along the Cotswold Way, clinging to the edge of the scarp and offering a close encounter with the Devil's Chimney, an oddly shaped limestone stack that is all that's left of Cheltenham's once-thriving quarrying industry atop **Leckhampton Hill**. The path then splits away to head down through quiet woods and eventually back to Seven Springs. Download full details at the Cotswold Way pages of ⓦescapetothecotswolds.org.uk – or pick up a leaflet at the Cheltenham tourist office.

Coberley

A few hundred yards south of Seven Springs, follow a minor road west to the tiny village of **COBERLEY**. Around a couple of bends, a sign for Coberley church points mutely at a little huddle of cottages beside an arched gatehouse. Open the gate, or the door beside it, to walk through to the Perpendicular **church of St Giles**, originally – like the cottages, the gatehouse and the cluster of stables and outbuildings around the adjacent courtyard – part of the grand Coberley Hall, built in the thirteenth century but now gone. The church, though, is full of atmosphere; originally Saxon and Norman, largely rebuilt 1870, it's worth visiting for its south chapel, founded by **Thomas de Berkeley**, a knight who fought at the Battle of Crécy (1346). The chapel still houses Berkeley's tomb alongside that of his wife, Lady Joan and, poignantly, an unnamed child – presumably their daughter. Local folk-history has it that Lady Joan, who outlived Berkeley and married again, was the mother of Dick Whittington, thrice Lord Mayor of London.

ARRIVAL AND DEPARTURE   SEVEN SPRINGS AND AROUND

By bus Seven Springs is served by bus #51 (Mon–Sat hourly) between Cheltenham (15min) and Cirencester (20min).

ACCOMMODATION AND EATING

★**Cowley Manor** Cowley, 5 miles south of Cheltenham ☎01242 870900, ⓦcowleymanor.com. Sensational country-house hotel, set in 55 acres, which follows none of the usual rules but instead showcases contemporary chic transplanted to this rural setting: interior clutter has been replaced by long, clean sightlines, fussy fittings superseded by witty, intelligent design. Expect low, square couches, elegant contemporary mood-lighting and guest rooms with curvaceous modern furniture. There's also an onsite spa. Fortunately, the service matches the style – relaxed, switched-on and intelligent. It's ferociously expensive, but if ever a Cotswold hotel merited a splurge, this is the one. **£225**

CHEESE ROLLING AT COOPER'S HILL

Amid woodland near **BROCKWORTH**, roughly four miles southeast of Gloucester – and six miles southwest of Cheltenham – rises **Cooper's Hill**, a vertiginous grassy hill which has been the site of an annual **Cheese Rolling Festival** (ⓦcheese-rolling.co.uk) for, some say, hundreds of years. On the last Monday in May, at noon, officials launch a round of double Gloucester cheese down the hill – whereupon dozens of intrepid and/or drunk souls with bravehearts run down after it, to the accompaniment of much revelry from the five thousand or so assembled onlookers. Whoever reaches the bottom first wins the cheese; second and third place win small cash prizes. In case you're tempted to take part, have a look at the website for images of just how steep Cooper's Hill is: it's not quite ninety degrees, but it might as well be. The resulting string of hospitalizations among competitors has resulted in the race often being banned; the 2010 event was officially cancelled – though cheeses were still rolled and people still ran – and in 2013 police advised the event's cheesemaker not to supply rounds of double Gloucester. That year foam replicas were rolled instead – and in 2014 Dutch cheesemakers stepped in to offer a 3kg round of Gouda. Expect road closures and parking restrictions in the area on the day.

Green Dragon Inn Cockleford ☎ 01242 870271, ⓦ green -dragon-inn.co.uk. Stone-flagged 17th-century pub in the next village south of Cowley and Coberley, with well-kept beer, good food (mains £9–17), wooden furniture in the bar crafted by "mouse man" designer Robert Thompson and nine pleasantly airy en-suite rooms upstairs. Mon–Sat 11am–11pm, Sun noon–10.30pm. **£95**

Star Bistro Ullenwood ☎ 01242 535984, ⓦ www .natstar.ac.uk/starbistro. This unusual lunch option is a collaboration between the Wiggly Worm, a charity run by the "Cotswold Chef" Rob Rees (ⓦ thecotswoldchef .com), and the National Star College of further education for young people with disabilities in Ullenwood, a mile west of Seven Springs. The seasonal, market-fresh cooking is consistently excellent, done in an open kitchen, service is warm and efficient – everything works. Two courses £14. It's popular: book ahead if you can. Mon–Fri 11am–4pm.

Gloucester

For centuries life was good for **GLOUCESTER**, which lies ten miles west of Cheltenham. The Romans chose this spot for a garrison to guard the River Severn and spy on Wales, and later for a *colonia*, or home for retired soldiers – the highest status a provincial Roman town could dream of. Commercial success came with traffic up the Severn, which developed into one of the busiest trade routes in Europe: the city's political importance hit its peak under the Normans, when William the Conqueror was a regular visitor. Gloucester became a religious centre too, as exemplified by the construction of what is now the cathedral, but by the fifteenth century it was on the slide: navigating the Severn this far upstream was so difficult that most trade shifted south to Bristol. In an attempt to reverse the

1

decline, a canal was opened in 1827 to link Gloucester to Sharpness, sixteen miles south on a broader stretch of the Severn. Trade picked up for a time, but it was only a temporary stay of economic execution.

Today, the canal is busy once again, though this time with pleasure boats, and the Victorian **docks** have undergone a facelift – shown off best for May's grand **Tall Ships Festival** (ⓦgloucestertallships.co.uk) – but the main reason for coming this way is to see Gloucester's awe-inspiring **cathedral**.

Gloucester Cathedral

College Green • Daily 7.30am–6pm • Free • ⓦ gloucestercathedral.org.uk

The superb condition of **Gloucester Cathedral** is striking in a city that has lost so much of its history; this one building still keeps seven masons in full-time employment. The Saxons founded an abbey here, and four centuries later, Benedictine monks arrived intent on building their own church. Work began in 1089. As a place of worship it shot to importance after the murder of Edward II in 1327 at Berkeley Castle (see p.71): Gloucester took his body and the king's shrine became a major place of pilgrimage. The money generated helped finance the conversion of the church into England's first and greatest example of the **Perpendicular style**, crowned by a magnificent 225ft tower. Henry VIII recognized the church's prestige by conferring the status of cathedral.

The nave and choir

Beneath the fourteenth- and fifteenth-century reconstructions, some Norman aspects remain, best seen in the **nave**, which is flanked by sturdy pillars and arches adorned with immaculate zigzag carvings. Only when you reach the choir and transepts can you see how skilfully the new church was built inside the old, the Norman masonry hidden beneath the finer lines of the Perpendicular panelling and tracery.

The **choir** has exceptional fourteenth-century misericords, and also provides the best vantage point for admiring the **east window**, completed in around 1350 and – at almost 80ft tall – the largest medieval window in Britain. Beneath it, to the left (as you're facing the east window) is the **tomb of Edward II** in alabaster and marble. In the nearby **Lady Chapel**, delicate carved tracery holds a breathtaking patchwork of stained-glass windows. In the **south ambulatory**, the tomb of Robert, duke of Normandy – eldest son of William the Conqueror – forms a painted wooden effigy dating from around 1290 (though Robert died in 1134). Dressed as a Crusader, he lies in a curious pose: his crossed arms and legs signify his length of military service.

The cloisters

The innovative nature of the cathedral's design is also evident in the beautiful **cloisters**, completed in 1367 and featuring the first fan vaulting in the country; the intricate quality of the work is outdone only by Henry VII's Chapel in Westminster Abbey, which it inspired. Take time to explore, not least to find the monks' **lavatorium** on the north side, a communal washing area with a long stone basin. The cloisters were used to represent the corridors of Hogwart's School of Witchcraft and Wizardry in the *Harry Potter* films.

Upstairs galleries and tower

Upstairs galleries April–Oct Mon–Fri 10.30am–4pm, Sat 10.30am–3.30pm • £2 Tower Wed–Fri 2.30pm, Sat 1.30pm & 2.30pm, in school hols also Mon & Tues 2.30pm • £4

The north transept serves as the entrance to the **upstairs galleries** where an exhibition explains the east window and allows you to view it at close quarters; in the **Whispering Gallery** you can pick up the tiniest sounds from across the vaulting. The fee also grants access to the **treasury**, of minor interest. You can climb the **tower** for exceptional views.

The Cross

Gloucester lies on the east bank of the Severn, its centre spread around a curve in the river. The city clusters around Northgate, Southgate, Eastgate and Westgate streets, all Roman roads; where they meet is dubbed the **Cross**, though no cross stands there. This is the location of the Friday **farmers' market**, overlooked by **St Michael's Tower**, all that's left of a fifteenth-century church – the tower now houses a heritage information centre for Gloucester Civic Trust, who run guided walks from here (see p.54).

Gloucester Folk Museum

99 Westgate St • Tues–Sat 10am–5pm, late July & Aug also Mon 10am–5pm • £3 • ☎ 01452 396868, ⓦ gloucestermuseums.co.uk

Westgate Street is the quietest and most pleasant of the city's four main thoroughfares – an odd mix of fast food outlets and pound shops with independent businesses and lively, locally run cafés. Near the cathedral grounds is the **Gloucester Folk Museum**, with displays on social history and changing exhibitions on local themes filling three floors of a handsome Tudor and Jacobean building.

Beatrix Potter Museum and Shop

9 College Court • Mon–Sat 10am–5pm, Sun noon–4pm • Free • ☎ 01452 422856, ⓦ tailor-of-gloucester.org.uk

One of the cottages on College Court, a lane between Westgate Street and the cathedral, was the workshop of John Pritchard, a Victorian **tailor** who was commissioned to make a new suit of clothes for the mayor. During the job, he returned one Monday morning to find the suit completed, apart from one buttonhole which bore a note reading "no more twist". Pritchard ascribed the miracle to fairies, though in truth two drunken employees had slept off their Saturday night excesses in the workshop rather than going home, and were then too embarrassed to be seen in the street by Sunday churchgoers, so stayed and worked. The bones of the story caught author Beatrix Potter's imagination when she visited in 1897; she sketched another, more picturesque house a few doors down at no. 9 to serve as the location for her children's story *The Tailor of Gloucester* – and that building has become "**The House of the Tailor of Gloucester**", now a **Beatrix Potter Museum and Shop**, with lots of Peter Rabbit trinkets for sale and a small room of Victorian memorabilia.

Gloucester City Museum and Art Gallery

Brunswick Rd • Tues–Sat 10am–5pm, late July & Aug also Mon 10am–5pm • £3 • ☎ 01452 396131, ⓦ gloucestermuseums.co.uk

A Victorian building a short stroll south of the centre houses **Gloucester City Museum and Art Gallery**. Reach it from Southgate Street via Greyfriars Lane, beside the chiefly fourteenth-century **St Mary de Crypt Church** and the gaunt, half-forgotten ruins of a Franciscan friary, founded here in 1231 and now just a skeletal ruin among the modern developments. The museum's archeological collection includes a decorative bronze mirror dating to about 50 AD and an exquisite set of twelfth-century bone and antler playing pieces – the Gloucester Tables Set – bearing designs representing everything from the signs of the zodiac to biblical stories, while the gallery displays works by Turner and Gainsborough, among others.

Gloucester Docks

ⓦ gloucesterdocks.me.uk

Roughly a third of a mile southwest of the city centre, **Gloucester Docks** holds fourteen warehouses built for storing grain following the opening of the Sharpness canal to the River Severn in 1827. Most have been turned into offices and shops, but there's still a good deal of atmosphere. Beside the main docks area is the Gloucester Quays shopping mall.

1

Gloucester Waterways Museum

Gloucester Docks • Daily: July & Aug 10.30am–5pm; rest of year 11am–4pm; boat trips May–Aug daily on the hour noon–3pm; April, Sept & Oct Sat & Sun only; 45min • £5.50; boat trip £6 • ☎01452 318200, ⓦ canalrivertrust.org.uk/gloucester-waterways-museum

At the docks, the southernmost Llanthony Warehouse is now occupied by the **Gloucester Waterways Museum**, which delves into every nook and cranny of the area's watery history, from the engineering of the locks to the lives of the horses that trod the towpaths, along with plenty of interactive displays. Out from the main building you can also practise "walking the wall" in the time-honoured manner of boatmen, who propelled their narrowboats through the tunnels by their feet, and explore the boats themselves moored up along the quayside. The museum runs regular **boat trips** out onto the Sharpness canal, with commentary.

Nature in Art gallery

Beside the A38 near Twigworth • Tues–Sun 10am–5pm • £5.25 • ☎01452 731422, ⓦ nature-in-art.org.uk • Bus #71 (Mon–Sat hourly; 10min)

About two miles north of Gloucester, eighteenth-century Wallsworth Hall is now home to the **Nature in Art** gallery. Dedicated exclusively to artistic portrayals of the natural world in all disciplines – from painting to decorative and applied arts – it includes a Byzantine mosaic alongside Lalique glassware, and works by Picasso beside Royal Doulton china, as well as a changing series of temporary exhibits by contemporary artists and craftspeople.

ARRIVAL AND GETTING AROUND   GLOUCESTER

By plane Gloucester's titchy airport (☎01452 857700, ⓦ www.gloucestershireairport.co.uk) lies beside junction 11 of the M5. It has a few domestic routes as well as pleasure flights run by ⓦ tigerairways.co.uk, ⓦ cotswold aeroclub.com & ⓦ ballooning-network.co.uk.

By train Gloucester station is on Bruton Way, a five-minute walk east of the centre. It is bypassed by many fast trains from the Midlands and the Southwest (change at Cheltenham Spa for connections).

Destinations Birmingham New St (hourly; 50min); Bristol (hourly; 40min); London Paddington (hourly, some change at Swindon; 1hr 55min), Stroud (hourly; 20min).

By bus National Express coaches from London and Heathrow Airport arrive at the bus station on Station Rd, opposite the train station: these are also a useful way to get to or from Cirencester on a Sunday, when local buses don't run. Some local buses depart from stops on

Clarence St nearby.

Destinations Burford (Mon–Sat 2 daily, 1 on Sun; 1hr 20min); Cheltenham (every 10min; 35min); Cirencester (Mon–Sat 4 daily; 1hr 10min); Dursley (Mon–Sat hourly, 2 on Sun; 50min); Nailsworth (Mon–Sat hourly; 1hr); Northleach (Mon–Sat 2 daily, 1 on Sun; 55min); Oxford (Mon–Sat 2 daily, 1 on Sun; 2hr); Painswick (2 on Wed; 25min); Slimbridge (Mon–Sat approx hourly, 2 on Sun; 40min); Stroud (twice hourly; 40min).

By car Waterwells park and ride (ⓦ gloucestershire.gov .uk/parkandride) is south in Quedgeley, off the A38 near M5 junction 12. Parking is free. Bus #507 runs to Southgate St in the centre (Mon–Sat every 12min 7.30am–6.30pm; £2.50 return, additional passengers £1.50).

By taxi Try Gloucester Taxi (☎01452 341341, ⓦ gloucester-taxi.co.uk) or AndyCars (☎01452 523000, ⓦ andycarsgloucester.co.uk).

INFORMATION AND TOURS

Tourist office 28 Southgate St (Mon 10am–5pm, Tues–Sat 9.30am–5pm; ☎01452 396572, ⓦ thecityofgloucester .co.uk & ⓦ cotswolds.com). They have details of self-guided walks on marked routes along the River Severn and Sharpness Canal.

Walking tours Gloucester Civic Trust runs guided walks

around the city centre from St Michael's Tower (April–Sept Mon–Sat 11.30am; 1hr 30min; £4; ☎07899 804853, ⓦ gloucestercivictrust.org). Gloucester Ghost Walks, led by paranormal investigator Lyn Cinderey, start from the tourist office (Wed 8pm, Thurs 6.30pm; £6; ☎07908 552855, ⓦ gloucesterghostwalks.co.uk).

ACCOMMODATION

Mulberry House 2a Heathville Rd ☎01452 720079, ⓦ the-mulberry-house.co.uk. Decent B&B in a modern family home roughly ten minutes' walk northeast of

the centre. Two en-suite doubles – small but spotless – are enhanced with quality breakfasts and a warm welcome. Cash only. __£55__

New Inn 16 Northgate St ☎01452 522177, ⓦnewinn -hotel.co.uk. This fourteenth-century galleried pub has 33 rooms in a convenient location right in the city centre. Quality is fairly basic, with corporate furniture despite the original wood beams; expect swirly carpets and late-night karaoke. **£54**

EATING AND DRINKING

Cafe Rene 31 Southgate St ☎01452 309340, ⓦcafe rene.co.uk. This lively, fancifully decorated pub, beside Greyfriars, serves decent burgers and steaks, with plenty for vegetarians (mains £9–14) and lighter lunches, as well as great Sunday barbecues in summer, and live blues, jazz and acoustic music twice a week. After 11pm on weekend nights, the cellar bar turns into a club (£2 admission), for loud local DJs. Sun–Thurs 11am–midnight, Fri & Sat 11am–4am.

New Inn 16 Northgate St ☎01452 522177, ⓦnewinn -hotel.co.uk. Pop into this fourteenth-century pub in the city centre to have a gander at the preserved interior – this is Britain's most complete surviving medieval courtyard tavern, ringed by galleries (and, reputedly, haunted) – and to sup a pint of one of their several cask ales. Mon–Thurs 11am– 11pm, Fri & Sat 11am–midnight, Sun noon–10.30pm.

Over Farm Market Over ☎01452 521014, ⓦoverfarm market.co.uk. Head about a mile west of the city centre to this wonderful farm shop, running for more than 30 years and often named best in the area. It's more like a rural food emporium, with deli and bakery – perfect to pick up a snack or several, along with wide ranges of local cheeses and beers. It also has events and activities for children. Mon–Sat 9am–6pm, Sun 9.30am–5pm.

So Thai Longsmith St ☎01452 535185, ⓦso-thai .co.uk. This fresh, appealing Thai restaurant has rapidly gained a reputation for quality and authenticity. The decor takes in vaulted brickwork, service is attentive and the food – including unusual northern Thai pork curry with pineapple, lamb *massaman*, and others – expertly prepared. Mains £9–16, two-course lunch menu £9. Tues– Sun 11am–10pm.

DIRECTORY

Hospital Gloucestershire Royal, Great Western Rd ☎0300 422 2222, ⓦwww.gloshospitals.nhs.uk.
Markets For farmers' markets, see p.45.
Pharmacy Boots, 38 Eastgate St ☎01452 423501,

ⓦboots.com (Mon–Sat 8am–6pm, Sun 10.30am–4.30pm).
Police station Longsmith St ☎101, ⓦgloucestershire .police.uk (daily 8am–8pm).
Post office Kings Sq (Mon–Sat 9am–5.30pm).

Painswick and around

Encompassing a ribbon of undulating terrain from the busy roads coming down off the Cotswold Edge into Cheltenham and Gloucester virtually as far as Bath, the south Cotswolds hold some of the region's best-loved countryside – as well as some of its most memorable hideaways.

Things get off to a cracking start at **PAINSWICK**, a congenial old wool town of legendary beauty seven miles southeast of Gloucester, or ten miles from Cheltenham, and almost 500ft up on a south-facing hillside. Ancient buildings jostle for space on its narrow, steep streets tumbling down off the regrettably busy A46. The relatively easy access means that Painswick can see promenading crowds in season, but its charm survives more or less intact. Just stroll the village's half-dozen lanes to sample the atmosphere, particular ancient Bisley Street, flanked by mostly fourteenth-century buildings.

St Mary's Church

Stroud Rd • Daily 9.30am–6pm; Nov–March closes 4pm • Free • ☎01452 814795, ⓦstmaryspainswick.org.uk

The spire of **St Mary's Church** dominates the village. Take your time to wander through the churchyard, where 99 **yew trees**, trimmed into bulbous lollipops, surround a fine collection of seventeenth- and eighteenth-century table tombs. And there are, apparently, exactly 99: the Devil himself, so storytellers say, brings death every time someone has tried to plant a hundredth. When every parish in the Gloucester diocese was given a yew tree to mark the millennium in 2000, eyes rolled in Painswick; the hapless tree was nonetheless planted – and remains healthy. Seven years later, though, one of the older yews toppled, implacably restoring the numerological balance. The **church** itself is a

1

Perpendicular beauty, though nothing remains of the pre-existing building mentioned in the Domesday Book. On the Sunday following September 19 each year, Painswick hosts the **clypping ceremony**, derived from an Anglo-Saxon word meaning to clasp or embrace: the village children process around the churchyard with flowers in their hair, then join hands to encircle the church and sing a special hymn, amid much festivity.

Painswick Rococo Garden

Gloucester Rd • Mid-Jan to end Oct daily 11am–5pm • £6.50 • ☎ 01452 813204, Ⓦ www.rococogarden.org.uk

Painswick's most promoted attraction – and a genuine one-off, unlike any other Cotswold garden – is the **Rococo Garden**, occupying most of the grounds of the privately owned eighteenth-century Painswick House, located about half a mile north of the village up the B4073 Gloucester road. Created in the 1730s in a deep valley behind the house by Benjamin Hyett, son of the original owner, the garden lay overgrown and abandoned for many years until restoration in the 1970s, thanks to a painting commissioned by Hyett in 1748 which showed the garden in its original form. This is England's only example of Rococo garden design, a short-lived fashion typified by a mix of formal geometrical shapes and more naturalistic, curving lines. In among the planting, expect to see statues and odd little follies, not least the spiked, curving **Exedra**, overlooking the diamond-shaped kitchen garden. For the best views, walk around anticlockwise. Winter is particularly special, with vast banks of snowdrops carpeting the slopes in February and March.

ARRIVAL AND INFORMATION   PAINSWICK

By bus Bus #46 (hourly) runs to/from Cheltenham (30min), Stroud (10min) and Nailsworth (30min). Bus #256 (2 on Wed) runs to/from Gloucester (25min).

Tourist office Painswick's summer-only tourist office (April–Oct Mon–Wed 10am–1pm, Thurs & Fri 10am–4pm, Sat 10am–1pm; ☎ 07503 516924, Ⓦ visitthecotswolds .org.uk & Ⓦ cotswolds.com) was, at the time of writing, temporarily housed in St Mary's Church ahead of a relocation to the gravedigger's hut in the churchyard.

WALKS AROUND PAINSWICK

Despite – or because of – the steep hills, there are some fine walks near Painswick, which lies plumb on the Cotswold Way. The Painswick tourist office has details of a leg-stretching **circular walk** (7 miles; 4hr) which heads north out of the village and up onto the Cotswold Way to panoramic vistas atop **Painswick Beacon** (929ft) clear into Wales, Shropshire and down to the Severn Estuary, before swinging around between farms to **Edge** and back up into Painswick. Another route leads southeast out of the village down Tibbiwell Lane, across the Painswick Stream and up Greenhouse Lane on the other side to reach the ridge-top at **Bull's Cross**, on the B4070 road, which offers views out over **Slad** (see p.58) and the Slad valley beyond. From Bull's Cross, pick a path north or south to descend back into the Painswick valley again.

An alternative circular **walk** (4 miles; 3hr) which takes in Cooper's Hill – site of the famous cheese-rolling festival (see p.50) – starts from **Cranham** village, a couple of miles north of Painswick, reached on bus #46 (hourly) between Stroud (15min) and Cheltenham (25min), or bus #256 (twice on Wed) from Gloucester (35min). It plunges straight into the ancient beech woods, climbing to join the Cotswold Way for the scenic stretch to the top of Cooper's Hill before descending on a path back to Cranham – where the traditional *Black Horse* (☎ 01452 812217, Ⓦ theblackhorsecranham.co.uk) is on hand for refreshment and decent meals; the pub garden is lovely. Download details of the walk at the Cotswold Way pages of Ⓦ escapetothe cotswolds.org.uk. The composer **Gustav Holst**, who stayed for a while in Cranham, often walked these paths; when he set Christina Rossetti's poem *In The Bleak Midwinter* to music for a hymnal published in 1906, he named his tune *Cranham*. The familiar melody is the perfect mental accompaniment for a chilly Christmas walk in Cranham Woods.

The website of Painswick Rococo Garden also offers downloadable details of four walks in and around Painswick.

ACCOMMODATION AND EATING

Cardynham House Tibbiwell St ☎ 01452 814006, ⓦ cardynham.co.uk. Lovely guesthouse with nine modern themed rooms – "Old Tuscany","Arabian Nights" – most with four-poster beds, all en suite, charmingly presented within a fifteenth-century building. It's a cosy, high-quality option, while the bistro (closed Sun eve & Mon), run by an outgoing Romanian couple, is a great place for simple, well-cooked nosh – cod loin, lamb cutlets, beef stroganoff and the like (mains £12–16). **£90**

Cotswolds88 Kemps Lane ☎ 01452 813688, ⓦ cotswolds88.com. Painswick's trump card, a glamorous design hotel crowbarred into the eighteenth-century vicarage. If it feels like a Soho boudoir inside, there's a reason: the hotel is owned by London design guru Marchella De Angelis, who is into numerology (hence the deeply significant "88" tag) and interiors that are either daringly avant-garde or tiresomely garish, depending on your taste. Expect chrome statues, psychedelic lighting, zebra-striped *chaises longues* and a cool service ethic which manages to blend genuine warmth with a rather enticing dash of contempt. Stay, eat, drink, smile – this is a playful bolthole to savour. **£110**

JK's at St Michaels Victoria St ☎ 01452 813832, ⓦ jks-restaurant.com. Upscale restaurant in a seventeenth-century building opposite the church, serving modern European cuisine based on locally sourced ingredients – pork in calvados gravy or chicken with basil and mozzarella (mains £10–16). Wed–Sat noon–11pm, Sun 12.30–3pm.

★ **Olivas** Friday St ☎ 01452 814774, ⓦ olivas.moonfruit .com. Brilliant (and much-loved) deli and café that does delicious Mediterranean-style lunches – Spanish soups and stews of chicken, chickpeas and chorizo, stuffed aubergines, loads of tapas including calamari, whitebait, olives, and more, all around £10. Daily 10am–5pm.

Prinknash Abbey and Bird Park

Abbey Shop and café daily 10am–4pm • ☎ 01452 812066, ⓦ prinknashabbey.org.uk **Bird Park** Daily 10am–5pm; Nov–Feb closes 4pm • £6.80 • ☎ 01452 812727, ⓦ thebirdpark.com

A couple of miles north of Painswick on the A46 Cheltenham road, signs point down off the hill to **Prinknash Abbey**. Prinknash – pronounced, bizarrely, *prinnidge* – is a functioning community of twelve Benedictine monks, who live in a sixteenth-century manor house below the car park which is off-limits to general visitors, as is the incongruous 1972 tower block which served as the monks' residence until 2008. Stop in at the modern **shop and café** for an earnest cup of tea and to sample the atmosphere – but otherwise head off down a signed lane to the separately run **Prinknash Bird and Deer Park**, a great rural retreat for families, with fallow deer, donkeys, bird-feeding and country paths to explore.

Sheepscombe

Follow the Painswick Stream up to its source and you come to **SHEEPSCOMBE**, tucked away off the B4070 amid beech woods at the head of the valley. This hidden, barely visited village sports classic Cotswold good looks and an isolation which has served it well: the lanes in and out are barely wide enough for a single car, yet the views yawn out over open countryside. As if by magic, it also lays claim to one of the Cotswolds' best-loved pubs. To stretch your legs, wander down through the village and over to the still, silent **church of St John** the Apostle, built in 1819, when the now-gone Sheepscombe mill supported twice the population the village has today. Few corners of the Cotswolds hold such resonance. Download details of a walk across the high ground of Sheepscombe Common at ⓦ nationaltrust.org.uk.

ARRIVAL AND DEPARTURE   SHEEPSCOMBE

By bus Bus #23 runs once on Thursday morning from Stroud (15min), returning the same afternoon.

EATING AND DRINKING

★ **Butchers Arms** Sheepscombe ☎ 01452 812113, ⓦ www.butchers-arms.co.uk. Marvellous village pub that simply gets everything right – beer, atmosphere, welcome, food... it's all spot on, neither fancy nor dour.

Mains – pork and apple sausages, salmon fishcakes, sundried tomato risotto, and the like – are £9–11. Mon–Thurs 11.30am–3pm & 6.30–11pm, Fri 11.30am–3pm & 6–11pm, Sat 11.30am–11pm, Sun noon–10.30pm.

1

Miserden

Bus #23 runs once on Thurs morning from Stroud (45min), returning the same afternoon. Also bus #256 from Gloucester (twice on Wed; 50min)

Over the ridges a couple of miles east of Sheepscombe – and past **WHITEWAY**, where a group of activists bought land in 1898 to establish an anarchist commune (which still survives), stands **MISERDEN**. Sapperton (see p.62) lies a few miles south, while steep lanes cross the valley and over to the Duntisbournes (see p.85), marking a **watershed**: on the ridge's western side, moisture drains into the Frome and thence to the Atlantic, while the eastern side drains to the Churn and the North Sea.

Misarden Park Gardens

Miserden • April–Sept Tues–Thurs 10am–4.30pm • £4 • ☎ 01285 821303, ⓦ misardenpark.co.uk

Poised above the valley of the River Frome near its source, the peaceful village of Miserden offers access to Misarden Park Gardens. The mismatch in spelling is accurate: the village and estate have an E, the gardens and manor house have an A, though nobody is sure why – and both are pronounced the same anyway. Up here, at over 800ft in elevation, breezes can be a little fresh, but the Lutyens-designed topiary remains immaculate and the herbaceous borders unruffled.

Slad

From **BIRDLIP**, a popular viewpoint up on the escarpment beside the A417, four or five miles east of Gloucester, the B4070 winds a scenic, undulating route southwest towards Stroud. Past turns for Sheepscombe, the road dips to scoot along the western slope of the Slad valley. **SLAD** itself, a little village strung out along and below the road, with a steep hillside behind, enjoys tumbling vistas down to the Slad Brook and beyond. This was the home for many years at the beginning and end of his life of **Laurie Lee**, author of the famous childhood memoir *Cider with Rosie* (see below).

Walks aside – and there are plenty: an easy four-mile route circumnavigates the village from Bull's Cross on the ridge above, coming down to the brook, past the quarries and back up to the ridge again – Slad's most obvious draw is the *Woolpack* pub on the main B4070 road, Lee's haunt for decades. On the slopes opposite the pub you'll find the writer's last resting-place, in the graveyard of the **Holy Trinity Church**. As it says on his stone: "He lies in the valley he loved."

ARRIVAL AND DEPARTURE   SLAD

By bus Bus #23 runs once on Thursday morning from Stroud (6min), returning the same afternoon. Also bus #63   from Stroud (1 on Sat; 5min).

LAURIE LEE IN SLAD

Laurie Lee is acclaimed as one of Britain's best twentieth-century writers. Born in Stroud in June 1914, he was raised by his mother in a Slad cottage; his father had left for London during World War I and never returned. Lee's most famous work *Cider with Rosie*, published in 1959 and often still given as a set text in schools, describes his childhood in Slad, evoking the atmosphere of the isolated rural village – before the appearance of cars – in beautifully vivid, engaging language. At the age of twenty, Lee left Slad for London and then travelled for four years through Spain, an experience recalled decades later in his masterpiece of travel writing *As I Walked Out One Midsummer Morning* (1969) and in *A Moment of War* (1991), a starkly affecting memoir of his time as a volunteer in the Spanish Civil War. Lee produced many other narrative books, essays and collections of poetry, yet seemed little taken with the London literary establishment. On the proceeds of *Cider with Rosie* he chose to buy a cottage in Slad, where he returned with his wife Kathy in the 1960s, remaining until his death in 1997.

FROM TOP WESTONBIRT ARBORETUM (P.68); STROUD FARMERS' MARKET (P.60) >

1

EATING AND DRINKING

Woolpack Slad ⊙01452 813429. Laurie Lee's old haunt remains unrenovated, a simple stone cottage inn, with thick walls, small windows and outside toilets. The beer (from the Uley brewery the other side of Stroud) suits the yawning views from the little terrace to a T, and decent food, a step above usual pub fare, adds to the allure (mains around £9–13). Daily noon–midnight (no food Sun eve).

Stroud and around

There are few reasons to stop in the market town of **STROUD**, once the centre of the local cloth industry. The best of this part of the Cotswolds lies in the **Five Valleys** surrounding Stroud – the Painswick Valley and Slad Valley to the north, the Toadsmoor Valley and Frome Valley to the east (the latter also known as the "Golden Valley") and the Nailsworth Valley to the south. Their topography of rushing streams, deep, narrow gorges and high common land for grazing sheep spurred the eighteenth- and nineteenth-century construction of textile mills galore, which in turn led to feats of engineering that transformed Stroud into a hub first for canal transport between the Severn and the Thames and, later, the railway.

Nowadays Stroud is big on independent retail. Leading the pack is the Saturday **farmers' market** (see p.45), a weekly jamboree of forty or fifty stallholders which fills the central streets, alongside music and impromptu happenings. In a similar vein, the Shambles, a medieval arcaded lane beside the church, hosts the **Shambles Market** (ⓦshamblesmarketstroud.co.uk) every Friday and Saturday – anything from books to cheese – and the **Sunday Market** (ⓦstroudsundaymarket .co.uk) adds crafts, food and entertainment on the first Sunday monthly. You could drop into the **Stroud Valleys Project** shop, 8 Threadneedle St (ⓦstroudvalleysproject .org), the front for a charity supporting environmentally sustainable local

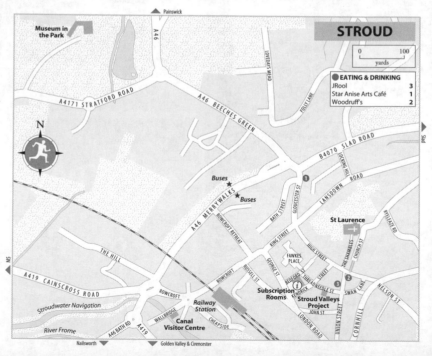

businesses, or browse the many unbranded local shops, cafés and delis dotted through the town centre.

Museum in the Park

Stratford Park • Tues–Fri 10am–5pm, Sat & Sun 11am–5pm; Aug also Mon 10am–5pm; Oct–March closes 4pm • Free • ☎ 01453 763394, ⓦ www.museuminthepark.org.uk

Stroud's legacy of textile excellence is celebrated at the **Museum in the Park**, with historical displays and a roster of changing temporary exhibitions on art and design housed in a splendid seventeeth-century wool merchant's mansion house on the northwestern fringes of town.

ARRIVAL AND INFORMATION   STROUD

By train From the station on Stratford Rd it's a short walk up through steep shopping streets into the town centre.
Destinations Cheltenham (hourly; 25min); Gloucester (hourly; 20min); Kemble (hourly; 15min); London Paddington (hourly, some change at Swindon; 1hr 30min).
By bus Stroud is a hub for bus routes and you may find yourself switching buses here. Most stop on Merrywalks, the main street west of the centre.
Destinations Cheltenham (hourly; 40min); Cirencester (Mon–Fri 5 daily, 3 on Sat; 35min); Dursley (hourly, 45min); Gloucester (hourly; 40min); Minchinhampton (Mon–Sat approx every 2hrs; 15min); Nailsworth (at least hourly; 20min); Painswick (hourly; 10min); Rodborough

Common (Mon–Sat 4 daily; 15min); Sapperton (Mon–Fri 5 daily, 3 on Sat; 25min); Selsley (hourly; 10min); Tetbury (Mon–Sat every 2hrs; 35min); Uley (Mon–Fri 4 daily; 50min); Wotton (Mon–Sat 4 daily; 40min).
Tourist office In the late-Regency Subscription Rooms on George St (Mon–Sat 10am–5pm; ☎01453 760960, ⓦvisitthecotswolds.org.uk & ⓦcotswolds.com). Among their racks of material are route descriptions for walks through nearby villages as well as towpath strolls west along the Stroudwater Navigation canal, which begins at Wallbridge just behind the station, where there's also a Canal Visitor Centre (Mon–Fri 10am–1pm, Sat 10am–4pm; ☎07582 286636, ⓦcotswoldcanals.com).

EATING AND DRINKING

JRool 12 Union St ☎01453 767123, ⓦjrool.co.uk. Lovely, relaxed bistro with a reputation for top-notch food, served from a small menu: wild mushroom gnocchi, pan-seared lemon sole, goat's cheese crumble, and so on. Mains £13–16, with more affordable set menu options too. Mon–Sat 10am–3pm, Thurs–Sat also 6.30pm–midnight.
★ **Star Anise Arts Café** 1 Gloucester St ☎01453 840021, ⓦstaraniseartscafe.com. This alternative-minded café at the bottom of Gloucester St has a lively, sociable buzz, with

tables spilling out onto the flagged courtyard. Food is decent, too, with bread and croissants baked onsite fresh daily and delicious veggie food, sourced locally (under £10). Mon–Fri 8am–5pm, Sat 8.30am–5pm.
Woodruffs 24 High St ☎01453 759195, ⓦwoodruffs organiccafe.co.uk. This was Britain's first organic café when it opened in 1998, and it remains a chatty, friendly place for a healthy, locally sourced lunch of mezze, beanburgers or stilton sandwiches (mains £5–9). Mon–Sat 8.30am–5pm.

The Golden Valley

Stroud may once have been a minor powerhouse of the Industrial Revolution, but today the money has moved out into the villages. Hemmed in by high slopes, the A419 and the railway head east into the valley of the River Frome, named the "**Golden Valley**" – so locals claim – by Queen Victoria when gazing through her train window; on an autumn afternoon, when low sunshine lights up the wooded slopes, aflame with colour, it's not hard to see her point. The seven miles to Sapperton, where the railway and the Thames and Severn Canal both duck into tunnels beneath the hills, at one time hosted 150 mills processing Cotswold wool and other textiles for distribution around the Empire.

Now the canal is long-disused (see ⓦwww.cotswoldcanalsproject.org for plans to revive it) and the villages are mostly quiet – but still virtually inaccessible, clinging to the forested slopes with only the narrowest of lanes to connect them. **CHALFORD**, the main settlement, was known as "Little Switzerland": its Alpine slopes are speckled with

1

mill-workers' cottages and threaded by a Lilliputian High Street barely wide enough to fit one car. Walk, instead, to find the distinctive **Round House** – a circular cottage that is still lived in – and to view the Arts and Crafts fittings in **Christ Church** on the main road.

On the slopes above, **FRANCE LYNCH** is named for exiled Huguenot weavers who settled here in the eighteenth century; find a route via the lanes above Chalford to reach pretty **BISLEY**, dominated by the spire of All Saints' Church and centred on the *Bear Inn*. Walking routes from the pub lead into the quiet, beech-filled **Toadsmoor Valley**.

At the upper end of the Golden Valley, **SAPPERTON** marks the "West Portal" of the canal tunnel; the "East Portal" is near Coates; see p.86.

ACCOMMODATION AND EATING   THE GOLDEN VALLEY

Bear Bisley ☎01452 770265, ⓦbisleybear.co.uk. A rather lovely seventeenth-century village pub, updated inside in an appealing, modern style, with good beer and one spick-and-span room for B&B. Mon–Sat noon–2.30pm & 6–11pm, Sun noon–10.30pm. **£65**

Bell Sapperton ☎01285 760298, ⓦbellsapperton .co.uk. This fine old pub in Sapperton village is known best for its food – well-presented modern British cooking in a cheerful, easygoing setting (mains £12–17). Book ahead if you can. Daily noon–2pm & 7–9.30pm.

Cotswold Yurts Chalford ☎07847 517905, ⓦcotswoldyurts.co.uk. Enjoy a spot of "glamping" (glamorous camping) in these four Turkoman-style yurts in meadows on Westley Farm, kitted out to luxury standards and bookable over the summer months for a minimum of three nights. **£385**

King's Head France Lynch ☎01453 882225, ⓦkings headfrancelynch.co.uk. A much-loved local pub in the middle of the village's narrow, winding lanes, with good beer and decent pub grub – steak, chicken in white wine sauce etc (mains £10–14). Mon–Sat noon–2.30pm & 6–11pm, Sun noon–10.30pm.

Selsley and around

Southwest of Stroud, the B4066 cuts a glorious route along the Cotswold Edge, worth driving simply for the sake of it. As you climb away from the Frome valley, **SELSLEY** – or, specifically, the saddleback tower of its glorious Arts and Crafts **church of All Saints** (ⓦallsaintsselsley.org.uk) – hoves into view, the church adorned with stained glass by William Morris.

Woodchester Mansion

Woodchester Park • April–Oct selected days 11am–5pm • £6.50 • ☎01453 861541, ⓦwoodchestermansion.org.uk & ⓦnationaltrust .org.uk • Access is only on foot from the car park – a walk of about a mile down the hillside – or with the free shuttle (see website for pickup points)

Above Selsley, on a left-hand curve, a signed turn leads left down a track to a valley-side car park. This is the closest you can drive to **Woodchester Mansion**, a rather spooky Victorian Gothic house in a hidden valley which was left part-built in 1873 and never completed. Around the mansion stretches **Woodchester Park**, with some silent walks beside a string of five lakes. Note that Woodchester village lies several miles away on the A46.

Uley and around

On the B4066, just past the turn for Nympsfield – a rather pretty village, unused to visitors – is a layby for the **Coaley Peak viewpoint**, the first of several along this stretch offering panoramic views out over the Severn Vale. Here is also the Neolithic burial mound **Nympsfield Long Barrow**, while just further along the road is the **Uley Long Barrow**, also known as **Hetty Pegler's Tump** after a seventeenth-century landowner (ⓦenglish-heritage.org.uk).

Before the road drops down off the ridge, to one side rises the mound of **Uley Bury**, among the largest Iron Age hill-forts in Britain. Fences prevent you from clambering on top of the bury, but you can walk around the edge – about two miles in total – and take in some staggering views. The atmosphere peaks on a winter's day, when bracing winds blow across the ridge while mist gathers in the valley below.

WALKS AROUND SELSLEY AND ULEY

Two easy **circular walks** using part of the Cotswold Way – and both downloadable at
Ⓦescapetothecotswolds.org.uk on the Cotswold Way pages – offer scenic routes flanking this
bit of the B4066. The first (5 miles; 4hr) begins at **KING'S STANLEY**, reached on bus #14
(hourly) from Stroud (20min) and Gloucester (55min), and heads up straight away onto Selsley
Common, offering grand views over the Severn. After a pause in Selsley village, the path drops
down for a towpath walk along the Stroudwater canal before the return to King's Stanley.

The second route (4 miles; 3hr 30min) begins at the *Old Crown* in **ULEY** (see below), reached
from Stroud on bus #21 (Mon–Fri 2 daily; 50min) or bus #35 (Mon–Fri 2 daily; 20min), climbing
steeply to Uley Bury and then out onto Cam Long Down for more all-round panoramic views
before circling back to the bury and down into Uley again.

Six miles out of Stroud, the B4066 finally drops down into **ULEY**, famed across this
part of the Cotswolds for its beer (Ⓦuleybrewery.com), whose village church lords it
over the small green. Beside Uley's *Old Crown* pub, Fiery Lane branches down through
dense woods to reach **OWLPEN**, home of the superb Arts and Crafts **Owlpen Manor**
(Ⓦowlpen.com), closed at the time of writing for long-term conservation work.

ACCOMMODATION AND EATING   SELSLEY AND AROUND

Old Crown 17 The Green, Uley ☎01453 860502,
Ⓦtheoldcrownuley.co.uk. Appealing old seventeenth-
century coaching inn in Uley – a traditional village local.
Excellent beer from the local brewery is enhanced by
straightforward pub grub (mains £9–10) and four cosy
en-suite guest rooms. **£75**
Thistledown Farm Tinkley Lane, Nympsfield

☎01453 860420, Ⓦthistledown.org.uk. Family-run
farm operating a range of eco-conservation schemes as
well as a rather lovely organic campsite, with a range of
camping fields plus the option to rent a pre-erected bell
tent (one night £90, three nights £170). They also run a
small farm shop (Fri–Sun 9am–6pm) and have plans for
a café. Pitches (plus £6 per adult) **£5**

Minchinhampton

Gazing down on Stroud from between the River Frome and the Nailsworth Stream,
vertiginous slopes reach up to **Rodborough Common** and, adjacent to the south,
Minchinhampton Common, six hundred acres of wildflower-speckled limestone
meadow which, in large part, are protected by the National Trust. Things can get a
little wild and woolly up here: the commons are gloriously exposed, much loved by
walkers, kite-flyers and other determined cobweb-blowers. Download details of a
Rodborough Common Butterfly Walk from Ⓦnationaltrust.org.uk or aim for one of
the ridge-top pubs, such as the cheery *Black Horse* (☎01453 872556), which has a
terrace offering stupendous views at the far (northern) side of the common: walk there
direct, or make a short detour around the western ridge via nearby Amberley.

MINCHINHAMPTON itself is quite a find, a village of considerable character, with its
handsome High Street culminating in the seventeenth-century **Market House**, raised on
pillars to protect one-time stallholders beneath. Across the way, **Holy Trinity Church** – of
ancient foundation but rebuilt in 1842 – looks rather emasculated: its unsafe spire was
pulled down in 1863 and a makeshift coronet hastily erected to preserve the stumpy
half-tower's dignity.

ARRIVAL   MINCHINHAMPTON

By bus Bus #28 (Mon–Sat every 2hrs) runs to/from
Stroud (30min) and Nailsworth (10min). Bus #29

(Mon–Sat every 2hrs) runs to/from Stroud (15min) and
Tetbury (20min).

ACCOMMODATION AND EATING

Bear of Rodborough Rodborough Common ☎01453
878522, Ⓦbearofrodborough.info. This castle-like hotel

– part of the Cotswold Inns & Hotels group – stands at the
top of the winding Bear Hill road, where Minchinhampton

1

Common blends into Rodborough Common. It's a stout, traditional property offering stout, traditional rooms: whether you're staying or just popping in for a cream tea, expect a sense of history overlaid with lots of dark, polished wood. **£140**

Burleigh Court Hotel Burleigh ☎ 01453 883804, ⓦ burleighcourthotel.co.uk. A rather stiff – but extremely quiet – country house property hidden on the slopes just below Minchinhampton. It's all very traditional inside, but the views are lovely. **£160**

Sophie's 20 High St, Minchinhampton ☎ 01453 885188, ⓦ sophiesrestaurant.co.uk. A highly respected, informal venue for mid-priced French country cooking and fine choices of French wines. Opt for duck and armagnac terrine and sea trout in *beurre blanc* – or the house speciality: fish soup. Three-course menu around £20. Beware their curious hours – the website has details – and always book ahead. Wed–Fri noon–2pm, plus selected Sat eves.

Tobacconist Farm Off Tetbury St, Minchinhampton ☎ 01453 883534, ⓦ tobacconistfarm.co.uk. Two hundred yards east of Minchinhampton High St, this small family-run farm offers visits for children, a great farm shop and camping (Easter–Sept). Pitches **£15**

★**Winstones Ice Cream** Greenacres, Bownham ☎ 01453 873270, ⓦ winstonesicecream.co.uk. On the eastern slopes of Rodborough Common, a step from the *Bear of Rodborough hotel*, Winstones have been making ice cream locally since 1925; today, as well as supplying cafés and restaurants all over the Cotswolds, they still sell direct from their shop counter all year round. Daily 9am–5pm.

★**Woefuldane Dairy** 3 Market Sq, Minchinhampton ☎ 01453 886855, ⓦ woefuldanedairy.co.uk. Minchinhampton's wonderfully named Woefuldane organic dairy operates a tiny farm shop beside the Market House: drop in to snaffle one or two of their award-winning artisan cheeses. Mon 10am–noon, Tues–Fri 9am–6pm, Sat 9am–2pm.

Nailsworth

Set down in a forested valley below Minchinhampton, about four miles south of Stroud via the A46, **NAILSWORTH** once hummed to the activity of thirteen textile mills. Most are now refurbished as modern business estates, though **Dunkirk Mill**, complete with its 12ft water wheel, and **Gigg Mill** are occasionally accessible to the public on open days; timings and arrangements are publicized by the Stroudwater Textile Trust (ⓦ stroud-textile.org.uk).

With its wooded surroundings and easygoing air, Nailsworth is a rather attractive little place. Drop into the tourist office for a chat and a bit of local insight before setting off to discover – well, not much. There's a late-Victorian church, an ironmonger, a crafts shop, the Yellow-Lighted Bookshop. What matters here is **food**: Nailsworth has a reputation for culinary quality as well as diversity, and its restaurants draw people from far and wide. Look out, too, for the monthly **farmers' market** (see p.45).

ARRIVAL AND INFORMATION
NAILSWORTH

By bus The most useful regular services include: Cheltenham (hourly; 1hr); Gloucester (Mon–Sat hourly; 1hr); Painswick (hourly; 30min); Stroud (at least hourly; 15min); Wotton (Mon–Sat 4 daily; 25min).

Tourist office Old Market (Mon–Fri 9.30am–5pm, Sat 9.30am–1pm; ☎ 01453 839222, ⓦ visitthecotswolds.org .uk & ⓦ cotswolds.com).

EATING AND DRINKING

IN TOWN

Egypt Mill Bridge St ☎ 01453 833449, ⓦ egyptmill .com. A charmingly renovated textile mill beside the River Frome in the town centre. The name recalls notorious eighteenth-century mill-owner Nathaniel Webb, who drove his workers so hard they nicknamed him Pharaoh and his mill Egypt. The days of bondage are thankfully past; now what you'll find is a cheerful clutter of memorabilia adorning a quirky, informal restaurant. Expect interesting approaches to familiar dishes: wild mushroom stroganoff with cognac, pork with black pudding, and the like. Mains are £12–16, but there are frequent cut-price offers,

especially at lunchtime. This is also Nailsworth's most congenial hotel, with a choice of fresh, unfussy rooms in the main building or larger alternatives in the adjacent Mill House annexe. Mon–Sat 10am–11pm, Sun noon–10.30pm. **£105**

★**Hobbs House** 4 George St ☎ 01453 839396, ⓦ hobbshousebakery.co.uk. Legendary Cotswold artisan baker, established in 1920 in Chipping Sodbury and now with outlets around the area, including this wonderful little bakery shop and bistro overlooking a free-flowing stream beside the street. It's great for coffee and light lunches, emphasizing British traditional dishes that are cooked with style from ingredients sourced locally. Mains £11–17. Mon–Sat 8am–3pm.

★**Olive Tree** 28 George St ☎01453 834802, ⓦtheolivetree-nailsworth.com. Cheery little café-restaurant with a menu of Italian-cum-Mediterranean salads and light bites that covers familiar pizza/pasta ground while also venturing into moussaka and Moroccan stews (mains £11–15). Mon–Sat 8.30am–3pm, plus Thurs–Sat 5–9pm.

Passage to India Old Market ☎01453 834063, ⓦthepassagetoindia.com. More than a simple curry house, this Indian restaurant has a gold-standard reputation for its perfectly authentic, perfectly cooked range of curries, even if service isn't the speediest in the world. Most mains are around the £10–13 mark. Alcohol not served. Sun–Thurs noon–2.30pm & 5.30–11.30pm, Fri 5.30pm–midnight, Sat noon–2.30pm & 5.30pm–midnight.

Wild Garlic 3 Cossack Sq ☎01453 832615, ⓦwild-garlic.co.uk. Highly regarded restaurant serving imaginative food rooted in local flavours and traditions. The menu is short, but quality of cooking, presentation and service are tip-top (mains £14–18). Also with three pleasant en-suite rooms for B&B, with wooden floors and bay windows. Wed 7–9.30pm, Thurs–Sat noon–2.30pm & 7–9.30pm, Sun noon–2.30pm. **£75**

★**Williams Food Hall** 3 Fountain St ☎01453 832240, ⓦwww.williamsfoodhall.co.uk. This avowedly upscale deli-cum-fish market-cum-oyster bar in the centre of Nailsworth is an impressive discovery. The smell of the sea hits you as soon as you step over the threshold, and their breakfasts and lunches are sensational – fishy specialities interspersed with posh takes on hearty English classics (mains £9–18). Mon–Sat 8am–5pm, also Fri 6.30–11.30pm.

OUT OF TOWN

Weighbridge Inn Avening Rd ☎01453 832520, ⓦweighbridgeinn.co.uk. A mile or so east of Nailsworth on the B4014, in the depths of the forest by a bridge, this old pub has reinvented itself with a very simple culinary idea: the "2 in 1 pie". Hefty pies, baked in the bowl, are split fifty-fifty – you choose a filling for one side (steak and mushroom, perhaps, or turkey and trimmings) and the chef supplies home-made cauliflower cheese for the other side. Pies are £12–£15, and there's also a menu of accomplished pub food (mains £10–13). Mon–Sat noon–11pm, Sun noon–10.30pm.

Matara Gardens

Kingscote Park • May–Sept Sun–Thurs 1–5pm • £5 • ☎01453 861050, ⓦmataragardens.com

For an unusually transcendental take on the Cotswold garden, a couple of miles south of Nailsworth and just west of the *Calcot Manor* hotel (see p.67) you'll find **Matara**, a meditative garden blending elements of Asian Zen design with Western planting, including a tea garden, labyrinth, healing spiral, Shinto woodland and more.

Tetbury and around

With Prince Charles's Highgrove estate on one side, his Duchy Home Farm on the other, and Princess Anne's Gatcombe Park estate just up the road near Avening, **TETBURY**'s claim to fame may be as the Cotswolds' most royal town – but, in truth, this attractive, engaging place has plenty going for it with or without the Windsors. Set on the Cotswold fringes, a mile or two from the Wiltshire border, Tetbury's combination of scenic countryside, a broad choice of accommodation, attractions both historic and – in the form of **Westonbirt Arboretum** – natural, plus good shopping and excellent food make this one of the best places in this entire chunk of the Cotswolds to hole up and chew the cud. It's given an extra shimmer of poshness by lots of antiques shops.

TETBURY FESTIVALS

In August, the **Festival of British Eventing** (ⓦgatcombe-horse.co.uk) just outside Tetbury, marks a crescendo in the town's equestrian poshness. By contrast, if you arrive on the last Monday in May you'll find local toughs hauling great overstuffed sacks past cheering crowds for the **Woolsack Races** (ⓦtetburywoolsack.co.uk), a dotty hangover from medieval days of wool wealth. The **Tetbury Food and Drink Festival** (ⓦtetburyfooddrinkfestival.com) sees a host of foodie events over a long weekend every September.

1

St Mary's Church

Church St • Daily 10am–4pm • ☎ 01666 500088, ⓦ tetburychurch.co.uk

Directly across the road from the tourist office rises Tetbury's **church** – curiously dedicated to both St Mary the Virgin and St Mary Magdalen. You enter beneath the tower, its spire soaring to 186ft; this was the only survival from a pre-existing church, demolished in 1777. The new church which resulted, completed in 1781, is acclaimed as one of the country's finest examples of **Georgian Gothic**: the view along the nave, with its dark box pews, candle chandeliers, slender wooden columns and enormous windows, is nothing short of breathtaking. The cloister-like ambulatory on the north side adds another dimension of eighteenth-century elegance.

Market House and Long Street

Tetbury's main crossroads is marked by the pillared, seventeenth-century **Market House**, which still hosts a general market every Wednesday and Saturday morning. From here, the village's main drag, the aptly named **Long Street**, heads away to the northwest, lined with shops and hotels; the old courthouse, at no. 63, now houses the **Tetbury Heritage Centre** (Mon–Fri 10am–3pm; free), chiefly dedicated to displays on the history of policing.

ARRIVAL AND INFORMATION TETBURY

By train Trains on the London–Swindon–Cheltenham line stop at Kemble station (see p.86), about seven miles northeast of Tetbury. From the station bus #881 (Mon–Sat every 2hrs) runs to Tetbury (25min). Taxis charge about £18 into Tetbury; local firms include Kemble Station Taxi (☎ 07817 450152, ⓦ kembletaxi.co.uk) and Kemble Taxis (☎ 0333 800 0750, ⓦ taxisofkemble.co.uk).

By bus Buses drop off in the village centre.

Destinations Cirencester (Mon–Sat every 2hrs; 40min); Malmesbury (thrice on Mon, Wed & Fri; 20min); Minchinhampton (Mon–Sat every 2hrs; 20min); Old Sodbury (Mon–Fri 5 daily, 3 on Sat; 25min); Stroud (Mon–Sat every 2hrs; 35min).

Tourist office 33 Church St (March–Oct Mon–Sat 10am–4pm; Nov–Feb Mon–Sat 11am–2pm; ☎ 01666 503552, ⓦ visittetbury.co.uk & ⓦ cotswolds.com). Staff offer encyclopedic quantities of information on attractions and services, including wine- or cheese-tasting excursions to nearby farms.

ACCOMMODATION

IN TOWN

The Close Long St ☎ 01666 502272, ⓦ theclose-hotel.com. A grand old sixteenth-century house, whose fifteen en-suite bedrooms exude classic good taste and quality, with just enough of a contemporary zing to keep things interesting without falling into the trap of designer edginess. **£160**

Oak House No.1 The Chipping ☎ 01666 505741, ⓦ oakhouseno1.com. Eye-popping super-posh B&B in this centrally located Georgian townhouse. Just three suites are available, furnished with antiques and state-of-the-art contemporary bathrooms, and the public areas wow with opulent settings of designer art and one-off modern furniture. **£275**

The Ormond 23 Long St ☎ 01666 505690, ⓦ theormondattetbury.co.uk. Good-value three-star hotel in an old building in the centre of town,

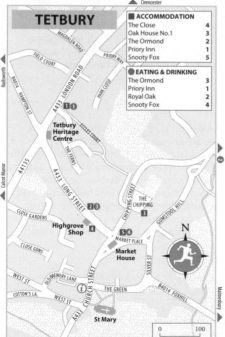

TETBURY

■ ACCOMMODATION
The Close	4
Oak House No.1	3
The Ormond	2
Priory Inn	1
Snooty Fox	5

● EATING & DRINKING
The Ormond	3
Priory Inn	1
Royal Oak	2
Snooty Fox	4

with a briskly engaging style of service and rooms which sport more taste and humour than you might expect for either the price, the location or the town. **£120**

★**Priory Inn** London Rd ☎01666 502251, ⓦthepriory inn.co.uk. Excellent family-friendly hotel on the edge of the centre – bright, breezy and cheerful. The fourteen rooms are neutral and unfussy, focusing on comfort rather than fripperies and refreshingly free of the desire to impress. **£99**

Snooty Fox Market Place ☎01666 502436, ⓦsnooty -fox.co.uk. Traditional old coaching inn in the centre of town, renamed by a former owner who was snubbed by the local hunt. These days it's been thoroughly updated: the buzzy, outgoing atmosphere is rather engaging, a nod to the traditional here, a touch of playful japery there. Nothing surprises, but this is a reassuringly safe pair of hands. **£80**

OUT OF TOWN

★**Calcot Manor** 4 miles west of Tetbury ☎01666 890391, ⓦcalcotmanor.co.uk. Stylish, relaxed, efficient, friendly – it's hard to know where to begin with what is widely acknowledged as one of the best hotels in England. Located by the A4135/A46 crossroads, in an expansive 220

acres of grounds, its 35 rooms are each individually designed, with smaller ones in the main farmhouse and larger options – including family rooms – ranged around the adjacent courtyard. Nothing is too much trouble: staff are fully engaged with every guest and every concern, busting a gut to make sure it all goes just as you'd want. **£280**

★**Hare and Hounds** 3 miles southwest of Tetbury ☎01666 881000, ⓦhareandhoundshotel.com. A fine, traditional country house hotel on the A433 just short of Westonbirt, offering a fresh, competent approach to four-star accommodation – nothing out of place and all bases covered. It's undoubtedly a cut above Tetbury's in-town hotels, and the quiet of the countryside location is lovely. Member of the Cotswold Inns & Hotels group. **£140**

Whatley Manor 4 miles south of Tetbury, near Easton Grey ☎01666 822888, ⓦwhatleymanor.com. A thoroughly upmarket, unabashedly lavish country hotel, set around a cobbled courtyard and offering a rare blend of warmth in design and a lack of pretension. Its 23 rooms and suites are fitted out to an exceptionally high standard – and, at this slight remove from the main touring zones of the Cotswolds, benefiting from an agreeably local feel. Member of the Relais & Châteaux group. **£300**

EATING AND DRINKING

Like Cirencester, Stow and one or two other Cotswold locations, Tetbury has a reputation for excellence in eating and drinking: the town hosts a clutch of fine restaurants and rather posh delis, with nearby country inns and hotels adding to the choice. As well as the dining options reviewed below, Crudwell (see p.70) and Nailsworth (see p.64) are within easy reach, and the tourist office has details of nearby vineyards offering wine-tasting.

IN TOWN

The Ormond 23 Long St ☎01666 505690, ⓦtheormondattetbury.co.uk. This celebrated restaurant focuses squarely on local suppliers, with an inventive range of classic, hearty dishes – think honey-roast ham, steak and ale pie or juniper duck with sausage – presented with style. It is, however, far from formal: good food and intelligent service mark it out. Mains £11–18. Food served Mon–Sat noon–2.30pm & 6.30–9.30pm, Sun noon–3pm & 7–9pm.

★**Priory Inn** London Rd ☎01666 502251, ⓦthepriory inn.co.uk. This cheerful, family-friendly spot emphasizes local credentials: ninety percent of their ingredients are sourced within thirty miles of Tetbury. Although the mains of Gloucester pork or Bibury trout are excellent (£12–18), the house speciality is wood-fired pizza (£8–12) – and they still manage to work in double Gloucester and local bacon as toppings. Food served Mon–Fri noon–3pm & 5–10pm, Sat & Sun noon–10pm.

Royal Oak 1 Cirencester Rd ☎01666 500021, ⓦtheroyaloaktetbury.co.uk. This longstanding inn recently reopened after a top-to-toe refit, and is now a great option for pleasantly upmarket organic dining:

warm asparagus salad, porcini mushroom burger, cider-braised pork belly, and so on. Mains £9–14 – or choose the "Workers' Pot" stew with bread or brown rice for £6 (Mon–Fri 5–6.30pm). Food served Mon–Fri noon–2.30pm & 5–9.30pm, Sat noon–2.30pm & 6.30–9.30pm, Sun noon–5pm.

Snooty Fox Market Place ☎01666 502436, ⓦsnooty -fox.co.uk. Pleasant, accommodating atmosphere in this popular inn, where uncomplicated English cooking is presented decently and charged moderately. Mains £11–21. Mon–Fri 7.30am–9.30pm, Sat 8am–9.30pm, Sun 8am–9pm.

OUT OF TOWN

★**Calcot Manor** 4 miles west of Tetbury ☎01666 890391, ⓦcalcotmanor.co.uk. This outstanding country hotel has two dining options. The posher is the *Conservatory* restaurant (mains £16–26), specializing in fish and shellfish – artfully done but less engaging than the adjacent *Gumstool Inn*, a rather bogus version of a country pub but nonetheless with much of the same food though priced considerably lower (mains £12–17), alongside a welter of upscale pub favourites, from fish pie to sausage

1

and mash. Conservatory: daily noon–2pm & 7–9.30pm. Gumstool Inn: Mon–Sat noon–2pm & 6–9.30pm, Sun noon–4pm & 6–9.30pm.

★**Hare and Hounds** 3 miles southwest of Tetbury ☎ 01666 881000, ⊛ hareandhoundshotel.com. This rural hotel has two choices for food. If you're prepared to push the boat out, the extremely good *Beaufort Restaurant* is a sound choice, with a solid reputation among the regulars from the polo club next door. Expect a small menu of carefully selected ingredients, explained and enhanced by the wait staff, and top-notch presentation. Two courses are £33. By contrast, the informal *Jack Hare's Bar* alongside

plays the "restaurant food in a pub setting" trick to perfection (mains £10–15). Beaufort: daily 7–9.30pm. Jack Hare's: daily noon–2.30pm & 7–9.30pm.

Trouble House 3 miles northeast of Tetbury ☎ 01666 502206, ⊛ thetroublehouse.co.uk. Intriguingly named old country pub on the A433 Cirencester road, with a past reputedly laden with ghosts and disasters – now reborn as an upmarket café-bar with a reputation for unpretentious good cooking: quiches, burgers, hearty salads, with a more expansive menu on weekend evenings. Mon–Thurs 8am–5pm, Fri 8am–5pm & 7–10pm, Sat 9am–5pm & 7–10pm.

Highgrove

Doughton • Garden tours: April–Oct selected days & times • From £24.50 • Booking essential: ☎ 020 7766 7310, ⊛ highgrovegardens.com

Highgrove, home of Prince Charles and Camilla, Duchess of Cornwall, lies about a mile southwest of Tetbury off the A433 in **DOUGHTON**. Two-hour tours of the **gardens** – led, needless to say, by a guide rather than HRH himself – operate in the summer. There's a waiting list of several weeks. Just the other side of Tetbury stands **Duchy Home Farm**, where Charles first experimented with organic farming on a large scale in the 1980s. It still operates as the leading source of produce for the Duchy Originals brand.

Rodmarton Manor

Rodmarton • May–Sept Wed & Sat 2–5pm • £8 • ☎ 01285 841442, ⊛ rodmarton-manor.co.uk

Arts and Crafts fans shouldn't miss **Rodmarton Manor**, a few miles outside Tetbury along the A433 towards Cirencester. The manor, designed by Arts and Crafts devotee Ernest Barnsley, was completed in 1929 using local materials and skilled craft workers. As well as the house – crammed with original furniture and design – the eight-acre garden is acclaimed as a Cotswold classic.

Chavenage House

Chavenage • May–Sept Thurs & Sun 2–5pm • £8 • ☎ 01666 502329, ⊛ chavenage.com

On minor roads a couple of miles northwest of Tetbury, **Chavenage House** is a captivatingly beautiful Elizabethan manor, still lived in as a family home and a regular star in TV costume dramas from *Lark Rise to Candleford* to *Tess of the D'Urbervilles*. One highlight is the Main Hall, with its Cromwell-era tapestries and minstrels' gallery.

Westonbirt: The National Arboretum

Westonbirt • Daily 9am–8pm; Sept–March closes 5pm • Guided walks March–Oct Wed 11am, Sat & Sun 2pm • £5–9 depending on season; guided walks free • ☎ 01666 880220, ⊛ forestry.gov.uk/westonbirt • Bus #27 (Mon–Fri 5 daily, 3 on Sat) to/from Tetbury (8min) and Old Sodbury (17min)

A little over three miles southwest of Tetbury via the A433, just before the village of **WESTONBIRT**, lies **Westonbirt: The National Arboretum**. Everything about the place relies on superlatives, from its role as protector of some of the oldest, biggest and rarest trees in the world to the display of natural colours it puts on in autumn, when even superlatives are insufficient. With seventeen miles of paths to roam, across six hundred acres and between sixteen thousand trees, it's worth making a day of it. There's plenty to do, including **self-guided trails**, guided walks, lots for kids and families, the annual **Treefest** in late August, which features wood sculpting and workshops, and more.

Malmesbury

1

The small Wiltshire hill town of **MALMESBURY** lies on the periphery of the Cotswolds, five miles southeast of Tetbury (and twelve miles south of Cirencester). It may have lost most of its good looks with a rash of modern development, but there's no gainsaying the stirring beauty of its partly ruinous Norman abbey. Note that if you're visiting on the last weekend in July, the mammoth **WOMAD** music festival (🐚womad.co.uk) attracts over eighty thousand people to Charlton Park, a mile northeast of Malmesbury off the B4040: be prepared for traffic delays and diversions.

The **High Street** begins at the bottom of the hill by the old silk mills and heads north across the river and up past a jagged row of ancient cottages on its way to the octagonal **Market Cross**, built around 1490 to provide shelter from the rain and now the venue for the fortnightly **farmers' market** (see p.45).

Malmesbury Abbey

Market Cross • Daily 10am–5pm; Nov–March closes 4pm • Free • ☎ 01666 826666, 🐚 malmesburyabbey.com

From the Market Cross the eighteenth-century **Tolsey Gate** leads through to **Malmesbury Abbey**, which was once a rich and powerful Benedictine monastery. The first abbey burnt down in about 1050, the second was roughed up during the Dissolution, but the beautiful Norman **nave** of the abbey church has survived, its south porch sporting a multitude of exquisite if badly worn Romanesque figures. Three bands of figures surround the doorway, depicting scenes from the Creation, the Old Testament and the life of Christ, while inside the porch the apostles and Christ are carved in a fine deep relief – stately figures in flowing folds surmounted by a flying angel. The tympanum shows Christ on a rainbow, supported by gracefully gymnastic angels. Within the main body of the church, the pale stone brings a dramatic freshness, particularly to the carving of the nave arches (look out for the Norman beak-heads) and of the clerestory. To the left of the high altar, the pulpit virtually hides the **tomb of King Athelstan**, grandson of Alfred the Great and the first Saxon to be recognized as king of England; the tomb, however, is empty and the location of the king's body is unknown. Malmesbury's local celebrities include **Eilmer the Monk**, who in 1005 attempted to fly from the abbey tower with the aid of wings: he limped for the rest of his life, but won immortal fame as the "flying monk".

Abbey House Gardens

Abbey House • Mid-March to end Oct daily 11am–5.30pm • £8 • ☎ 01666 827650, 🐚 abbeyhousegardens.co.uk

Beside the abbey, the splendid five-acre **Abbey House Gardens** are particularly photogenic, acclaimed by Alan Titchmarsh and gloriously lush in the summer months. Abbey House has also gained popularity as the home of the "Naked Gardeners", Ian and Barbara Pollard, who featured on TV in the 2000s; they offer a few "clothes optional" visiting days each summer, detailed on the website.

Athelstan Museum

Cross Hayes • April–Oct daily 10.30am–4.30pm; Nov–March Mon–Sat 10.30am–4.30pm, Sun 11.30am–3.30pm • Free • ☎ 01666 829258, 🐚 athelstanmuseum.org.uk

Malmesbury's engaging and well-presented local history collection is in the **Athelstan Museum**, ranging from local lace to hoards of Roman and Saxon coins as well as multiple images of the abbey, an eighteenth-century fire engine and a very early Victorian tricycle.

ARRIVAL AND INFORMATION   MALMESBURY

By bus Buses drop off on Cross Hayes, round the corner from the Market Cross.

Destinations Chipping Sodbury (Mon–Sat 4 daily; 50min); Cirencester (Mon–Sat 5 daily; 50min); Crudwell (Mon–Sat 5 daily; 25min); Old Sodbury (Mon–Fri 4 daily; 50min);

Tetbury (3 on Mon, Wed & Fri; 20min).

Tourist office Town Hall (Mon–Thurs 9am–5pm, Fri 9am–4.30pm, June–Sept also Sat 10am–4pm; ☎ 01666 823748, 🐚 malmesbury.gov.uk & 🐚 visitwiltshire.co.uk).

1

ACCOMMODATION AND EATING

Old Bell Abbey Row ☎01666 822344, ☯oldbellhotel
.co.uk. Originally built as a guest house for the abbey and
dating back to the thirteenth century, this is now a fine,
atmospheric hotel, famed especially for its splendid wood-
floored restaurant, serving modern British cooking with a
twist – venison, bacon and stout pie, for example, or salt-
baked celeriac. Mains £13–20. Daily noon–2.30pm &
6.30–9pm.

Smoking Dog High St ☎01666 825823, ☯sabrain
.com/smokingdog. Despite the weird name, this is a fine
old drinkers' pub, with excellent beer and surprisingly
good food – peach and blue cheese salad, beer-battered
haddock, board of Welsh cheeses, and all. Mains £9–16.
Mon–Thurs noon–11pm, Fri & Sat noon–midnight,
Sun noon–10.30pm.

Crudwell

Four miles north of Malmesbury on the A429 Cirencester road, and easily reached
on back roads east of Tetbury, **CRUDWELL** is an unremarkable village at the very
northern edges of Wiltshire made remarkable by the success of its rural hotel and
restaurant businesses.

ACCOMMODATION AND EATING   CRUDWELL

★**Potting Shed Pub** Crudwell ☎01666 577833, ☯the
pottingshedpub.com. A gently contemporary conversion of
an old village boozer, this is now one of the leading rural
restaurants in the Cotswolds. The bar has light Shaker-style
wood panelling, there are flagstones underfoot and an
eponymous *faux*-potting shed extension sports artfully
placed garden paraphernalia under a high pitched ceiling.
Aside from knowing how to pull a pint, they've also brought a
whiff of panache to country pub dining: their chips are triple-
cooked, their autumn burger made from local pheasant, their
mash laced with basil, their cod served with chorizo. Mains

are £14–17. Mon–Sat 11am–midnight, Sun 11am–11pm.
★**Rectory** Crudwell ☎01666 577194, ☯therectory
hotel.com. Adding to Crudwell's allure, this tasteful
twelve-bedroom country house hotel delivers comfort and
quiet without attempting to spring surprises – other than
in the tea menu, which lists eleven varieties from Lahloo
smokey to Darjeeling second flush. Rooms are simple,
fresh and a bit flowery, while the dining room (two-course
set menu £27) offers some intriguing options – seared
monkfish with oxtail, rabbit and pea pie, and so forth. Food
served Sun–Thurs 7–9pm, Fri & Sat 7–9.30pm. **£105**

Dursley and around

Tucked into a fold of the Cotswold escarpment, the valley-floor town of **DURSLEY**
doesn't have much to say for itself. A couple of old buildings and a grand church in
its centre are overshadowed by humdrum modern commerce, fuelled by Dursley's
location astride a network of main roads, including the A4135 from Tetbury, which
links to the Gloucester–Bristol A38. Slimbridge (see p.72) and Berkeley (see p.71)
lie two or three miles west. The Cotswold Way footpath passes through and, in truth,
so should you.

EATING AND DRINKING   DURSLEY

Old Spot Inn 2 Hill Rd ☎01453 542870, ☯oldspotinn
.co.uk. Just about the best thing in Dursley, this old
pub has won a barrelful of awards, not least CAMRA
National Pub of the Year, for the quality of its beer and its
determinedly unreconstructed interior: an ordinary old

fireplace, bookcase in the corner, plain tile floor, and so on.
Hunt it out for a pint – and an honest pub lunch – to
savour: it's hidden away off Dursley's main street. Mon–Sat
11am–11pm, Sun noon–11pm.

Tyndale Monument

Soaring above Dursley and its adjoining neighbour **CAM** is **Stinchcombe Hill**, famed as
the westernmost point of the Cotswolds; struggle up to the scenic golf course on the
top, or follow the wiggly B4060 as it circumnavigates the hill. Once you've come
around you'll spot on a shoulder of the hills ahead what looks like a tall obelisk. This is

the 111ft **Tyndale Monument**, built in 1866 to commemorate William Tyndale, the first person to translate the Bible into English, who was born around these parts in about 1490. Paths lead up to it from **NORTH NIBLEY** at its base, and you can normally enter to climb the interior staircase for exceptional views from the top. Paths around the summit – short, steep ones and longer, gentler ones – lead back to North Nibley.

Wotton-under-Edge and around

The B4060 coils around to enter **WOTTON-UNDER-EDGE**, passing first the cheery, well-stocked **Wotton Farm Shop** (☏01453 521546, ⌨wottonfarmshop.co.uk). Wotton itself, crammed beneath high slopes, makes for a picturesque diversion: **Long Street**, as well as ordinary shops and banks, has some good-looking old buildings. Turn left onto Market Street to reach the **Chipping** market square, where you'll pass the **Electric Picture House** (⌨wottoncinema.com), a popular art-house cinema run by Wotton volunteers: taking the weight off for a couple of hours in front of a flickering screen is, oddly, a great way to support the local economy.

A gentle **walk** of four and half miles leads down from the Chipping on signed paths southwest to **KINGSWOOD** village, where a grand sixteenth-century gatehouse (⌨english-heritage.org.uk) is the only remnant of a demolished Cistercian abbey. Paths lead on through the fields in a circuit back to Wotton.

Southeast of Wotton near **OZLEWORTH** stands the Tudor hunting lodge **Newark Park** (March–Oct Wed–Sun 11am–5pm; £7.10; ⌨nationaltrust.org.uk), reached from Wotton on a rising and falling **circular walk** (6.5 miles; 5hr; downloadable at the Cotswold Way pages of ⌨escapetothecotswolds.org.uk) that also takes in a chunk of the Cotswold Way.

ARRIVAL AND INFORMATION   WOTTON-UNDER-EDGE

By bus Bus #40 (Mon–Sat 4 daily) to/from Stroud (40min) and Nailsworth (25min). Bus #84 (Mon–Sat hourly) to/from Chipping Sodbury (35min). Bus #201 (Mon–Fri once daily) to/from Gloucester (55min).
Tourist office Wotton's Heritage Centre doubles as the

tourist office, on the Chipping (Tues, Thurs & Fri 10.30am–12.30pm & 2–4pm, Sat 10am–1pm; April–Oct also Sun 2.30–5pm; ☏01453 521541, ⌨wottonheritage. com & ⌨visitthecotswolds.org.uk).

The Vale of Berkeley

Flanking the M5 southwest of Gloucester, and tucked between the Cotswold Edge and the River Severn, the **Vale of Berkeley** is somewhat tangential to a Cotswolds holiday, but hosts a sprinkling of noteworthy sights that might draw you down to the marshy ground beside the river. Best known is the **Slimbridge Wetland Centre**, an internationally renowned wildlife reserve with tons of activities alongside its core attraction of birdwatching. **Berkeley Castle**, scene of medieval regicide, is another highlight, as is a scattering of quiet pubs and byways in the Severn-side villages – notably an outstanding seafood restaurant in far-flung **Arlingham**.

Berkeley

Bolingbroke: How far is it, my lord, to Berkeley now?
Northumberland: Believe me, noble lord, / I am a stranger here in Gloucestershire: / These high wild hills and rough uneven ways / Draws out our miles, and makes them wearisome.   Shakespeare, Richard II

He could have just said "not far". Off the A38, secluded within a swathe of meadows and gardens beside the little village of **BERKELEY**, looms the grandly impressive presence of the castle, about fifteen miles south of Gloucester.

1

Berkeley Castle

April–Oct Sun–Wed 11am–5pm • £10 • ☎ 01453 810303, 🌐 berkeley-castle.com

Berkeley Castle looks the part. The stronghold has a turreted medieval appearance, its twelfth-century austerity softened by its gradual transformation into a family home (the Berkeleys have been in residence here for almost 900 years). The interior is packed with mementoes of its long history, including its grisliest moment when, in 1327, **Edward II** was murdered here – purportedly by a red-hot poker thrust into his backside. You can view the cell where the event took place, along with dungeons, dining room, kitchen, picture gallery and the Great Hall, with its painted sixteenth-century wooden screen. It's a hugely impressive historical jaunt, liberally scattered with portraiture and antique furniture, Brussels tapestries in the Morning Room and beer barrels in the cellar. Outside, the grounds include a **Butterfly House**, with British and exotic examples flying freely.

Edward Jenner Museum

Church Lane • April–Sept Sun–Wed noon–5pm; July & Aug also Sat noon–5pm • £6.95 (£1 discount if you show a ticket for Berkeley Castle or Slimbridge) • ☎ 01453 810631, 🌐 jennermuseum.com

Within easy walking distance of the castle, in Berkeley village itself, stands the excellent **Edward Jenner Museum**. Jenner, who discovered the principle of vaccination, was born in Berkeley in 1749; after studying in London, he returned here in 1772 to practise as a doctor and conduct his experiments. The museum occupies his former house, the Chantry, with rooms devoted both to Jenner's work and also to well-designed displays on modern stories of vaccination.

EATING AND DRINKING   BERKELEY

Salutation Inn Ham ☎ 01453 810284, 🌐 the-sally-at-ham.com. Follow Berkeley's High St south for less than a mile to this unpretentious garden pub that really knows its beer, holding a fistful of CAMRA awards, and has a modest food menu. It's easy to put together a circular walk of about two hours from Berkeley to Ham and the Severn. Mon 5–11pm, Tues–Fri noon–2.30pm & 5–11pm, Sat noon–11pm, Sun noon–10.30pm.

Slimbridge Wetland Centre

Slimbridge • Daily 9.30am–5.30pm; Nov–March closes 5pm • £11.18 • ☎ 01453 891900, 🌐 wwt.org.uk/slimbridge

Heading south along the A38 past **CAMBRIDGE** (pronounced as it looks – the village has a bridge over the River Cam), a roundabout marks the turn down towards the Severn for **SLIMBRIDGE** and the neighbouring **Slimbridge Wetland Centre**. This was the first Wildfowl and Wetlands Trust reserve, founded in 1946 by naturalist Peter Scott. Its primary purpose is to study and protect the numerous resident and migratory species of ducks, geese and swans – but within its 750 acres it also has a large area open to the public. The quantity (and quality) of stuff you can do here is impressive, from boat rides and Land Rover safaris to canoeing, birdwatching and loads of educational play activities for children. There are guided walks, late-afternoon commentaries in the winter months as migratory swans come into land, tours of the heated Tropical House, and more, all detailed on the website. Come early; stay late.

Frampton-on-Severn

Along the A38 about nine miles southwest of Gloucester, near junction 13 of the M5, a turning marks the B4071's departure north onto a peninsula framed by an oxbow of the River Severn. The first village you come to, off to the left, is **FRAMPTON-ON-SEVERN**, a pretty place of Georgian and Tudor houses draped around what is purportedly the longest village green in England – effectively an

1

THE SEVERN BORE

The Severn Estuary has the second-highest tidal range in the world (after the Bay of Fundy in Nova Scotia), its water levels varying by an extraordinary 50ft or more. During the highest tides, the rising water is funnelled up the narrowing river with ever-increasing force, forming a foaming wave up to 6ft high known as the **Severn Bore**. It's an obvious draw for river-surfers, but also attracts crowds of onlookers, both for the rush of the bore and the transformation of a calm river into a torrent which appears to flow upstream for an hour or more after the bore itself has passed. Connoisseurs have identified a number of prime viewpoints along the Severn near Gloucester. The best is on the west bank at **MINSTERWORTH**, where the *Severn Bore Inn* (☎01452 750318, ⓦsevernboreinn.co.uk) offers parking and a good vantage point. A decent alternative on the east bank is at **STONEBENCH**, but the narrow lanes here are often crowded with vehicles, making access difficult; further downstream, the *Old Passage* at **ARLINGHAM** (see below), though not a tip-top location (it stands on a broad curve), is a good second-best – and they host highly acclaimed "Bore Breakfasts" on the mornings that the wave rushes past.

Exact timings for different viewpoints are published a year in advance by enthusiast websites such as ⓦsevern-bore.co.uk. Each bore is given a star-rating on the basis of its likely height and speed: four- and five-star events (meaning a tidal range above 16ft) tend to occur most frequently in spring and autumn.

open meadow, some 22 acres in area. When your whistle first at the rather refined *Bell* (☎01452 740346, ⓦthebellatframpton.co.uk), at the top end of the green, and by the time you've walked to the other end – past Frampton Court, an eighteenth-century mansion set in a groomed, gated estate – you'll be grateful for refreshment at the *Three Horseshoes* (☎01452 742100, ⓦthreehorseshoespub.co.uk), a beer-drinkers' local. Past the *Three Horseshoes*, turn right towards the river to reach the isolated **St Mary's Church**, consecrated in 1315 and beautifully tranquil; its lead Romanesque font is probably older than the building.

Saul and Arlingham

North of the Frampton turn, the B4071 crosses the Gloucester and Sharpness Canal, immediately afterwards bending right to enter **SAUL** village. Follow signs through the village to find **Saul Junction**, the point where the Stroudwater Navigation, a canal built in the 1770s from Framilode (on the Severn nearby) east to Stroud, was crossed in 1827 by the newfangled Gloucester and Sharpness Canal. The Stroudwater, long fallen into disrepair, is now the subject of intensive restoration efforts by the Cotswold Canals Trust (ⓦwww.cotswoldcanalsproject.org). The junction-point, dotted with pleasure craft, has a good deal of atmosphere, especially in the misty mornings: you could walk from here to the Severn at Framilode, then make a loop back past Fretherne to settle in for lunch at Frampton's *Bell* (see above).

Beyond Saul, if you keep going straight you'll come to **ARLINGHAM** village – quiet and muddy. The main reason to come out this far lies even further ahead at the end of the peninsula: the B4071 eventually peters out on the banks of the Severn, offering views across to the Forest of Dean and Newnham church, dramatically perched on the cliffs opposite.

INFORMATION	SAUL AND ARLINGHAM
Canal Visitor Centre Saul Junction (April–Oct Sat 12.30–5pm, Sun 10am–5pm; rest of year Sat & Sun 12.30–4pm; ☎07854 026504, ⓦcotswoldcanals.com).	A hut on the towpath – pick up information and light refreshments, and details of short boat trips which run on summer Sundays, on demand (25min; £4).

1

★ **Old Passage** Arlingham ☎ 01452 740547, ⊛ theold passage.com. At the isolated western end of the B4071 road, overlooking the Severn, this classy restaurant specializes in immaculately presented fish and seafood: fresh lobster (Welsh or Cornish), oysters, crab, mussels and more, interspersed with seasonal dishes – including meat and vegetarian options – and market-fresh fish. Mains £17–22, or two-course lunch menu (Tues–Fri) £15. Book well ahead to eat, or for their three pretty, simply furnished rooms. Tues–Sat noon–2pm & 7–9pm, Sun noon–2.30pm. **£110**

Chipping Sodbury

South of Dursley and Tetbury, although you're still in the Cotswolds, character and mood shift irrevocably: landscapes are plainer and less grandly open, and the characteristically golden yellow Cotswold limestone is slowly replaced by a silvery, greyer variety – nice, but not the same. Knocking on Bristol's door, **CHIPPING SODBURY** is a pleasant, busy market town with a long history: its name is Saxon, deriving from "Soppa's burg" (though no record survives of who Soppa was), prefixed by *ceapen*, meaning market.

Its **High Street** is purportedly one of the widest in England, formerly flanked by market stalls. Partway along, the centrally placed **clock tower** is the location of Sodbury's twice-monthly **farmers' market** (see p.45). Further east, **Broad Street** has a number of handsome facades; a Tudor house survives on nearby Hatters Lane. On Horse Street, past the post office, you'll spot an eighteenth-century milestone marking the distance of 108 miles to Hyde Park Corner in London.

ARRIVAL AND INFORMATION
CHIPPING SODBURY

By bus Buses drop off by the clock tower on the High St. Destinations Malmesbury (Mon–Sat 4 daily; 50min); Old Sodbury (Mon–Fri at least 4 daily; 6min); Wotton (Mon–Sat hourly; 30min).

Tourist office At the clock tower on the High St (Mon–Sat 10am–5pm, Oct–March closes 4pm; ☎ 01454 888686, ⊛ www.yateandchippingsodbury.co.uk & ⊛ visitchipping sodbury.com).

ACCOMMODATION AND EATING

Hamptons 21A High St ☎ 01454 854745, ⊛ thehamptons deli.co.uk. Super-classy upmarket deli and café on the High St – aim for their trademark eggs Benedict or steak sandwiches in ciabatta, or opt for paninis and salads. Mon–Sat 8am–5.30pm, Sun 9am–3pm.

Moda House 1 High St ☎ 01454 312135, ⊛ modahouse .co.uk. A fine old Georgian house in the town centre, offering a warm welcome and eleven en-suite rooms furnished beautifully with contemporary fabrics and a sense of style. **£75**

Old Sodbury and around

Less than a mile east of Chipping Sodbury stands **OLD SODBURY**, a silent residential village topped by the ancient **church of St John the Baptist**: a Saxon-style T-shaped stone in the external east wall, carved with four rounded crosses, suggests that the church's knoll has been a place of worship for many centuries, if not millennia. It's got bags of atmosphere. A **circular walk** (2.5 miles; 2hr) from the church runs north along the Cotswold Way to **LITTLE SODBURY** and back across the fields; download details at ⊛ escapetothecotswolds.org.uk.

A couple of miles east of Old Sodbury, **BADMINTON** village is famed for its May horse trials (⊛ www.badminton-horse.co.uk) and the adjacent **Badminton House**, residence of the dukes of Beaufort for more than three hundred years (but closed to the public).

ARRIVAL
OLD SODBURY

By bus Services include: Chipping Sodbury (Mon–Sat at least 4 daily; 6min); Malmesbury (Mon–Sat 4 daily; 40min); Tetbury (Mon–Fri 5 daily, 3 on Sat; 25min); Westonbirt (Mon–Fri 5 daily, 3 on Sat; 15min).

Castle Combe

East of the Sodburys – and only ten miles north of Bath – the B4039 sidles south over the M4, from where signposted back lanes give access to **CASTLE COMBE**, often called the prettiest village in England. This remarkable (but often very crowded) medieval settlement has almost entirely kept its looks. It goes without saying that the best times to explore the lower village – the part of interest – and surrounding valleyside paths are morning and evening, before or after the bulk of visitors roam.

Walking down from the car park, your first sight of the village is the multi-gabled Dower House, built around 1700. Then you come down to the titchy main square, marked by the medieval **Market Cross**, its square tiled roof supported on four thick stone pillars. The view down the main street is exceptional: although evidence of 21st-century life does exist (road markings, signs, a bus stop), Castle Combe's appearance has changed little in 500 years. It shares a Cotswold history: the Bybrook stream, which is the village's *raison d'être*, at one time ran three textile mills – most of Castle Combe's houses are weavers' cottages. Off to the right is the **church of St Andrew**, an unusually grand wool church which shelters the tomb of Walter de Dunstanville, a Crusading knight (and Baron of Castle Combe) who died in 1270.

The Norman **castle** for which the village is named survives only as barely discernible foundations, now out of bounds on a hilltop golf course. Up on top, too, is **Castle Combe Circuit** (wcastlecombecircuit.co.uk) – the perimeter track of an old airfield – which hosts rally and touring car championships, as well as have-a-go track day events.

ARRIVAL AND INFORMATION
CASTLE COMBE

By car There's nowhere to park in the old village, and the streets are almost too narrow to drive through. The best advice is to leave your car in the free car park just off the B4039 and walk the few minutes down the hill into the village.

By bus Bus #37 to/from Malmesbury (1 on Wed; 40min).
Information The community website wcastle-combe .com is packed with detail.

ACCOMMODATION AND EATING

Castle Inn 01249 783030, wcastle-inn.info. This lovely hotel in the old village is just about the poshest choice for dining, its modern British cooking overlaid with a Mediterranean influence (mains £12–19). There's also a more straightforward bar menu (£11–14), cream teas, and so forth. The eleven en-suite rooms are smoothly luxurious, with contemporary boutique flair in fabrics and colours. £135

White Hart 01249 782295, wwadworth.co.uk. Rather good pub by the Market Cross – a medieval half-timbered inn which, centuries on, still focuses on beer, serving surprisingly good pints and pub grub to the promenading visitors. Daily 11am–11pm.

The central Cotswolds

BIBURY

The central Cotswolds

Few main roads cross the Cotswold hills. Two east–west corridors – the A40 and A44 – more or less follow valley contours, linking Oxford with Cheltenham and Evesham respectively, but through history Cotswold topography hasn't lent itself to many easily definable north–south routes. In that regard, not much has changed since the Romans: their Fosse Way road – now the A429 – is still the only north–south artery through the region, cutting a more or less straight line from the wilds of Warwickshire through the central Cotswolds to Cirencester and on south towards Bath. This leaves the best of the region tucked into the hills either side: beautiful landscapes, quiet villages, splendid country churches.

The southern parts of the region are anchored by the presence of **Cirencester**, a lovely, old-fashioned market town which, these days, is the epitome of what has turned Gloucestershire into "Poshtershire" – a polo-playing hideaway on the fringe of classic countryside, yet with speedy links to Cheltenham and London, and now sporting upmarket bars, delis and department stores. It's easy, though, to take what you want and leave the rest behind: Cirencester's Roman museum, for instance, is a cracker, as are the villages of the quiet **Coln Valley** nearby – and humble **Fairford** hosts a church as splendid as any in the Cotswolds.

Pretty **Northleach** is thankfully bypassed by both the A40 and A429 at their crossroads, though riverside **Bibury** has become a very popular mid-Cotswolds stop. **Bourton-on-the-Water** is one of the most visited but perhaps least satisfying of all Cotswold destinations, and nearby **Stow-on-the-Wold** and **Moreton-in-Marsh**, though visually attractive, lie slap bang in the eye of the Cotswold tourism hurricane.

As always, head away from the main routes to find the best of the area: **Blockley** village, between Moreton and Chipping Campden, is a beauty, while the high wolds west of Stow are speckled with horsey hamlets flanking the splendid **Cotswold Farm Park** rare-breeds centre, itself only a spit from the famously beautiful twin villages of **Upper** and **Lower Slaughter**.

Cirencester

Plumb astride the A429 fifteen miles southeast of Cheltenham, pleasantly old-fashioned **CIRENCESTER** was a provincial capital under the **Romans**. The town flourished for three centuries: its grand forum was one of the largest in northern Europe, and in the province of Britannia "Corinium" was second in size and importance only to "Londinium" (London). The **Saxons** put paid to all that, largely destroying the Roman town. The **wool** boom of the Middle Ages saw a revival, and today, with its handsome stone buildings, Cirencester is an affluent little place that lays claim to be capital of the Cotswolds. Come, chiefly, for the outstanding **Roman museum** and the **Church of St John the Baptist** – but also make time to tap into the

LOWER SLAUGHTER

Highlights

❶ Cirencester The "capital of the Cotswolds" – a friendly market town with a grand church, quiet old lanes and good food. **See p.78**

❷ Fairford Come to this attractive village near the Thames to crick your neck at the superb medieval stained glass in the church. **See p.88**

❸ Bibury A one-street riverside village with perhaps the most photographed cottages in England. **See p.90**

❹ Northleach This charming, unspoilt mid-Cotswolds village merits a detour. **See p.93**

❺ The Slaughters Winningly handsome twin villages, with idyllic scenery and top-rated hotels – great for a luxury retreat. **See p.97**

❻ Cotswold Farm Park A brilliant day out: rare breeds showcased on a working farm, perfect for families. **See p.98**

❼ Batsford Arboretum Fine walks in beautiful parkland just outside Moreton-in-Marsh. **See p.105**

❽ Blockley A typically charming Cotswold village: quiet, attractive and – most importantly – out of the way. **See p.106**

HIGHLIGHTS ARE MARKED ON THE MAP ON P.80

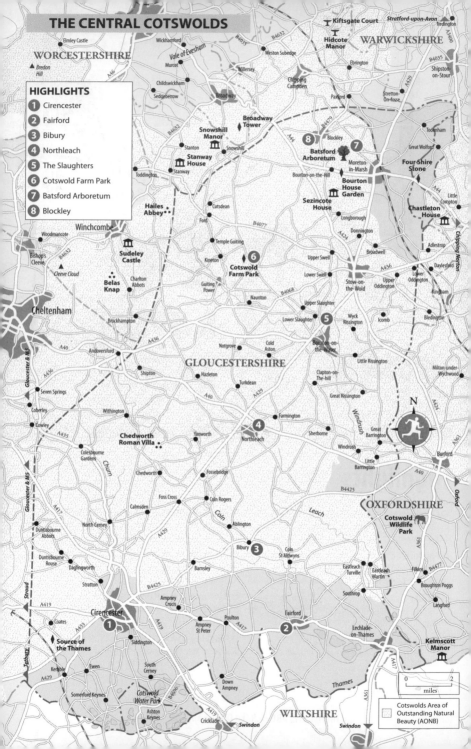

THE CENTRAL COTSWOLDS

WORCESTERSHIRE

WARWICKSHIRE

HIGHLIGHTS

1. Cirencester
2. Fairford
3. Bibury
4. Northleach
5. The Slaughters
6. Cotswold Farm Park
7. Batsford Arboretum
8. Blockley

GLOUCESTERSHIRE

OXFORDSHIRE

WILTSHIRE

Bredon Hill

Elmley Castle

Wickhamford

Vale of Evesham

Murcot

Childswickham

Sedgeberow

Willersey

Broadway

Weston Subedge

Chipping Campden

Paxford

Ebrington

Kiftsgate Court

Hidcote Manor

Stratford-upon-Avon

Tredington

Shipston-on-Stour

Stretton-On-fosse

Todenham

Great Wolford

Four Shire Stone

Little Compton

Broadway Tower

Snowshill Manor

Stanton

Snowshill

Blockley

Batsford Arboretum

Moreton-in-Marsh

Chastleton House

Stanway House

Stanway

Toddington

Bourton-on-the-Hill

Bourton House Garden

Sezincote House

Longborough

Adlestrop

Chipping Norton

Hailes Abbey

Cutsdean

Ford

Temple Guiting

Kineton

Donnington

Broadwell

Daylesford

Kingham

Winchcombe

Woodmancote

Bishop's Cleeve

Cleeve Cloud

Sudeley Castle

Charlton Abbots

Belas Knap

Upper Swell

Lower Swell

Stow-on-the-Wold

Upper Oddington

Lower Oddington

Bledington

Cheltenham

Brockhampton

Guiting Power

Naunton

Cotswold Farm Park

Upper Slaughter

Lower Slaughter

Wyck Rissington

Icomb

Andoversford

Shipton

Notgrove

Cold Aston

Bourton-on-the-Water

Little Rissington

Seven Springs

Coberley

Cowley

Hazleton

Turkdean

Clapton-on-The-hill

Milton-under-Wychwood

Withington

Farmington

Great Rissington

Chedworth Roman Villa

Yanworth

Northleach

Sherborne

Windrush

Great Barrington

Burford

Colesbourne Gardens

Chedworth

Fossebridge

Little Barrington

Calmsden

Foss Cross

Coln Rogers

Cotswold Wildlife Park

North Cerney

Ablington

Duntisbourne Abbots

Bibury

Coln St Aldwyns

Eastleach Turville

Eastleach Martin

Filkins

Broughton Poggs

Duntisbourne Rouse

Daglingworth

Barnsley

Southrop

Langford

Stratton

Ampney Crucis

Cirencester

Coates

Source of the Thames

Siddington

Ampney St Peter

Poulton

Fairford

Lechlade-on-Thames

Kelmscott Manor

Kemble

Ewen

South Cerney

Cotswold Water Park

Down Ampney

Somerford Keynes

Ashton Keynes

Cricklade

Swindon

Swindon

Thames

SWINDON

0   2
miles

Cotswolds Area of Outstanding Natural Beauty (AONB)

N

FARMERS' MARKETS

Dates may change around Christmas and New Year. See also ⓦ localfoods.org.uk.

Bourton-on-the-Water 4th Sun of month 9am–12.30pm ⓦ fresh-n-local.co.uk.
Cirencester 2nd & 4th Sat of month 8.30am–1pm ⓦ cirencester.gov.uk.
Stow-on-the-Wold 2nd Thurs of month 9am–1pm ⓦ fresh-n-local.co.uk.

2

upmarket food-and-shopping lifestyle that has made Cirencester the unlikely hub of so-called "Poshtershire". Alongside a developing hinterland of quality food producers, the town now has genuinely good **restaurants** – often populated, entertainingly, by a very distinctive breed of ladies who lunch.

Market Place

Cirencester's heart is the delightful, swirling **Market Place**, busy with traffic and commerce, and packed with traders' stalls for the Monday and Friday markets, and the fortnightly Saturday farmers' market. Plans are afoot to redesign the whole square, improving pedestrian circulation and shifting some of the traffic away: expect changes – or, perhaps, improvements – when you visit.

Church of St John the Baptist

Market Place • Daily 10am–5pm; Oct–March closes 4pm • Free • ☎ 01285 659317, ⓦ cirenparish.co.uk

An irregular line of eighteenth-century facades along the north side of Market Place contrasts with the heavier Victorian structures opposite, but the parish church of **St John the Baptist**, built in stages during the fifteenth century, dominates. The flying buttresses that support the tower had to be added when it transpired that the church had been constructed over the filled-in Roman ditch that ran beside Ermin Street, the Gloucester–Silchester road, which passed this way. The grand three-tiered south **porch**, the largest in England and big enough to function at one time as the town hall, leads to the nave, where slender piers and soaring arches create a superb sense of space, enhanced by clerestory windows that admit a warm light. The church contains much of interest, including a colourful wineglass **pulpit**, carved in stone around 1450 and one of the few pre-Reformation pulpits to have survived in Britain. Set into a display case nearby is the **Boleyn Cup**, a gilded silver goblet made in 1535 for Anne Boleyn. To the left of the chancel, superb fan vaulting hangs overhead in the **chapel of St Catherine**, who appears in a vivid fragment of a fifteenth-century wall painting. Climbing the **tower** is permitted on a few selected days each year. Outside, one of the best views of the church is from the **Abbey Grounds**, site of the Saxon abbey demolished in 1539 during the Dissolution, and now a small park skirted by the small River Churn and a fragment of the Roman city wall.

New Brewery Arts

Brewery Court • Mon–Sat 9am–5pm; April–Dec also Sun 10am–4pm • Free • ☎ 01285 657181, ⓦ newbreweryarts.org.uk

Just south of the Market Place off shop-lined Cricklade Street, the **New Brewery Arts** centre has more than a dozen resident artists, whose studios you can visit and whose work you can buy. It's worth popping by to see who is working and exhibiting – and, perhaps, to catch some live music.

Corinium Museum

Park St • Mon–Sat 10am–5pm, Sun 2–5pm; Nov–March closes 4pm • £4.95 • ☎ 01285 655611, ⓦ coriniummuseum.org

From the Market Place, walk down Black Jack Street to access Cirencester's most handsome quarter, centred on Park, Thomas and Coxwell streets – all of them narrow

CIRENCESTER

■ ACCOMMODATION

Corinium	2
Fleece	4
Ivy House	6
Mayfield Park	1
No. 12	3
Organic Farm Shop	5

● CAFÉS & RESTAURANTS

Graze	3
Indian Rasoi	1
Jack's	4
Jesse's Bistro	2
Made By Bob	6
New Brewery Arts Café	7
Organic Farm Shop	8
Soushi	5

and lined by stone houses dating mostly from the seventeenth and eighteenth centuries. One of those on Park Street houses the sleek, state-of-the-art **Corinium Museum**, offering the chance for an absorbing couple of hours taking in the town's Celtic, Roman and Saxon heritage. Mosaics abound, including large, floor-sized pavements, there's a trove of Bronze Age gold, an excellent video on Cotswold life in the Iron Age, a reconstruction of a Romano-British garden, and more. Less ancient items include a hoard of silver and gold coins totalling a dizzy £18 that was buried in a lead pipe during the Civil War and unearthed in 1981.

Cirencester Park

Daily 8am–5pm • Free; polo £10 • ⓦ cirencesterpark.co.uk & ⓦ cirencesterpolo.co.uk

Outside the Corinium Museum on Park Street, a yew hedge the height of telegraph poles conceals **Cirencester House**, the Earl of Bathurst's residence. At no point can you actually see the building (it's rather plain anyway), but you can stroll the attached three-thousand-acre **park**, accessed via **Cecily Hill**, a lovely street which rises to an eccentric-looking castle – actually a Victorian barracks – beside the park gates. The park's **polo** grounds attract some of the country's top players, with games held virtually every weekend between May and September.

ARRIVAL

By train Trains on the London–Swindon–Cheltenham line stop at Kemble station (see p.86), about five miles southwest of Cirencester. From the station bus #881 runs to Cirencester (Mon–Sat every 2hr; 15min), as does bus #855 (Mon–Fri 1 daily; 25min). Taxis charge about £10; local firms include Kemble Station Taxi (☎ 07817 450152, ⓦ kembletaxi.co.uk) and Kemble Taxis (☎ 0333 800 0750, ⓦ taxisofkemble.co.uk).

By bus In addition to services listed below, National Express long-distance coaches serve Cirencester direct from central London and Heathrow airport, stopping on London Rd (5min east of Market Place): they are also a useful way to get to and from Cheltenham or Gloucester on a Sunday, when local buses don't run.

Destinations Barnsley (Mon–Sat 4 daily; 10min); Bibury (Mon–Sat 4 daily; 15min); Bourton-on-the-Water (Mon–Sat 4 daily; 35–50min); Cheltenham (Mon–Sat hourly; 40min); Crudwell (Mon–Sat 4–5 daily; 25min); Fairford (Mon–Sat 6 daily; 30–55min); Gloucester (Mon–Sat 4 daily; 1hr 10min); Lechlade (Mon–Sat 6 daily; 50min–1hr 5min); Malmesbury (Mon–Sat 4–5 daily; 50min); Moreton-in-Marsh (Mon–Sat once daily; 1hr 20min); Northleach (Mon–Sat 5–6 daily; 20–40min); Stow-on-the-Wold (Mon–Sat 1 daily; 1hr 10min); Stroud (Mon–Fri 5 daily, 3 on Sat; 35min); Tetbury (Mon–Sat 5 daily; 40min).

By car Driving into Cirencester may try your patience. There is a bypass-cum-ring road – but it's less of a ring, more of a lop-sided horseshoe, punctuated by poorly signed round-abouts. As you go round, the A429 and A419 battle for supremacy, with signs for Swindon and Bristol often super-seding closer-at-hand destinations. The bypass is itself bypassed by the A417 (which, inconveniently, turns into the A419 at one point). Add to that a fiendish one-way system, and you may wonder what Cirencester has got to hide.

By taxi Local firms include 2&Fro (☎ 01285 640088, ⓦ 2andfro.tel) and A2B (☎ 01285 655651, ⓦ a2btaxisof cirencester.co.uk).

INFORMATION AND TOURS

Tourist office At the Corinium Museum on Park St (Mon–Sat 10am–5pm, Sun 2–5pm; Nov–March closes 4pm; ☎ 01285 654180, ⓦ cotswolds.com & ⓦ cotswold .gov.uk).

Walking tours The Cirencester Civic Society runs guided walks in summer (May–Sept Sun at 3pm, also June–Aug Wed at 3pm; 1hr 30min; £2; ⓦ ccsoc.org.uk), starting from the church in Market Place.

ACCOMMODATION

For a town with history, location and money on its side, Cirencester's **accommodation** is a touch disappointing: quality is good, but the range is a bit limited. Book well ahead for the places below – or day-trip from a nearby base at, say, Tetbury (see p.65), Coln St Aldwyns (see p.90) or North Cerney (see p.84). By the time you read this, the revamped *King's Head* (ⓦ kingshead-hotel.co.uk) will have opened on Market Place as Cirencester's first five-star hotel: worth a look.

Corinium 12 Gloucester St ☎ 01285 659711, ⓦ corinium hotel.com. Decent three-star family-run hotel in a historic sixteenth-century property on this attractive, narrow street a short walk northwest of the centre. Only fifteen rooms, modestly priced and adequately furnished. **£105**

Fleece Market Place ☎ 01285 658507, ⓦ thefleece cirencester.co.uk. This old town-centre inn has been freshly updated to a smart, contemporary look. The 28 rooms now feel like calm, stylish boltholes: low ceilings and seventeenth-century beams are enhanced by swanky en-suite bathrooms – and a great location. **£94**

Ivy House 2 Victoria Rd ☎ 01285 656626, ⓦ ivyhouse cotswolds.com. Of a string of B&Bs along Victoria Rd, this is one of the more attractive options, a high-gabled Victorian house with four en-suite guest rooms, modestly done up. **£80**

Mayfield Park Cheltenham Rd ☎ 01285 831301, ⓦ mayfieldpark.co.uk. Well-equipped campsite on the A435 near Perrotts Brook, a couple of miles north of town. Pitches **£19**

No.12 12 Park St ☎ 01285 640232, ⓦ no12cirencester .co.uk. A stolid Georgian townhouse virtually opposite the museum hides this swanky, very nicely presented B&B-cum-boutique pad. Four rooms, with tasteful, muted colours set off by silks and velvets, have luxury pretensions: a free-standing claw-foot bath here, an antique leather sleigh bed there. **£120**

★ **Organic Farm Shop** Abbey Home Farm, Burford Rd ☎ 01285 640441, ⓦ theorganicfarmshop.co.uk. This top-rated farm shop and café off the B4425 two miles east of Cirencester has self-catering accommodation, including a lakeside cabin, a woodland yurt let by the night (two-night minimum stay) and a "leave no trace" campsite. Pitches **£5**, yurt **£60**

EATING AND DRINKING

Cirencester has a welter of noteworthy **restaurants and pubs**. Rob Rees, an award-winning chef and local food entrepreneur who goes by the title "The Cotswold Chef" (ⓦ thecotswoldchef.com), runs a Food Centre at the Royal Agricultural College on the edge of town, offering short **cookery courses** and bespoke **food tours**; see his website for details. Look out for the **Cotswold Show and Food Festival**, held in Cirencester Park in early July (ⓦ cotswoldshow.co.uk).

IN TOWN

Graze 3 Gosditch St ☎ 01285 658957, ⓦ bathales.com. Gazing across at the church, just round the corner from the Market Place, this splendid old building – its neo-Gothic façade concealing what was a thirteenth-century tithe barn, added to in the fifteenth century, still with some

2

2

original timbers over Roman column bases – is now a rather good gastropub, run by the independent Bath Ales mini-chain. Subtitling itself a brasserie and chophouse, it turns out locally sourced pork and lamb chops, steaks and burgers (£12–17) to an easygoing, food-savvy local crowd. Mon–Thurs 11am–11pm, Fri 11am–midnight, Sat 9am–midnight, Sun 9am–11pm.

Indian Rasoi 14 Dollar St ☎01285 644822, ⓦindianrasoi.org. An up-to-date, contemporary styled restaurant serving probably the best curry in Cirencester (which is not such faint praise as you might imagine). Go for the classic dishes, and especially the mouth-watering choice of lamb curries. Mains £8–12. Mon–Sat noon–2pm & 5.30–11.30pm, Sun noon–2pm & 5.30–11pm.

Jack's 44 Black Jack St ☎01285 640888. Attractive little independent daytime café in an old building (and covered alleyway) beside the Corinium Museum – salads, soups, cakes and big cups of coffee. Cash only. Mon–Sat 9am–5pm, Sun 10.30am–5pm.

★**Jesse's Bistro** The Stableyard, 14 Black Jack St ☎01285 641497, ⓦjessesbistro.co.uk. Wonderful little hideaway, in a courtyard off the street between the museum and the main square. The speciality here is fish and seafood – as you walk in, you'll get a whiff of the fish counter beside the door, freshly caught beasties whisked over direct from the Cornish coast. The menu changes daily; expect crab salad or *moules marinière*, oven-roasted mackerel or pepper-crusted bream alongside meaty favourites such as rump steak or calves' liver – hearty food, expertly prepared and served with smooth informality. Mains roughly £12–14. Mon noon–2.30pm, Tues–Sat noon–2.30pm & 7–9.30pm.

Made By Bob The Corn Hall, 26 Market Place ☎01285 641818, ⓦfoodmadebybob.com. Striking, buzzy daytime café-restaurant just off the main square

– very hip, serving outstanding food and snacks in a smart yet casual ambience. Opens for breakfast (Bircher muesli, kippers, eggs Benedict, all the way up to a full English; £5–10), and stays open after lunch for posh afternoon tea. The kitchen is placed centrally: watch the chefs prepare anything from fish soup with gruyère or red pepper tart to grilled squid or ribeye steak, from a daily changing menu (mains £9–18) – or just drop by the deli section for swanky sandwiches (£5–6), olives, fresh-baked bread and the like. Mon–Wed 7.30am–5.30pm, Thurs & Fri 7.30am–5.30pm & 7–9pm, Sat 8am–5.30pm.

New Brewery Arts Café Brewery Court, off Cricklade St ☎01285 657181, ⓦnewbreweryarts.org.uk. Pleasant daytime café in this buzzing arts centre – good for a coffee or a light lunch (£5–8), with some delicious veggie options. Mon–Sat 9am–4.45pm, Sun 10am–3.45pm.

Soushi 12 Castle St ☎01285 641414, ⓦsoushi.co.uk. Modest little Japanese restaurant with a reputation for excellence. As well as sushi platters and bento boxes for lunch, there's a full evening menu of sushi and sashimi, alongside specialities such as chicken skewers, sweet ginger tofu, slow-cooked pork belly, tempura, and more (mains £9–17) – all very fresh, and authentically prepared by the Japanese chef. It's a small place, hidden away down a side-alley: expect good food, rather than lavish atmosphere. Tues–Sat noon–2.30pm & 6–9.30pm.

OUT OF TOWN

★**Organic Farm Shop** Abbey Home Farm, Burford Rd ☎01285 640441, ⓦtheorganicfarmshop.co.uk. This wonderful farm shop off the B4425 two miles east of Cirencester includes an award-winning café serving delicious soups, stews and roasts from organic, locally sourced produce, always with a vegan option – and it's licensed for alcohol. Mains around £10. Tues–Sat 9am–4.30pm, Sun 11am–3.30pm.

DIRECTORY

Hospital Cheltenham General, Sandford Rd, Cheltenham (☎0300 422 2222, ⓦwww.gloshospitals.nhs.uk).
Markets General market on Market Place (Mon & Fri 9am–3pm; ⓦcirencester.gov.uk), as well as regular farmers markets (see p.81).
Pharmacy Boots, 39–43 Cricklade St ☎ 01285 653019,

ⓦboots.com.
Police station The Forum (Mon–Sat 9am–5pm; ☎101, ⓦgloucestershire.police.uk).
Post office Castle St (Mon–Fri 9am–5.30pm, Sat 9am–12.30pm).

North Cerney

If you want to move on quickly from Cirencester to Cheltenham, take the speedy A417 dual carriageway (though expect traffic at the bottleneck around Birdlip). For a more pleasant drive, opt for the slower A435, passing first through **NORTH CERNEY**, home of acclaimed goat's cheese producer Cerney Cheese (no public access; ⓦcerneycheese.com) and the adjacent **Cerney Gardens** (late Jan to late Oct daily 10am–5pm; £5; ⓦcerneygardens.com), a fragrant hideaway centred on a Victorian walled garden.

ACCOMMODATION AND EATING   **NORTH CERNEY**

Bathurst Arms North Cerney ☎01285 831281, ⓦ bathurstarms.com. An award-winning traditional inn – log fires, wooden beams – updated to high standards in drinking, dining and lodging. Much of the food is sourced from Gloucestershire farms, from Cerney goat's cheese starters to Old Spot pork, Churn Valley venison and Cotswold lamb (mains £12–17). The six well-presented rooms are a bargain. Mon–Fri noon–2pm & 6–9pm, Sat noon–2.30pm & 6–9.30pm, Sun noon–3pm & 7–9pm. **£80**

Colesbourne Gardens

2

Colesbourne Park • Feb & early March Sat & Sun 1–4.30pm • £7.50 • ☎ 01242 870567, ⓦ colesbournegardens.org.uk

In the valley of the River Churn, on the A435 halfway between Cirencester and Cheltenham, **COLESBOURNE**, centred on a 2,500-acre estate, is renowned for its ten-acre gardens, opened to the public over five weekends in late winter specifically for the spectacular array of snowdrops – thousands of them, celebrated by *Country Life* magazine as "England's greatest snowdrop garden".

The Duntisbournes

Northwest of Cirencester, the hills start to rear up on the approach to Stroud, forming a folded landscape of high tops and deep, damp valleys. Minor roads off the A417 first reach **DAGLINGWORTH** – about a picturesque and unvisited a Cotswold village as you could dream up – before penetrating the narrow valley of the **Duntisbournes**. This succession of tiny communities – barely even hamlets, most of them – includes **MIDDLE DUNTISBOURNE** and **DUNTISBOURNE LEER** before culminating in **DUNTISBOURNE ABBOTS**, with a Norman church overlaid by Victorian restoration. The walk from Cirencester is lovely, roughly five miles altogether.

Duntisbourne Rouse

Look carefully for a carved wooden finger-post on the single-track road between Daglingworth and Middle Duntisbourne. This marks the otherwise indiscernible location of **DUNTISBOURNE ROUSE**, neither a village nor a hamlet, but effectively just a church – and a real beauty. Dedicated to St Michael, this tiny country building of Saxon origin stands alone on grassy slopes beside a wood, reached via a lychgate by the roadside. The chancel is Norman, the tower and bells fifteenth-century (with the saddleback top added later), but the power of the place is its age – and its isolation.

The Ampneys and Poulton

East of Cirencester, the A417 makes short work of the thirteen miles to Lechlade. Past pretty **AMPNEY CRUCIS**, beside a turnoff to Ampney St Mary in what is termed **AMPNEY ST PETER** (though there are no signs), stands the small *Red Lion*, one of England's most noteworthy **historic pubs**. It hasn't been done up in decades but remains entirely free of the usual studied pub character – no horse-brasses or tankards hanging from the beams. This is just two plain rooms in a three-hundred-year old stone cottage – and there's no bar. Instead, the landlord perches on a stool in the corner, pulling pints from two handpumps and passing them over the back of a wooden bench to his customers, who sit together around one table by the fireplace. The other room has the same set-up: a bench around two walls, and one table by the fire. There's no food, and nowhere for loners to hide: the only option is to introduce yourself to the regulars. At the time of writing opening hours were very restricted (see p.86).

From the next-door village of **POULTON**, back roads cut north for two or three miles to Barnsley (see p.91) and Bibury (p.90), and south the same distance to **DOWN AMPNEY**, birthplace of the composer Ralph Vaughan Williams, also with a strikingly beautiful thirteenth-century church.

2

EATING AND DRINKING

Falcon Inn Poulton ☎01285 850878, ⓦfalconinn poulton.co.uk. Another high-quality makeover of a traditional village tavern into a swanky Cotswolds gastropub. This time, the food is good enough to draw fine-dining buffs out from Cirencester (which is really saying something) – sample dishes include osso buco with polenta, rabbit pie and duck breast with celeriac (£11–17),

everything benefiting from smooth, engaging service and a relaxed, family-friendly atmosphere. Tues–Sat noon–3pm & 5–11pm, Sun noon–4pm.

Red Lion Ampney St Peter ☎01285 851596. This ancient pub sports a historic interior that hasn't been touched in decades (see p.85) – indeed, the current licensee is only the fourth since 1851. Mon, Fri & Sat 6–9pm, Sun noon–2pm.

Kemble and around

Southwest of Cirencester, three roads diverge, towards Stroud, Tetbury and Malmesbury. The last of these – the A429 – passes first through **KEMBLE**, a mundane little village which happens to have one of the Cotswolds' few main-line **railway stations**, with services to Swindon, Reading and London in one direction, and Stroud, Gloucester and Cheltenham in the other.

Kemble is surrounded by water meadows that are traditionally regarded as the **source of the River Thames** – and the *Thames Head Inn* on the A433 just by the railway bridge has made a good living out of folk seeking the river's origins. Bar staff (and a big sketch-map hanging in the pub's porch) can point you onto the short walk of about fifteen minutes from the pub to **THAMES HEAD**, a point by a copse in open fields, where a stone marker declares a shallow depression to be the river's source. However, if you're keen to see flowing water, check at the pub beforehand: Thames Head, confusingly, is often dry (see box below).

In **EWEN**, about a mile east of Kemble, the *Wild Duck Inn* – an ivy-clad stone building dating from 1563, set in its own gardens – was formerly one of the area's leading restaurants. As this book went to press in 2014 it had just reopened under new management, and may be worth a look if you're in the area. Check online (ⓦthewildduckinn.co.uk) for the latest.

Tunnel House Inn

On the wild back lanes between **COATES** and **TARLTON** villages, north of Kemble, signs will lead you to the *Tunnel House Inn* (see opposite), reachable by car only along a narrow, rutted track which climbs beside the now-defunct Thames & Severn Canal to the grand Georgian "East Portal". This is the point where the canal enters the Sapperton Tunnel – once the longest canal tunnel in Britain – on its way towards Sapperton (see p.62) and Stroud. The pub stands directly above the portal.

THAMES HEAD

When you reach **Thames Head**, don't be disappointed if there's no water in sight. The River Thames is fed by groundwater, and the water table rises and falls throughout the year; the Environment Agency continuously tracks the river's source, which shifts along a line of several miles of boggy ground between Thames Head and Ashton Keynes, southeast near Cricklade.

To cast further aspersions, this bit of the river is shorter than the River Churn, which rises at Seven Springs (see p.49) on the Cotswold Edge and flows south through Cirencester to join the Thames near Cricklade. Because Seven Springs flows year-round, and because the distance from Seven Springs to the confluence is over twelve miles longer than from Thames Head to the confluence, many say that the stream rising at Thames Head is, in fact, insignificant and the true Thames rises at Seven Springs. By this reasoning, the Churn should in fact be regarded as the Thames.

But logic is no match for tradition. Thames Head remains the focus of attention – indeed, the marked **Thames Path** (ⓦnationaltrail.co.uk) starts here: walk it direct to the Thames Barrier at Woolwich in southeast London, 184 miles away.

COTSWOLD AIRPORT

What was once RAF Kemble, an airfield located off the A433 four miles southwest of Cirencester – home for many years to the famous Red Arrows aerobatic display team – has now become the titchy **Cotswold Airport** (☎ 01285 771177, ✆ cotswoldairport.com). It has no scheduled flights and is used only by private jets, but there are occasional public events and air shows.

2

Two **long-distance paths** pass the *Tunnel House*: the Cirencester–Tetbury stage of the Monarch's Way, and the Macmillan Way (see p.32) en route to Sapperton. Casual walkers could otherwise opt for a post-prandial ramble around the pub on woodland paths above the silted-up canal. The **Cotswold Canals Partnership** (✆ www.cotswold canalsproject.org) has the long-term goal of reopening this once-thriving link between the Severn and the Thames, but it's long, slow work: they are currently dredging and rebuilding in order to reconnect Stroud to the national waterways network. Reopening the full route to Lechlade is a distant dream.

ARRIVAL AND DEPARTURE   KEMBLE AND AROUND

By train and bus Kemble is served by trains on the London–Swindon–Cheltenham line. From Kemble station bus #881 (Mon–Sat every 2hr) runs to Cirencester (15min) and Tetbury (25min). Bus #855 also runs to Cirencester (Mon–Fri 1 daily; 25min). Taxi firms include Kemble Station Taxi (☎ 07817 450152, ✆ kembletaxi.co.uk) and Kemble Taxis (☎ 0333 800 0750, ✆ taxisofkemble.co.uk).

ACCOMODATION AND EATING

Thames Head Inn ☎ 01285 770259, ✆ thameshead inn.co.uk. This congenial pub stands by the railway bridge on the A433 about half a mile north of Kemble, plumb between Cirencester and Tetbury. Stop in for a drink, decent food (mains £9–12) or to sleep: they have four very spick-and-span rooms in a converted modern annexe. Mon–Sat 11am–11pm, Sun noon–10.30pm. **£75**
Tunnel House Inn ☎ 01285 770280, ✆ tunnelhouse .com. This isolated seventeenth-century inn feels like a country haven, with its vintage memorabilia, fireside sofas, bookshelves and stuffed owl. Nonetheless, and despite the location, it can get busy, with locals and visitors alike arriving for a country pint or a decent pub meal (mains £10–15). Under new management at the time of writing: things might have changed a bit when you visit. Daily noon–11pm.

Cotswold Water Park

Gateway Information Centre Off the B4696 "Spine Rd", four miles southeast of Cirencester • Daily 9am–5pm • ☎ 01793 752413, ✆ www.waterpark.org • **Cotswold Country Park and Beach** Feb, Nov & Dec Wed–Sun 10am–4pm; March & Oct daily 10am–5pm; April & May daily 10am–6pm; June & Sept daily 10am–7pm; July & Aug daily 10am–8pm • £2–6, depending on season • ☎ 01285 868096, ✆ cotswoldcountrypark.co.uk

Covering an area of forty square miles straddling the Gloucestershire–Wiltshire border, the **Cotswold Water Park** takes in no fewer than 147 lakes. Created over several decades by sand and gravel extraction, the lakes vary widely in size, beauty and accessibility. Some are owned by individuals or clubs, many are given over to second-home developments, but plenty are protected as Sites of Special Scientific Interest: twenty thousand waterfowl overwinter here, fourteen of the UK's seventeen species of bat are resident, beavers are monitored as part of a reintroduction project, there are 23 species of dragonfly to find, and so on. Leisure is also big: private operators on several of the lakes offer activities from angling to waterskiing.

Your first port of call should be the **Gateway Information Centre** – they have full information on the water park's facilities, including details of walks in the nature reserves dotted around the lakes, bike rental, kayaking, camping, and more.

From the Gateway Information Centre, the B4696 towards **SOMERFORD KEYNES** leads to the water park's biggest draw, the **Cotswold Country Park and Beach**. This cluster of adjacent lakes, set in seventy acres of grounds – which includes the UK's largest inland beach – has kids' activities galore, as well as some quieter corners.

Butts Farm

South Cerney • Farm Shop: Tues–Fri 10am–6pm, Sat 8.30am–2pm; visits: April–Sept Tues–Sun 10.30am–5pm • Visits £5 • ☎ 01285 862224, ⓦ buttsfarmrarebreeds.co.uk

Off the A419 beside **SOUTH CERNEY**, just north of the Cotswold Water Park, you'll find the wonderful **Butts Farm**. This working farm specializes in rare breeds, and the shop is crammed with home-cured bacon, exotic sausages and pâtés, alongside more familiar local produce. The farm itself is also open for **visits**, when kids can bottle-feed lambs, milk goats, ride ponies and take a tractor safari.

Fairford and around

FAIRFORD, on the River Coln about six miles east of Cirencester, and just a couple of miles south of Coln St Aldwyns (see p.90), has a busy, narrow main road carrying the A417, but is still rather pretty, with a tight dog-leg bridge and ancient, silver-stoned cottages – some half-timbered – lining the street. Once you squeeze into the centre, the broad **Market Place** opens off the A417 (which is here named as London Road or London Street). Look out for the very popular **Royal International Air Tattoo** (ⓦ airtattoo.com), held over a weekend in mid-July at RAF Fairford nearby.

St Mary's Church

High St • Daily 10am–5pm, Oct–March closes 4pm • ☎ 01285 712611, ⓦ stmaryschurchfairford.org.uk

It's a pleasant, short stroll up the Market Place to reach Fairford's main attraction, the elegant **St Mary's Church**. Built in the 1490s over ancient predecessors, this is a splendid example of Perpendicular Gothic, broad and lofty, constructed around an earlier tower. It is famed for its unique array of late-medieval **stained glass**. Created in the first decade or so of the sixteenth century by Barnard Flower, glazier to the king (Henry VII), at his workshop in Westminster, the glass survives intact as a complete set of 28 windows. Guides in the church can explain the themes, which include episodes from the life of Christ and depictions of prophets and apostles – look out for Mary's parents apparently cuddling and kissing in the north aisle; St Apollonia, patron saint of dentists, holding forceps and a just-plucked tooth in the south aisle; and the great west window showing the Last Judgement (with, to the right, Cain killing Abel). The choir stalls hide a fine set of **misericords** dating to the early fourteenth century.

ARRIVAL AND DEPARTURE   FAIRFORD

By bus Buses drop off in the Market Place.
Destinations Cirencester (Mon–Sat 5–6 daily; 30–55min);

Lechlade (Mon–Sat 8 daily; 5–10min); Southrop (Tues, Thurs & Sat 1 daily; 25min).

ACCOMMODATION AND EATING

7a Coffee Shop 7a London St ☎ 01285 712918, ⓦ 7acoffeeshop.co.uk. Much-loved café in the centre of Fairford, serving up paninis, salads, light bites and sensational chocolate brownies in multiple varieties. It's open limited hours, though. Mon 10am–3pm, Tues–Fri 9am–5pm, Sat 8.30am–12.30pm.

Colosseo 1 London St ☎ 01285 239238, ⓦ colosseo fairford.com. This family-run Italian restaurant had only just opened at the time of writing – but the welcome is warm and the cheerful menu of upscale pizzas, pastas and meaty mains (£8–16) was getting a thumbs-up from locals. Tues–Sun noon–3pm & 6–10.30pm.

Lechlade-on-Thames

Four miles east of Fairford – and just a couple of miles from fascinating
Kelmscott Manor (see p.161) – **LECHLADE-ON-THAMES**, oddly, is a port town.
This is the highest navigable stretch of the River Thames and, in the nineteenth-
century heyday of the Thames & Severn Canal, Lechlade functioned as a
transshipment point for cargo moving between the canal and the river. In truth,
though, there's not much left, and the town now labours under the weight of road
traffic on the east–west A417 and the north–south A361. They cross by the
wedge-shaped **Market Place**, overlooked by the spire of the splendid fifteenth-
century church of **St Lawrence** (ⓦstlawrencelechlade.org.uk). Roam the interior,
with its Tudor east window, and then stroll the churchyard, as Shelley did in 1815:
his poem *A Summer Evening Churchyard, Lechlade*, is commemorated by a carved
stone at the entrance.

The **Ha'penny Bridge** nearby carries the A361 over the Thames, overlooked by the
pleasant *Riverside* pub. From here you can follow the Thames Path for the short
walk west to **INGLESHAM**, where the River Coln and the canal enter (there are plans
afoot to restore the lock here – see ⓦcotswoldcanalsproject.org), or the slightly
longer walk east to **St John's Lock**, near where the River Leach enters. The lock is
marked by an 1854 **statue of Old Father Thames** by Raffaelle Monti which originally
stood in London's Crystal Palace, then was moved to Thames Head (see p.86) before
ending up here.

ARRIVAL AND ACTIVITIES   LECHLADE-ON-THAMES

By bus Buses drop off in the Market Place.
Destinations Cirencester (Mon–Sat 6 daily; 50min–1hr
5min); Fairford (Mon–Sat 9 daily; 5–10min); Southrop
(Tues, Thurs & Sat 1 daily; 5min).

Boat trips Half-hour river cruises start from Riverside Park
on the south side of Ha'penny Bridge (April–Sept Sat & Sun
plus some weekdays 11am–5pm; £4; ☎07787 485294,
ⓦlechladetripboat.co.uk).

EATING AND DRINKING

Riverside Park End Wharf ☎01367 252534, ⓦriverside
-lechlade.com. Attractive, popular pub on the Thames
beside Ha'penny Bridge, pleasant for a pint, handy for a
pub lunch (two courses £12), and also with good-value
en-suite rooms. Mon–Sat noon–3.30pm & 5–11pm, Sun
noon–11pm. **£84**

Trout Inn St John's Lock ☎01367 252313, ⓦthetrout
inn.com. Friendly old riverside pub slightly outside
Lechlade, best for a reviving pint or two by the water, also
with a programme of live jazz, blues and folk events.
Mon–Sat 11am–11pm, Sun noon–11pm.

Southrop

Northeast of Fairford, country lanes cross over into the valley of the River Leach
at **SOUTHROP** (pronounced "sutherop"), bang on the Gloucestershire–Oxfordshire
border. Stop in for a glimpse of the Grade 1 listed **St Peter's Church**, dating from the
twelfth century, with its slate roof and Norman arches – and also for a lunch to
remember, either here at the *Swan* or a mile to the east at the *Five Alls* in Filkins (see
p.160). Download details of a four-mile circular walk that begins at the *Swan* at
ⓦfriendsofthecotswolds.org.

EATING AND DRINKING   SOUTHROP

Swan Southrop ☎01367 850205, ⓦtheswanat
southrop.co.uk. A classic updating of an ivy-swathed
seventeenth-century village inn into a landmark country
restaurant, this place exudes charm. The bar is still a
locals' retreat, while the restaurant showcases inventive,
upmarket, but not overly fussy cooking, with plenty for

carnivores to get their teeth into (including local Kelmscott
pork) and a good choice of fish and veggie options. Mains
are £15–25, with cheaper options at the bar (£10–15).
Book well ahead. Mon–Thurs noon–2.30pm & 6–9pm,
Fri noon–2.30pm & 6–9.30pm, Sat noon–3pm &
6–9.30pm, Sun noon–3.30pm.

Coln St Aldwyns

A couple of miles north of Fairford, and about the same south of Bibury, **COLN ST ALDWYNS** sits down in the valley of the River Coln. It's a quiet, typical estate village, with a square-towered church – originally dedicated to St Athelwine – that retains a Norman doorway, enveloped by chevron designs. The main draw is the rather wonderful *New Inn*, a sixteenth-century stone-built pub.

ACCOMMODATION AND EATING

New Inn Coln St Aldwyns ☎ 01285 750651, ⊚ new-inn .co.uk. Out of the Cotswold hubbub, but not hard to find, this country inn is a great base from which to explore the whole region, from Cirencester to Burford and everywhere in between. Previously known – and widely reviewed – as a gastronome's bolthole, the place came under new management in 2013, with a fresh approach that toned down the fine-dining aspirations (and prices). The menu now takes in steaks, smoked haddock fishcakes, duck confit and so on (mains £9–15), while the fourteen rooms are lovely, featuring contemporary design touches and luxury bathrooms. Mon–Thurs 8am–10.30pm, Fri & Sat 8am–11pm, Sun 8am–9pm. **£120**

Bibury and around

Hidden away on the B4425 between Cirencester and Burford, at the point where the road crosses the River Coln, **BIBURY** – like Broadway, Burford and Bourton-on-the-Water – is a hugely popular Cotswolds tourism honeypot. Winningly attractive (and famously dubbed "the most beautiful village in England" by Victorian designer William Morris), it draws crowds by the coachload. Yet there's even less to do here than in its alliterative compadres: strolling the village lanes is the thing, but everybody else has had the same idea.

At the east end of the village you'll pass the splendid, quiet church of **St Mary**, with Gothic windows, Saxon elements surviving above the chancel arch and a fifteenth-century timber ceiling.

Arlington Row

Set back from Bibury's main road is the focus of every photographer's attention. **Arlington Row**, originally built around 1380 as a wool store, was converted in the seventeenth century into a line of cottages to house weavers working at nearby Arlington Mill. It was this glimpse of hound's-tooth gables, warm yellow stone and wonky windows which stole William Morris's heart – and which is now immortalized in the UK passport as an image of England.

Rack Isle

To reach Arlington Row from the main road, you have to cross a diminutive patch of boggy meadow known as **Rack Isle** (it's where clothes were once hung on racks to dry). Now protected by the National Trust, the wildflower-strewn isle has several pretty footpaths winding across it to the little bridge over the Coln at the far end, a couple of hundred yards away.

Bibury Trout Farm

Arlington • Daily 8am–6pm; March & Oct closes 5pm; Nov–Feb closes 4pm • £3.95 • ☎ 01285 740215, ⊚ biburytroutfarm.co.uk

By a tiny bridge over the River Coln stands the **Bibury Trout Farm**. Unsurprisingly popular, since it's the only paying attraction in a heavily touristed village, the fishery has footpaths leading out across a network of ponds to scenic picnic spots (you can buy fresh and smoked trout in the shop for barbecuing) and also offers a catch-your-own section, with all equipment provided.

A WALK AROUND BARNSLEY AND BIBURY

A scenic, quiet **walk** (11 miles; 5hr) links a series of trails to cover some rough terrain between Barnsley and Bibury. From the centre of Barnsley, paths head north across Barnsley Park and on, over the fields and across Fosscross Lane to Winson village, alongside Coln Rogers (see below) in the wooded Coln Valley. Climb to Lamborough Banks for a great view, then turn south to drop down to Bibury. The return leads on paths behind Arlington to cut southwest across the fields, through Deadlands Copse and back to Barnsley.

2

ARRIVAL AND DEPARTURE   BIBURY

By train and taxi A taxi to Bibury from Kemble station (see p.86) is about £25.

By bus Bus #855 (Mon–Sat 5 daily) runs to Cirencester (20min) and Northleach (20min).

ACCOMMODATION AND EATING

Bibury Court Bibury ☎ 01285 740337, ☻ biburycourt .com. Out of harm's way at the east end of the village, this place looks ravishing, a Jacobean mansion to die for. Tranquil in its own grounds, it offers untrammelled peace and quiet: people come, people whisper, people go, and the loudest noise is the church bells. The restaurant is excellent (afternoon tea is a bit of a local institution), but the rooms might disappoint – not quite as elegant nor as well-appointed as the price might indicate. Two larger rooms, bizarrely, have no en-suite bathroom. **£145**

Catherine Wheel Bibury ☎ 01285 740250, ☻ catherine wheel-bibury.co.uk. Just up from the trout farm, Bibury's

only pub is, in many ways, your best bet – a busy but cheery place, with a modest gastropub menu (mains £11–17), as well as sandwiches and stone-baked pizzas, and four pleasant, beamed double rooms in a separate building. Mon–Sat 11am–11pm, Sun 11am–10.30pm. **£65**

Swan Bibury ☎ 01285 740695, ☻ swanhotel.co.uk. This decent enough hotel by the bridge in the village centre – a member of the Cotswold Inns & Hotels group – is a spruce, comfortable and welcoming place in a stand-out setting, with rooms in the main building and posher suites in the separate garden cottage. The brasserie isn't up to much, though. **£150**

Barnsley

Between Cirencester and Bibury, the B4425 passes through **BARNSLEY**, once a little-regarded cluster of houses, now firmly on the map of five-star Cotswold tourism for the conversion of a country house on the edge of the village into one of the region's swankiest hotels. *Barnsley House* is a phenomenally expensive place to stay, but – if there's not a wedding on – there's nothing to stop you dropping in to roam the spectacular gardens among laburnum avenues and hidden statues (daily 10.30am–4.30pm; £10 including tea).

ACCOMMODATION AND EATING

Barnsley House Barnsley ☎ 01285 740000, ☻ barnsley house.com. This luxury hotel occupies a glorious Jacobean mansion – but its style is anything but Jacobean. Inside, you could be in the flashiest of boutique pads: state-of-the-art styling announces that, here, money is no object. The restaurant is outstanding (Italian-inspired mains £11–27) and there's an onsite spa that breathes contemporary minimalism. **£325**

★ **Village Pub** Barnsley ☎ 01285 740421, ☻ thevillage pub.co.uk. If the *Barnsley House* hotel gives your wallet the

wobbles, repair instead across the road. The same design team who created the hotel have transformed Barnsley's village pub into – you guessed it – *The Village Pub*, a super-sleek, urban stylist's ironic take on country ways, sporting a *papier-mâché* stag's head above the fireplace, heavy swag curtains, designer settles and pub grub so immaculate it borders on fine dining (mains £12–15). They also have six rooms, finished to a superbly high standard. Food served Mon–Fri noon–2.30pm & 6–9.30pm, Sat noon–3pm & 6–9.30pm, Sun noon–3pm & 6–9pm. **£135**

Coln Rogers

A thicket of narrow, empty lanes crisscrosses its way north from Bibury back up the Coln valley towards Fossebridge on the A429. Once past **Arlington** and **Ablington**, on Bibury's doorstep, you could aim for tiny **COLN ROGERS**, named for Roger of Gloucester, a twelfth-century knight, and today almost lost in the forest. Here, reached down a track off a back road, stands the **Saxon church** of St Andrew – simple, but resonant with age. With a good map, you could put together a circular walk following tracks through and behind Coln Rogers: it's extraordinary to find a place so scenic, and so quiet, this deep in the heart of the Cotswolds.

2 Fossebridge

Either side of the A40 junction, the arrow-straight A429 – which follows the line of the Roman road Fosse Way – takes on rollercoaster aspirations, shooting down one hillside and immediately whizzing straight up the next. About three miles south of Northleach, a particularly steep dip, which marks the valley of the River Coln, shelters the **Inn at Fossebridge**, a rather atmospheric three-hundred-year-old coaching inn. Roads here turn off west to Chedworth Roman villa and east into the maze-like Coln Valley.

ACCOMMODATION AND EATING FOSSEBRIDGE

Hare and Hounds Foss Cross ☎ 01285 720288, ⓦ hareandhoundsinn.com. This country inn two miles south of Fossebridge has turned itself into a rather good gastropub – roast Cotswold lamb, fillet of beef with *bok choi*, or couscous-stuffed peppers served in a cosy, flagstoned dining room. Mains £14–19. Also with ten spacious en-suite rooms. Food served daily 11am–2.30pm & 6–9.30pm. **£110**

Inn at Fossebridge On the A429 Fosse Way,

Fossebridge ☎ 01285 720721, ⓦ fossebridgeinn.co.uk. This landmark eighteenth-century coaching inn a couple of miles south has built up a gold-standard reputation: its nine rooms are comfortable and traditionally styled, a lovely back garden offers lakeside strolls, and the food – familiar English pub dishes – is reliably good (mains £12–18). However, at the time of writing the long-standing owners had put the place on the market: check the situation before you visit. **£125**

Chedworth Roman Villa

Yanworth • April–Oct daily 10am–5pm; Feb, March & Nov closes 4pm • £9 • NT ☎ 01242 890256, ⓦ nationaltrust.org.uk

From Fossebridge, roads west off the A429 show "Roman Villa" signs – a twisting and turning drive along hilly country lanes above the River Coln for three miles or more to reach **Chedworth Roman Villa**. In the fourth century AD, when this villa was built, it would have been one of the largest country houses in Britain – a giant mansion of fifty rooms or more, arrayed on three sides around a large courtyard, with its own spring, two bath-houses, heated living rooms, and more. Today, you pass first through an interpretation centre before exiting to the open site, which retains a sense of drama: it's not difficult to imagine the grandeur of the house, set in remote countryside. Mosaic floors survive, and the spring – probably holy, with a shrine or temple built around it – still flows, flanked by bath-houses. A Victorian shooting lodge, plonked beside the grassy courtyard, now houses a small museum of finds.

Note that the villa is misleadingly named: **CHEDWORTH** village lies a mile or more to the south, known for a rather fine church with a twelfth-century tower. To the chagrin of local residents, its last pub – the tumbledown *Seven Tuns* – recently closed.

ACCOMMODATION AND EATING CHEDWORTH

Chedworth Farm Shop Denfurlong Farm, Fields Rd ☎ 01285 720721, ⓦ chedworthfarmshop.co.uk. This family-run farm has a shop selling all kinds of local goodies, as well as a decent café serving up light lunches (£6–8), bottomless breakfasts (Sat & Sun 8.30–11.30am; £6) and

– above all – home-made ice cream, made on the farm: "from cow to cone in 12 hours," they say (ⓦ cotswold -icecream.co.uk). There's also simple camping. Mon–Wed 9am–5.30pm, Thurs & Fri 9am–9pm, Sat & Sun 8.30am–5.30pm. Pitches **£15**

Northleach

Secluded in a shallow depression ten miles northeast of Cirencester – and the same distance southwest of Stow – **NORTHLEACH** is one of the central Cotswolds' more appealing villages. Despite the fact that the A40 Oxford–Cheltenham road and the A429 Fosse Way cross at a large roundabout just north of the town, virtually no tourist traffic makes its way into the centre.

West End leads into the town, growing ever narrower as it curves into the centre. As you walk the last bit, as long as you were slightly short-sighted and had some luck with the sunshine, you could perhaps for a brief minute imagine yourself in a rather pleasant, self-possessed little town in Bordeaux or the Dordogne, characterized by silvery limestone facades and refreshingly free from signs of commerce.

The Old Prison

On the A429 • Daily 9.30am–4.30pm • Free • ☎ 01451 861563, ⊛ escapetothecotswolds.org.uk

First stop is the old Georgian **prison**, now the headquarters of the Cotswolds Conservation Board, just outside the town and less than a mile south of the A40/A429 roundabout. Enter through the café or directly into the prison, which has interesting displays in the old cells on the history of crime and punishment in Gloucestershire. This leads through to "**Escape to the Cotswolds**", an excellent modern visitor centre explaining the work of the conservation board in maintaining the Cotswolds Area of Outstanding Natural Beauty. Outside you can explore a "rural life" exhibition of old wagons and carts.

Church of St Peter and St Paul

Mill End • Daily 9am–5pm • Free • ☎ 01451 861432, ⊛ northleach.org

In the town centre, around the quiet, sloping **Market Place**, cluster rows of late-medieval buildings, with more framing the adjoining **Green**, some half-timbered. The outstanding feature is the handsome Perpendicular **church of St Peter and St Paul**, erected in the fifteenth century at the height of the wool boom. Its porch – suitably ostentatious – is overseen by a set of finely carved corbel heads, while wide clerestory windows light the beautifully proportioned nave. The floor is inlaid with an exceptional collection of **memorial brasses**, marking the tombs of the merchants whose endowments paid for the church. On several, you can make out the woolsacks laid out beneath the owner's feet – a symbol of wealth and power that survives today in the House of Lords in London, where a woolsack is placed on the Lord Chancellor's seat.

ARRIVAL AND INFORMATION   NORTHLEACH

By bus Buses drop off in the Market Place.
Destinations Bibury (Mon–Sat 5–6 daily; 20min); Bourton-on-the-Water (Mon–Sat every 1–2hr; 15–35min); Burford (Mon–Sat 2–4 daily, 1 on Sun; 15min); Cheltenham (Mon–Sat every 1–2hr, 1 on Sun; 30–35min); Cirencester (Mon–Sat 5–6 daily; 20–40min); Gloucester (Mon–Sat 2–4 daily, 1 on Sun; 1hr); Lower Slaughter (Mon–Sat every 2hr; 20min); Minster Lovell (Mon–Sat

2–4 daily, 1 on Sun; 20min); Moreton-in-Marsh (Mon–Sat every 2hr; 45min); Oxford (Mon–Sat 2–4 daily, 1 on Sun; 1hr); Stow-on-the-Wold (Mon–Sat every 2hr; 30min); Witney (Mon–Sat 2–4 daily, 1 on Sun; 30min).
Tourist office The "Escape to the Cotswolds" centre at the Old Prison (daily 9.30am–4.30pm) doubles as a mini tourist office, with volunteer staff occasionally on hand.

ACCOMMODATION AND EATING

Cotswold Lion Café Old Prison ☎01451 861563, ⊛escapetothecotswolds.org.uk. Friendly daytime café within the Old Prison on the edge of the town, serving up teas, coffees, cakes and light lunches (under £10).

Daily 9.30am–4.30pm.
Far Peak Camping 1 mile south of Northleach ☎01285 721090, ⊛farpeakcamping.co.uk. This countryside activity centre has an indoor climbing wall,

fitness training, a woodland rope course, nature trails, space for caravans and camping options – in one of three huts or on a grass pitch. Pitches £14, huts £40
Wheatsheaf West End ☎ 01451 860244, ⓦ cotswolds wheatsheaf.com. At this excellent former coaching inn in Northleach town centre, the old stone exterior has been left intact, but the public areas have been remodelled in a bright modern style softened by period furniture, book-cases and etchings of favourite livestock – this is very much a pub devoted to country pursuits, organizing regular riding, shooting and fishing parties (chiefly for weekending Londoners). Its restaurant is first-rate, presenting upscale Mediterranean-influenced cuisine – lamb shank with polenta, aubergine and apricot tagine and so forth. Mains £13–18. There are fourteen comfortable, en-suite guest rooms. Food served Mon–Sat noon–3pm & 6–9pm, Sun noon–3.30pm & 6–9pm. £140

Sherborne Estate and around

East of Northleach, the A40 powers towards Burford (see p.156), scooting past the National Trust-owned **Sherborne Estate** (dawn–dusk; free), a working estate crisscrossed with walking trails. The focus of attention is **Lodge Park** (March–Oct Fri–Sun 11am–4pm; £5.45; ☎ 01451 844130, ⓦ nationaltrust.org.uk), England's only surviving example of a seventeenth-century grandstand – it's a curious visit, imagining all the banqueting and gambling that went on here from the balcony and rooftop viewpoints. Download details of a Sherborne Family Fun Walk at ⓦ nationaltrust.org.uk.

The villages nearby hold a couple of culinary success stories: the Bensons fruit juices and "Chilly Billy" lollies you see sold at cafés and markets all over the Cotswolds (ⓦ bensonstotallyfruity.co.uk) are made on Sandy Hill Farm outside **Sherborne**, while at tiny **Windrush** Pinchpool Farm produces the top-rated Windrush goat's cheese, another market staple. From **Great Barrington**, the last village inside Gloucestershire, a pleasant **walk** (see p.159) leads from the popular *Fox Inn* (☎ 01451 844385, ⓦ foxinnbarrington.com) alongside the River Windrush into Burford.

Bourton-on-the-Water

BOURTON-ON-THE-WATER stands at the centre of Cotswold tourism. Set just east of the A429 Fosse Way, its old quarter straddles the tiny **River Windrush**. Beside the village green – flanked by photogenic Jacobean and Georgian facades in yellow Cotswold stone – five picturesque little **bridges** describe a series of arcs over the shallow water, dappled by shade from overhanging trees. Bourton looks lovely, but its proximity to main roads means that it's invariably packed: tourist coaches cram in all summer long and the village, inevitably, has changed to accommodate them.

High Street

The little **High Street**, alongside the green, now concentrates on souvenirs, banks and teashops, interspersed with purpose-designed tourist attractions: a Model Village here, a Dragonfly Maze there. You'll find a model railway exhibition, a motoring museum packed with vintage cars and period memorabilia, even a bird park by the river showing off flamingos and king penguins. Kids might enjoy it, but they might enjoy the Cotswold Farm Park (see p.98), ten minutes' drive away, more.

Cotswold Perfumery

Victoria St • Mon–Sat 9am–5pm, Sun 10am–5pm • Shop free; tour £5, booking essential; one-day course £195, including lunch & gifts •
☎ 01451 820698, ⓦ cotswold-perfumery.co.uk
Curiously, the Bourton attraction which, on the surface, appears the most contrived is perhaps the most genuinely interesting. The **Cotswold Perfumery** isn't just another

fancy souvenir shop, but one of Europe's very few manufacturers and retailers of perfume, offering informative **factory tours** of their modest little site, taking in the perfume garden, laboratory and compounding room. They also have one-day **perfumery courses**, covering how to create and blend a fragrance.

Cotswold Brewing Company

Stow Rd • Shop: Mon–Fri 9am–5pm • Tours daily 11am & 2pm, booking essential • £15 including gifts • ☎ 01451 824488, ⓦ cotswoldbrewing.com

Just outside Bourton on the main A429 is the home base of the **Cotswold Brewing Company**. Unlike most artisan brewers hereabouts they make only one ale, Cotswold Cask, but focus mainly on producing a range of European-style lagers, sold in pubs and restaurants around the area (and in London). They sell direct from their shop, and also offer **brewery tours**, looking at the site's history and brewing techniques, and including a guided tasting.

Greystones Farm Nature Reserve

Greystones Lane • Always open • Free • ☎ 01451 810853, ⓦ gloucestershirewildlifetrust.co.uk

A short walk east of Bourton, the barely-visited **Greystones Farm Nature Reserve** is a working organic livestock farm which includes Salmonsbury Meadows, a Site of Special Scientific Interest around the River Eye that forms a patchwork of ponds and islands sheltering water birds and wildflowers such as the rare marsh orchid. Footpaths lead to a Neolithic earthwork nearby, possibly an enclosed settlement above the wetlands.

Wyck Rissington

If you've come to Bourton seeking Cotswold tranquillity, make a beeline for **WYCK RISSINGTON**, a crowd-free village barely a mile to the northeast. The silent church, largely twelfth- and thirteenth-century – with a plaque on the organ noting that Gustav Holst was organist here in 1892 and 1893 – is entrancing, and the old bench in the churchyard outside has exactly what you're looking for.

WALKS AROUND BOURTON-ON-THE-WATER

THE RISSINGTON ROUND

Download details of the easy "Rissington Round" walk (3.5 miles; 2hr) at ⓦ escapetothe cotswolds.org.uk. The walk starts in **GREAT RISSINGTON** at the pleasant *Lamb Inn* (☎ 01451 820388, ⓦ thelambinn.com), reachable from Bourton on bus #802 (Mon–Sat every 2hr; 6min), and leads across the fields to **Little Rissington** before descending to skirt a fishing lake on the return to Bourton.

THE WARDEN'S WAY AND WINDRUSH WAY

Two paths cross the high wolds west of Stow, both linking Bourton-on-the-Water with Winchcombe (see p.127) – a distance of fourteen miles – and both graded as easy. The **Warden's Way** winds through the villages of Lower and Upper Slaughter, Naunton and Guiting Power before passing through woodland and skirting Sudeley Castle to enter Winchcombe. Its neighbour, the **Windrush Way**, is a lonelier affair, following the river out of Bourton to Harford Farm, then branching west to take a hilltop route to Winchcombe via Hawling and Spoonley Wood. Both can be tackled in either direction: many people choose to combine the two in a circular route, either to/from Bourton or to/from Winchcombe. Pick up information and maps at local tourist offices.

2

2

ARRIVAL AND GETTING AROUND

By bus Buses stop on the High St. The Witney Shuttle minibus (☎0800 043 4633, ⓦwitneyshuttle.com) runs several times a day between Heathrow Airport and Bourton-on-the-Water; advance booking essential.
Destinations Barnsley (Mon–Fri 2 daily, once on Sat; 35min); Bibury (Mon–Fri 2 daily, once on Sat; 30min); Burford (1 on Wed & Fri; 25–35min); Cheltenham (Mon–Sat every 1–2hr; May–Sept also 2 on Sun; 30–45min); Chipping Norton (1 on Thurs, Fri & Sat; 45min–1hr 5min); Cirencester (Mon–Fri 2 daily, 1 on Sat; 45min); Lower

BOURTON-ON-THE-WATER

Slaughter (Mon–Sat every 1–2hr; May–Sept also 2 on Sun; 5–10min); Moreton-in-Marsh (Mon–Sat every 1–2hr; May–Sept also 2 on Sun; 25min); Northleach (Mon–Sat every 1–2hr; May–Sept also 2 on Sun; 15min); Stow-on-the-Wold (Mon–Sat every 1–2hr; May–Sept also 2 on Sun; 10min).
By bike Hartwells on the High St rents bikes from £14/day, with tandems, tag-along bikes and trailers also available (Mon–Sat 9am–6pm, Sun 10am–5.30pm; ☎01451 820405, ⓦhartwells.supanet.com).

INFORMATION AND TOURS

Tourist office Beside the perfumery on Victoria St (Mon–Fri 9.30am–5pm, Sat 9.30am–5.30pm; Oct–March closes 1hr earlier; ☎01451 820211, ⓦbourtoninfo.com).

Walking tours The "Bloody Bourton" walking tour starts from the war memorial (Fri & Sat 7pm; £6) – book at the tourist office or by phone (☎07954 182016).

ACCOMMODATION

Broadlands Clapton Row ☎01451 822002, ⓦbroadlandsguesthouse.com. High-quality B&B in a houseproud little nook a short stroll away from the village centre, with a range of double, king-size and family rooms, spotlessly clean and with a warm welcome. Breakfast is served in a Victorian conservatory. **£70**
Chester House Victoria St ☎01451 820286, ⓦchesterhousehotel.com. Busy independent hotel in the village centre, with smoothly updated contemporary country-style interiors and something of a quirky spirit of fun in both service and design. **£95**
Clapton Manor Clapton-on-the-Hill ☎01451 810202, ⓦclaptonmanor.co.uk. Head up the slopes south of Bourton to titchy Clapton-on-the-Hill for the gorgeous views and this picture-perfect Tudor-Jacobean mansion – still a family home – offering two rooms for B&B, grand breakfasts and a wealth of local knowledge. **£110**

Dial House High St ☎01451 822244, ⓦdialhousehotel.com. Family-run hotel occupying a seventeenth-century building in the village centre, with bags of atmosphere, pleasant gardens and a decent restaurant. All rooms are individually decorated in contemporary style – rich fabrics, sleek bathrooms and careful detailing – but the location commands a premium. **£159**

CAMPING

Field Barn Park ☎01451 820434, ⓦfieldbarnpark.com. A mile or so south of Bourton on the road towards Clapton Hill is this quiet campsite, reserved exclusively for the over-30s. Closed Oct–March. Pitches **£20**
Folly Farm ☎01451 820285, ⓦcotswoldcamping.net. This small, basic farm campsite lies two and a half miles west of Bourton off the A436, an easy stroll to the pub in Cold Aston village – this and other local walks and cycle rides are detailed on its website. Pitches **£16**

EATING AND DRINKING

It feels like almost every other business in Bourton is offering some form of snack fodder – though for decent dining there's more choice up the road in Lower Slaughter (see p.97). Bourton's farmers' market (see p.81) is held on the fourth Sunday of every month at Countrywide Stores on Station Rd.

Croft Victoria St ☎01451 820286, ⓦchesterhousehotel.com. Reliable, informal restaurant within a popular hotel beside the river, with breakfasts, soup and salad, and staple mains of burgers, bangers and mash, and traditional puddings. Mains £9–11. Daily 9am–9pm.
Dial House High St ☎01451 822244, ⓦdialhousehotel.com. Bourton's poshest restaurant, offering an appealing range of light bites at lunchtime – including tasting platters mixing samples of fish, meat or veg for sharing (£13) – as well as posh afternoon tea with Champagne (£21) and a fine-dining menu in the evenings that raises the ante, with artfully presented French-influenced cuisine (two courses £35). Mon &

Tues noon–2.30pm, Wed–Sun noon–2.30pm & 6.30–9pm.
★Toast the Cotswolds Moore Rd ☎01451 821306, ⓦtoastthecotswolds.com. Just back from the High St, this cheery, family-run farm shop is closely linked with local food producers. The owners – who themselves produce "Love My Cow" beef in Bourton, and who also set up Bourton's Cotswold Food and Farming Festival, a one-day event in late August – stock all sorts of yummy treats from around the region. This is one of the few outlets for *mhencha*, a deliciously fragrant Moroccan sweet pastry made by Bourton's own one-woman Mhencha Company: sample it at the in-store coffee bar. Mon–Sat 8.30am–5.30pm, Sun 10am–4pm.

The Slaughters

A hop and a step outside Bourton-on-the-Water, the **Slaughters** (as in *slohtre*, Old English for a marshy place, cognate with "slough") are much more enticing than their neighbour, though still on the day-trippers' circuit. Pop by to take in some of the most celebrated village scenery in the Cotswolds.

Lower Slaughter

First comes **LOWER SLAUGHTER**, a mile or so northwest of Bourton. Here, the River Eye snakes its way shallowly through the village, overlooked by a string of immaculate honeystone Cotswold cottages. The village church of **St Mary** blends in well, but in fact it's largely Victorian. There is a small **museum** (and souvenir shop) signposted in a former mill, but the main attraction of the five-minute stroll through the village is to stop in for a little something at one of the several rather grand hotels occupying gated mansions on both sides of the village.

Upper Slaughter

From Lower Slaughter it's an easy hour's walk up the river valley to **UPPER SLAUGHTER**, another pretty village tucked into a wooded dell. Its church of **St Peter**, a Saxon foundation rather mucked about with in the 1870s, might entice you to dally – as might another, rather lovely country hotel.

ARRIVAL AND DEPARTURE   THE SLAUGHTERS

By bus Buses serve only Lower Slaughter.
Destinations Bourton-on-the-Water (Mon–Sat every 1–2hr; May–Sept also 2 on Sun; 5–10min); Burford (1 on Wed & Fri; 30–40min); Cheltenham (Mon–Sat every 1–2hr; May–Sept also 2 on Sun; 55min); Moreton-in-Marsh (2 on Tues & 1 on Fri; 20–45min); Northleach (Mon–Sat every 1–2hr; May–Sept also 2 on Sun; 25–40min); Stow-on-the-Wold (Mon–Sat every 1–2hr; May–Sept also 2 on Sun; 5–10min).

ACCOMMODATION AND EATING

★**Lords of the Manor** Upper Slaughter ☎01451 820243, ⓦlordsofthemanor.com. This luxurious hotel occupies the old rectory beside the church in Upper Slaughter. The building dates from 1649, added to in the nineteenth century. Set grandly in its own park, it screams "traditional country house hotel", but is actually presented extremely tastefully – modern, but not overpoweringly contemporary. The 26 rooms are in a similar vein: sumptuous without being brash. Clocks tick, the parquet creaks; it's all rather restful. The restaurant is one of the best in the area, awarded a Michelin star for its innovative French-influenced fine dining (three courses £69) – it operates every evening and for Sunday lunch; at other times, there's only a lighter bar menu. Food served Mon–Sat noon–2.30pm & 6.45–8.45pm, Sun 12.30–1.30pm & 6.45–8.45pm. **£200**

Lower Slaughter Manor Lower Slaughter ☎01451 820456, ⓦlowerslaughter.co.uk. This glorious old manor house plays its (visual) part perfectly, drawing on a thousand years of history to wow the many deep-pocketed visitors the Cotswolds attracts. There's a hint of style over substance here – the rooms are spacious and elegant, with a fresh ambience and pleasing contemporary style – but prices are uncompromisingly high. The restaurant works better, with accomplished fine dining that is starting to pick up awards; aim for the "farm to fork" lunch menu (two courses £21–26) as the most accessible entry-level option. Food served Mon–Thurs 12.30–2pm & 7–9pm, Fri &

CHEESE FROM THE DAIRY

From the church in Lower Slaughter, the country lane Copsehill Road drifts gently northeast towards the village of Lower Swell. Before you get there, a turnoff leads to Kirkham Farm, where Simon Weaver and his team produce the famous organic **Cotswold Brie**. They make the cheeses fresh just about every day, and you can turn up and buy direct from the creamery door (Mon–Fri 9am–5pm; ☎01451 870852, ⓦsimonweaver.net).

Sat 12.30–2pm & 7–9.30pm, Sun 12.30–3pm & 7–9pm. **£450**
The Slaughters Country Inn Lower Slaughter ☎ 01451 822143, ⓦ theslaughtersinn.co.uk. An altogether lighter prospect than its neighbours, though owned by the same team as *Lower Slaughter Manor* across the road. Still a seventeenth-century building, still in honeyed limestone, it has nonetheless been transformed inside, with gently contemporary decor and a breezy, interested service ethic. Notably family friendly, the hotel has little time for Cotswold stuffiness, offering thirty bedrooms featuring bold modern fabrics and design touches, alongside an informal restaurant (mains £13–20). Daily noon–9pm. **£85**

2

Cotswold Farm Park

Near Guiting Power • Daily 10.30am–5pm; Feb–March & Nov–Dec closes 4pm • £8.95 • ☎ 01451 850307, ⓦ cotswoldfarmpark.co.uk • No public transport; see website for detailed driving directions

In a region bedevilled by "visitor attractions", the **Cotswold Farm Park** stands out. Although aimed squarely at families looking for a fun day out, the park – with its adventure playground, kiddie tractor-driving and maze quest – remains part of a working farm, displaying an authentic, educational atmosphere. It was established in 1971 by farmer Joe Henson to showcase his collection of rare traditional breeds of sheep, pigs, cattle and horses, and is now owned and run by his TV presenter son, Adam. The park occupies a large area, with plenty to see on a wander around (or let the Farm Safari tractor take the strain), including information about the different breeds of farm animals on view, from rare Gloucester cattle and Bagot goats to the ancient Soay breed of sheep, brought here from a Scottish island in the 1960s. Demonstrations take place throughout the season of **lambing** (Feb–April), **milking** (May–Oct) and **shearing** (May & June). You could also tackle the easy two-mile **wildlife walk** signposted through the adjacent Barton Bushes. There are full restaurant and picnic facilities onsite. It's a brilliant day out.

The Guitings and around

Just west of the Cotswold Farm Park, back roads will take you to the **Guitings** (rhymes with "sightings"). To the north, almost lost in the woods on the banks of the titchy River Windrush, is quiet **TEMPLE GUITING**, named for having been granted in 1120 to the Knights Templar, a group of French Crusaders headquartered at the site of Solomon's temple in Jerusalem. A couple of miles south is its slightly larger twin, **GUITING POWER**, on the slopes above the river. Guiting Power's originally Norman church of **St Michael**, isolated in fields on the southern edge of the village, stands beside the route of the **Warden's Way** path (see p.95). Come in late July and you'll find the **Guiting Festival** (ⓦ guitingfestival.org) in full swing, Guiting Power's village hall managing, somehow, to pull in jazz and classical music performers of world renown.

ARRIVAL AND DEPARTURE   THE GUITINGS

By bus Bus #819 (1 on Fri) to/from Bourton-on-the-Water (20min) to Guiting Power and Temple Guiting.

ACCOMMODATION AND EATING

Guiting Guest House Guiting Power ☎ 01451 850470, ⓦ guitingguesthouse.com. Lovely, personally-run B&B in an old stone farmhouse, with a mix of en-suite rooms – twin, queen, king and four-poster – and a wealth of local knowledge about walks in the breezy countryside around. **£80**
Hollow Bottom Guiting Power ☎ 01451 850392, ⓦ hollowbottom.com. The better of Guiting Power's two pubs, this friendly inn, much-loved by racing devotees and workers from the stables hereabouts, has decent beer, good food (mains £10–15) and four fresh, immaculately presented rooms for B&B (with two more due to be completed by the time you read this). Food served Mon–Fri 10am–2pm & 6–10pm, Sat & Sun 10am–4pm & 6–10pm. **£80**

Ford

The high wolds west of Stow are horse country: this close to Cheltenham, the villages and countryside host lots of stables and many of the pubs are full of jockeys and stable-hands getting the dust out of their throats. The best-known – and, many say, the best – is the *Plough Inn* at **FORD**, on the B4077 less than a mile from Temple Guiting. Located directly beside Jackdaw's Castle, ex-jockey Jonjo O'Neill's training yard, this atmospheric old inn, once voted "Racing Pub of the Year", is bedecked in equestrian memorabilia, saddles and brasses. A pleasant **circular walk** (6 miles; 3hr) starts at the pub, heads to **CUTSDEAN** village nearby and follows a back lane to skirt Jackdaw's Castle, picking up the Gloucestershire Way to return to Ford alongside the "gallops".

A couple or so miles west of Ford, the B4077 drops down scenically off the Cotswold Edge, passing near Stanway House (see p.126).

2

ACCOMMODATION AND EATING   **FORD**

Plough Inn Ford ☎01386 584215, ⊛theplough innford.co.uk. This famous old racing pub is perfect for a pint, or a traditional meal in its Georgian-style restaurant extension (mains £10–16). It also has three decent en-suite rooms – though bear in mind they will be booked during the Cheltenham races. Food served Mon–Thurs 12.15–2.15pm & 6–9.15pm, Fri–Sun noon–9.15pm. **£80**

Stow-on-the-Wold

When outsiders want to poke fun at the Cotswolds, they invariably aim first at **STOW-ON-THE-WOLD**. Over the last ten or fifteen years, a succession of metropolitan journalists from the London papers – visiting chiefly to review one or other of the restaurants – have taken delight in tearing strips off Stow for its supposed docility and predictability. *Sunday Times* critic A.A. Gill was apoplectic, dubbing Stow "the worst place in the world" (before going on to declare, apparently seriously, "In Britain all the

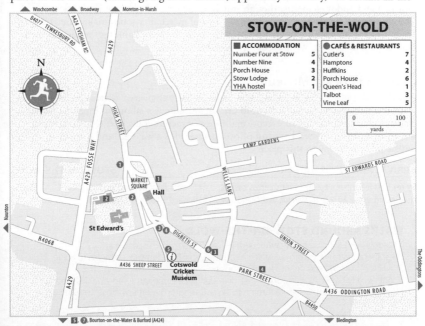

really innovative food is made in cities. Well, one city. London."). Stow is a symptom of a terrible malaise, comes the bleat. It's ruining the Cotswolds.

The answer, of course, is that not everybody likes urban culture, and not everybody wants boutique hotels and gastropubs. People don't come to Stow to be thrilled, challenged or intrigued. It's a historic Cotswold market town, gentrified but largely unprettified: people come to have a stroll around the old square, a browse in the shops and a nice meal. The town delivers on all fronts. To some, that makes the place infuriating, a parody of itself. But frankly, Stow doesn't give a damn.

The market square

Perched at 700ft above sea level, Stow is the highest town in the Cotswolds. It sucks in a disproportionate number of visitors for its size and attractions, which essentially comprise an old **market square** surrounded by seventeenth- and eighteenth-century coaching inns, cafés and antique shops. The square was the scene, on March 21, 1646, of the last battle of the English Civil War, when Royalist armies, routed on a nearby battlefield, were pushed back into the town by victorious Roundheads. The slaughter was such that, legend has it, ducks were seen swimming in the blood: some claim that the lane leading east out of the square, Digbeth Street, is named for "Duck Bath". In quieter times, the narrow walled alleyways, or "tchures", running into the square would have funnelled sheep into the market, which is now dominated by an imposing Victorian **hall**, flanked on one side by a medieval **cross** (though the headstone is a modern replacement) and on the other by a set of stocks (also modern) adorning a small, triangular green.

St Edward's Church

Behind the square • ⓦ scats.org.uk

Behind the square, the church of **St Edward**, with its 88-ft Perpendicular tower, has Norman and Tudor elements, though much in the broad, light interior is Victorian. The churchyard hosts three "bale tombs" of wool merchants – and make sure you stroll around to the photogenic **north porch**, where two yew trees flanking the old wooden door appear to have grown into the stonework.

Cotswold Cricket Museum

Brewery Yard • Tues–Sat 9.30am–5pm, Sun 9.30am–3.30pm • £3.50 • ☎ 01451 870083, ⓦ cotswoldcricketmuseum.co.uk

Just off the square, the small **Cotswold Cricket Museum** is a labour of love: the owner Andy Collier has built up an exceptional range of memorabilia over 25 years, from blazers and balls to signed bats and photos galore. He's always around for a chat: cricket buffs could lose a day to this place.

ARRIVAL AND INFORMATION   STOW-ON-THE-WOLD

By car Eight roads from all points of the compass meet at Stow, including the A429 from Moreton and Cirencester, A424 from Broadway and Burford, A436 from Chipping Norton and B4068 from Cheltenham.

WALKS AROUND STOW-ON-THE-WOLD

"Meadows and Mills" is an easy **walk** (4 miles; 2hr 30min) downloadable at ⓦ escapetothecotswolds.org.uk, which heads downhill from Stow across fields to Lower Slaughter (see p.97) and on into Bourton-on-the-Water (see p.94). An alternative route, dubbed "From Wold to Water" (6 miles; 3hr) – also downloadable at the same site – passes through Maugersbury and Icomb before turning to Wyck Rissington and then across water meadows into Bourton.

By train A taxi from Moreton railway station (see p.103), five miles north, costs around £12.

By bus Buses stop on or near the market square. The Witney Shuttle minibus (☎0800 043 4633, ⓦwitney shuttle.com) runs several times a day between Heathrow Airport and Stow; advance booking essential.

Destinations Bourton-on-the-Water (Mon–Sat every 1–2hr, May–Sept also twice on Sun; 10–20min); Burford (1 on Wed & Fri; 35–45min); Cheltenham (Mon–Sat every 1–2hr, May–Sept also twice on Sun; 1hr); Chipping Norton (1 on Tues, 2 on Wed, 1 on Thurs, 1 on Fri; 25min–1hr 15min); Lower Slaughter (Mon–Sat every 1–2hr, May–Sept also twice on Sun; 5min); Moreton-in-Marsh (Mon–Sat every 1–2hr, May–Sept also twice on Sun; 10min); Northleach (Mon–Sat every 1–2hr, May–Sept also twice on Sun; 20–30min).

Tourist office In the Cricket Museum, Brewery Yard (Tues–Sat 9.30am–5pm, Sun 9.30am–3.30pm; ☎01451 830341, ⓦstowinfo.co.uk).

ACCOMMODATION

IN TOWN

Number Nine 9 Park St ☎01451 870333, ⓦnumber -nine.info. Pleasant old house offering quality B&B just down from the town square. The three bedrooms feature low beams but contemporary styling – and the rates are a bargain. **£65**

Porch House Digbeth St ☎01451 870048, ⓦporch -house.co.uk. Purportedly the oldest inn in Britain, with parts of the building dated at 947 AD (though the interiors have been freshly modernized). The thirteen traditionally styled, hessian-floored rooms look good, with some retro design touches, but the standard doubles are rather poky: superior and feature rooms let you breathe a bit. **£100**

Stow Lodge The Square ☎01451 830485, ⓦstow lodge.co.uk. An eighteenth-century rectory set in its own grounds off the main square, this is a Cotswolds hotel from the old school – antique prints, old bookcases, saggy sofas and all. Run by the same family for over fifty years, it feels it – rooms, service and clientele are very traditional – but there's an idiosyncratic charm to the place nonetheless. **£135**

YHA hostel The Square ☎0845 371 9540, ⓦyha.org .uk. This good-looking Georgian townhouse on the main square is the Cotswolds' only youth hostel – an excellent choice for a budget stay, with small dorms and a choice of family rooms (4–6 beds) as well as kitchen facilities, a garden and a little café. Reception closed 10am–5pm. Dorms **£19**, doubles **£50**

OUT OF TOWN

Number Four at Stow Fosse Way ☎01451 830297, ⓦhotelnumberfour.co.uk. A real find in a difficult location, about a mile south of Stow (and down a steep hill), jammed into the V of the junction between the busy A424 and busier A429. Despite the unromantic setting, this is a very pleasant little country hotel, family owned and run by two sisters; it's their fourth such venture, hence the name. Inside, road noise is barely detectable. Interiors are all very tastefully modern – fabrics and colours work together, and the eighteen bedrooms are simply but stylishly furnished. It's elegant, but not overpowering, and the warm welcome is a breath of fresh air. **£160**

EATING AND DRINKING

Stow hosts a clutch of noteworthy restaurants, but you could also venture slightly further afield to try outstanding places in nearby villages: Bourton-on-the-Hill (see p.106), the Oddingtons (see p.102), the Slaughters (see p.97) or Kingham (see p.169), to name a few. In among its antique shops, butchers and ironmongers, Stow has some fine, upmarket delis stocking local produce – and the market square hosts a monthly farmers' market (see p.81).

IN TOWN

Hamptons 1 Digbeth St ☎01451 831733, ⓦhamptons finefoods.co.uk. One of the best of Stow's delis, groaning with local produce: people come from miles around for the cheeses in particular. Just down the road is a specialist in wine and olives, and there are others, too. Mon–Sat 9am–5pm, Sun 11am–4.30pm.

★**Huffkins** The Square ☎01451 832870, ⓦhuffkins .com. Legendary Cotswold tearoom – top spot in town for afternoon tea, but also good for snacks and light meals (around £10). Mon–Fri 9am–5pm, Sat 9am–5.30pm, Sun 10am–5pm.

Porch House Digbeth St ☎01451 870048, ⓦporch -house.co.uk. Purportedly the oldest inn in Britain, with parts of the building dated at 947 AD (though the interiors have been freshly modernized). The restaurant is a comfortably posh affair, with fish pie or roast lamb mains (£12–17) served in a cosily renovated dining area, while the pub – complete with wonky beams – has a cheaper, simpler bar menu. Food served in the pub: Mon–Sat noon–9.30pm, Sun noon–8.30pm; restaurant Mon–Sat 6.30–9.30pm.

Queen's Head The Square ☎01451 830563, ⓦdonnington-brewery.com. Traditional old Donnington pub that provides good beer, good service and a pleasant, chatty atmosphere. Food is a level above standard pub grub (mains roughly £9–11). Mon–Sat 11am–11pm, Sun noon–10.30pm.

2

★**Talbot** The Square ☎ 01451 870934, ⓦ thetalbot.net. Ex-coaching inn on the main square, now a genial middle-of-the-road pub – great for a sociable drink or an uncomplicated meal, with options enhanced unusually by Mediterranean dishes such as grilled halloumi or shell-on prawns from a long menu of tapas. Mains £10–15; tapas £3–5. Mon–Sat noon–2.30pm & 6.30–9.30pm, Sun 12.30–4pm.

Vine Leaf 10 Talbot Court ☎ 01451 832010, ⓦ thevine leaf.co.uk. Cheery little daytime café-cum-restaurant off the square which does light lunches – salads, risotto, mezze platters – as well as steaks, belly of pork and devilled kidneys. Mains £10–17. Tues–Sat 11.30am–9pm.

OUT OF TOWN

Cutler's At Number Four hotel, Fosse Way ☎ 01451 830297, ⓦ hotelnumberfour.co.uk. A great choice just south of town – a formal, contemporary-styled restaurant serving excellent, upmarket seasonal cuisine: you might find saddle of lamb or sirloin steak on the menu alongside partridge, lobster or an innovative veg option. Mains £16–22; two-course lunch £17. Mon–Sat noon–2pm & 7–9pm, Sun noon–2.30pm.

The Oddingtons

A mile or so east of Stow, signs off the A436 point you to **UPPER ODDINGTON** – one half of a village which is split not just in name. This is the more down-to-earth bit, still with a strong local community. Down the way, **LOWER ODDINGTON** – just that tiny bit closer to swanky Daylesford and Kingham (see p.169) – is tangibly posher, with a greater proportion of holiday cottages and second homes. The contrast is intriguing.

EATING AND DRINKING   THE ODDINGTONS

Fox Lower Oddington ☎ 01451 870555, ⓦ foxinn.net. Now under the husband-and-wife team who formerly ran the celebrated *Old Butchers* restaurant in Stow, this rather studied take on the traditional country pub has gained a new lease of life for its food – bold, confident cooking that blends British classics with European styles and flavours: Cornish seabass jostles with French snails, pumpkin risotto with liver and onions. Mains £14–22. Mon–Sat noon–2pm & 6.30–9.30pm, Sun noon–3pm & 7–9pm.

Horse and Groom Upper Oddington ☎ 01451 830584, ⓦ horseandgroom.uk.com. This bright, hearty locals' pub has been updated to include a straightforwardly good restaurant, showcasing an accomplished, innovative approach to old favourites, from salmon poached in white wine to Old Spot pork braised in cider. Mains £14–17 – and don't miss the home-made desserts. Mon–Sat noon–2pm & 6.30–9pm, Sun noon–2.30pm & 7–9pm.

Longborough

ⓦ longborough.net

North of Stow and south of Moreton, between the fork of the A424 and A429, **LONGBOROUGH** is perhaps best known hereabouts for having, remarkably, its own opera house, the venue every summer for the prestigious **Longborough Festival Opera** (ⓦ lfo.org.uk). A finstroke away is the **Donnington Trout Farm** (ⓦ donningtontrout. co.uk), supplying fresh and smoked trout to farmers' markets across the region, as well as the nineteenth-century **Donnington Brewery** (ⓦ donnington-brewery.com), still a family-run concern, with seventeen pubs across the local area.

EATING AND DRINKING   LONGBOROUGH

Cotswold Food Store Longborough ☎ 01451 830469, ⓦ cotswoldfoodstore.co.uk. This is effectively a rather upmarket farm shop on the A424 outside Longborough village, with a wide range of local and organic food – including a great deli counter – and a terrace café alongside for coffees and light lunches. Mon–Sat 9am–5.30pm, Sun 10am–4.30pm; café closes 30min earlier.

Moreton-in-Marsh

A key transport hub and one of the Cotswolds' more sensible towns, **MORETON-IN-MARSH**, though relatively low-lying – hills rise to east, west and south – isn't in a marsh at all. A now-vanished wetland nearby – a popular spot for local waterfowl – became known as the hen-marsh: it didn't take long for "Moreton Henmarsh" to be mangled into the current formulation. The A429 Fosse Way runs north–south through the town as the High Street, meeting the east–west A44 in the town centre at a dog-leg of mini-roundabouts. Despite a lack of attractions within the town, Moreton has always been an important access point for the countryside and remains so with its **railway station**, served by regular trains on the Cotswold Line direct link between London, Oxford and Worcester (see p.23).

If you're around in early September, don't miss the huge **Moreton Show** (ⓦmoretonshow.co.uk), a traditional celebration of local agriculture, also with showjumping, falconry, motocross and go-karting.

High Street

Moreton's **High Street** is a broad, handsome affair, dating from its origins in the thirteenth century as a market town and enhanced with many Jacobean and Georgian facades from its heyday as a stop for London–Worcester coaches. Plumb in the centre, the **Redesdale Hall** – dating from 1887, though built in a medieval style – is named for Lord Redesdale, father of the infamous Mitford sisters (among them Nancy, a writer; Diana, wife of British wartime fascist leader Oswald Mosley; and Unity, a close companion of Adolf Hitler), who spent part of their childhood years at Batsford House, just west of Moreton. Nearby, on the corner of Oxford Street, the **Curfew Tower** is Moreton's oldest building, dating from the sixteenth century and once used as the town jail, while opposite, a short stroll west along the Bourton Road brings you to the **Wellington Aviation Museum** (Sun 10am–noon & 2–4pm; £2.50; ⓦwellingtonaviation.org), displaying memorabilia from the wartime RAF base located beside Moreton.

MORETON-IN-MARSH

Dorn & Shipston ▲

ACCOMMODATION

Acacia Guest House	1
Fosseway Farm	5
Manor House	4
Old School	2
Redesdale Arms	3

Warner's Budgens

Railway Station

Redesdale Hall

Curfew Tower

Wellington Aviation Museum

CAFÉS & RESTAURANTS

Cotswold Cheese Co.	2
Marshmallow	1
Mulberry	3

Stow-on-the-Wold ▼

ARRIVAL AND DEPARTURE

MORETON-IN-MARSH

By train Moreton is served by trains on the London–Oxford–Worcester line. The station is a two-minute walk from the High St. Local taxi firms include Cotswold Taxis (ⓣ07710 117471, ⓦcotswoldtaxis.com) and Moreton Taxis (ⓣ07800 957646, ⓦmoretontaxis.co.uk).
Destinations Charlbury (hourly; 20min); Kingham (hourly; 20min); London Paddington (hourly; 1hr 35min); Oxford (hourly; 25min); Worcester (hourly; 35min).
By bus Buses stop on the High St. Irregular routes

include many Tuesday buses, serving Moreton's weekly market.
Destinations Blockley (Mon–Sat 8 daily; 10min); Bourton-on-the-Hill (Mon–Sat 8 daily; 5min); Bourton-on-the-Water (Mon–Sat hourly; June–Sept also 2 on Sun; 25–30min); Broadway (Mon–Sat 3 daily; 25min); Cheltenham (Mon–Sat hourly; June–Sept also 2 on Sun; 1hr 15min;); Chipping Campden (Mon–Sat 8 daily; 30min); Lower Slaughter (Mon–Sat hourly; June–Sept also 2 on

2

THE FOUR SHIRE STONE

East of Moreton, the A44 soon crosses into Oxfordshire for the brief run towards wonderful Chastleton House (see p.172), the Rollright Stones (see p.173) and Chipping Norton (see p.170). As it does so, it passes the tall, eighteenth-century **Four Shire Stone**, which once marked the point where Gloucestershire, Oxfordshire, Warwickshire and Worcestershire touched noses. Today, only the first three still meet here; boundary changes in 1931 transferred Blockley parish, whose ragged borders extended to this point, from Worcestershire to Gloucestershire.

Sun; 20min); Northleach (Mon–Sat hourly; June–Sept also 2 on Sun; 40min); Shipston-on-Stour (Mon–Sat 2 daily; 10min); Stow-on-the-Wold (Mon–Sat hourly; June–Sept also 2 on Sun; 10min); Stratford-upon-Avon (Mon–Sat 10 daily; 1hr–1hr 15min).

INFORMATION AND ACTIVITIES

Tourist office High St (Mon 8.45am–4pm, Tues–Thurs 8.45am–5.15pm, Fri 8.45am–4.45pm, Sat 10am–1pm; Nov–March Sat closes 12.30pm; ☎01608 650881, ⓦcotswold.gov.uk & ⓦcotswolds.com).

Outdoor activities Rob Ireland Activity Days (☎01386 701683, ⓦrobireland.co.uk) runs archery, clay-pigeon shooting and quad-biking at a rural site just north of Moreton. There's also Cotswold Paintballing (☎07836 657397, ⓦcotswoldpaintballing.com). Book ahead for either. Contact the Old Farm at Dorn, a mile north of Moreton (☎01608 650394, ⓦoldfarmdorn.co.uk), for details of farm visits for groups and a range of courses, from sausage-making and bacon-curing to sheep-shearing and butchery.

ACCOMMODATION

IN TOWN

Acacia Guest House 2 New Rd ☎01608 650130, ⓦacaciainthecotswolds.co.uk. Simple, decent little B&B on the short street connecting the station to the High St – very handy for arrivals and departures by train or bus. **£60**

Manor House High St ☎01608 650501, ⓦcotswold -inns-hotels.co.uk. Pleasant four-star hotel occupying a sixteenth-century former coaching inn in the centre, with a nice garden centred on an ancient mulberry tree and well-kept, stylish rooms. **£120**

Redesdale Arms High St ☎01608 650308, ⓦredesdalearms.com. Relaxed three-star hotel with notably good service and 34 rooms – traditionally styled ones in the main building and more contemporary ones in a newer annexe. **£120**

OUT OF TOWN

Fosseway Farm Stow Rd ☎01608 650503, ⓦfosseway farm.co.uk. Good-value, traditional farmhouse B&B set back from the A429 a few minutes' walk south of the town centre, also including a large caravan park and campsite. Pitches **£17**, doubles **£60**

Old School Little Compton ☎01608 674588, ⓦtheoldschoolbedandbreakfast.com. Award-winning, upscale little B&B in this village four miles east of Moreton, offering four en-suite rooms in a Victorian schoolhouse that includes beautiful church-style windows in the swanky guest lounge. Hosts are knowledgeable and forthcoming; bedrooms are spacious and thoughtfully kitted out. **£120**

EATING AND DRINKING

There's nothing wrong with Moreton's restaurants, but you could also venture slightly further afield to try outstanding places nearby: Bourton-on-the-Hill (see p.106), the Oddingtons (see p.102), the Slaughters (see p.97) or Kingham (see p.169), to name a few. The Old Farm at Dorn, a mile north of Moreton, has a good farm shop (Wed–Sat 9.30am–5pm; ☎01608 650394, ⓦoldfarmdorn.co.uk).

Cotswold Cheese Company 5 High St ☎01608 652862, ⓦcotswoldcheese.com. Splendidly aromatic deli and cheese emporium on the High St, selling fragrant goodies from all round the Cotswolds. Mon–Sat 9am–5pm, Sun 10am–4pm.

Marshmallow High St ☎01608 651536, ⓦmarshmallow-tea-restaurant.co.uk. This pleasant tearoom north along the High St has an outstanding choice of speciality teas, from Gunpowder to Nilgiri. High tea – scone, smoked salmon sandwiches and all – is £13, and the place doubles as a casual restaurant for light meals (mains £9–11). Mon 8.30am–6pm, Tues 10am–6pm, Wed & Thurs 8.30am–8pm, Fri & Sat 8.30am–8.30pm, Sun 10.30am–5pm.

Mulberry At Manor House Hotel, High St ☎01608 650501, ⓦcotswold-inns-hotels.co.uk. The top restaurant in town – a rather posh setting, with muted contemporary styling (and a smart casual dress code), serving highly acclaimed modern British cuisine prepared from Cotswold ingredients, such as wild rabbit terrine followed by tenderloin of local pork. Three courses are £39, with good vegetarian options available; there's also an eight-course tasting menu at £60. Daily noon–2.30pm & 7–9.30pm.

Batsford Arboretum

Batsford • Daily 10am–5pm • £7 • ☎ 01386 701441, ⓦ batsarb.co.uk

West of Moreton there's plenty of rural interest, as the hills of the Cotswolds Area of Outstanding Natural Beauty (ⓦescapetothecotswolds.org.uk) rise towards Chipping Campden and the Cotswolds scarp. Accessed directly from the A44 just over a mile west of Moreton – rather than from the quiet village of **BATSFORD** itself, which lies to the north – **Batsford Arboretum** sprawls delightfully across 56 acres of hilly, south-facing countryside. Designed at the end of the nineteenth century by Algernon Mitford, later the first Lord Redesdale, and greatly expanded in the 1950s, its oriental planting and design are enhanced by more than 1500 tree varieties. Batsford is particularly stunning in the autumn months. Aim first for the waterfall, but also take in the huge Cathedral Lime, a grove of redwoods, reputedly England's largest "handkerchief tree" (*Davidia involucrata*) and the beautiful Peaches Walk. A Japanese rest house offers peaceful views.

Cotswold Falconry Centre

Batsford Park • Flying displays daily 11.30am, 1.30pm & 3pm; April–Oct also 4.30pm • £10 • ☎ 01386 701043, ⓦ cotswold-falconry.co.uk

Immediately beside Batsford Arboretum, and reached via the same driveway off the A44, the **Cotswold Falconry Centre** is home to around a hundred birds of prey, from owls and vultures to hawks, kestrels, eagles and various species of falcon – saker, lanner, aplomado and peregrine. One-hour displays show off the birds' abilities, with plenty of educational info alongside the aerobatic thrills.

Sezincote House

Near Batsford • House and gardens: May–Sept Thurs & Fri 2.30–5.30pm • Gardens only: Jan–Nov Thurs & Fri 2–6pm • House & gardens £10, gardens only £5 • ☎ 01386 700444, ⓦ sezincote.co.uk

On the south side of the A44, directly opposite the Batsford Arboretum driveway, stands the gate of **Sezincote House**. Built in the few years after 1805, Sezincote – whose name derives from *Cheisnecote*, a blend of French and Old English meaning "home among the oaks" – is remarkable for its exterior, designed by architect Samuel Pepys Cockerell and artist Thomas Daniell in Indian Mogul style. The house sports scalloped peacock-tail arches above the windows, a large "iwan" arch above the main door, a glorious Orangery wing sweeping round to an ornate, pinnacled pavilion and – most prominently – an onion dome atop the main building. Its interiors, though, are less of a draw than the **gardens**, featuring an Indian bridge flanked by Brahmin bulls which preludes lavish planting in a Persian garden and extensive water gardens topped by a Hindu temple.

Bourton House Garden

Near Bourton-on-the-Hill • April–Oct Wed–Fri 10am–5pm • £6 • ☎ 01386 700754, ⓦ bourtonhouse.com

Alongside Sezincote House, a driveway off the A44 gives into the grounds of **Bourton House Garden**, generally less visited than neighbouring attractions. The house – a grand affair – is not open to the public. You approach through the sixteenth-century **tithe barn**, emerging into the flamboyant **garden**, particularly fine in late summer. Past the formal White Garden, an eighteenth-century raised path offers views over the hills, leading round to the Knot Garden, centred on a basket pond recovered from the 1851 Great Exhibition, and a parterre featuring fanciful topiary. Walks cross the seven-acre pasture opposite the garden, to take in the splendour of the trees.

2 Bourton-on-the-Hill

Spreading up the steep A44 west of Moreton-in-Marsh, the little village of **BOURTON-ON-THE-HILL** offers a picturesque cluster of cottages wrapped around the handsome church of **St Lawrence**, with wonderful views back over Moreton and the Evenlode valley below. Stop in for liquid or culinary refreshment at the village's outstanding *Horse and Groom* pub.

ARRIVAL AND DEPARTURE   BOURTON-ON-THE-HILL

By bus Buses serve Blockley (Mon–Sat 8 daily; 5min) and Moreton-in-Marsh (Mon–Sat 8 daily; 5min).

ACCOMMODATION AND EATING

★**Horse and Groom** Bourton-on-the-Hill ☎01386 700413, ⓦ horseandgroom.info. Occupying a Georgian building of Cotswold stone at the top of Bourton-on-the-Hill village, just before the turn to Blockley, this award-winning free house has a fine reputation locally for good beer, friendly service and – above all – excellent food. The menu changes frequently, taking in pork, lamb and beef sourced from local farmers, and seasonal veg, filled out with fresh fish and seafood, cooked with style but without pretension: this place impresses without even trying (mains £10–20). But it's popular: always book ahead. There are also five appealing rooms, some with views, one with French doors opening onto the garden. Mon–Fri 11am–2.30pm & 6–11pm, Sat 11am–3pm & 6–11pm, Sun noon–3.30pm. **£120**

Blockley

Gracing the hills between Moreton and Chipping Campden (see p.112), **BLOCKLEY** is one of the prettier villages hereabouts, fortunately with roads that are too narrow for tourist coaches to penetrate. A former centre for silk processing – in the late nineteenth century mills kept several hundred people in work here – it's still a prosperous little place, with one notable employer being Britain's biggest manufacturer of motorbike sidecars. Blockley's houses of Cotswold stone, tiered above a rushing brook, are set off by the particularly fine church of **St Peter and St Paul**, originally Norman, its nave lit by three large fifteenth-century windows and sporting a Jacobean pulpit, while one end of the village hosts the charming **Mill Dene Garden** (March–Oct Tues–Fri 10am–5pm, Sat 9am–2pm; £6; ⓦ milldenegarden.co.uk). As tempting a reason to visit, though, is Blockley's **shop** (Mon–Fri 8am–6pm, Sat 8.30am–6pm, Sun 8.30am–1pm; ⓦ blockleyshop.com), owned and run by villagers themselves. It's a cheery spot, and the hub of village life: have a chat with the locals, grab a newspaper and hole up at the café for coffee or a light lunch.

Several good **walks** include a circular route of just under five miles which skirts the fields to Batsford village before turning to follow a short stretch of the Monarch's Way – a long-distance path from Staffordshire to Devon – and Heart of England Way back into Blockley.

ARRIVAL AND DEPARTURE   BLOCKLEY

By bus Several buses stop in the village centre. **Destinations** Bourton-on-the-Hill (Mon–Sat 8 daily; 5min); Broadway (Mon–Sat 3 daily; 15min); Chipping Campden (Mon–Sat 8 daily; 20min); Moreton-in-Marsh (Mon–Sat 8 daily; 10min); Stratford-upon-Avon (Mon–Sat 8 daily; 50min–1hr 5min).

ACCOMMODATION AND EATING

Crown Blockley ☎01386 700245, ⓦcrownhotel blockley.co.uk. An old inn with great potential. There's nothing actually bad – the 24 rooms are comfortable enough (though the "budget" rooms are really too small), and the dinner (three courses £20) is fine – but you can't help feeling such a quiet, attractive village as Blockley deserves a bit better. £89

Great Western Arms Blockley ☎01386 700362, ⓦthegreatwesternarms.net. This friendly village local – a Hook Norton pub – has been recently refurbished. It's a decent place for an honest pint and simple pub food (£6–8). Mon 6–11pm, Tues–Fri noon–3pm & 6–11pm, Sat & Sun 11am–11pm.

Lower Brook House Blockley ☎01386 700286, ⓦlowerbrookhouse.com. A lovely B&B occupying a seventeenth-century stone house just below the village centre, with six fresh, individually styled bedrooms – super-quiet, super-comfortable. £110

2

The north Cotswolds

CHIPPING CAMPDEN

The north Cotswolds

Taking in the northernmost fringes of the Cotswolds Area of Outstanding Natural Beauty (ⓦescapetothecotswolds.org.uk), the terrain between Stratford-upon-Avon and Moreton-in-Marsh – what we've termed the north Cotswolds – covers a swathe of diverse terrain in the far northern reaches of Gloucestershire and the far southern extremities of Worcestershire, where both of them sidle up against the borders of Warwickshire and Oxfordshire. It holds some of the Cotswolds' best-loved attractions: green hills, ancient villages and magnificent gardens.

Many people, visitors and locals alike, say the Cotswolds' single most beautiful destination is **Chipping Campden**. This picture-perfect village of honeystone Jacobean gables set against forested hills manages single-handedly to tick every Cotswold box, while still retaining full command of poise and dignity. Minor villages nearby, notably **Stanton** and **Ebrington**, remain almost impossibly picturesque. Formal gardens at **Hidcote** and **Kiftsgate** add to the seduction, and some fine hill **walks** add memorable breadth to those on a long, slow journey of Cotswold discovery.

Campden's near-neighbour, **Broadway** feels somewhat over-celebrated by comparison – heart-warming, historically significant and undoubtedly beautiful, but unrelentingly given over to peak-season tourism. Just beyond, though tangential to the region, the low-lying **Vale of Evesham** offers undramatic diversion from Broadway's overplayed hand.

The high, open wolds west of Stow reach the Cotswold Edge at **Winchcombe**, a small town with a long history that is now a prime base for independent-minded types keen to explore the great outdoors. Winchcombe has become one of the Cotswolds' great walking centres, with footpaths to suit all tastes and abilities enveloping the town – not

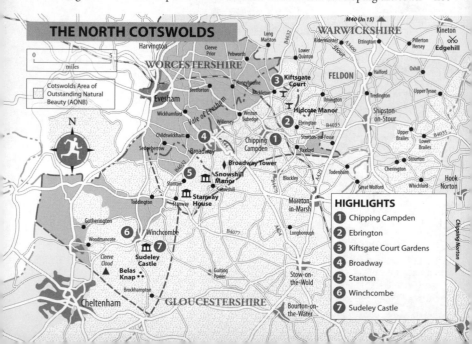

THE NORTH COTSWOLDS

WARWICKSHIRE

WORCESTERSHIRE

Cotswolds Area of Outstanding Natural Beauty (AONB)

Evesham

Vale of Evesham

Broadway

Chipping Campden

Broadway Tower

Snowshill Manor

Stanway House

Stanton

Winchcombe

Sudeley Castle

Cleeve Cloud

Belas Knap

Cheltenham

GLOUCESTERSHIRE

HIGHLIGHTS

1 Chipping Campden
2 Ebrington
3 Kiftsgate Court Gardens
4 Broadway
5 Stanton
6 Winchcombe
7 Sudeley Castle

SUDELEY CASTLE

Highlights

❶ Chipping Campden Simply one of the loveliest of all Cotswold towns. Unmissable for its architecture, its sense of history, its atmosphere and its hospitality. **See p.112**

❷ Ebrington Thatched cottages, peace and quiet and a great pub lift this charming backwater village out of the ordinary. **See p.118**

❸ Kiftsgate Court Gardens Bewitching displays of roses at this lesser-known hillside stately home, alongside the much more visited National Trust gardens at Hidcote. **See p.119**

❹ Broadway A leading light of Cotswold tourism – certainly a pretty village but also

perhaps a touch too busy. Now enhanced by two excellent museums. **See p.119**

❺ Stanton This quietly magnificent honeystone village is bypassed by most visitors: make time to walk its lanes and byways, if you can. **See p.126**

❻ Winchcombe A historic walkers' village that makes a great base for exploring the area, with memorably down-to-earth charm. **See p.127**

❼ Sudeley Castle A stunningly handsome medieval castle, which can boast impeccable royal heritage and evocative formal gardens. **See p.130**

HIGHLIGHTS ARE MARKED ON THE MAP ON P.110

least the **Cotswold Way**, which shadows the Edge from north to south. Within easy reach of Winchcombe are a magnificent castle at **Sudeley**, a ruined abbey at **Hailes** and the evocative prehistoric burial mound of **Belas Knap**, which squats atop **Cleeve Hill**, the Cotswolds' highest point, a stone's throw from Cheltenham.

3 Chipping Campden

CHIPPING CAMPDEN, twelve miles south of Stratford-upon-Avon, gives a better idea than anywhere else in the Cotswolds as to what a prosperous wool town might have looked like in the seventeenth century. The wonderfully elegant, almost perfectly preserved High Street is hemmed in by ancient houses, whose undulating, weather-beaten roofs jag against each other, above twisted beams and mullioned windows. Its name derives from the Saxon term *campadene*, meaning cultivated valley, and the Old English *ceapen*, or market.

More than being merely picturesque, though, Campden (the name is invariably shortened) has atmosphere. There are coach parties, of course, and urbanite weekenders, and muddy-booted hill-walkers – but there is also a thriving, rooted local community, some having been here all their lives, many having arrived to tap into a wellspring of creativity which has underpinned the town since the days of the nineteenth-century Arts and Crafts movement (see p.160). **Charles Ashbee**, an Arts and Crafts devotee, relocated the London-based Guild and School of Handicraft here in 1902 and though that venture failed, it bequeathed a legacy of independent artisans in art and design which continues to enrich Campden life. The "**Creative Campden**" website explains more (ⓦcreativecampden.co.uk).

Campden is perched atop the Cotswold scarp, and from **Dover's Hill**, just northwest of the town, views yawn out over a broad swathe of three counties. The town also marks the northern end-point of the **Cotswold Way** (see p.32), a long-distance path which hugs the high ground all the way to Bath, a hundred miles south.

Beautiful, inspiring, creative and with a strong sense of its own history, Campden could melt the hardest of hearts. Roam in the evening and early morning, when the streets are empty and the golden hues of the stone are at their richest.

High Street

Make time to stroll along Campden's **High Street**, past **Grevel House**, Campden's oldest building (built in around 1380), and more Tudor, Jacobean and the odd Georgian façade. Behind many lurk fancy hotels, upscale design boutiques – and ordinary shops. Midway along, Campden's pint-sized **Town Hall** sports a plaque on one corner marking the start (and end) of the Cotswold Way.

Market Hall
High St • Always open
Chipping Campden happens to host what might be the single most atmospheric, and emblematic, building in the Cotswolds: the seventeenth-century open-sided **Market Hall**. With its uneven floor of worn stones, its simple design – five arches long, two arches wide – its origin as a gift to Campden from the local lord Sir Baptist Hicks, and its

physical placement at the centre of village life, this barn-like building in the middle of the High Street, where dairy farmers once sold their wares, summons up more Cotswold ghosts than any number of stately homes or grand gardens. Dawdle here.

The Old Silk Mill

Sheep St • Daily 10am–5pm • **Hart Silversmiths** Mon–Fri 9am–5pm, Sat 9am–noon • ☎ 01386 841100, ⓦ hartsilversmiths.co.uk

Partway along the High Street, a turn down Sheep Street brings you to the **Old Silk Mill**, which Ashbee took over for the Guild of Handicraft. Today, as well as housing galleries of local art and ceramics, the old building rings with the noise of chisels from the resident stone carvers and hammering from the upstairs workshop of **Hart**, a silversmith firm which came out to Campden with Ashbee in 1902 and has been based here since. You're free to wander into their workshop – like stepping into an old photograph, with metalworking tools and half-finished pieces strewn everywhere under low ceilings, and staff perched by the windows working by hand on decorative items or jewellery.

Court Barn Museum

Church St • Tues–Sun 10am–5pm; Oct–March closes 4pm • £4 • ☎ 01386 841951, ⓦ courtbarn.org.uk

The history and work of Ashbee's Guild of Handicraft, and its leading exponents, is explained at the superb **Court Barn museum**. Sited opposite a magnificent row of seventeenth-century Cotswold stone **almshouses** in Church Street, the museum displays the work of Ashbee and eight Arts and Crafts cohorts, placing it all in context with informative displays and short videos – the bookbinding of Katharine Adams, stained-glass design of Paul Woodroffe, furniture design of Gordon Russell (who has his own museum in Broadway; see p.120), the silver of Hart's and Robert Welch, and more.

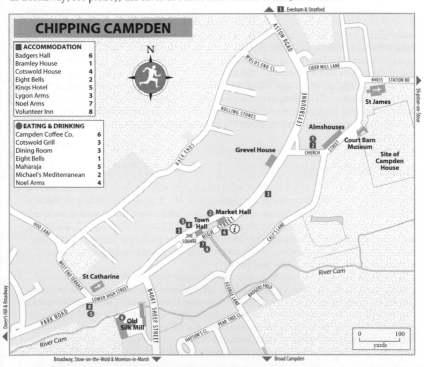

CHIPPING CAMPDEN'S FESTIVALS

Chipping Campden hosts the **Literature Festival** (ⓦcampdenlitfest.co.uk) and **Music Festival** (ⓦcampdenmusicfestival.co.uk), which both run annually in May, as well as events throughout the year around the **BITE food festival** (ⓦthebite.co).

Old Campden House Gateway

Church St • ☎ 01628 825925, ⓦ landmarktrust.org.uk

The top end of Church Street is dominated by a splendidly ornate Jacobean **gateway** – but if you peek through the gates, there's nothing there but more or less empty fields. The gateway was once the main entrance to the Campden House estate created in the 1610s by **Baptist Hicks**, a textile merchant knighted by James I and later Lord Mayor of London. Centred on an imposing three-storey mansion, whose dome was illuminated at night, the estate took in eight acres of formal gardens – but during the Civil War, less than forty years after its construction, Hicks's grandson had the house burnt to the ground rather than allow it to fall into Parliamentarian hands. What survives today, leased by the Landmark Trust, is the gatehouse, some foundation remnants and a pair of modest **banqueting houses** that are now very posh self-catering accommodation. Check on their website for details of the few open days each year that the public are admitted to the banqueting houses and grounds.

St James' Church

Church St • March–Oct Mon–Sat 10am–5pm, Sun 2–6pm; Nov–Feb Mon–Sat 11am–4pm, Sun 2–4pm; closes 3pm in Dec & Jan • Free • ⓦ stjameschurchcampden.co.uk

At the top of the village, approached by an avenue of lime trees, rises **St James' Church**. Built in the fifteenth century, the zenith of Campden's wool-trading days, this is the archetypal Cotswold wool church, beneath a magnificent 120ft tower. Inside, the airy nave is bathed in light from the clerestory windows and there's a delicate and carefully considered balance between height and length. The South Chapel holds the ostentatious **funerary memorial** of the Hicks family, with the fancily carved marble effigies of Sir Baptist and Lady Elizabeth lying on their table-tomb overlooked by the standing figures of their daughter and son-in-law, Edward Noel, who came a fatal cropper fighting the Parliamentarians in the Civil War. The church is also the venue for the prestigious **Chipping Campden Music Festival** (ⓦcampdenmusicfestival.co.uk), held each May.

Dover's Hill

A fine panoramic view rewards those who make the short but severe hike up the first stage of the Cotswold Way, north from the centre of Chipping Campden to **Dover's Hill**. From the Lower High Street, turn beside St Catharine's Church to follow West End Terrace and then Hoo Lane onwards, doglegging along Kingcombe Lane and up onto the hill (which is also accessible by car, with a car park near the summit). The topograph at the highest point, 740ft above sea level, affords breathtaking vistas extending to the Malvern Hills and beyond.

Since 1612 this natural amphitheatre has been the stage for an Olympics of rural sports, though the event was suspended in the mid-nineteenth century just as games like shin-kicking were taking hold. A more civilized version, the **Cotswold Olimpicks** (see p.116), has been staged here annually since 1966 with tug-of-war, falconry and hammer-throwing plus a bit of shin-kicking for old times' sake.

There are maps and notes at the Cotswold Way pages of ⓦescapetothecotswolds .org.uk explaining how to turn this walk into a circuit back to Campden (3 miles; 2hr), or how to include **Lynches Wood** just below the summit – carpeted with bluebells in May – to make a longer loop (4.5 miles; 3hr).

ARRIVAL AND DEPARTURE
CHIPPING CAMPDEN

By train The nearest station is Moreton-in-Marsh (see p.102), eight miles away, on the London–Oxford–Worcester line. From there take bus #21 or #22 (linked timetables; Mon–Sat every 1–2hrs; 45min) or a taxi (about £25; see p.103 for taxi numbers).
By bus Absurdly, considering the popularity of the place,

Chipping Campden has no buses on Sundays. The rest of the week, buses stop on the High St.
Destinations Blockley (Mon–Sat every 1–2hr; 20–30min); Broadway (Mon–Sat 3 daily; 20min); Cheltenham (1 on Thurs; 1hr 5min); Moreton-in-Marsh (Mon–Sat every 1–2hr; 45min); Stratford-upon-Avon (Mon–Sat every 1–2hr; 35min).

INFORMATION AND TOURS

Tourist office High St (March–Oct daily 9.30am–5pm; Nov–Feb Mon–Thurs 9.30am–1pm, Fri–Sun 9.30am–4pm; ☎01386 841206, ⊛ campdenonline.org).

Walking tours The Cotswold Voluntary Wardens offer a guided town walk in summer (April–Oct Tues 2.30pm & Thurs 10am; £3.50), starting from the Market Hall.

3

ACCOMMODATION

Chipping Campden's **accommodation** is excellent: the high profile of the village and its relatively well-heeled brand of overnight visitor mean that standards are high. Many places insist on a two-night minimum stay, especially during the summer peak.
For extra-special **self-catering**, contact the Landmark Trust (☎01628 825925, ⊛ landmarktrust.org.uk) to book one of the Jacobean banqueting halls (see p.114) – even in such an atmospheric place as Campden, they are exceptional. Four nights in high season could cost £800–1400.

HOTELS & INNS
Cotswold House The Square ☎01386 840330, ⊛ cotswoldhouse.com. On the High St in the centre of Campden, this plush – perhaps overly plush – hotel occupies an immaculately maintained Regency townhouse and its older neighbours. Quality is exceptional, both in the main house and the cottages and suites behind: expect mood lighting, underfloor heating, stone baths, free DVDs, six kinds of pillow – the whole nine yards. There's also a spa, with a full range of treatments and therapies. **£180**
★ **Eight Bells** Church St ☎01386 840371, ⊛ eightbells inn.co.uk. Seven individually done-up bedrooms at this much-loved pub between the High St and the church. The style is calm – smartly modern without struggling for the designer boutique look – and being at a slight remove from the town centre is a bonus. **£115**
Kings Hotel The Square ☎01386 840256, ⊛ www .kingscampden.co.uk. Charming luxury hotel hiding behind an eighteenth-century frontage on the High St.

Eclectic contemporary styling, reminiscent of an urban boutique hotel, characterizes the nineteen bedrooms, including five extra-special rooms in a renovated cottage, but good offers during the week can make rates surprisingly affordable; prices jump at weekends. Sister to Stratford's *Arden* hotel (see p.145). **£110**
Lygon Arms High St ☎01386 840318, ⊛ lygonarms .co.uk. Not to be confused with the venerable top-end *Lygon Arms* in nearby Broadway, this is a decent midrange ex-coaching inn (pronounced "liggon") that's been around for five hundred years or so – though now with rather bland, refurbished rooms. A decent stop-gap. **£80**
★ **Noel Arms** High St ☎01386 840317, ⊛ noelarms hotel.com. Sister property of *Cotswold House*, directly opposite but considerably more down to earth. Housed in a sixteenth-century former coaching inn, with a traditional wood-panelled bar and log fires, it has 28 bedrooms – pleasant and very comfortable but not flashy – and a solid reputation for service and quality. **£95**

DAY-TRIPPING BY BUS FROM CHIPPING CAMPDEN
From a base in Chipping Campden, it's possible to use the limited public transport to put together a **day-trip by bus** – not on Sundays, though, when no buses run. Using bus #21 or #22 (Mon–Sat every 1–2hrs), you could start from Campden around 9am, have a couple of hours in Broadway, then move on to Bourton-on-the-Hill for lunch and a stroll around Sezincote House, Batsford Arboretum or the nearby gardens, catching the last bus back from Batsford to Campden around 6.30pm. In the other direction, the same buses could give you a full day in Stratford-upon-Avon: visit on the first or third Saturdays of the month to browse Stratford's excellent farmers' market.

3

THE COTSWOLD OLIMPICKS

Centuries before the revival of the ancient Greek tradition of the Olympic Games – generally recognized to be at Athens in 1896 – the Gloucestershire village of Chipping Campden was staging its own Olympic celebration of athletic prowess. In 1612, local lawyer **Robert Dover** organized a series of competitions on a hilltop site outside Campden (subsequently renamed Dover's Hill in his honour) – running, jumping, hammer-throwing, sword-fighting, wrestling, horse-racing and more, partly it seems in order to give the local people something to cheer about, and partly perhaps to select prime athletes for military service in defence of King James, who was an enthusiastic supporter of Dover's enterprise. Within a few years, the games had become known as the "**Olimpicks**", commemorating the Greek tradition, and included music and festivities, games of cards and chess and a grand fireworks display.

After a pause for the Civil War the games rolled on, though largely losing their noble ideals: bottle-throwing grew increasingly popular and wrestling morphed into contests of shin-kicking between opponents in hobnail boots. During the Victorian era, the games drew tens of thousands, before their final demise in 1852, when the division of common land meant Dover's Hill passed into private ownership.

Some 76 years later the National Trust bought the hill, hosting a one-off games in 1951 before local enthusiasts revived the tradition in earnest in 1966. Since then the **Cotswold Olimpicks** have been staged annually on Dover's Hill, on a Friday in late May or early June, with a range of competitions including tug-of-war, wrestling and, of course, shin-kicking. Find more information at ⓦolimpickgames.com.

The day after the games has, for a couple of centuries at least, been given over to the **Scuttlebrook Wake**, a traditional knees-up formerly featuring a smoking contest, a gorging contest, climbing a greasy pole and other entertainments, now comprising a costumed procession through Chipping Campden, accompanied by floats, morris dancing and funfair rides. Full details at ⓦscuttlebrookwake.org.

Volunteer Inn Lower High St ☎01386 840688, ⓦthevolunteerinn.net. Great budget option at this friendly, outgoing pub and Indian restaurant at the end of the High St – often used by walkers on the Cotswold Way and cycle enthusiasts (you can rent bikes onsite; see p.117). The nine rooms are modest but perfectly adequate – the only drawback can be noise from the bar, particularly on Friday and Saturday nights. **£60**

B&B

Badgers Hall High St ☎01386 840839, ⓦbadgershall

.com. Popular, atmospheric choice for B&B, in an old stone house on the High St, above their own tearoom. All the guest rooms are en suite and come complete with period detail – beamed ceilings and so forth; advance bookings are advised. **£110**

Bramley House 6 Aston Rd ☎01386 840066, ⓦbramleyhouse.co.uk. Fine little B&B in a modern(-ish) Cotswold stone house a few minutes' walk off the High St – only three guest rooms, all cosy, but the difference comes in the personal touch: great service and locally sourced breakfasts. **£75**

EATING AND DRINKING

Aside from places to eat and drink within Chipping Campden village, more excellent dining options lie within easy reach nearby – for example in Ebrington (see p.118), Broadway (see p.119) or Bourton-on-the-Hill (see p.106), not forgetting the gut-busting *Pudding Club* in Mickleton (see p.119).

CAFÉS

Badgers Hall High St ☎01386 840839, ⓦbadgershall .com. This tearoom in the middle of the village has won awards and international acclaim for its inch-perfect take on traditional English tea and cakes, all freshly made daily. Also light lunches (under £10). Mon–Sat 10am–4.30pm, Sun 11am–4.30pm.

★**Campden Coffee Company** Old Silk Mill, Sheep St ☎01386 849251, ⓦcampdencoffeecompany.co.uk. Hole up at this bright and breezy café within the Old Silk

Mill for coffees, paninis, teas, cakes and light lunches (£4–7), sourced locally from independent suppliers. Mon–Fri 9am–4.30pm, Sat & Sun 10am–4.30pm.

RESTAURANTS

Cotswold Grill At Cotswold House hotel, The Square ☎01386 840330, ⓦcotswoldhouse.com. Upmarket modern British cooking in a contemporary setting, focusing on steaks and meaty mains (£13–20), as well as traditional Sunday lunch. Food served Mon–Fri

10.30am–2.30pm & 6.30–9.30pm, Sat & Sun 10.30am–9.30pm.

The Dining Room At Cotswold House hotel, The Square ☎ 01386 840330, ⓦ cotswoldhouse.com. Elegant fine-dining restaurant, presenting innovative modern British cuisine in a distinctly cosmopolitan ambience, using locally sourced ingredients on a short, artfully presented menu. Four courses around £45. Thurs–Sat 7–9.30pm.

★ **Eight Bells** Church St ☎ 01386 840371, ⓦ eightbells inn.co.uk. This charming old stone inn is a particularly cosy place to eat – also with a great reputation – with a menu encompassing dishes such as pheasant with mushrooms, pork with apricots and chestnuts or lamb's liver on bubble and squeak. Mains £13–17. Food served Mon–Thurs noon–2pm & 6.30–9pm, Fri & Sat noon–2.30pm & 6.30–9.30pm, Sun noon–9pm.

Maharaja At Volunteer Inn, Lower High St ☎ 01386 840688, ⓦ maharajacatering.net. This much-loved midrange Indian restaurant is attached to the *Volunteer Inn*, though run separately from it. The menu takes in all the classics, as well as unusual – and fiery – Bangladeshi fish and chicken curries, fruity Kashmiri dishes and even venison curry. Mains £8–17. Sun–Thurs 5–10.30pm, Fri & Sat 5–11pm.

Michael's Mediterranean High St ☎ 01386 840826, ⓦ michaelsmediterranean.co.uk. Warm and welcoming Greek-Cypriot restaurant in an eighteenth-century house on the High St, focusing – for a refreshing change – on modern Greek and Mediterranean cuisine, featuring an array of mezze starter dishes (hummus, halloumi cheese, kalamari) followed by moussaka, *kleftico*, yoghurt-marinated kebabs and steaks, with *baklava* to finish. Mains £11–19. Tues–Sat 11am–2.30pm & 7–10pm, Sun noon–3pm.

Noel Arms High St ☎ 01386 840317, ⓦ noelarmshotel .com. Thanks to its chef, who has several times won Great British Pub Awards for Best Curry, this popular inn serves some of the best Indian pub food in the country, including Sri Lankan black lamb (£16) and a unique yellow seafood curry of monkfish, king prawns and baby squid (£15). The menu also takes in more familiar burgers, risottos, battered haddock and roasts (mains £12–17). Mon–Sat noon–3pm & 6–9.30pm, Sun noon–4pm & 6–9.30pm.

WALKING AND CYCLING AROUND CHIPPING CAMPDEN

There's a wealth of **walking and cycling** in the hills and countryside around Chipping Campden. For ideas, maps and guidance, drop in to Campden's well-equipped tourist office, whose knowledgeable staff can point you in the right direction.

LONG-DISTANCE WALKS

Top choice locally is the **Cotswold Way** (see p.32), which starts (or ends) at Chipping Campden, extending to Broadway, Winchcombe and on south to Bath. The first stage, between Campden and Broadway (6 miles; 4hr), is a great introduction to the walk, with several hilltop viewpoints and bags of Cotswold character. It starts with the walk to Dover's Hill (see p.114), then heads down through Campden Woods to climb the infamous Fish Hill to Broadway Tower, ending with the steep descent into Broadway village, where there are plenty of accommodation options and – if you time things right – buses to return you to Campden.

Chipping Campden is also a midway point on the **Heart of England Way**, with stages linking north down the scarp to Mickleton and Bidford-on-Avon (14 miles) and south over the hills to Bourton-on-the-Water (15 miles) – and it forms one end of the **Cotswold Link**, which facilitates access to the Macmillan Way's Cross-Cotswold Path, 21 miles east at Banbury (see p.189).

SHORTER WALKS

Of the numerous shorter walks around Campden, one of the best starts from the archway of the *Noel Arms* on the High Street, beneath which a trail cuts south to join the road into picturesque **BROAD CAMPDEN** village, a mile or so away in its own valley. To one edge of the village stands the fine old *Bakers Arms* (☎ 01386 840515, ⓦ bakersarmscampden.co.uk), with top-quality local ales and good food. The walk back takes you past Broad Campden's church – the house opposite was converted from a Norman chapel by Charles Ashbee in 1905 – across a stream and between the fields back to Chipping Campden.

CYCLING

Cycle Cotswolds (daily 9am–9pm; ☎ 01789 720193 or 07933 368074, ⓦ cyclecotswolds.co.uk), based at Chipping Campden's *Volunteer Inn* (see p.116), have 21-speed "Trek" bikes for rent (£12/day), with child bikes and child seats/tag-alongs also available. They offer free delivery and collection within a radius of four miles around Chipping Campden, subject to a minimum order of £24.

Ebrington and around

On the approach to Chipping Campden from the east, just inside the Gloucestershire county boundary lies **EBRINGTON**, a lovely old thatched village of classically Cotswold good looks secreted into the folded landscape. The ancient **church of St Eadburgha** – a Saxon name, recalling the granddaughter of King Alfred – retains early Norman foundations in its bell tower and a canopied seventeenth-century oak pulpit within, while beside the triangular village green is one of the loveliest pubs in the area.

A mile to the south, **PAXFORD** – like its near-neighbour Blockley (see p.106) – is another almost absurdly photogenic one-car-an-hour village, sporting a row of traditional Cotswold cottages – one is the village shop, still with its vintage Hovis sign – and, across the way, a Victorian chapel standing perfectly framed before open countryside. Paxford's *Churchill Arms* was formerly one of the Cotswolds' leading gastropubs; it closed in 2014, but may have been revived when you visit.

EATING AND DRINKING · EBRINGTON AND AROUND

★Ebrington Arms Ebrington ☎01386 593223, ⓦtheebringtonarms.co.uk. This heart-warming seventeenth-century inn has not only won a fistful of CAMRA Pub of the Year awards but also pops up in the *Good Food Guide*. Duck the oak beams and antlers on the wall to sup your choice of Cotswold ales in a genial, easygoing atmosphere – log fires in winter, walled garden in summer – or try food that is sophisticated without being pretentious: John Dory with local tomatoes and bok choi, Gloucester Old Spot pork chops or Cotswold lamb with wild garlic. Mains £14–18, or lunch special £8 (Mon–Fri). Five comfortable rooms, freshly refurbished with modern en-suite bathrooms, make for high-quality B&B. Food served Mon–Thurs noon–2.30pm & 6–9pm, Fri & Sat noon–2.30pm & 6–9.30pm, Sun noon–3.30pm & 6–8.30pm. **£112**

Hidcote Manor Garden

Hidcote Bartrim • May–Aug daily 10am–7pm; Sept daily 10am–6pm; March & April Sat–Wed 10am–6pm; Oct Sat–Wed 10am–5pm; Nov, Dec & Feb Sat & Sun 11am–4pm; Jan shop only Sat & Sun 11am–3pm • £10 • NT ☎01386 438333, ⓦnationaltrust.org.uk • Taxi from Chipping Campden about £15

Well-signposted down country lanes four miles north of Chipping Campden, beside **HIDCOTE BARTRIM** village, **Hidcote Manor Garden** is often described as one of the greatest gardens of the twentieth century. On the edge of the Cotswold scarp overlooking the Vale of Evesham, it was created by Lawrence Johnston, a private and rather enigmatic character, between 1907 and 1930 as a sequence of outdoor "rooms", fully furnished (with plants) and connected by corridors and designed spaces. It's an intriguing concept, executed across a large area, which demands considerable attention: this isn't an attraction to dip in and out of. If gardens are your thing, plan to spend the best part of a day here exploring at leisure, to get under the skin of the place – and to tune out the perambulating crowds.

Hidcote was the first property acquired by the National Trust (in 1947) purely for its garden. They inherited a mature, sophisticated estate which nonetheless eschews many of the usual features associated with such properties. Instead of making the manor a centrepiece from which the garden radiates, Johnston sidelined the house, subtly shifting his garden's focus away from a celebration of human creativity in nature to, rather, a display of natural harmony under human influence. He made no attempt to introduce architecture – no pergolas, summer-houses or stone pathways – other than in the clipping of yew trees and planting of beech avenues to mimic buildings and streets. Aside from a couple of open areas – the **Theatre Lawn** and **Long Walk** – almost every part of Johnston's garden is compact, intimate and intricate, with close, detailed planting. Highlights include the **Red Border**, a sumptuous display in summer of lilies, lobelias, dahlias and more, the **Stilt Garden**, ringed by angular hornbeams, and the **Rose Garden** – but there's lots more. There is, deliberately, no labelling; instead, leaflets describing the planting, and an excellent garden guidebook by Anna Pavord, are available at the ticket desk. Various events run throughout the year, including dawn walks, painting workshops and apple-pressing: check the website for details.

THE PUDDING CLUB

An old village at the foot of the escarpment below Hidcote, where the B4632 Stratford–Broadway road meets the B4081 zipping down from Chipping Campden, **MICKLETON** is pretty – but not quite pretty enough to merit a stop, were it not for the **Pudding Club** (Ⓦ puddingclub.com). A bit of gastronomic fun, devised in 1985 to help save traditional British puddings from apparently imminent demise, this once-weekly communal consumption of spotted dick, sticky toffee pudding, syrup sponge and other custard-draped favourites, has gained worldwide fame, hosted – as from day one – at Mickleton's *Three Ways House Hotel* (Ⓣ 01386 438429, Ⓦ threewayshousehotel.com).

The hotel, like the village, has charm but isn't quite top-drawer: some rooms, though well equipped and with nice bathroom freebies, are a touch smaller and plainer than you might expect. Plump instead for one of the bigger, cheerier pudding-themed rooms in the Garden Wing (from £220). Any shortcomings, though, tend to be overshadowed by the genial service – and the puddings. Book well ahead for Pudding Club "meetings" (open to all; £37 per person), which generally happen on Friday evenings: you get a light main course followed by access to the legendary Parade of Seven Puddings. Strict rules apply: only one pudding at a time, you must finish one pudding before you can get another, and so on. The record, just so you know, is 24 helpings.

Kiftsgate Court Gardens

Kiftsgate • May–July Sat–Wed noon–6pm; Aug Sat–Wed 2–6pm; April & Sept Sun, Mon & Wed 2–6pm • £7.50 • Ⓣ 01386 438777, Ⓦ www.kiftsgate.co.uk • Taxi from Chipping Campden about £15

If your heart sinks at the prospect of yet another garden, take courage. Located barely half a mile from Hidcote, **Kiftsgate Court Gardens** sees a fraction of the visitors who pile into its better-known neighbour – and, more to the point, as one plain-spoken admirer put it, "There's not a National Trust teapot in sight." Still privately owned by the granddaughter of Heather Muir, who bought the estate in 1918, this is a simply lovely retreat, perched, like Hidcote, on the very edge of the Cotswold scarp, with breathtaking panoramic views. The house (no public access, apart from a tearoom in one corner) sports a striking Georgian facade with a high Classical portico which originally formed part of Mickleton's manor: in 1887 it was detached, transported up the hill and a new house constructed behind. Around it, Muir and her daughter (and, now, granddaughter, who lives here with her family) created a glorious, low-key garden that is famed, in particular, for its **roses** – lavish, aromatic borders full of them, in numerous varieties, including its own *Rosa filipes "Kiftsgate"*. Contemporary sculptures dot the grounds, and don't miss the **Water Garden**, a former tennis court behind clipped yew hedges converted into a Zen-like space for contemplation, featuring a square pool reflecting a small, square island "planted" with 24 gilded bronze philodendron. It is stunning.

Broadway

"Broadway and much of the land about it are the perfection of the old English rural tradition."   Henry James

Wedged into an outlying corner of Worcestershire five miles west of Chipping Campden (and sixteen miles northeast of Cheltenham), **BROADWAY** is a handsome little village at the foot of the steep escarpment that rolls along the western edge of the Cotswolds. It seems likely that the Romans were the first to settle here, but Broadway's zenith was as a stop for stagecoaches plying between London and Worcester. This has defined much of the village's present appearance – its long, broad main street framed by honeystone cottages and former coaching inns shaded beneath chestnut trees. It's undeniably attractive and, like Campden, can attract more visitors than is comfortable – but unlike its neighbour Broadway feels less able to absorb them. Ordinary, everyday life exists here somewhere, away from the tearooms, souvenir shops and neatly mown roadside lawns,

Mickleton & A44 Moreton ▲

BROADWAY N

BLOXHAM ROAD

SPRINGFIELD LANE

NEVILL CLOSE

MORRIS ROAD

MILLS CL

STATION ROAD

CHELTENHAM ROAD

B4632

GORDON CLOSE

LEAMINGTON ROAD

ORCHARD AVENUE

HIGH STREET

Evesham

Winchcombe & Cheltenham

LIFFORD GARDENS

BACK LANE ℹ
RUSSELL
SQUARE

BACK LANE

Gordon Russell
Museum

COLLETTS FIELDS

2 HIGH STREET

The
Green

1
4

2
3

HIGH STREET

3 4

Ashmolean
Museum Broadway

6

CHURCH STREET

5

5

6
7

CHURCH CLOSE

0   200
     yards

St Edburgha & Snowshill ▼

3

ACCOMMODATION	
Abbots Grange	6
Broadway Hotel	5
Crown & Trumpet	7
Lygon Arms	3
Olive Branch	2
Russell's	4
Windrush House	1

EATING & DRINKING	
Broadway Deli	3
Crown & Trumpet	6
Lygon Arms	2
Market Pantry	4
Russell's	1
Tisanes Tea Rooms	5

but in truth there's not much sign of it. Visit the two outstanding museums, and enjoy an early-morning stroll while the streets are empty, but then move on. The **Broadway Arts Festival** (⊚ broadwayartsfestival.com) fills a fortnight in early June.

High Street

Broadway is named for its chestnut-lined **High Street**, a wide thoroughfare that previously formed part of the road linking London and Wales, via Worcester. Now blocked at its upper end, on the slopes of Fish Hill – and thankfully bypassed by the A44 – the High Street is still flanked by ex-coaching inns, set back behind broad grass verges. You're likely to approach from the west along Station Road; at the time of writing, construction work was under way here to rebuild Broadway's old station to be a stop on the Gloucester Warwickshire heritage line (see p.127): trains may be running by the time you visit.

The further up the High Street you go, the quieter things become: beyond the Leamington Road turning, which leads back out to the A44, the **Upper High Street** – now a cul-de-sac – is a lovely place to meander, its fine old houses now mostly residential and free from commerce. The **Cotswold Way** long-distance trail runs the length of the High Street, disappearing off southwards (signposted) partway along the Upper High Street to climb to Broadway Tower (see p.124).

Gordon Russell Museum

Russell Sq • Tues–Sun 11am–5pm; Nov–Feb closes 4pm; closed Jan • £5 • ☎ 01386 854695, ⊚ gordonrussellmuseum.org

Battle a path between the teashops and take either of a couple of lanes ducking off the High Street to reach the signposted **Gordon Russell Museum**, a superbly presented showcase of the work and influence of this noted furniture designer (1892–1980), whose father moved to Broadway in 1904 to run the *Lygon Arms* and whose company, headquartered in the village for sixty years, is still in operation (⊚ hands.co.uk). Housed in a curved building – dubbed locally "The Banana" – which was formerly Russell's

FROM TOP CHIPPING CAMPDEN (P.112); KIFTSGATE COURT GARDENS (P.119) >

workshop, the museum displays drawings, photographs and notebooks alongside videos of interviews with Russell, but the glory of it is the collection of original Russell furniture. It's gorgeous work, ranging from Arts and Crafts to 1930s modernism and beyond: of particular note are the radio cabinets in the upstairs galleries – intricate, highly polished evocations of an age past.

Ashmolean Museum Broadway

65 High St • Tues–Sun 10am–5pm • £6 • ☎ 01386 859047, ⓦ www.ashmoleanbroadway.org

Tudor House, a former coaching inn on Broadway's High Street, has now been converted to hold a new annexe of the **Ashmolean Museum**. Objects across four floors of displays are mostly on loan from the main museum in Oxford (see p.229), covering four hundred years of history up to the present day – embroidered tapestries and furniture in the panelled ground floor rooms, Worcester porcelain, glass, examples of William Morris tiles and pottery from Winchcombe on the upper levels. Highlights include paintings by Gainsborough and Reynolds, and the temporary exhibits on the top floor. It's a fascinating addition to Broadway's cultural life.

St Eadburgha's Church

ⓦ stmichaelsbroadway.org

Off Broadway's Green, unobtrusive Church Street leads south towards Snowshill, bringing you after a mile or so to the parish **church of St Eadburgha**, a twelfth-century building over a Saxon foundation, named for the granddaughter of King Alfred and wonderfully tranquil and remote from the fluster of the village centre. An unexplained arson attack in 2014 destroyed its twelfth-century door, but the interior of medieval stonework and a Jacobean communion table survived.

ARRIVAL AND DEPARTURE   BROADWAY

By train The closest station is Honeybourne (6 miles), though Moreton-in-Marsh (10 miles) and Evesham (8 miles) are about as good. Check with the tourist office for taxi information.

By bus Broadway has no buses on Sundays. On other days, buses stop on the High St.

Destinations Cheltenham (Mon–Sat 4 daily; 1hr); Chipping Campden (Mon–Sat 3 daily; 20min); Evesham (Mon–Sat 5 daily; 25min); Moreton-in-Marsh (Mon–Sat 3 daily; 25min); Stanton (Mon–Sat 4 daily; 5min); Stratford-upon-Avon (Mon–Sat 3 daily; 50min); Winchcombe (Mon–Sat 4 daily; 35min).

INFORMATION AND TOURS

Tourist office Russell Sq (April–Oct Mon–Sat 10am–5pm, Sun 11am–3pm; Feb, March, Nov & Dec closes 4pm; Jan closed; ☎ 01386 852937, ⓦ beautifulbroadway.com).

Tours A fine way to get under the skin of the place is with the private art tours run on demand by local artist Jeremy Houghton (£25 per person; ⓦ broadwayarttours.co.uk).

John Singer Sargent's *Carnation, Lily, Lily, Rose* (1887), which firmly established his London reputation, was painted in Broadway, at a time when a group of artists and illustrators which included novelist Henry James lived and worked here; Houghton's tours cover places where Sargent and others worked.

ACCOMMODATION

HOTELS & INNS

Broadway Hotel The Green ☎ 01386 852401, ⓦ cotswold-inns-hotels.co.uk. Fine old hotel perfectly sited on the village green at the busy end of the High St, originally a sixteenth-century bolthole for the abbots of Pershore and still with period features. Rooms are comfortable, if a touch flowery, and all named after National Hunt champions and Cheltenham Gold Cup stars: depending on your personal situation, you could stay in the "Best Mate" superior double – or the "War of Attrition" twin room. **£80**

Crown and Trumpet 14 Church St ☎ 01386 853202, ⓦ cotswoldholidays.co.uk. Traditional seventeenth-century coaching inn just round the corner off the High St – and a much-loved option for decent, unpretentious, midrange accommodation, with five simple en-suite rooms and a warm welcome. It's a popular choice: book well ahead. **£70**

★**Lygon Arms** High St ☎01386 852255, ⓦthehotel collection.co.uk. A grand, sprawling coaching inn (pronounced "liggon"), in classic style. Known to have been an inn since 1532 (though probably much older: one of the bedrooms has a fourteenth-century fireplace set into its 4ft-thick stone walls), it has long had noble and royal associations, hosting both Charles I (in 1645) and Cromwell (in 1651) in rooms which retain their original panelling and fittings. It is now owned by a national chain, though, to their credit, the corporate atmosphere is largely held at bay. The 78 bedrooms vary from modern styles through to original period suites, all fitted out to an extremely high standard; there's also a spa with swimming pool. **£112**

★**Russell's** 20 High St ☎01386 853555, ⓦrussellsof broadway.co.uk. Outstanding restaurant which also doubles as a relaxed, super-stylish boutique hotel. Just seven rooms are presented with scrupulous attention to detail: mood-lighting enhances feature headboards or walls of exposed stone, textiles set off unusual furniture design, bathrooms host huge stand-alone tubs and showers-for-two, and so forth. A splendid option, unusually keenly priced: book well ahead. **£115**

B&BS

Abbots Grange Church St ☎020 8133 8698, ⓦabbots grange.com. Exceptional B&B in an eye-popping medieval mansion with a venerable history which dates back to the early fourteenth century – and also encompasses Henry James and John Singer Sargent, who lived and worked in the house, among a group of artists and illustrators, in the 1880s. It offers three rooms in what, despite the grandeur, is a private family home – two four-poster rooms

and one twin, all with access to the eight-acre grounds (which include a private tennis court and croquet lawn). It's expensive, but unique. **£160**

Olive Branch 78 High St ☎01386 853440, ⓦtheolive branch-broadway.com. Award-winning guesthouse in an old stone house on the upper part of the High St, out of the fluster. It may be a touch pastel-and-chintz for some tastes, but is otherwise cosy and well run; some rooms have king-size beds and access to the rear garden. **£102**

Windrush House Station Rd ☎01386 853577, ⓦwindrushhouse.com. Four-star guesthouse located just a step out of town, rather more tasteful than many of the competition, with five stylishly decorated rooms, another excellent breakfast and owners who really know the value of extending a warm welcome. **£80**

OUT OF TOWN

Buckland Manor Buckland ☎01386 852626, ⓦbucklandmanor.co.uk. A couple of miles south of Broadway (and just yards inside Gloucestershire), this is an extraordinarily opulent country hotel, part of the Relais & Châteaux group. All the details are in order – stone fireplaces, mullioned windows, four-poster beds, cream teas, sweeping views and, as one journalist commented, "bathrooms so big you could live in them". That said, there are only fifteen rooms: this is luxury on a human scale. **£260**

Dormy House Willersey Hill ☎01386 852711, ⓦdormy house.co.uk. Lavish independent four-star country hotel beside the golf club a few miles out of town, on a hillside with great views. Rooms are sleekly modern, with a good deal of style – this is a very swish, romantic place to hole up and relax. **£230**

EATING AND DRINKING

★**Broadway Deli** 29 High St ☎01386 853040, ⓦbroadwaydeli.co.uk. For picnic supplies or foodie souvenirs, in the absence of a regular farmers' market (markets are held only two or three times a year; check dates at the tourist office), you could do worse than pop into this exceptionally good deli, spread across two floors, also with a great café section for coffees and paninis. Mon–Sat 8am–5.30pm.

Crown and Trumpet 14 Church St ☎01386 853202, ⓦcotswoldholidays.co.uk. This cheery, historic local tavern is one of the better watering-holes in town, with decent beers, a lively atmosphere, solid, old-fashioned Sunday roasts and regular sessions of live blues and jazz. Mains £6–12. Mon–Fri 11am–3pm & 5–11pm, Sat 11am–11pm, Sun noon–4pm & 6–10.30pm.

Lygon Arms High St ☎01386 852255, ⓦthehotel collection.co.uk. Broadway's famous old hotel hosts easily the most atmospheric dining room in town, the dramatic Jacobean Great Hall, with its oak panelling, minstrels' gallery, open fireplace and barrel-vaulted ceiling. Fortunately, the

food matches up – hearty, traditional English cooking of the highest quality (three-course menu £34). The hotel brasserie has more affordable fare – burgers, toad in the hole, goat's cheese pizzas, and so on (mains £10–15). Great Hall Sun–Fri 12.30–2pm & 7–9.30pm, Sat 7–9.30pm. Brasserie daily 10am–10pm.

Market Pantry 31 High St ☎01386 858318, ⓦmarket pantry.co.uk. Pleasant little café offering coffees, freshly baked cakes and light lunches in an easygoing atmosphere of shabby-chic furniture and buzzy conversation. Mains £6–9, posh afternoon tea £13. Mon–Fri 9am–5pm, Sat 9.30am–5pm, Sun 10am–5pm.

★**Russell's** 20 High St ☎01386 853555, ⓦrussellsof broadway.co.uk. Far and away the best and most alluring restaurant in – or near – Broadway, with a stylish, contemporary interior and relaxed, efficient service. Take in the classic Modern British menu, featuring produce from the Vale of Evesham and the Cotswolds: local lamb chops with honey-roasted figs, lamb and sweetbreads, monkfish with bulghur wheat and pomegranate, and so on, presented

3

WALKS AROUND BROADWAY

The countryside around Broadway is packed with good **walking** opportunities. A long, full-day stage of the **Cotswold Way** (12 miles; 7hr) branches southwest to Winchcombe, initially heading towards Buckland before diverting through beech woods to Stanton, Stanway and Hailes; with some pre-planning you could catch bus #606 (Mon–Sat) from a midway point back to Broadway. There's also a **circular route** (7.5 miles; 4hr 30min) which follows the Cotswold Way, then branches off at Stanton church to return north through Laverton and Buckland, rejoining the Cotswold Way at Broadway Coppice for the last short section back into Broadway. A shorter **circular walk** (4 miles; 3hr; downloadable at the Cotswold Way pages of ⓦ escapetothecotswolds.org.uk) heads up to Broadway Tower: starting from Broadway High Street, cutting south across fields to join Coneygree Lane off the Snowshill road, climbing steeply to the tower, then following the Cotswold Way path back down onto Broadway High Street again. Full details, maps and information are at the tourist office.

3

with elegance. Mains £17–24, or two-course set menu £17. Daily noon–2.30pm & 6–9.30pm.

Tisanes Tea Rooms 21 The Green ☎01386 853296, ⓦ tisanes-tearooms.co.uk. If you're going to indulge in a tearoom, best make it this one. It's uncompromisingly traditional, with tootling vintage music, tea-cakes and shortbread – but, unusually, also plenty of gluten-free options. Daily 10am–5pm.

Broadway Tower

Near Broadway • Daily 10am–5pm; shorter hours in bad weather • £4.80 • ☎01386 852390, ⓦ broadwaytower.co.uk

Atop Fish Hill, a mile southeast of Broadway village, **Broadway Tower** stands at the second-highest point in the Cotswolds (the highest is Cleeve Hill; p.132). The tower itself, a turreted folly built in 1798, has become an icon of the Cotswolds, perched at more than 1,000ft above sea level with stupendous views on all sides that purportedly encompass thirteen counties. The Pre-Raphaelite artists of Broadway and Chipping Campden loved it – Morris, Burne-Jones, Rossetti and others frequently came up here to take the air and dream of England.

The reality today is a touch more prosaic. Now privately owned, the tower stands alongside a family activity park, comprising an adventure playground, snack bar and picnic area. Inside, the tower's three compact levels now hold displays on the history of the building – but aside from a rather nice topographical model of the Cotswold hills, they're unlikely to inspire. Pay your admission to climb the 71 steps to the roof, for those views.

Childswickham

Two miles west of Broadway, the charmingly named village of **CHILDSWICKHAM** has less to do with the Cotswolds than with the Vale of Evesham (see p.132) – its countryside is flat and its agricultural preoccupations are market gardening and arable. It's nonetheless a pretty place, spread out below the fifteenth-century spire of the originally Norman **church of St Mary**.

EATING AND DRINKING   CHILDSWICKHAM

Childswickham Inn Childswickham ☎01386 852461, ⓦ childswickhaminn.co.uk. Stop in at this family-friendly country pub for a pint or a decent meal in their updated brasserie, serving roasts, steaks and fishcakes in a cheerful, unpretentious atmosphere. Mains £11–17. Food served Mon–Sat noon–2pm & 6–9pm, Sun noon–6pm.

Snowshill

Along the country lane south of Broadway, a mile or so past St Eadburgha's Church you come to **SNOWSHILL**, about as sleepy and picturesque a Cotswold village as you could imagine. Its cottages huddle around the **church of St Barnabas** – unusual for being entirely Victorian, though with a beautiful fifteenth-century Tudor font and seventeenth-century carved pulpit.

Snowshill Manor

Snowshill • July & Aug Wed–Mon 11am–5pm; April–June, Sept & Oct Wed–Sun noon–5pm; Nov garden only Sat & Sun 10.30am–3.30pm • £9.80 • NT ☎ 01386 852410, ⓦ nationaltrust.org.uk

On the edge of the village, **Snowshill Manor** is a good-looking Cotswold manor house holding a trove of exotic curiosities. The architect, craftsman and poet Charles Wade (1883–1956) – inspired as a boy by his grandmother's Chinese cabinet in black and gold lacquer, now on display in the house – spent decades hunting down objects that were not rare or valuable but "of interest as records of various vanished handicrafts". The results of his forays include model carts, boneshaker bicycles, children's prams, wooden toys, beds, beetles, all kinds of musical instruments and other curios; they were crammed into the house, while he himself lived in a cottage in the garden.

It makes for a fascinating rummage through a jumbled mind – rooms across all three floors of the house remain stuffed with all manner of bits and bobs. On the ground floor, the **Turquoise Room** holds Wade's favourite piece, a nineteenth-century wooden model of a Japanese mask-maker. "Grannie's Cabinet" takes pride of place in the **Zenith Room**, while most dramatic is the arrangement of 26 Samurai warriors dating from the seventeenth to the nineteenth centuries in the **Green Room** upstairs. Note that it's a ten-minute walk to reach the house from the car park.

Also of significance is the manor's **garden**, created by Wade in the Arts and Crafts style and now maintained organically, without chemicals. It has been described by gardening expert Monty Don as "overwhelmingly English – soft, subtle and entirely in harmony with the surrounding countryside". All the doors and gates opening onto the garden, and the furniture within it, are painted in "Wade blue", a shade developed by Wade specifically to complement the natural tones of his planting.

Cotswold Lavender

Hill Barn Farm, Snowshill • mid-June to mid-Aug daily 10am–5pm • £2.50 • ☎ 01386 854821, ⓦ cotswoldlavender.co.uk

Snowshill is known for its lavender. If you're around in high summer, which is the only time when the lavender blooms, drop into **Cotswold Lavender** just outside the village to see their 53 acres of fields, browse their fragrant giftshop and scoff lavender scones in the tearoom.

ACCOMMODATION   SNOWSHILL

Snowshill Hill Snowshill ☎ 01386 853959, ⓦ www .snowshill-hill.co.uk. A couple of miles outside Snowshill, within walking distance of the lavender fields, this working farm with sheep and Galloway cattle offers great B&B – only three rooms, all on the ground floor, with locally sourced ingredients for breakfast and a warm welcome. **£80**

WALKING FROM STANTON TO SNOWSHILL

Numerous fine **walks** pass through or near Stanton. A **circular trail** (6 miles; 4hr 30min; map and notes downloadable at the Cotswold Way pages of ⓦ escapetothecotswolds.org.uk) begins in Stanton village, following the Cotswold Way signposts to climb steeply up Shenberrow Hill, eventually branching off onto a path through quiet Littleworth Wood and down into Snowshill village. From Snowshill you turn west again, climbing to follow another track beside Buckland Wood before rejoining the Cotswold Way to walk south, back up to the edge of Littleworth Wood. From here a minor track offering views west over Stanton and across to the Severn Vale leads you down to the *Mount Inn* (see p.126) and back into Stanton. You could shorten the route by eliminating the Snowshill loop and using Littleworth Wood as the furthest point of the circuit (2.5 miles; 2hr 30min).

Bus 606 (Mon–Sat) runs once from Broadway High Street around 9am to Stanton, returning from the Stanton turn on the B4632 a bit after 5pm. Note that the *Mount Inn* closes at 3pm.

Stanton

The B4632 Cheltenham Road scoots south from Broadway, passing a succession of attractive villages adorning the escarpment on the left. **BUCKLAND** and **LAVERTON** are pretty – but **STANTON**, three miles south of Broadway, takes the biscuit. As unspoilt Cotswold villages go, there are few (if any) better: the entire village is built of warm Cotswold stone, the Norman spired **church of St Michael** is a beauty both inside and out, everywhere you look there are Jacobean gables and mullioned windows and (deliberately) not a shop or a tearoom in sight – it's a stunner.

Above the village, a lane leads up Shenberrow Hill to **Stanton Guildhouse**, perched above the village. Built in the 1960s in inch-perfect traditional style by social worker and proponent of Arts and Crafts philosophy Mary Osborn, it operates as a kind of community hub and rural conference centre, hosting spiritual retreats and a regular cycle of weekly classes in skills such as pottery, art, woodwork, furniture restoration and stained glass. The house is generally not open to walk-in visitors, but check the website for details of what's on.

ARRIVAL AND DEPARTURE   STANTON

By bus Bus #606 (Mon–Sat 4 daily) serves Broadway (5min), Winchcombe (30min) and Cheltenham (55min).

ACCOMMODATION AND EATING

★ **Mount Inn** Stanton ☎ 01386 584316, ⓦ themount inn.co.uk. Stanton's only nod to commercialization is this seventeenth-century walkers' pub hidden away at the top of a steep slope above the village centre, offering spectacular views from its terrace alongside uncomplicated meals (mains £11–14) and fine Donnington ales. Daily noon–3pm & 6–11pm.

Stanton Guildhouse Stanton ☎ 01386 584357, ⓦ stantonguildhouse.org.uk. The *Guildhouse* has seven bedrooms, but generally doesn't provide B&B for individuals. However, it's possible to rent the whole property as a self-catering cottage over the weekend (sleeps up to 15). Enquire about arrangements and prices well in advance. Three nights from around £1200

Stanway House and Fountain

Stanway • June–Aug Tues & Thurs 2–5pm • £7, grounds only £4.50 • ☎ 01386 584469, ⓦ stanwayfountain.co.uk

A mile south of Stanton, just before you reach the B4077, which cuts east-west between Stow and Tewkesbury, **STANWAY** hamlet is dominated by the presence of **Stanway House** – most prominently its magnificent triple-storied, triple-gabled **gatehouse** in buttery yellow Cotswold stone. A Jacobean manor house as splendid as any in the region, it awes from the outside – even if, inside, it's all a bit ramshackle: the limited opening hours are an indication that Lord and Lady Neidpath (the Earl and Countess of Wemyss), whose home this is, are unequivocally not in the museum business. Much of the house's furniture is original, including a 22ft-long shuffleboard table built in 1620, but there's no literature to help you navigate a path through the distinctly lived-in rooms – the only way is to wander, admiring the well-worn armchairs and family portraits as you go. The main attraction, though, lies outside: Stanway's **water garden**, designed in the 1720s and featuring a canal running on a high terrace with an impressively long cascade, is now home to the **world's tallest gravity fountain** (and the tallest fountain of any kind in Britain), installed in 2004 and driven from a half-million-litre reservoir located 580ft up in the nearby hills. It's activated twice during the afternoons that the house is open to the public, spouting to 300ft above the lawns.

Hailes Abbey and around

Near Winchcombe • Daily 10am–6pm; April–June & Sept–Oct closes 5pm • £4.50 • NT • EH ☎ 01242 602398, ⓦ nationaltrust.org.uk & ⓦ english-heritage.org.uk

Hailes Abbey, signposted just off the B4632 a couple of miles north of Winchcombe, was once one of England's great Cistercian monasteries, founded in the 1240s. Pilgrims came from all over the country to pray before the abbey's phial of Christ's blood – that is

GLOUCESTERSHIRE WARWICKSHIRE STEAM RAILWAY

Based nominally at **TODDINGTON** – though its station is in fact located east of Toddington beside the roundabout where the B4632 meets the B4077 – the **Gloucestershire Warwickshire Steam Railway** (☎01242 621405, ⓦgwsr.com) keeps alive a section of the old Great Western line from Birmingham and Stratford to Bristol, originally opened in 1906 and closed to regular services in 1976. It's a prodigiously successful operation, relying on more than six hundred volunteers and drawing thousands of fare-paying passengers each month. From Toddington, the line runs south to Winchcombe and then on a scenic route down off the Cotswold Edge to end at Cheltenham Racecourse. Trains run pretty much year-round, most frequently in June, July and August, dropping to weekends only in winter (no service Jan & Feb). An all-day ticket, valid on any route, is £15. The twelve-mile journey takes just over half an hour each way.

Plans are afoot to extend the line north of Toddington: a section to Laverton is already open, and trains may already be running to Broadway by the time you read this. Nonetheless it will be some years before the railway – despite its name – actually reaches Warwickshire.

until 1538, when, during the Dissolution, the relic was discredited as "honey coloured with saffron". The abbot was forced to surrender the abbey to Henry VIII's commissioners the following year, and shortly thereafter the buildings were demolished.

What survives is chiefly an assortment of foundations, but some cloister arches remain, worn by wind and rain. The grassy ruins may lack drama, but Hailes is still worth visiting for its onsite **museum**, where you can examine thirteenth-century bosses at close quarters, and for **Hailes Church**, just across the road, which is older than the abbey and contains beautiful wall paintings dating from around 1300. Its cartoon-like hunting scene was probably a warning to Sabbath-breakers.

Hayles Fruit Farm

Near Hailes Abbey • Tearoom daily 9am–5pm • ☎01242 602123, ⓦhaylesfruitfarm.co.uk

Located just past the abbey, **Hayles Fruit Farm** is famed chiefly for its apples and pears – and its legendary Badger's Bottom cider, a mainstay at farmers' markets across the Cotswolds. Stop in at the well-stocked **farm shop and tearoom**, tackle their family-friendly **nature trail** or stay overnight: a year-round **campsite** takes tents and caravans. Farm staff maintain doggedly that their spelling (with a Y) is original, and that it was a meddling bureaucrat in 1936, when English Heritage took over responsibility for the abbey, who decided that Hailes (with an I) looked more decorous. There may be truth in this: railway records show that, as late as 1928, a newly opened station nearby was named for "Hayles Abbey". Then again, medieval spelling was so hit-and-miss it's doubtful the odd vowel made much difference either way.

Farmcote

Farmcote Herbs: May–Sept Fri–Sun 10.30am–5.30pm • ☎01242 603860, ⓦfarmcoteherbs.co.uk

To stretch your legs, you could follow an old track southeast from Hailes Abbey up the steep hill overlooking the ruins, past the fruit farm, for a mile or so to **FARMCOTE** village, where the tiny **St Faith's Church** once hosted pilgrims on their way to or from Hailes, and **Farmcote Herbs** sells locally grown medicinal herbs, chilli pepper plants and chutneys. Return to the abbey, or continue a couple of miles further across the high wolds to reach the welcoming *Plough Inn* at Ford (see p.99).

Winchcombe

About eight miles southwest of Broadway – and nine miles northeast of Cheltenham – **WINCHCOMBE** has a long main street flanked by a fetching medley of limestone and half-timbered buildings, the former pure Cotswolds, the latter more typical of

Evesham (see p.132). It's an unprettified working town which nonetheless holds itself with considerable grace, rooted in an unusually long history and offering engaging attractions to complement beautiful surroundings – notably magnificent **Sudeley Castle** on the outskirts and some fine **walks**.

Brief history

With the proximity of the **Stone Age** burial mound Belas Knap and the **Iron Age** hill forts on Cleeve Hill, the area around Winchcombe was of considerable importance long before the **Romans**. By the eighth century, Winchcombe was capital of the kingdom of **Mercia**, and its **abbey**, centred on the shrine of **St Kenelm**, a ninth-century boy-martyr, long predated Hailes Abbey down the road. **Winchcombeshire** even survived as a fully fledged English county for a few years in the eleventh century, before being subsumed into Gloucestershire. Until the Dissolution, when Winchcombe Abbey was completely destroyed, the constant flow of pilgrims helped support the town, which also flourished during the medieval wool boom.

3

St Peter's Church

Gloucester St • ⓦ winchcombeparish.org.uk

One of the grand results of Winchcombe's medieval prosperity was **St Peter's Church**, a mainly fifteenth-century structure distinguished by forty alarming gargoyles that ring the exterior. Inside, aside from a bold Jewish Star of David adorning the original painted cover of the seventeenth-century **font** – evidence, it seems, of newfound Protestant zeal to return to the fundamental roots of Christianity – the church's most striking feature is its broad chancel and Victorian east window: the medieval wooden screen which formerly stood in front was removed to the west end of the church in the 1980s, giving the interior unusual airiness.

High Street and around

The best of Winchcombe is sampled wandering the **High Street** and the few streets around. **Castle Street** dips down to cross the trickling River Isbourne – claimed to be the only river in England to flow north for its entire length – on the short stroll to **Sudeley Castle** (see p.130), while a mile north, just off the B4632 beside **GREET** village, you'll find Winchcombe's station on the preserved **Gloucestershire Warwickshire Steam Railway** (see p.127) right by **Winchcombe Pottery** (Mon–Fri 8am–5pm, Sat 10am–4pm; May–Sept also Sun noon–4pm; ⓦ winchcombepottery.co.uk), a craft enterprise that has been going here since 1926.

Winchcombe Folk and Police Museum

High St • April–Oct Mon–Sat 10am–1pm & 2–4.30pm • £1.50 • ☎ 01242 609151

The Victorian town hall now hosts the **Winchcombe Folk and Police Museum**, displaying historical bits and bobs as well as a collection of police memorabilia. The old stocks outside have seven holes, purportedly to enable an infamous one-legged scoundrel of old to get his come-uppance here alongside three pals.

ARRIVAL AND INFORMATION **WINCHCOMBE**

By bus Bus #606 (Mon–Sat 4 daily) to/from Stanton (30min), Broadway (35min) and Cheltenham (25min).

By steam train From Cheltenham, you could take a local bus to Cheltenham Race Course station for the Gloucestershire Warwickshire Steam Railway to Winchcombe station, a mile north of the town centre. Check days of running carefully on the GWSR website (see p.127).

Tourist office High St (April–Oct daily 10am–4pm; ☎ 01242 602925, ⓦ winchcombe.co.uk & ⓦ winchcombe welcomeswalkers.com).

Walking tours Guided walks around the town (April–Oct Sun 2pm; 1hr 15min; free) start from the tourist office.

WALKS AROUND WINCHCOMBE

With access to the Cotswold Way as well as a host of lesser walks round and about, Winchcombe has set itself up as the **walking** capital of the Cotswolds. Take a look at the Ordnance Survey Explorer map covering the Cotswolds and you'll find Winchcombe hunched like a spider amid a web of trails reaching out on all sides. Aside from the **Cotswold Way** – see p.131 for a circular route to Belas Knap – there's the **Windrush Way** and **Warden's Way** (see p.95), both connecting Winchcombe to Bourton-on-the-Water; the **Gloucestershire Way** to Stow or Tewkesbury; and two long-distance routes heading north into Worcestershire, the 42-mile **Wychavon Way** and 59-mile **St Kenelm's Way**.

The dedicated website ⓦ winchcombewelcomeswalkers.com has full information. There you can download details of a circular walk (2 miles; 1hr) from Winchcombe to Sudeley Castle (see p.130) as well as a scenic loop (5 miles; 3hr) through Spoonley Wood, two miles southeast of town. It starts in the same place as the Cotswold Way walk, by the war memorial on Abbey Terrace, opposite Winchcombe's church, but shortly after peels left to cross the grounds of Sudeley Castle and follow the contour of the hill to **Spoonley Wood**, site of a ruined Roman villa with a beautifully preserved **mosaic** *in situ*. From there, strike uphill to a farm track, which you can follow southwest, turning right at Cole's Hill towards abandoned Waterhatch Farm. The path then drops gently down to river level and wends its way back to Winchcombe.

Many other options exist for short, circular walks around town, including the figure-of-eight Winchcombe Way, comprising two pleasant countryside circuits outlined at ⓦ winchcombe.co.uk.

ACCOMMODATION

★ **Lion Inn** 37 North St ☎ 01242 603300, ⓦ thelion winchcombe.co.uk. A lovely contemporary inn in a renovated old building in the village centre, hosting seven freshly modern rooms, all of them en suite and done up with taste. **£100**

Sudeley Castle Cottages Sudeley Castle ☎ 01242 602308, ⓦ sudeleycastle.co.uk. It's not often you have the chance to stay on a royal estate. These eleven self-catering cottages, tucked into a corner of the grounds between Sudeley Castle and Winchcombe village, sleep three, four or five people. Some are modern, others are renovated from existing older buildings, all are simply and elegantly appointed. Prices vary greatly – a long weekend

in high season starts from around **£450**

Wesley House High St ☎ 01242 602366, ⓦ wesley house.co.uk. Rather classy small hotel wedged into a house where eighteenth-century preacher John Wesley stopped over, featuring five upscale rooms, individually decorated and immaculately presented. **£75**

White Hart High St ☎ 01242 602359, ⓦ whitehart winchcombe.co.uk. A good-looking old inn on the main street with wooden floors and benches to suit its cheerful atmosphere. Eight en-suite rooms are decorated in traditional-meets-folksy manner, and there are also three cheaper "ramblers" rooms with shared bath. **£70**

EATING AND DRINKING

Food Fanatics 12 North St ☎ 01242 604466, ⓦ food -fanatics.co.uk. Cheerful local deli in the middle of the village, well-stocked with local produce galore and also with a small coffee-shop section. Mon–Fri 8am–7pm, Sat 8am–6pm, Sun 10am–5pm.

★ **Juri's Tearoom** High St ☎ 01242 602469. Pop into this self-styled "Olde Bakery and Tea Shoppe" for an award-winning cream tea to remember (£16) in the rose garden, say, or the vine-shaded conservatory. Top quality cakes and sweet treats are baked onsite, there are fifteen varieties of tea, handmade scones – and Juri herself is Cordon Bleu-trained. Thurs & Fri 10am–5pm, Sat 10.30am–5pm, Sun 11am–5pm.

Lion Inn 37 North St ☎ 01242 603300, ⓦ thelion winchcombe.co.uk. This fifteenth-century ex-coaching inn has been thoroughly updated, now doubling as a contemporary, family-run village bolthole. The menu relies on seasonal local produce – duck and chicken terrine, or lamb

with parsnip puree, but also ventures into light, modern European styles for tagines or seafood dishes. Mains £13–17. Food served daily noon–3pm & 6–9.30pm.

Wesley House High St ☎ 01242 602366, ⓦ wesley house.co.uk. A highly acclaimed traditional restaurant – lamb, pan-roasted halibut, roast guinea fowl and the like (two courses £22) – in an airy, calm setting, alongside a more contemporary styled wine bar and grill (closed Mon), for tapas, burgers and risotto of the day (mains £11–16, or two-course lunch £11). Tues–Sat noon–2pm & 6.30–9pm, Sun noon–3pm.

Wine and Sausage At White Hart, High St ☎ 01242 602359, ⓦ wineandsausage.co.uk. A great place to eat. The speciality here is hearty British cooking, with a focus on sausages in gourmet varieties such as venison and red wine or pork and stilton, and other meaty mains (£10–20). Two-course lunch £10, or three-course meal for two with wine £50. Food served daily 8am–9pm.

Sudeley Castle

Winchcombe • April–Oct daily 10am–5pm • £14 • ☎ 01242 604244, ⊛ sudeleycastle.co.uk

Rising amid a magnificent estate on Winchcombe's southern edge, and surrounded by immaculate gardens, **Sudeley Castle** manages to combine ravishing good looks with a long and fascinating history. The Cotswolds may have more than its fair share of stately homes and grand country piles – but this is a genuine beauty. Spare Sudeley an afternoon, at least.

Brief history

Sudeley's royal history stretches back before **Domesday**: a Saxon manor house here was **Ethelred the Unready**'s wedding present to his daughter, Goda. The house or castle on the Sudeley site was destroyed during the reign of **Stephen**, though the family lived on: legend has it that **William de Sudeley**, son of the local lord in the early thirteenth century, was one of the four knights who murdered Thomas à Becket at Canterbury. The present buildings date chiefly from the mid-fifteenth century, when Ralph Boteler, a senior military commander under Henry V and Henry VI, was created the **1st Baron Sudeley** and set about building a castle to befit his status. He had precious little time to enjoy what became known as one of the finest properties in England: in 1469, during the Wars of the Roses, the new king **Edward IV** confiscated Sudeley. Boteler never saw it again. **Richard III** was the owner-resident for several years, and in 1535 **Henry VIII** spent a week at Sudeley with Anne Boleyn.

Sudeley's golden age centres on a few years in the 1540s. After Henry VIII died in 1547, **Edward VI** gave the castle to **Sir Thomas Seymour**, brother of Henry's third wife, Jane – and a legendary womanizer. His affair with **Katherine** (or **Catherine**) Parr, Henry's sixth and final wife, began as early as 1543; within six months of Henry's death, Seymour and Parr were married. Shortly thereafter they moved into Sudeley with a household numbering more than a hundred, including **Lady Jane Grey**, who was living under Seymour's protection, and Elizabeth Tudor, daughter of Henry VIII by Anne Boleyn. The calm was short-lived: Parr died at Sudeley in 1548 after giving birth to a daughter, Mary (whose subsequent life is a mystery – most historians believe she died young), and the political tide quickly turned against Seymour, who was executed for treason in 1549.

Sudeley remained in the spotlight. **Elizabeth I** stayed for three days in 1592, and during the **Civil War** Sudeley acted as a Royalist garrison, coming under repeated attack and eventually suffering near-demolition. The remains mouldered grandly, attracting the attention of **George III**, who fell down a crumbling flight of stairs on a visit in 1788. Katherine Parr's coffin was rediscovered amid the ruins in 1782, though it wasn't until more than fifty years later that John and William Dent, industrialists from Worcester, purchased the derelict estate and began what was, for the time, surprisingly sensitive restoration of the surviving Elizabethan shell. Emma Dent, a niece, continued their work, collecting antiques and Tudor furnishings for the castle and engaging in good works for the townsfolk of Winchcombe, which included funding new roads and a public swimming bath. The current owner, **Elizabeth Ashcombe**, wife of the 4th Baron Ashcombe, has lavished energy particularly on the castle **gardens**, which today have become as much of a draw as the castle itself.

The castle

From the **visitor centre**, paths lead on circuitous routes through the grounds, past a ruined medieval **tithe barn**, wildflower meadow and herb garden on the approach to the battlemented castle, its tall chimneys rising romantically above the trees. You **enter** via the original fifteenth-century west wing, where a series of rooms are given over to **historical exhibits**, from a collection of replica Tudor costumes and original lacework to stories of Henry VIII and a lock of Katherine Parr's hair. Drop into the adjacent **coffee shop**, housed in what was formerly the castle kitchens and now bedecked with heraldic banners – but the main reason to visit Sudeley is to spend time outdoors: appreciating the architecture and gardens as you stroll trumps the exhibition rooms ten times over.

DAY-TRIPS BY BUS FROM WINCHCOMBE

It's fairly straightforward to put together enticing day-trips into the Cotswolds countryside around Winchcombe by **bus** – though not on a Sunday, when these routes don't operate. From Winchcombe, bus #606 goes to Broadway for a couple of hours' break mid-morning, after which bus #21 can take you to Batsford Arboretum or Moreton-in-Marsh for the afternoon. The return journey retraces your steps. Alternatively, you could create a day-trip from Winchcombe to Cheltenham on bus #606, and then to Painswick on bus #46, again easily retracing your steps in the afternoon.

Art tour

Mon–Thurs 3.30pm • £10 extra • book before 1.30pm same day

If you can't get enough of Sudeley, special **art tours** offer guided visits to the Ashcombes' private apartments in the east wing, taking in the castle's grandest rooms, bedecked with Tudor finery as well as artworks by Van Dyck, Rubens and others.

The grounds

Behind the west wing, alongside the towering ruins of the Elizabethan **Banqueting Hall** – left romantically untouched during the Victorian restoration – explore the pretty **Knot Garden** and stroll through a grove of mulberry trees to reach the spectacular **Queen's Garden**, surrounded by yews and filled with summer roses. Alongside, presaged by the **White Garden** – an all-white array of passion flowers, roses, peonies, clematis and spring tulips – stands the Perpendicular Gothic **St Mary's Church**, rebuilt by George Gilbert Scott in 1863; inside, a rather beautiful Victorian tomb marks the final resting-place of Katherine Parr. Beyond, a **pheasantry** holds fifteen endangered species of pheasant from around the world, while in the far corner of the grounds, kids may be rather more entertained by a giant **adventure playground**.

Belas Knap

Always open • Free • ⓦ english-heritage.org.uk

South of Winchcombe, up on the eastern ridge of Cleeve Hill, the Neolithic long barrow of **Belas Knap** occupies one of the wildest – and highest – spots in the Cotswolds. Dating from around 3000 BC, this is the best-preserved burial chamber in England, stretched out like a strange sleeping beast cloaked in green velvet, 178ft long, 60ft wide and 14ft high. Its name derives from the Old English *cnaepp*, meaning hilltop, along with, most likely, *bel* meaning beacon, though some theorize a link with the Latin word *bellus* (beautiful).

The best way to get there is to **walk**, undertaking the two-mile climb up the Cotswold Way from Winchcombe. The path strikes off to the right near the entrance to Sudeley Castle; when you reach the country lane at the top, turn right and then left for the ten-minute hike to the barrow. Details of this route incorporated into a circular walk (5.3 miles; 4hr) to/from Winchcombe – also with a shorter variation (3.5 miles; 3hr) – can be downloaded at the Cotswold Way pages of ⓦescapetothecotswolds.org.uk. It's also possible to **drive** to Belas Knap; heading out of Winchcombe on the B4632, follow signs into a lay-by, then join the steep, narrow Corndean Lane up to a hillside pull-in where you can park for the short walk up to the site.

What you see first is the **false portal** on the north side, set back between two horned prominences – probably designed to put grave-robbers off the scent. Four other entrances around the barrow give into small **burial chambers** that would originally have held several bodies each. The views over the surrounding countryside are exceptional.

For an exhilarating, lonely drive, continue south on Corndean Lane, scuttling over the hills and through dense woods past **CHARLTON ABBOTS** to eventually join the A436 Cheltenham–Stow road near **ANDOVERSFORD**.

Cleeve Hill

Southwest of Winchcombe, the B4632 clings to the shoulders of the Cotswold Edge, offering stupendous views out towards Tewkesbury from the cliff-edge village of **CLEEVE HILL**, named for the expanse of grassed limestone which rears above. This is wild, windswept countryside: when Cheltenham, some 900ft below, is swathed in valley mists, the great rolling expanse of **Cleeve Common**, atop the ridge and speckled with wildflowers in season, can bask in glittering sunshine, rising to the **highest point in the Cotswolds**. The true summit – at 1,083ft – is a flattish area at the southern edge of the common; aim instead for the better views from the northern edge around what is dubbed **Cleeve Cloud**, at roughly 1,040ft, and easily reached by a stiffish walk up from a parking area near the golf course, signed off the B4632. See the Cotswold Way pages of ⓦescapetothecotswolds.org.uk for downloadable details of the **Cleeve Hill Common Ring**, a circular walk (6 miles; 4hr 30min) from the car park, with a shorter alternative (4 miles; 3hr), that takes in the best of the open hilltops and viewpoints.

3

The Vale of Evesham

A low-lying semicircle of Worcestershire defined by the River Avon, the **Vale of Evesham** – with a history stretching back to the thirteenth-century baron Simon de Montfort – is best known for **asparagus**. The area has been a centre of market gardening since the 1950s; today, besides its orchards of apples, cherries and plums, the Vale lies at the heart of the British asparagus industry, hosting thousands of migrant farm workers over the spring and summer months. Restaurants all across the region – and beyond, into the Cotswold hills – devise fresh asparagus dishes of all kinds throughout the harvest season of May and June. Watch for festivities around the **British Asparagus Festival** (ⓦbritishasparagusfestival.org), held each spring.

In Cotswold terms the Vale is fairly tangential. Despite some nice walks (and its own Plum Festival in August) Pershore to the northwest is too far-flung. The main focus is the old abbey town of **Evesham**, an easy day-trip from Broadway or Chipping Campden that can provide a refreshing blast of modern-day commerce. Make a circuit of it by stopping in at **Bretforton**, one of the loveliest of the villages.

Evesham

The A44 whisks you into **EVESHAM**, about six miles northwest of Broadway. Protected by a loop of the Avon, the town was once home to a huge Benedictine abbey, founded around 700 AD after a local swineherd, Eof, had a vision of the Virgin Mary (the town's name derives from "Eof's *ham*", or home). The abbey was almost completely destroyed in 1540 during the Dissolution – though what remains is impressive enough.

Abbey Park

From pedestrianized Bridge Street in the shop-heavy town centre, make your way through to the **Abbey Park**, where stand two churches and the surviving abbey bell tower. First is **All Saints' Church** (daily 9.30am–4pm), entered through a Tudor porch, with a Norman arch surviving in the west wall; the interior, though largely Victorian, includes the small sixteenth-century Lichfield Chapel off the south aisle, with some lovely fan-vaulting overhead. Across the lawns – originally where the abbey stood – looms the 110ft-tall **Bell Tower**, in Perpendicular Gothic style, elaborately carved and sprouting four tall pinnacles; you can walk beneath its central arch out to sloping riverside gardens beyond. Opposite All Saints stands **St Lawrence's Church** (daily 9.30am–4pm), also remodelled in the nineteenth century, though with older parts including, again, a fan-vaulted chapel in the south wall.

Almonry Heritage Centre

Abbey Gate • Mon–Sat 10am–5pm; March–Oct also Sun 2–5pm • Museum £5 • ☎ 01386 446944, ⓦ almonryevesham.org

Across the Abbey Park, beside the busy north–south Vine Street, stands Evesham's oldest building, the fourteenth-century **Almonry Heritage Centre**, which doubles as the tourist office. The centre includes a rather good **museum**, hosting displays on the abbey, Saxon burial jewellery and other elements of Evesham's history.

Battlefield Trail

ⓦ simondemontfort.org

Abbey aside, Evesham's other claim to fame is as the location of an epic battle in 1265 between **Simon de Montfort** and Prince Edward (later Edward I), which marked the victory of royalist forces over de Montfort's nascent baronial parliament. The site of the clash, a mile or so north of Evesham near Greenhill, now has a self-guided **Battlefield Trail** leading across the fields – see the website for details of how to walk it. A memorial to de Montfort stands in the abbey park, near the Bell Tower.

ARRIVAL AND DEPARTURE EVESHAM

By train Evesham is served by trains on the London–Oxford–Worcester line. The station is a ten-minute walk along the High St from the Abbey Park.
Destinations Charlbury (hourly; 35min); Kingham (hourly; 25min); London Paddington (hourly, 1hr 50min), Oxford (hourly; 40min); Worcester (hourly; 20min).
By bus Buses stop on the High St.
Destinations Broadway (Mon–Sat 5 daily; 25min); Stratford-upon-Avon (Mon–Sat hourly, plus 3 on Sun; 45min).

INFORMATION AND TOURS

Tourist office In the Almonry Heritage Centre (Mon–Sat 10am–5pm; March–Oct also Sun 2–5pm; ☎ 01386 446944, ⓦ eveshamtowncouncil.gov.uk).
Boat trips From Abbey Park (April–Oct every 30min 11am–4.30pm; £3.50; ☎ 07860 895416, ⓦ handsam boatcompany.co.uk).
Walking tours Guided town walks (May–Aug Tues 2.30pm; £1; 1hr; ⓦ eveshamvaletourguides.co.uk) start from the tourist office.

Bretforton

Around four miles east of Evesham, just off the B4035 (which goes on to climb to Chipping Campden), **BRETFORTON** is about the prettiest village in the Vale. Its **church of St Leonard** is of Norman foundation, with a fifteenth-century tower, but the reason to come this way is the wonderful old **Fleece Inn** alongside. One of only three pubs to be owned by the National Trust, it remained in the same family from around 1400, when it was built as a farmhouse, right through to 1977, when the last owner died. Duck to enter – and keep ducking: the rambling interior, largely unchanged from the fifteenth century, is barely believable, with its bowed beams, tiny old windows, cracked flagstones, high-backed settles, open fires with tin kettles – and, in one of the snugs, a pewter service that was reputedly Cromwell's. The old courtyard outside is the setting for the annual **Asparagus Auction**, usually held on Bank Holiday Monday at the end of May, when thousands pack in to bid for bundles of the choicest fresh-cut spears.

Bretforton is also known for **Spot Loggins** ice cream (ⓦ spotloggins.com), made on a nearby farm and available at the *Fleece Inn* as well as across the Cotswolds.

ACCOMMODATION AND EATING BRETFORTON

★ **Fleece Inn** Bretforton ☎ 01386 831173, ⓦ thefleece inn.co.uk. The beer is good in this ancient pub, and in recent years even the food has taken a step up in quality – now expect well-prepared hearty British cooking (mains £11–15) – but the main thing is the atmosphere. If you get stuck, they have one room upstairs for B&B – cosy enough, and en suite. Daily 10am–11pm. Food served Mon–Sat noon–2.30pm & 6.30–9pm, Sun noon–4pm & 6.30–8.30pm. **£98**

Stratford-upon-Avon and the Feldon

COMPTON VERNEY

Stratford-upon-Avon and the Feldon

Just beyond the Cotswolds' northernmost limit, Stratford-upon-Avon has gained worldwide fame for its associations with England's national poet, William Shakespeare – historical (Shakespeare was born here), architectural (the town is full of Elizabethan and Jacobean frontages) and cultural (you can watch world-class theatre here all year round). Whether you base yourself in Stratford, or visit for the day – despite the crowds – you shouldn't miss it.

Stratford lies a good ten miles north of what's normally considered as the Cotswolds. To the southeast, gentle hills line the Warwickshire-Oxfordshire border, offering views out over the flatlands of the **Feldon** which envelop the little-regarded market town of **Shipston-on-Stour**. There's some pleasant walking and cycling, but of more interest are the unusually good fine-art collections and exhibitions at **Compton Verney**.

Stratford-upon-Avon

Despite its worldwide fame, **STRATFORD-UPON-AVON** is at heart an unassuming market town with an unexceptional pedigree. Its first settlers forded, and later bridged, the River Avon, and developed commercial links with the farmers who tilled the surrounding flatlands. A charter for Stratford's weekly market – a tradition continued to this day – was granted in the twelfth century, and the town later became an

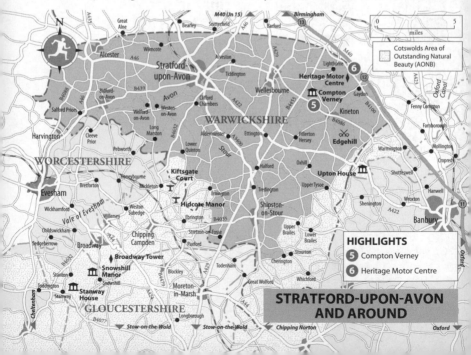

HIGHLIGHTS
5 Compton Verney
6 Heritage Motor Centre

STRATFORD-UPON-AVON
AND AROUND

HERITAGE MOTOR CENTRE

Highlights

❶ **Royal Shakespeare Company** Take in a world-class production of a Shakespeare play: it's neither as expensive, nor as inaccessibly high-brow as you might think. **See p.139**

❷ **MAD Museum** Rather fun collection of clanking kinetic sculptures in this quirky town-centre museum. **See p.141**

❸ **Holy Trinity Church** This beautiful old church in meadows by the River Avon is the Bard's final resting-place. **See p.143**

❹ **Stratford farmers' market** Stratford's fortnightly farmers' market is one of the region's best, a jovial introduction to town life amid the tourism. **See p.147**

❺ **Compton Verney** A modern, inspiring art gallery set in a fine country house outside Stratford, also with a good restaurant, and beautiful grounds to explore. **See p.148**

❻ **Heritage Motor Centre** Heaven for petrolheads – a well-presented collection of vintage Jaguars, Land Rovers and other vehicles. **See p.149**

HIGHLIGHTS ARE MARKED ON THE MAPS ON P.136 & P.138

important stopping-off point for stagecoaches between London, Oxford and the north. Like all such places, Stratford had its clearly defined class system; John and Mary **Shakespeare** occupied the middle rank, and would have been forgotten long ago had their third child, **William**, not turned out to be the greatest writer ever to use the English language.

A consequence of their good fortune is that this picturesque little town is nowadays all but smothered by package-tourist hype: in summer, its central streets groan under the weight of thousands of tourists, all seemingly trying to get into the **Birthplace Museum** at the same time. Don't let that deter you: Stratford still has the ability to surprise and delight, whether in the excellence of some of its restaurants, the gentle river views beside **Holy Trinity Church** or, most notably, in the world-class drama on offer. The revamped **Royal Shakespeare Theatre** is a beauty, but its smaller neighbour the **Swan** is, perhaps, even better: watching Shakespeare (or anything else) in this Elizabethan-style wooden galleried theatre, famous actors performing virtually within touching distance, is a memorable Stratford experience. Book well ahead for it.

Spreading back from the River Avon, Stratford's **town centre** is flat and compact, filling out a simple gridiron two blocks deep and four blocks long. The main drags are Bridge Street, Wood Street and High Street (all shopping), Sheep Street (restaurants) and pedestrianized Henley Street (terrace cafés and Shakespeariana). All of the town's key attractions are dotted nearby, including **Shakespeare's Birthplace**, **Hall's Croft** and **Nash's House/New Place**, all three of which are managed by the Shakespeare Birthplace Trust. The other star turns are set amid gardens on the banks of the Avon – the theatres of the **Royal Shakespeare Company** (RSC) in the centre and, further

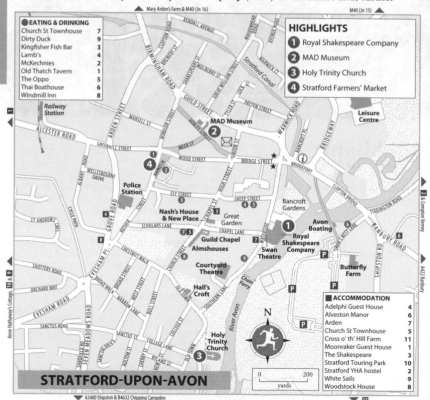

4

●EATING & DRINKING

Church St Townhouse	7
Dirty Duck	9
Kingfisher Fish Bar	3
Lamb's	4
McKechnies	2
Old Thatch Tavern	1
The Oppo	5
Thai Boathouse	6
Windmill Inn	8

HIGHLIGHTS

1. Royal Shakespeare Company
2. MAD Museum
3. Holy Trinity Church
4. Stratford Farmers' Market

■ ACCOMMODATION

Adelphi Guest House	4
Alveston Manor	6
Arden	7
Church St Townhouse	5
Cross o' th' Hill Farm	11
Moonraker Guest House	1
The Shakespeare	3
Stratford Touring Park	10
Stratford YHA hostel	2
White Sails	9
Woodstock House	8

STRATFORD-UPON-AVON

south, **Holy Trinity Church**, where Shakespeare lies buried. There are two outlying Shakespearean properties to north and west: **Anne Hathaway's Cottage** in Shottery and **Mary Arden's Farm** in Wilmcote.

Bancroft Gardens

Spanning the Avon at more or less the point where a ford in Saxon times gave rise to the town's name, the multi-arched **Clopton Bridge** – paid for by Hugh Clopton, a Stratford boy who became Lord Mayor of London in 1491 – has carried traffic for more than five hundred years. It is still the main entry into Stratford from the east and south; pedestrians use the car-free **Tramway Bridge** alongside, which offers views of the nesting ducks and swans on midriver islands to left and right. Both lead to the canal basin, terminus of the Stratford Canal, a 25-mile link to the Avon from the Grand Union Canal further north which was completed in 1816 just before the arrival of the railways. The basin is usually packed with narrowboats – many on permanent moorings as cafés or mini-galleries – and all around are the lawns of the waterside **Bancroft Gardens**, a popular place to stroll or relax on the grass with an ice cream. By the bridge is the finely sculpted **Gower Memorial** of 1888 – a seated Shakespeare surrounded by characters from his plays – while near the middle of the park stands the elaborately spiky **Swan Fountain**, unveiled in 1996.

From here, two streets storm up into the centre of town: **Sheep Street** dead ahead, or parallel to the right is **Bridge Street**, lined with eighteenth-century facades – once coaching inns, now high-street stores.

Royal Shakespeare Theatre

Waterside • Mon–Sat 10am–7pm or so, Sun 10am–5pm • Tours: days and times vary; check website for details and booking; £6–10 •
☎ 0844 800 1110, ⊛ rsc.org.uk

Gazing down on Bancroft Gardens from the south stands the **Royal Shakespeare Theatre**. There was no theatre in Stratford in Shakespeare's day; the first hometown drama festival in his honour was held only in 1769, more than 150 years after his death, at the behest of London-based actor-manager David Garrick. Thereafter, the idea of building a permanent home in which to perform Shakespeare's works slowly gained momentum, and finally, in 1879, the Shakespeare Memorial Theatre was opened on land donated by local beer baron Charles Flower. After fire destroyed it in 1926, architect Elisabeth Scott won a competition to design a replacement; her cinema-like red-brick edifice, opened in 1932 and though elegant in parts, was later widely criticized as unsuitable. In the end, the building – which includes the adjacent **Swan Theatre**, created in the 1980s with a galleried Elizabethan-style wooden interior for staging "in-the-round" productions – was closed for a complete rebuild.

Unveiled in 2010 behind the curving 1930s facade (the only element of Scott's building to survive), the new theatre now incorporates a thrust stage bringing the actors and audience much closer together, vastly improved facilities linking the RST and the Swan for the first time, a landmark brick-built tower rising to one side, a rooftop restaurant and more. Historical flummery notwithstanding, Stratford's biggest draw is **world-class theatre**: if you do nothing else in the town, watch a play.

Drama aside, there are options almost every day (sometimes several times a day) to go behind the scenes on a **theatre tour** – including tours targeted at children, and ghost walks – as well as loads of public talks, readings and workshops.

Waterside chain ferry

Waterside • Easter–Sept daily 10am–5pm roughly every 15min • 50p

Beyond the Royal Shakespeare Theatre, you could stroll along **Waterside** past the famous *Dirty Duck* pub – or on the lovely riverside footpath through the Avonbank Gardens – to where a quaint little hand-operated **chain ferry** trundles across the river to more gardens on the other bank. It's a quirky way to reach the gardens and the Butterfly Farm on the east bank of the Avon (see p.143).

Shakespeare's Birthplace

Henley St • Daily: July & Aug 9am–5.30pm, April–June & Sept–Oct 9am–5pm, Nov–March 10am–4pm • Five House Pass £23.90 or Birthplace Pass £15.90 (see opposite) • ☎ 01789 204016, ✆ shakespeare.org.uk

Top of everyone's bardic itinerary is **Shakespeare's Birthplace**, located halfway along pedestrianized Henley Street. You enter via a modern visitor centre, whose displays poke into every corner of Shakespeare's life and times, making the most of what little hard evidence there is, filled out with clips from famous films and performances of Shakespeare's plays over the years.

Next door stands the heavily restored, half-timbered building where the great man was purportedly born – actually two dwellings knocked into one. The northern, much smaller and later part was the house of Joan, Shakespeare's sister, and it adjoins the main family home, which was bought by John Shakespeare in 1556 and today looks something like it would have done then. It includes a glover's workshop, where Shakespeare's father beavered away (though some claim that he was a wool merchant or a butcher), and a bedroom done up as a sixteenth-century birthing room, with cradle, washing-tub and toys – despite the fact that it is not certain that Shakespeare was even born in this building. The house has been attracting visitors for centuries regardless and upstairs one of the old mullioned windows, now displayed in a glass cabinet, bears the **scratch-mark signatures** of some of them, including Thomas Carlyle and Walter Scott.

You exit into the lovely **gardens**, where costumed actors perform excerpts from some of the more famous plays.

ROYAL SHAKESPEARE COMPANY PERFORMANCES

One of the world's leading theatre companies, the **Royal Shakespeare Company** had its roots in the Victorian ideal of a permanent troupe of actors based in Stratford, but the concept only came to fruition in the 1950s under the artistic directorship of Anthony Quayle and then Peter Hall. Today the company works on a repertory system: you could stay in Stratford for a few days and see three or four different plays – all Shakespeare if you like, but the RSC also produces work by Shakespeare's contemporaries as well as new writing and even the occasional musical.

The RSC's three stages in Stratford are the **Royal Shakespeare Theatre** and **Swan Theatre**, which form one building on the banks of the Avon, and the **Other Place** at the Courtyard Theatre, a temporary structure nearby on Waterside, where redevelopment plans are afoot.

Tickets (☎ 0844 800 1110, ✆ rsc.org.uk) go on sale months in advance, with prices ranging from £12 for restricted-view seats at off-peak times to more than £60 for the best seats in the house on weekend evenings. Young people aged 16–25 qualify for £5 tickets at all performances, and there are also discounts for families and people over 60. Occasionally, students and those under 25 or over 60 can pick up **standby tickets** in person on the day of performance – and it's always worth asking at the theatre about **returns** – but don't rely on it. Always plan ahead.

TICKETS FOR THE SHAKESPEARE HOUSES

There are **five historic houses** connected with Shakespeare that are open to the public in and around Stratford. Three are in the town centre – the Birthplace, Hall's Croft and Nash's House/New Place – and two more, Anne Hathaway's Cottage and Mary Arden's Farm, are on the outskirts. All five are owned and run by the **Shakespeare Birthplace Trust** (☎01789 204016, ⓦ shakespeare.org.uk). Rather than individual tickets, you have to buy a **Five House Pass** for all five properties (£23.90) – or there's a **Birthplace Pass** for the three in the town centre (£15.90). Both are valid for a year, and include access to Shakespeare's grave in Holy Trinity Church. Discounts apply for families. Either buy direct from the trust – online or in person at any of the five houses – or look out for discount deals in combination with tickets for other attractions around town.

MAD Museum

4 Henley St • Daily 10.30am–5.30pm; Oct–March closes 5pm • £6.80 • ☎01789 269356, ⓦ themadmuseum.co.uk

If you've got kids in tow – or just if you need a break from Stratford's relentlessly Bardic tourism – duck into the charming **MAD Museum**. Although undoubtedly a bit dotty, the museum is named for "Mechanical Art and Design": it's packed with whirring, trundling, creaking examples of kinetic sculpture – bits of metal and other stuff intricately formed into pointless machines that do nothing except please and fascinate.

High Street

Stratford's **High Street** is lined picturesquely with Tudor buildings but shamelessly devoted to modern commerce, with familiar brand names on both sides. Partway along, beside the crooked *Garrick Inn*, stands **Harvard House**, an elaborate half-timbered building which may be flying the Stars and Stripes: John Harvard, grandson of the original owners, studied at Cambridge University before emigrating to America in 1637 and founding a seat of learning in Cambridge, Massachusetts which still bears his name. The house (administered by the Birthplace Trust) was closed at the time of writing with no plans for reopening.

Nash's House and New Place

Chapel St • Closed at the time of writing • Formerly: March–Oct daily 10am–5pm, Nov–March 11am–4pm • Formerly: Five House Pass £23.90 or Birthplace Pass £15.90 (see above) • ☎01789 204016, ⓦ shakespeare.org.uk

Along Chapel Street, with the Guild Chapel in view dead ahead, is another Birthplace Trust property, **Nash's House and New Place**, closed at the time of writing for complete renovation, with reopening planned for 2016. Expect some changes from the account given here.

Once the property of Thomas Nash, first husband of Shakespeare's granddaughter, Elizabeth Hall, the house's ground floor is kitted out with a pleasant assortment of period furnishings. Upstairs, one display provides a potted history of Stratford, including a scattering of archeological bits and pieces, and another focuses on the house with a cabinet of wood-carvings made from the **mulberry tree** that once stood outside. Reputedly planted by Shakespeare, the tree was chopped down in the 1750s by the owner, a certain Reverend Francis Gastrell, who was fed up with all the tourists. An enterprising woodcarver bought the wood and carved Shakespearean mementoes from it – hence the carvings in the cabinet.

The adjacent **gardens** contain the foundations of **New Place**, Shakespeare's last residence, which was demolished by the same Reverend Gastrell, but for different reasons: he was in bitter dispute with the town council over taxation. The foundations have prompted all sorts of speculation and queries that may be resolved by archeologists, who have been working here – and at the adjacent **Great Garden of New Place** – for several years.

Guild Chapel

Church St • Daily 9am–4.30pm roughly • Free • ☎ 01789 207111, ⊛ stratfordtowntrust.co.uk

Across from Nash's House stands the fifteenth-century **Guild Chapel**, whose chunky tower and sturdy stonework shelter a plain, though atmospheric interior enlivened by some simple stained-glass windows and elaborate **wall-paintings** above the chancel arch; they survived the Reformation under whitewash and were rediscovered in 1804 – but then virtually erased by ill-conceived "renovations". Only faint outlines survive today and it's almost impossible to tell what's what. The chapel had a new organ installed in 2014. Outside, the adjoining **King Edward VI Grammar School**, where it's assumed Shakespeare was educated, incorporates a creaky line of photogenic fifteenth-century **almshouses** running along the south side of Church Street.

Hall's Croft

Old Town • Daily: April–Oct 10am–5pm, Nov–March 11am–4pm • Five House Pass £23.90 or Birthplace Pass £15.90 (see p.141) • ☎ 01789 204016, ⊛ shakespeare.org.uk

Stratford's most impressive medieval house is **Hall's Croft**. The former home of Shakespeare's elder daughter, Susanna, and her doctor husband, John Hall, the immaculately maintained Croft, with its beamed ceilings and rickety rooms, holds a good-looking medley of period furniture and – mostly upstairs – a fascinating display on **Elizabethan medicine**. Hall established something of a reputation for his medical know-how and after his death some of his case notes were published in a volume entitled *Select Observations on English Bodies*. You can peruse extracts from Hall's book – noting that Joan Chidkin of Southam "gave two vomits and two stools" after being "troubled with trembling of the arms and thighs" – and then suffer vicariously at the displays of eye-watering forceps and other implements. The best view of the building itself is at the back, in the neat walled garden.

SHAKESPEARE: A LIFE

Other than the plays and sonnets he left behind – and even their authorship is disputed – very little about the life of England's national poet can be pinned down with certainty. From civic archives, it is known that **John Shakespeare** – described variously as a glove-maker, a butcher or a merchant in wool or corn – and his wife, **Mary** (née **Arden**), baptized their son, **William**, at Holy Trinity Church in Stratford on April 26, 1564. It's presumed that the boy was born in Stratford in the few days beforehand, but the date and location are unknown; it has long, though, been an irresistible temptation to place the birth three days earlier, on the feast day of St George, patron saint of England (April 23), in the Shakespeare family house which survives on Henley Street. William went to a local grammar school and, at the age of 18, married **Anne Hathaway**, a local woman almost eight years his senior. The marriage was a rushed affair: less than six months later, Anne gave birth to a daughter, Susanna, followed in 1585 by twins, Hamnet (who died at the age of 11) and Judith.

The trail then goes cold until 1592, by which time Shakespeare was in London, earning a high-profile reputation as a playwright and actor, drawing royal attention from Elizabeth I and, after 1603, her successor James I. His output in the 1590s and 1600s was extraordinary: 38 plays appeared in barely a decade. By 1597 he was clearly a wealthy man, purchasing New Place, an imposing mansion in central Stratford for himself and his family, even while maintaining a house in London. He also invested in the construction of London's Globe Theatre in 1599, where many of his greatest plays were first performed, including *Hamlet*, *Othello* and *King Lear*.

After around 1606 Shakespeare's writing tailed off and he seems to have retired from literary life, spending more time in Stratford than in London. He died on or about his 52nd birthday, on April 23, 1616, and is buried in Holy Trinity Church.

Those are the bare bones – and, in truth, they are of little interest. What Shakespeare did or didn't do hardly matters at all, considering the quality of what he wrote.

Holy Trinity Church

Old Town • April–Sept Mon–Sat 8.30am–6pm, Sun 12.30–5pm; March & Oct Mon–Sat 9am–5pm, Sun 12.30–5pm; Nov–Feb Mon–Sat 9am–4pm, Sun 12.30–5pm • Free; Shakespeare's grave £2 (free with Five House Pass or Birthplace Pass) • ☎ 01789 266316, Ⓦ stratford-upon-avon.org

By the war memorial at the foot of Old Town, a footpath leads to **Holy Trinity Church**, whose mellow, honey-coloured stonework dates from the thirteenth century. Enhanced by its riverside setting and flanked by the yews and weeping willows of its graveyard, the dignified proportions of this quintessentially English church are the result of several centuries of chopping and changing, culminating in the replacement of the original wooden spire with today's stone version in 1763. Inside, the nave is flanked by a fine set of stained-glass windows, some of which are medieval, and bathed in light from the clerestory windows up above. You'll see that the nave is quite unusually built on a slight skew from the line of the chancel – supposedly to represent Christ's inclined head on the cross. In the north aisle, beside the transept, is the **Clopton Chapel**, where the large wall-tomb of George Carew is a Renaissance extravagance decorated with military insignia appropriate to his job as master of ordnance to James I. But poor old George is long forgotten – unlike William Shakespeare, who lies buried in the **chancel**, his remains overseen by a sedate and studious memorial plaque and effigy added seven years after his death.

Butterfly Farm

Swan's Nest Lane • Daily 10am–6pm; March & Oct closes 5.30pm; Nov–Feb closes 5pm • £6.25 • ☎ 01789 299288, Ⓦ butterflyfarm.co.uk

Of the many other tourist attractions around Stratford – a brass-rubbing centre or wizardry show here, a Tudor museum or multimedia Shakespeare experience there – one of the loveliest, and the one most likely to appeal to parents and Tudor'd-out children alike, is the **Butterfly Farm**, across the river. More than 250 species of tropical butterfly roam a huge landscaped greenhouse, along with parrots and a South American iguana. Also explore the caterpillar room, "insect city" and "arachnoland", complete with black widows and tarantulas.

Anne Hathaway's Cottage

Shottery • Daily: April–Oct 9am–5pm, Nov–March 10am–4pm • £9.50 or Five House Pass £23.90 (see p.141) • ☎ 01789 204016, Ⓦ shakespeare.org.uk • Signposted footpath (1.3 miles/30min) from Evesham Place, off Rother St

Just over a mile west of the centre in the well-heeled suburb of **SHOTTERY** stands **Anne Hathaway's Cottage**, Anne's home before she married Shakespeare in 1582. The cottage – actually an old farmhouse – is an immaculately maintained, half-timbered affair with a thatched roof and quaint little chimneys, its interior displaying a comely combination of period furniture, including a finely carved four-poster bed. The garden is splendid too, crowded with bursting blooms in the summertime. The adjacent orchard and **Shakespeare Tree Garden** features a scattering of modern sculptures and more than forty trees and shrubs mentioned in the plays, each with a plaque bearing the appropriate quotation.

Mary Arden's Farm

Wilmcote • April–Oct daily 10am–5pm • £12.50 or Five House Pass £23.90 (see p.141) • ☎ 01789 204016, Ⓦ shakespeare.org.uk • Free parking; also reachable on the City Sightseeing tour bus (see p.145)

The final piece in the Shakespeare properties jigsaw is **Mary Arden's Farm**, three miles northwest of the town centre in the village of **WILMCOTE**. Mary was Shakespeare's mother and the only unmarried daughter of her father, Robert, at the time of his death in 1556. Unusually for the period, Mary inherited the house and land, thus becoming one of the neighbourhood's most eligible women – John Shakespeare, eager for self-improvement, married her within a year. The site covers several acres, taking in

TRIPS INTO THE COTSWOLDS

From Stratford the most direct **driving route** into the Cotswolds is the B4632 via Mickleton (see p.119), which lies at the foot of the scarp within easy reach of Broadway and Chipping Campden. On the way, near **Upper Quinton**, you'll pass the **Lower Clopton farm shop** (Tues–Fri 9.30am–5pm, Sat 8.30am–4.30pm; ☎01386 438236, ☒lowerclopton.co.uk) – impressively well stocked, also with short nature trails leading up to a scenic picnic area on Meon Hill.

A COTSWOLDS DAY-TRIP BY BUS

If you're based in Stratford, it's straightforward to use bus #21/22 (linked routes: Mon–Sat approx hourly) for a Cotswolds **day-trip by bus**. A departure around 9am would give you a couple of hours mid-morning in either Broadway (see p.119) or Blockley (see p.106), depending on your taste, from either of which you can be in Chipping Campden (see p.112) for lunch, returning to Stratford around 6 or 7pm.

the Arden house, a well-furnished example of an Elizabethan farmhouse, as well as neighbouring Palmer's Farm, outbuildings, nature trails and fields where longhorn cattle and Cotswold sheep graze. Costumed re-enactments of what life on a Tudor farm might have been like enhance your wanderings.

ARRIVAL AND GETTING AROUND   STRATFORD-UPON-AVON

BY TRAIN

Stratford-upon-Avon's sleepy railway station is on the western edge of town, ten minutes' walk from the centre, served by Chiltern Railways from London Marylebone, and London Midland trains from Birmingham Moor St. On both routes Stratford is the end of the line.
Destinations Banbury (5 daily; 1hr); Birmingham Moor St (hourly; 40min); London Marylebone (6–8 daily; 2hr).

BY BUS

Buses are plentiful, except on Sundays. Most arrive and depart from the lower (eastern) end of Bridge St. If you're coming direct from Oxford or Cheltenham, the train is a bit long-winded: your best bet may be a National Express long-distance coach, all of which pull into the Riverside bus station, on the east side of the town centre, off Bridgeway.
Destinations Banbury (Mon–Sat every 2hr; 1hr 10min); Blockley (Mon–Sat every 1–2hr; 1hr); Bourton-on-the-Hill (Mon–Sat every 1–2hr; 1hr 5min); Broadway (Mon–Sat 3 daily; 50min); Chipping Campden (Mon–Sat every 1–2hr; 35min); Chipping Norton (4 daily; 45min); Evesham (Mon–Sat hourly, 3 on Sun; 45min); Moreton-in-Marsh (Mon–Sat every 1–2hr; 1hr 10min); Shipston-on-Stour (Mon–Sat hourly, Sun every 2hr; 25min).

BY CAR

Stratford lies about an hour's drive from both Oxford and Cheltenham. The often busy town-centre car parks cost

about £10 for 24 hours.

Park and ride Stratford has two park and ride options. Bishopton Park and Ride (Mon–Sat 7.30am–11.30pm; April–Sept also Sun 9.30am–7.30pm; ☎01926 412929, ☒warwickshiretravel.co.uk) is about a mile north of the centre by the A46/A3400 roundabout, beside Stratford Parkway rail station. Parking is free and buses run into town every 10–15 minutes (£2 return). Rosebird Park and Ride (Mon–Sat 7am–7pm; ☎01564 797070, ☒rosebird centreparkandride.co.uk) is south of town, by the A3400/ B4632 roundabout. Parking is free and buses go every half-hour (£1.70 return).

BY TAXI

There are taxi ranks at the railway station, Bridge St and elsewhere around town. Otherwise try Main Taxis (☎01789 414514, ☒maintaxis.co.uk) or A1 Taxis (☎01789 433444, ☒a1taxitravel.com).

BY BIKE

Stratford Bike Hire (☎07711 776340, ☒stratfordbikehire .com) has bikes for rent from £15/day, including helmet, locks and repair kit – and they will deliver and collect free of charge within six miles around Stratford. Child bikes and trailers are available, and they also offer discounts on admission to all five Shakespeare properties, as well as details of a self-guided nine-mile cycle trail that links them.

INFORMATION

Tourist office Bridgefoot (Mon–Sat 9am–5.30pm, Sun 10am–4pm; ☎01789 264293, ☒discover-stratford.com). As well as booking accommodation (£5 fee), they have

discounted tickets for the Shakespeare houses, MAD Museum, boat trips and other attractions.

ACCOMMODATION

With the quantity of visitors passing through, Stratford has loads of accommodation options – but quality standards aren't always focused on encouraging repeat business. There are lots of chain hotels offering bland interiors, impersonal service and ho-hum food – obvious ones, in hulking modern blocks, but also secret ones, hidden away behind alluringly half-timbered facades in the centre, or masquerading as country houses out of town. Looks may deceive. Note that in the peak summer months and during the Shakespeare's Birthday celebrations around April 23 (ⓦ shakespearesbirthday.org.uk), it's essential to book ahead.

HOTELS

Alveston Manor Clopton Bridge ⓣ 01789 205478, ⓦ macdonaldhotels.co.uk. Although chiefly a hotel for weddings and events, this chain property can double as an undemanding leisure option, offering a wide choice of traditionally styled rooms. The convenience of the location, set back in private grounds away from the tourist maelstrom, but only a short stroll over the river from the town centre, is a deciding factor. **£126**

Arden Waterside ⓣ 01789 298682, ⓦ theardenhotel stratford.com. Owned by the RSC and located in prime central position, directly opposite the theatres, this extremely fancy boutique hotel oozes contemporary elegance throughout, from spacious suites with luxurious fabrics and marble bathrooms to the Champagne Bar and waterfront brasserie. Very posh, very formal – yet booking ahead could net a discounted deal. Sister property to the *Kings* hotel in Chipping Campden. **£190**

★**Church Street Townhouse** 16 Church St ⓣ 01789 262222, ⓦ churchstreettownhouse.com. A pretty little independent boutique hotel in two adjacent buildings in the town centre – one dating from 1768, with a Victorian

---

STRATFORD-UPON-AVON TOURS

A city as heavily touristed as Stratford has loads of options for tours, both within the city and further afield. The popularity of all these means it's a good idea to book in advance.

ON FOOT

The two-hour **Stratford Town Walk** starts from the fountain in Bancroft Gardens on Waterside (Mon–Thurs 11am, Fri 2pm, Sat & Sun 11am & 2pm; £5; ⓣ 07855 760377, ⓦ stratfordtownwalk .co.uk). The same guides also do a **Ghost Walk** (Mon & Thurs–Sat 7.30pm; £6), starting from the same place. Another costumed caper is the **Shakespeare Walking Tour**, led by the Bard himself (mid-Jan to Nov Sat 2pm; £5; ⓣ 01789 298070, ⓦ falstaffexperience.co.uk), starting from the Falstaff Experience Tudor World, 40 Sheep St.

BY BOAT

For boat trips on the Avon, **Bancroft Cruisers** runs a continuous cycle of 45-minute cruises from their landing stage by the *Holiday Inn*, near the tourist office (daily 10.30am–5.30pm; shorter hours in winter; £5.50; ⓣ 01789 269669, ⓦ bancroftcruisers.co.uk). **Avon Boating** has forty-minute cruises departing about every twenty minutes from their landing stage at Bancroft Gardens by the Royal Shakespeare Theatre (April–Oct daily 10.30am–5.30pm; £5.50; ⓣ 01789 267073, ⓦ avon-boating.co.uk). For both, there's no need to book: just turn up and board. Avon Boating also rents rowing boats, punts and canoes (£5/hr) and small motor boats (£30/hr). Once a month (March–Sept) you can book for Bancroft Cruisers' Saturday-evening **Ghost Cruise** (£12; ⓣ 07855 760377, ⓦ stratfordtownwalk.co.uk) – a chug along the river with spooky stories and an onboard bar; check online for dates and booking.

BY OPEN-TOP BUS

City Sightseeing runs a one-hour open-top **bus tour** (April–Oct every 15–30mins; first bus 9.30am, last bus Aug 5.30pm, May–July & Sept 5pm, April & Oct 4pm; ⓣ 01789 412680, ⓦ www.city sightseeing-stratford.com), which starts on Bridgefoot and has stops all round the town centre, including at Anne Hathaway's Cottage and Mary Arden's Farm. A hop-on-hop-off ticket is £13 (valid 24hr) or £19.50 (valid 48hr). Family discounts are available, and they also sell **discounted tickets** for other attractions, including the Shakespeare properties and river cruises; details on the website.

BY TRAIN

The **Shakespeare Express** (ⓣ 0121 708 4960, ⓦ shakespeareexpress.com) is a historic steam-train excursion between Stratford and Birmingham Snow Hill. It runs every Sunday in summer (July to early Sept), departing Stratford around 12.30pm, arriving back just after 3pm. The return trip costs £15, or £55 in Premier Class including lunch served onboard.

4

CYCLING AROUND STRATFORD

The fairly flat countryside around Stratford is ideal for **cycling** – and Stratford has a great bike hire shop (see p.144). A five-mile stretch of disused railway between Stratford and Long Marston is now the **Stratford Greenway** (see ⓦ stratfordbikehire.com for details), a surfaced path for walkers and cyclists with *Carriages Café* (ⓦ carriagescafe.co.uk), an old converted railway carriage, offering refreshments partway along at Milcote. At Long Marston, you can turn round and retrace your route, or continue onwards to make a day of it – the Greenway forms part of the Sustrans **National Route 5**, which runs on for 25 miles through Shipston to Banbury, from where trains bring you back to Stratford. Alternatively, you could combine the Greenway with village routes back to Stratford to form a roughly twelve-mile circuit – details at ⓦ www.warwickshire.gov.uk/cycling. Also check with **Cotswold Cycling Tours** (ⓣ01789 721108, ⓦ cycling-tours.org.uk), based in Lower Quinton south of Stratford, for ideas about countryside rides up to Chipping Campden.

facade and high ceilings, the other of seventeenth-century origin with gnarled oak beams. The lobby and reception decor may be a touch glitzy for some, but the twelve bedrooms are more restrained – nonetheless with super-kingsize beds, feature headboards, rainfall showers and complimentary port and shortbread in every room. The owners – two sharp Stratford businesswomen – know the value of good service: expect a warm welcome. Minimum two-night stay Fri & Sat. **£110**

The Shakespeare Chapel St ⓣ01789 294997, ⓦ mercure.com. Now part of a chain, this distinctive old hotel bang in the centre of town, with its mullioned windows and half-timbered Tudor facade, is one of Stratford's best known. The interior has retained its low beams and open fires in a fairly successful amalgamation of old and new, and the corporate atmosphere – though present in the public areas and most of the rooms – isn't quite as intrusive as at many of its competitors. Plump, if you can, for a four-poster suite. **£129**

B&B

Adelphi Guest House 39 Grove Rd ⓣ01789 204469, ⓦ adelphi-guesthouse.com. Relaxed, cosy B&B in a good-looking Victorian townhouse a short walk from the centre. The owners have accumulated all sorts of interesting bric-à-brac – from vintage theatre posters to ornate lamp stands – and (bar a small single) the six guest rooms are all en suite. The best room, which comes complete with a four-poster bed and views, is in the attic. Delicious home-cooked breakfasts too. **£80**

Cross o' th' Hill Farm Clifford Lane ⓣ01789 204738, ⓦ cross-o-th-hill-farm.com. Once you've mastered the name, this is a lovely, quiet B&B option, at a farm located up a lane off the Shipston Rd a mile or two southeast of the town centre, easily walkable. The atmosphere is quiet, rural and relaxed, amid meadows and pasture, and the interior style matches up – easygoing contemporary, with a minimum of clutter, while the food is either home-grown or sourced locally. No credit cards. **£96**

Moonraker Guest House 40 Alcester Rd ⓣ01789 268774, ⓦ moonrakerhouse.com. This well maintained place, in a large suburban house, has seven en-suite guest rooms, each decorated in smart modern-meets-period style (canopied beds, mini-chandeliers and so forth). Great breakfasts, too – either full English or vegetarian. Just beyond the railway station, about half a mile west of the centre. **£80**

White Sails 85 Evesham Rd ⓣ01789 550463, ⓦ white-sails.co.uk. Very classy four-room B&B about ten minutes' walk west of the centre, with boutique-style airs and graces – smartphone dock, in-room espresso machine, Champagne-stocked minibar, all rooms en suite (king, superking or four-poster). Quality is excellent, from the cheery welcome onwards. **£100**

Woodstock House 30 Grove Rd ⓣ01789 299881, ⓦ woodstock-house.co.uk. A smart and neatly kept B&B five minutes' walk west of the centre. It has five comfortable bedrooms, all en suite, decorated in frilly modern style. **£80**

HOSTEL

Stratford YHA hostel Hemmingford House, Alveston ⓣ0845 371 9661, ⓦ yha.org.uk. Fine hostel occupying a Georgian mansion on the edge of Alveston, two miles east of Stratford on the B4086. It has dorm beds (around £18–22) plus doubles and family rooms, some of which are en suite, as well as laundry, cycle rental, parking, kitchen facilities and cut-price breakfasts and evening meals. Get there on foot or by bike: cross the Clopton Bridge and follow Tiddington Rd out of town. Stratford–Leamington buses #18/18A (daily) and #X15/X18 (not Sun) stop outside, as does Stratford–Banbury bus #269 (not Sun). **£35**

CAMPING

Stratford Touring Park Stratford Racecourse, Luddington Rd ⓣ01789 201063, ⓦ stratfordtouringpark .com. Decent, well-kept caravan and camping site by the racecourse, a couple of miles southwest of the town centre. Closed Nov–March. Pitches **£13**

EATING AND DRINKING

Stratford is accustomed to feeding and watering thousands of visitors: finding refreshment is never difficult. But many places are geared up to serve the day-tripper as rapidly as possible – not a recipe for much gastronomic delight. There is a scattering of notable **restaurants**, some of which have been catering to theatre-goers for many years. Most restaurants in the centre (Sheep St is lined with them) offer a **pre-theatre menu** between 5pm and 7pm, with prices for two courses around £11–14.

RESTAURANTS AND CAFÉS

Church Street Townhouse 16 Church St ☎01789 262222, ⓦchurchstreettownhouse.com. This choice small, well-placed hotel offers well-priced, high-quality food sourced locally wherever possible and presented with style, in a cheery, informal dining room that is far enough back into the town centre to catch more locals than theatre-goers. Mains £11–18. Daily 11am–10pm.

Kingfisher Fish Bar 13 Ely St ☎01789 292513. The best fish-and-chip shop in town. Takeaway and sit-down available – and only a five-minute walk from the theatres. Mon–Sat 11.30am–1.45pm & 5–10pm.

Lamb's 12 Sheep St ☎01789 292554, ⓦlambs restaurant.co.uk. Smart and appealing central restaurant with a solid reputation serving a mouth-watering range of stylish English and continental dishes in antique premises – beamed ceilings and so forth. Two-course set menu £14, other mains £12–19. Mon 5–9pm, Tues–Sat noon–2pm & 5–9pm, Sun noon–2pm & 6–9pm.

McKechnies 37 Rother St ☎01789 299575, ⓦmckechnies-cafe.co.uk. Great little independent daytime-only café beside the Market Place offering what's been voted as the best coffee in Stratford, as well as hearty all-day breakfasts and light lunches (around £10). Mon–Sat 8am–5.30pm, Sun 9.30am–4.30pm.

★**The Oppo** 13 Sheep St ☎01789 269980, ⓦtheoppo.co.uk. Universally shortened to "The Oppo" from its full name, *The Opposition Bistro*. Serves international cuisine in a busy but amiable atmosphere in pleasant old premises next door to (and with the same owners as) *Lamb's*. It's generally a lighter, easier-going option than its neighbour, with some slightly more adventurous options: dishes of the day, chalked up on a board inside, are good value at around £9–10, otherwise mains are £11–17. Mon–Thurs noon–2pm & 5–9pm, Fri & Sat noon–2pm & 5–11pm.

Thai Boathouse Swan's Nest Lane ☎01789 297733, ⓦthaigroup.co.uk. Informal, much-loved restaurant occupying an old boathouse on the river's edge just over the bridge from the town centre, serving up exquisite Thai specialities in a pleasant ambience – book ahead for a window table. Mains are £9–18 or go for a multi-course set menu (£23–31). Sun–Fri noon–2.30pm & 5.30–10.30pm, Sat 5.30–10.30pm.

PUBS

★**Dirty Duck** 53 Waterside ☎01789 297312, ⓦwww .dirtyduck-pub-stratford-upon-avon.co.uk. Properly the *Black Swan*, but this archetypal actors' pub, yards from the theatres and stuffed to the gunwales every night with a vocal entourage of RSC employees and hangers-on, was playfully renamed during World War II by American GIs camped nearby. Ales are served up in somewhat spartan, wood-panelled premises and there's a terrace for hot-weather drinking. A long menu encompasses pork sausages, beef and ale pie, fish and chips, steaks and the like; the food wins no awards, but it's decent enough and well priced (mains £8–15). Daily 11am–11pm or later.

Old Thatch Tavern 23 Greenhill St ☎01789 295216, ⓦoldthatchtavernstratford.co.uk. Popular, comfortable pub bang in the town centre, on the corner of the Market Place. It's the only thatched building left in central Stratford, with low-beamed ceilings and a good range of beers that attracts a mixed crew of tourists and locals. Mon–Sat 11.30am–11pm, Sun noon–6pm.

Windmill Inn Church St ☎01789 297687, ⓦgkpubs .co.uk. Four-hundred-year-old pub with rabbit-warren rooms and low-beamed ceilings. Many say they serve Stratford's best pints of cask ale, and the menu has had a brush-up in recent years – now worth a look. Nothing fancy, but unusually affordable (mains £6–11). Daily 11am–11pm.

STRATFORD FARMERS' MARKET AND FOOD FESTIVAL

Shakespeariana aside, Stratford is renowned locally – and across the region – for its excellent **farmers' market** (ⓦstratforduponavonmarkets.co.uk), held on the **first and third Saturdays** of every month 9am–3pm on Rother Street, by the American Fountain. It's a friendly, jovial glimpse of real life amid all the tourism, and a key point of regional contact – the most northerly market for brewers, bakers and cheesemakers from Oxfordshire and Gloucestershire, and the southernmost market for producers from Birmingham and the West Midlands. Look out, too, for late May's **Stratford Food Festival** (ⓦstratfordfoodfestival.co.uk), which runs alongside a weekend of racing at Stratford Racecourse.

DIRECTORY

Hospital Warwick Hospital, Lakin Rd ☎01926 495321, ⓦ www.swft.nhs.uk.

Markets General market on Rother St (Fri 9am–4pm; ⓦ stratforduponavonmarkets.co.uk). For farmers' market, see p.147.

Pharmacy Boots, 11 Bridge St ☎01789 292173, ⓦ boots .com (Mon–Sat 8.30am–6pm, Sun 10.30am–4.30pm).

Police station Rother St ☎ 101, ⓦ warwickshire.police.uk (daily 8am–8pm).

Post office 2 Henley St (Mon–Sat 8.30am–6pm).

The Feldon

Many of the attractions around Stratford-upon-Avon lie beyond the remit of a Cotswolds guide, most notably magnificent Warwick Castle, eight miles northeast. West of Stratford the B439 leads to **Evesham** (see p.132), while south of Stratford the A3400 Oxford road scoots across a region known as the **Feldon**. The name derives from an Old English term referring to land cleared for agriculture: this flattish farming country, ideal for pasturing livestock, fills much of southeast Warwickshire, very distinct from its counterpart – the forest of Arden, referred to by Shakespeare – which covers the northwest of the county.

The main attraction is the country-house art gallery at **Compton Verney**, though you could also divert to the **Heritage Motor Centre** – both lie midway between Stratford and Banbury. Routes south towards the old market town of **Shipston-on-Stour** introduce some quiet villages on the Cotswolds fringe.

Compton Verney

9 miles east of Stratford • Tues–Sun 11am–5pm • £7.25, or £13.60 including temporary exhibitions • ☎01926 645500, ⓦ comptonverney.org.uk

On the B4086 between Stratford and Banbury, signs mark **Compton Verney**, a surprising – and wonderful – oasis of fine art in the depths of open country. From the car park it's a short stroll through beautiful wooded grounds and across a fine Capability Brown-designed bridge, guarded by four lead sphinxes, to **Compton Verney house**. Originally built in the 1440s as the manor for an adjacent village, now gone, the house was extensively remodelled in the 1760s by Scottish architect **Robert Adam**. The owner who commissioned Adam, John Peyto Verney, also brought in **Capability Brown** to landscape the grounds. The family later fell on hard times, and eventually sold up in 1921; the house decayed quietly until purchased by a trust in 1993 with the express purpose of opening it to the public as an art gallery.

Theirs is a splendid achievement. The house itself – an imposing U-shaped mansion amid tree-shaded, lakeside lawns – has been beautifully restored: the galleries are light and airy, notes and artistic interpretation are excellent and there's a cycle of world-class **temporary exhibitions** throughout the year. The **permanent collection** starts on the ground floor with scenes from seventeenth- and eighteenth-century Naples, medieval German works and a room of British portraits. Upstairs are the Chinese galleries, with Neolithic pottery alongside colourful Ming-dynasty enamel and gilt, while the top floor is given over to a delightful collection of **British folk art** – teapots, shop signs, portraits of favourite livestock and scenes of everyday life from bare-knuckle boxing to tooth-pulling.

Afterwards, wander among the lime trees, cedars, yew and Wellingtonia, and stroll through a coppice to an echoing **ice-house**. An entertaining podcast of a walk through the grounds is downloadable at ⓦ talkingthewalk.co.uk. There's also a kids' woodland adventure playground, alongside a picnic spot.

ARRIVAL AND DEPARTURE   COMPTON VERNEY

By bus Bus #269 (Mon–Sat 2 daily) to/from Stratford (20min) and Banbury (45min). Note that the more frequent Stratford–Banbury bus #270 follows a different route that avoids Compton Verney.

By car Compton Verney is on the B4086 between Wellesbourne and Kineton, six miles from the M40 junction 12, and well signed on local roads. Parking is free.

EATING AND DRINKING

★**Compton Verney Restaurant** Compton Verney House ☎01926 645500, ⌨ comptonverney.org.uk. An unusually good place for lunch – risotto with local goat's cheese, ham hock terrine, grilled sea bass, and so forth (mains £8–11). There's plenty for kids, and good vegetarian options. They also do afternoon cream tea, and can pack a picnic for you to take into the grounds (£15). Tues–Sun 11am–4.30pm.

Heritage Motor Centre

Gaydon • Daily 10am–5pm • £12; Land Rover Experience £9 extra • ☎ 01926 641188, ⌨ heritage-motor-centre.co.uk

Directly beside junction 12 of the M40, **GAYDON** is car country. Aston Martin is headquartered here, as is the Land Rover brand, with a clutch of other famous automotive names in the vicinity: Banbury hosts the Prodrive and Marussia Formula 1 teams, Silverstone is just down the road, Lotus, Mercedes and Williams are nearby, Red Bull and Honda are in Milton Keynes, BMW Mini is based at Oxford – the list goes on.

From the motorway, signs direct you a mile north on the B4100 to the **Heritage Motor Centre**. A purpose-designed showroom occupying one corner of an old RAF base, whose runways now serve as a test track for Jaguar Land Rover's research team based alongside, this is an impressively laid-out evocation of the British car industry. The display floor includes a time-line of vehicles from 1896 to the present. You can be a passenger for a short Land Rover Experience driving demo over rough terrain (book ahead if you want to get behind the wheel yourself) and at bank holidays and over the summer the centre stages a variety of rallies and classic car events.

Halford and around

Just north of where the A3400 meets the arrow-straight A429 Roman road **Fosse Way** (see p.78) lies **HALFORD**. Almost everybody thunders past, but you could stop off to wander the lanes down into Halford village – tranquil, picturesque and lined with fine old cottages. Halford's old manor house has clung onto its Tudor façade, and nearby **St Mary's Church**, with elements of Romanesque and Norman design, a Gothic font and pre-Raphaelite stained glass, is bewitchingly still.

A little south, the over-neat village of **TREDINGTON** clusters around the tall spire of **St Gregory's Church**, which retains parts of the narrow windows of its Saxon predecessor high up above the nave, though most is fourteenth-century. A mile or so south a turning towards the estate village of **HONINGTON**, built around the grand seventeenth-century Honington Hall (no public access), crosses the River Stour at an elegant old limestone **bridge** of the same date, listed as an ancient monument.

EATING AND DRINKING HALFORD AND AROUND

★**Bell** Alderminster ☎01789 450414, ⌨thebellald .co.uk. Renovated eighteenth-century coaching inn five miles south of Stratford (and far from the crowds). There's a good deal of atmosphere in the bar, while the nine guest rooms have been done up well, in an appealingly flamboyant, upmarket contemporary style – plump for the top-floor suite and you get oak beams and a free-standing bath. The restaurant steps beyond the ordinary: try a starter of tikka-battered mackerel or cider-barbecue glazed pork, a main of fillet steak with crab or beetroot and asparagus risotto (£12–18) – quality is excellent and service warmly forthcoming. Mon–Wed 9.30am–3pm & 5.30–11pm, Thurs–Sun 9.30am–11pm. £95
Halford Halford ☎01789 748217, ⌨thehalford.co.uk. Big, sixteenth-century coaching inn on the A429 Fosse Way, now given a top-to-toe refit in thoroughly swanky contemporary country style. The bedrooms have feature walls, silky cushions and curious artworks to go with exposed

CLASSIC CAR RENTAL

If you've caught the classic car bug, contact The Open Road (☎0845 070 5142, ⌨theopenroad .co.uk), a firm based near Gaydon which specializes in **classic car rental** – anything from an MGB roadster (£150/day) to a 1970 Jaguar E-Type (£330/day).

beams and original fireplaces, while the restaurant is remarkably good, serving modern British food from Gressingham duck in plum sauce to gourmet fish and chips (mains £12–17). March–Dec daily 11am–11pm; Jan & Feb Tues–Sat 11am–11pm, Sun 11am–3pm. £75

Old Manor House Halford ☎01789 740264, ⓦoldmanor-halford.co.uk. Lovely option for B&B, in Halford village's sixteenth-century manor house, set in 3 acres of gardens sloping down to the River Stour. The three bedrooms are cosy and houseproud – all very tasteful and quiet. £100

Peacock Oxhill ☎01295 688060, ⓦthepeacockoxhill

.co.uk. Popular small pub on the Feldon flatlands midway between Stratford and Banbury, off the A422. Make the detour to eat – this is top-notch British locally sourced food, cooked properly and served without pretension from daily-changing menus. Mains £10–18, also with sharing platters for two and a range of £10 set meals. Food served Mon–Sat noon–2pm & 6–9pm, Sun noon–8pm.

Talton Mill Farm Shop Newbold-on-Stour ☎01789 459140, ⓦtaltonmill.com. Decent local farm shop and deli just off the A3400 south of Alderminster, selling a good range of local foods and condiments. Mon–Sat 9am–5pm, Sun 9.30am–12.30pm.

Shipston-on-Stour

ⓦ shipstononline.org

Purists will snort to see **SHIPSTON-ON-STOUR** even mentioned in a Cotswolds guide: not only is it in Warwickshire (not a Cotswolds county, according to some), but it lies in flatlands between the hills and also lacks the appearance and atmosphere of its Cotswold near-neighbours such as Moreton-in-Marsh, eight miles south, and Chipping Campden, the same distance west. On the other hand, if that doesn't bother you, this genial old town could make for a pleasant diversion away from the crowds. Shipston's unpretentious mood is set by its name, derived from the Saxon term *Scepwaeisctune*, or "Sheep-Wash Town": this is where local farmers gathered to dip their livestock in the river.

Sheltered beside a meeting-point of roads from four points of the compass, Shipston's little **High Street** is boxed in at both ends, giving it a cosy, enclosed ambience; erase the supermarkets and it could almost be Trumpton.

A few coaching inns survive – dodge the Georgian-fronted *White Bear* in favour of the attractively renovated *George*, or pop round the corner to the no-nonsense, seventeenth-century *Horseshoe* on Church Street, a step from **St Edmund's Church**, of ancient foundation but rebuilt in 1855.

You can download an entertaining podcast of a town **walk** at ⓦtalkingthewalk.co.uk – then lose yourself in the little tangle of lanes off the High Street.

The Brailes

ⓦ brailesvillage.co.uk

The B4035 climbs east from Shipston on its way to Banbury, fourteen miles distant. Three or so miles out of town you pass through the twin villages of the Brailes – first neat **UPPER BRAILES** and then, almost contiguous, **LOWER BRAILES**, dominated by the **church of St George**, dubbed the "Cathedral of the Feldon". It's a magnificent sight, set back behind an Edwardian lychgate, largely thirteenth- and fourteenth-century, with high clerestory windows, an elaborate Gothic east window and,

---

SHIPSTON SHOPS

Shipston is home to a surprising number of independent businesses: galleries, crafts outlets, haberdashers and, above all, food and drink. Sample award-winning **pork pies** at Rightons butchers, 16 Sheep St (ⓦrightonsofshipston.co.uk), and drop into the cheery **Taste of the Country**, 2 Market Place (ⓦtasteofthecountry.co.uk), which sells a wide range of local foods and fresh-baked breads – it would take a will of iron to glimpse the pile of home-made jam tarts in their window and walk on by. Sheldons, **wine** merchants of venerable vintage, offer **tours** of their Victorian cellars on New Street with wine-tastings (£20; ⓦsheldonswines.com).

SHIPSTON AND ITS VILLAGES BY BUS

With a bit of planning, it's possible to day-trip by bus between Stratford, Shipston and Banbury/Chipping Norton. You could use a sequence of departures on the linked **buses #50 and 50A** (hourly), leaving Stratford around 9am for a couple of hours in Shipston. Then use bus #50A (every 2hr) to reach Lower Brailes for the church and lunch at the *George Inn* opposite (☎01608 685788, ⓦthegeorgeatbrailes.co.uk), then continue on the #50A – visiting Broughton for the castle, if you match their opening days (see p.194), or Sibford Gower for a village stroll and a pint at the *Wykham Arms* (see p.196) – and finish up in Banbury (see p.184) at around 5 or 6pm. Stay overnight in Banbury, or jump on an evening train back to Stratford.

Alternatively, leave Stratford for a lazy lunch in Shipston, and then move on that afternoon on bus #50 (3 daily) to Chipping Norton (see p.170) – note that this is the only option on Sundays, when the #50A doesn't run.

Shipston has a network of scheduled once-a-week village routes (extending as far as Moreton, Banbury and Chipping Norton), served by private volunteer minibuses. Full details at ⓦ shipstonlink.co.uk.

unusually, three *sedilia* (medieval stone seats for officiating priests) surviving against the south wall of the chancel. East of Brailes, the road continues over Gallow Hill before eventually bumping its way down to Broughton Castle (see p.194) on the edge of Banbury.

The "**Cotswold and Feldon Cycle Route**" (map and notes downloadable at ⓦescapetothecotswolds.org.uk) links Shipston and Lower Brailes in a mostly flat fourteen-mile circuit. It initially heads south to **CHERINGTON**, where the modest *Cherington Arms* serves its own Cherington Ale, then continues to Brailes and between the fields back to Shipston, while an optional extra seven-mile loop (which includes some hill-climbs) heads out from Cherington via **WHICHFORD**, notable for its fine old Hook Norton pub *The Norman Knight* overlooking an attractively unkempt village green.

Stretton-on-Fosse and around

ⓦ strettononfosse.com

West of Shipton, once you cross the "Portobello Crossroads" – where the B4035 meets the A429 Fosse Way – you re-enter classic Cotswolds territory. The main draw hereabouts is Chipping Campden (see p.112) but before you cross the Warwickshire-Gloucestershire border you could detour south a mile or so to **STRETTON-ON-FOSSE**, a quiet village declared a conservation area for its historic Cotswold-stone cottages.

Nearby, picturesque **ILMINGTON** (ⓦilmington.org.uk), the highest village in Warwickshire, clusters around the lovely old **church of St Mary**, with its Norman belltower, oak pews carved by twentieth-century English furniture-maker Robert Thompson and the embroidered **Apple Map**, a copy of medieval maps showing the location of each of the village's orchards. Ilmington still holds **Apple Walks**, most often in October, where villagers gather to view the Apple Map and then ramble the nearby lanes to find each of the 38 apple varieties grown locally.

EATING AND DRINKING   STRETTON-ON-FOSSE

Plough Stretton-on-Fosse ☎01608 661053, ⓦstretton onfosse.com. Overlook the slightly cramped interior, with beer mugs hanging from the beams and a big inglenook fireplace: this friendly old pub – an independently run free house – has good beer, good food (around £10–15) and, more to the point, is closely bound into its local community. Mon 6–11pm, Tues–Sat 11am–11pm, Sun 11am–3pm.

Simple Suppers Farm Shop Ditchford Mill Farm ☎01608 650399, ⓦsimplesuppers.co.uk. Just south of Stretton-on-Fosse, between Todenham village and the A429, nestling beside the Knee Brook – a tributary of the River Stour – this family-run farm business has won national acclaim for its pork pies. Mon 9.30am–noon, Tues & Thurs–Sat 9.30am–5pm.

4

The Oxfordshire Cotswolds

BURFORD

5

The Oxfordshire Cotswolds

In Cotswold terms often playing second fiddle to Gloucestershire next door, Oxfordshire nonetheless hosts much that is most beautiful about the region – rolling, hilly landscapes chiefly given over to agriculture, crossed by ancient roads and dotted with equally ancient villages of honey-coloured ironstone. Oxfordshire's difference, if one can be discerned at all, stems perhaps from its position closer to the centre of national events. A key battleground throughout the Civil War, and tightly bound into the later rush of economic development – thanks, chiefly, to the canals and railways serving towns at the fringes of the high ground – Oxfordshire has long found itself serving as a trunk route for both ideas and conflicts moving between Birmingham and London. In truth the wider county has less to do with its academic city-capital than most observers suppose.

Royal patronage has also played its part. The ancient hunting forest of Wychwood once covered the hills northwest of Oxford: one of the county's most attractive small towns, **Woodstock**, developed as an adjunct to a royal hunting lodge nearby. That lodge, destroyed during the Civil War, was rebuilt in the eighteenth century as **Blenheim Palace**, a monument to the glory of the dukes of Marlborough and, in 1874, the birthplace of Winston Churchill.

But for the most part, highlights of what is now marketed as the **Oxfordshire Cotswolds** (⊚www.oxfordshirecotswolds.org) are rural. The fulcrum of the area is the titchy **River Evenlode**, which winds west–east from its source across the county border in Gloucestershire, past the lovely village of **Kingham** – tiny, but with a railway station offering direct Oxford/London trains and so replete with places to stay, eat and walk – around the remnants of the ancient Wychwood forest near **Charlbury**, also on the rail line, and onwards to meet the Thames. Its gentle valley, and the neighbouring valley of the **River Windrush**, offer charming Cotswolds scenery in spades, not least around photogenic **Minster Lovell**.

Within Oxfordshire's part of the Cotswolds Area of Outstanding Natural Beauty (⊚escapetothecotswolds.org.uk), there is a fairly well-developed rural infrastructure, which centres on the only significant town, **Burford** – pretty, but rather fancy and very busy. Burford is often cited as the "Gateway to the Cotswolds", but you don't really need a gateway. Opt, instead, to meander from pillar to post, getting as far away from main roads as possible – down, for example, to **Kelmscott Manor**, the remote farmhouse where Victorian designer William Morris developed his hugely influential "Arts and Crafts" ideas, or across to the hugely atmospheric Jacobean

BLENHEIM PALACE

Highlights

❶ Burford Busy, rather posh little town that slopes down prettily to a bridge over the River Windrush. **See p.156**

❷ Kelmscott Manor This isolated Thames-side farmhouse preserves superb Victorian Arts and Crafts furnishings in a memorably atmospheric setting. **See p.161**

❸ Minster Lovell A crumbling, ruined Jacobean manor house by a babbling river, straight out of central Cotswolds casting. **See p.164**

❹ Kingham Lovely Cotswold village that manages to combine ritzy pubs, fine views and great country walks. **See p.169**

❺ Chastleton House Perhaps the most rewarding stately home visit in the area – gloriously impressive Jacobean architecture offset by an endearing air of timeworn neglect. **See p.172**

❻ Rollright Stones This unsung, rarely visited, deeply evocative prehistoric stone circle stands alone in fields bang on the Oxfordshire-Warwickshire border. **See p.173**

❼ Blenheim Palace One of England's great stately homes, perched on the edge of the attractive small town of Woodstock, displaying taste and hubris in equal measure. **See p.177**

HIGHLIGHTS ARE MARKED ON THE MAP ON P.156

5

stately home at **Chastleton** and equally atmospheric standing stones at **Rollright**, both just outside the market town of **Chipping Norton**. Everywhere, of course, there are long, lonely **walks** to tackle and heart-warming village **pubs** to offer succour and refreshment.

Burford

Many visitors get their first real taste of the Cotswolds twenty miles west of Oxford at **BURFORD**, where the long and wide **High Street**, which slopes down to a bridge over the River Windrush, is magnificent, despite the traffic. The street is flanked by a remarkably homogeneous line of old buildings that exhibit almost every type of peccadillo known to the Cotswolds, from wonky mullioned windows and half-timbered facades with bendy beams through to spiky brick chimneys, fancy bow-fronted stone houses, and grand horse-and-carriage gateways. The tourist office has a free leaflet describing a **walk** around town, but you'd do just as well to take your chances and absorb the fluster of daily life – coach parties browsing at souvenir shops, BMWs disgorging immaculate women outside

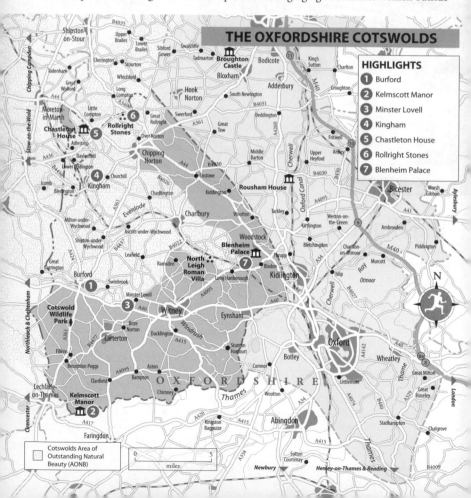

hair salons or interiors boutiques, country types chatting by family butchers… it's all very Cotswolds.

Tolsey Museum

126 High St • April–Oct Tues–Sun 2–5pm • Free • Ⓦ tolseymuseumburford.org

At the High Street's corner with Sheep Street stands a Tudor timber-framed building on stone pillars where traders once paid their tolls. This now houses the **Tolsey Museum**, exhibiting town maces, charters and old industrial artefacts, as well as a fancy doll's house, furnished in the style of the early nineteenth century.

St John the Baptist Church

Church Green • Ⓦ burfordchurch.org

Near the bottom of Burford's hill, where a row of sixteenth-century weavers' cottages stand by **Burford Bridge**, lanes cut through to the fascinating **St John the Baptist Church**, with architectural bits and pieces surviving from every phase of its construction, beginning with the Normans and ending in the wool boom of the seventeenth century. Very unusually, its clutter of mausoleums, chapels and chantries survived the Reformation. The most impressive **mausoleum** is that of Lawrence Tanfield, James I's Chancellor of the Exchequer, who lies on his canopied table-tomb with his wife, both decked out in their Jacobean finery. Even more striking, however, is the **funerary plaque** of Edmund Harman, Henry VIII's barber and surgeon, stuck to the wall of the nave and sporting four Amazonian figures, the first representation of Native Americans in Britain. It is unlikely that Harman met any, but rather he seems to have been linked to a Spanish company trading with South America. Outside, the **churchyard** is strewn with so-called "bale tombs", unique to the area, their rounded tops reminiscent of a bale of wool.

BURFORD

ACCOMMODATION
Angel 5
Bay Tree 2
Bull 4
Burford House 3
Lamb Inn 1

EATING & DRINKING
Angel 3
Bull 2
Huffkins 1
Inn for All Seasons 4

FARMERS' MARKETS

For details see Ⓦ tvfm.org.uk. Dates may change around Christmas and New Year. See also Ⓦ www.localfoods.org.uk.

Charlbury Quarterly on 2nd Sat 9am–1pm.
Chipping Norton 3rd Sat of month 8.30am–1.30pm.
Witney 4th Fri of month 8.30am–1.30pm.
Woodstock 1st Sat of month 8.30am–1pm.

5

THE LEVELLERS

A modern plaque beside the entrance to Burford church pays tribute to "three **Levellers**, executed and buried in this churchyard, 17th May 1649". Earlier that month, some eight hundred Roundhead soldiers in Cromwell's New Model Army – who had been fighting without pay and who were angry at their leaders' betrayal of the notion that all men possessed equal rights under the law – mutinied. These "Levellers", as they became known (from their desire to level out social inequalities), arrived in Burford on May 14. That night, Cromwell attacked the town with cavalry, seizing 340 of the Levellers and locking them in the church. One, Anthony Sedley, carved his name into the font (it is still visible). After 48 hours of incarceration, the supposed ringleaders – the three men named on the plaque – were dragged out into the churchyard and shot.

Burford now hosts **Levellers Day** (⊕ levellersday.wordpress.com) on the Saturday closest to May 17 every year, commemorating the Levellers' pre-socialist ideals with music, processions and debates on themes of social justice.

ARRIVAL AND INFORMATION
BURFORD

By bus The Oxford–Cheltenham bus stops by the A40 at the top of Burford; other buses stop on or near Burford's High St. **Destinations** Bourton-on-the-Water (1 on Wed & Fri; 25min); Charlbury (Mon–Fri 2 daily; 35min); Cheltenham (Mon–Sat 2–4 daily, 1 on Sun; 45min); Chipping Norton (Mon–Sat hourly; 30min); Kingham (1 on Wed & Fri; 20min); Minster Lovell (Mon–Sat hourly; 10min); Northleach (Mon–Sat 2–4 daily, 1 on Sun; 15min); Oxford (Mon–Sat 2–4 daily, 1 on Sun; 45min); Stow-on-the-Wold (1 on Wed & Fri; 35min); Witney (Mon–Sat at least hourly, 5 on Sun; 15min); Woodstock (Mon–Sat hourly; 50min).

Tourist office 33a High St (Mon–Sat 9.30am–5pm, Sun 10am–4pm; ☎01993 823558, ⊕www.oxfordshire cotswolds.org).

Walking tours Guided town walks (April–Sept Tues–Sun 10am, 11am, noon, 2pm & 3pm; rest of year Wed & Sun 11am & 2.30pm, Sat 10.15am, noon & 2.30pm; £5; 45min; ⊕ theburfordtour.com) start from the Tolsey Museum.

ACCOMMODATION

IN TOWN

Angel 14 Witney St ☎01993 822714, ⊕theangelat burford.co.uk. This sixteenth-century inn just off the main High St is particular renowned for its restaurant, but also has three en-suite guest rooms decorated in a pleasantly tasteful version of traditional style. **£90**

Bay Tree Sheep St ☎01993 822791, ⊕cotswold-inns -hotels.co.uk. First-class hotel in a lovely location off the High St, occupying a wisteria-clad stone house dating from the sixteenth century. Its twenty-odd rooms, in the main house and a couple of annexes, are done up in a distinctly lavish rendition of period character. **£180**

Bull 105 High St ☎01993 822220, ⊕bullatburford .co.uk. This venerable old inn on Burford's High St has been hosting guests for more than three hundred years – Charles II dallied here with Nell Gwynne, as did Lord Nelson with Lady Hamilton. It is known chiefly for its restaurant, though also has several traditionally styled rooms, some featuring dark wood panelling and four-poster beds. **£100**

Burford House 99 High St ☎01993 823151, ⊕burford -house.co.uk. Outstanding choice – a historic eight-room timber-framed townhouse hotel that makes an art of the personal touch. The owners, invariably on hand, are unfailingly courteous and have done a fine job with the interiors, retaining classic features but managing effort-lessly to refine and update. Memorably charming and comfortable. **£185**

Lamb Inn Sheep St ☎01993 823155, ⊕cotswold-inns -hotels.co.uk. On the same street as the *Bay Tree*, but a tad more traditional than its neighbour, from the bar's flagstoned floor up. Quality is exceptional, from the seventeen carefully presented guest rooms to the splendid gardens. **£160**

OUT OF TOWN

Swan Swinbrook ☎01993 823339, ⊕theswan swinbrook.co.uk. A mile or two east of Burford, on the banks of the River Windrush, this self-declared "boutique Cotswolds inn" offers plenty of peace and quiet along with a rather upmarket sense of style in its eleven bedrooms, lifted well out of the ordinary with contem-porary decor, modern-rustic bathrooms and – from five rooms – river views. Shooting day-packages draw weekending Londoners, but this remains an atmospheric hideaway nonetheless. **£120**

EATING AND DRINKING

Burford's dining is, in the main, posh. Aside from our recommendations here, other options within easy reach by car include at Filkins (see p.160), Southrop (see p.89) and Northleach (see p.93).

IN TOWN

Angel 14 Witney St ☎01993 822714, ⊛theangela tburford.co.uk. This old inn is a fine place to eat, highly regarded for its careful presentation and lively, creative menu – a madeira jus enlivening roast chicken, coriander and chilli adding zip to crab linguine, and so on. Mains £14– 18, or two-course set menu £18. Food served Mon–Sat noon–3pm & 6–9.30pm, Sun noon–4pm & 6–8.30pm.

Bull 105 High St ☎01993 822220, ⊛bullatburford .co.uk. A formal setting for memorable fine dining, grafting French and Mediterranean influences onto local ingredients – such as local pork done three ways in calvados – with particular emphasis on fish and seafood. The style might be a touch over-fussy for some, but there's no doubting the range and ability on display. Mains £16–21, with a cheaper bar menu. Food served Mon–Sat noon–3pm & 6–9.30pm, Sun noon–4pm & 6–9pm.

Huffkins 98 High St ☎01993 822126, ⊛www .huffkins.com. Legendary tearoom offering afternoon tea and cakes to remember. Also not a bad stop for lunchtime soup and salad and light bites (around £10). Mon–Sat 9am–5pm, Sun 10am–5pm.

OUT OF TOWN

Inn For All Seasons On A40, three miles west of Burford ☎01451 844324, ⊛innforallseasons.com. Known for its unusually wide range of Devon-sourced fish and seafood, alongside local venison, pork, lamb and so on, this pleasant pub restaurant on the main A40 road offers a slightly more down-to-earth atmosphere than many places in Burford, marked by an easygoing, unaffected service style. Mains £13–20. Food served Mon–Sat noon–3pm & 6–9.30pm, Sun noon–4pm & 6–9pm.

Swan Swinbrook ☎01993 823339, ⊛theswan swinbrook.co.uk. This fine country inn restaurant, once owned by the Dowager Duchess of Devonshire, the last of the Mitford sisters and who died in 2014, has a strong reputation for local, seasonal cooking with Mediterranean influences – chicken breast with a walnut pesto, saffron risotto, chorizo and bresaola. Mains £14–19. Food served Mon–Thurs noon–2pm & 7–9pm, Fri noon–2pm & 6.30–9.30pm, Sat noon–2.30pm & 6.30–9.30pm, Sun noon–3pm & 6.30–8.30pm.

Upton Smokery Upton Downs Farm ☎01993 823699, ⊛uptonsmokery.co.uk. One of the most celebrated Cotswold food producers, this family-run farm just west of Burford on the B4425 Bibury road specializes in smoked meats and fish, selling a wide range of their own products alongside other deli items from cheeses to jams in an onsite farm shop. Mon–Sat 10am–5.30pm, Sun 11am–2pm.

Cotswold Wildlife Park

Bradwell Grove • Daily 10am–6pm; Nov–Feb closes 5pm; last admission 90min before closing; miniature train April–Oct only; penguin-feeding daily 11am & 3pm • £14.50; miniature train £1 extra • ☎01993 823006, ⊛cotswoldwildlifepark.co.uk

Two miles south of Burford, the **Cotswold Wildlife Park** is a massively popular visitor attraction, drawing happy families by the thousand to see zebras and rhinos, gibbons and giant tortoises, lions, penguins and tarantulas – to name a few. Kids have a whale

---

RIVERSIDE WALKS BESIDE BURFORD

Two particularly lovely **walks** cover terrain on the banks of the River Windrush to either side of Burford; download maps and notes for both at the Car-Free Walks page of ⊛escapetothe cotswolds.org.uk.

West of Burford, for walk 5 ("Great Barrington–Burford"; 5 miles; 2hr) take bus #853 west along the A40 to the Lodge at **Little Barrington** (ask the driver for the right stop). From here walk down to the Windrush and cross to wander through **Great Barrington** before returning to the river and following a lane beside the meadows which eventually joins Sheep Street in Burford.

East of Burford, for walk 9 ("Villages of the Windrush Valley"; 4 miles; 2hr), take bus #853 east to the turning for **Asthall**; you approach the village, whose Elizabethan manor house was formerly home to the Mitford sisters, on foot. Over the Windrush, walk on into **Swinbrook**, where the twelfth-century church of St Mary has a monument showing six members of the Fettiplace family reclining comically on their elbows, the Tudor effigies rigid and stony-faced, their Stuart counterparts stylish and rather camp. Just before the church consider a refreshment stop at the *Swan* (see above). A stroll further brings you to **Widford**, a deserted hamlet of which only the isolated St Oswald's Chapel is left, in the middle of a field (built over a Roman villa), its fourteenth-century murals still discernible inside. A beautiful footpath along the Windrush takes you back into Burford.

A mile or so east of Swinbrook lies **Minster Lovell** (see p.164).

5

of a time, riding the **miniature train** around the park, petting the goats and letting off steam in the adventure playground. Best make a day of it: bring a picnic and laze the afternoon away on the lawns – but there's not much peace and quiet to be had, either way. Among other events, **penguin-feeding** happens daily.

Filkins and Broughton Poggs

Ⓦ filkins.org.uk

Around five miles south of Burford, and a couple of miles north of Lechlade-on-Thames (see p.89), the beautiful old honeystone village of **FILKINS** lies just off the main road, separated from its neighbour **BROUGHTON POGGS** by a trickle of water known as the Broadwell brook: in practice, they are one village. As well as the small **Swinford Museum** (May–Sept 1st Sun of month 2.30–5pm; free), displaying rural craft and agricultural tools, the village houses the **Cotswold Woollen Weavers** (Mon–Sat 10am–6pm, Sun 2–6pm; Ⓦ cotswoldwoollenweavers.co.uk), a shop, café and small textile museum attached to the studios of this upmarket designer, producing fashion collections in Cotswold wool as well as everyday clothing, rugs and home accessories. Stop in for a lunch to remember, either here at the *Five Alls* or a mile to the west at the *Swan* in Southrop (see p.89).

ACCOMMODATION AND EATING   FILKINS

Five Alls Filkins ☎ 01367 860875, Ⓦ thefiveallsfilkins .co.uk. After an extensive refit, this once-dowdy old village pub has been rejuvenated as one of the swankiest of Cotswolds country gastro-inns, drawing A-list celebs far out into the sticks. The food has won most plaudits, a contemporary rethinking of modern British cuisine, drawing in Italian influence and "turf to table" cool – starters of ciabatta or potted shrimps, mains of roast lamb with beans or French sausage stew, and puddings to die for. Mains £12–23, or opt for the cheaper bar menu. The rooms, as you'd expect, are all en suite, with comfy beds and art on the walls. Food served Mon–Sat noon–2.30pm & 6.30–9.30pm, Sun noon–3pm. **£120**

WILLIAM MORRIS AND THE PRE-RAPHAELITES

Socialist, artist, writer and craftsman **William Morris** (1834–1896) had a profound influence on his contemporaries and on subsequent generations. In some respects he was an ally of Karl Marx, railing against the iniquities of private property and the squalor of industrialized society, but – in contrast to Marx – he believed machines enslave the individual, and that people would be liberated only through a sort of communistic, crafts-based economy. His prose/poem story *News from Nowhere* vaguely described his Utopian society, but his main legacy turned out to be the **Arts and Crafts Movement**.

Morris's career as an artist began at Oxford, where he met **Edward Burne-Jones**, who shared his admiration for the arts of the Middle Ages. After graduating they both ended up in London, painting under the direction of Dante Gabriel Rossetti, the leading light of the **Pre-Raphaelites**, a loose grouping of artists intent on regaining the spiritual purity characteristic of art before Raphael and the Renaissance "tainted" the world with humanism. In 1861 Morris founded **Morris & Co** ("The Firm"), whose designs came to embody the ideas of the Arts and Crafts Movement, one of whose basic tenets was formulated by its founder: "Have nothing in your houses that you do not know to be useful or believe to be beautiful." Rossetti and Burne-Jones were among the designers, though Morris's own designs for fabrics, wallpapers and numerous other products were to prove a massive influence in Britain. The Laura Ashley aesthetic is a lineal descendant of Morris's rustic nostalgia.

Not content with his artistic endeavours, in 1890 Morris set up the **Kelmscott Press**, named after (but not located at) his summer home, whose masterpiece was the so-called *Kelmscott Chaucer*, the collected poems of one of the Pre-Raphaelites' greatest heroes, with woodcuts by Burne-Jones. Morris also pioneered interest in the architecture of the Cotswolds and, in response to the Victorian penchant for modernizing churches and cottages, he instigated the **Society for the Protection of Ancient Buildings** (Ⓦ spab.org.uk), still an active force in preserving the country's architectural heritage.

Kelmscott Manor

Kelmscott • April–Oct Wed & Sat 11am–5pm • £9 • ☎ 01367 252486, ⓦ kelmscottmanor.org.uk • From the car park it's a pleasant ten-minute walk to the house

Beside **KELMSCOTT** village, amid water meadows on the banks of the Thames, a small, relatively modest Tudor farmhouse was where author and designer **William Morris** created a country home from 1871 to his death in 1896. Its very simplicity is what attracted Morris, who wrote: "This is what I came out to see, this many-gabled old house built by the simple country-folk of the long-past times, regardless of all the turmoil that was going on in cities and courts…"

Built around 1600 by the Turners, local yeoman farmers, and now known as **Kelmscott Manor** – though it's not, and never was, a manor house – the house is enhanced by the furniture, fabrics, wallpapers and tapestries created by Morris and his Pre-Raphaelite friends, including Burne-Jones and Rossetti. It could easily fill a pleasant half-day. There is limited space, so admission is by timed ticket; it's wise to call ahead to confirm arrangements.

Inside, knowledgeable guides are stationed in every room. From the entrance passage, turn right into the **Old Hall**, once a dining-room and still with its original table and – flanking the fire – seventeenth-century oak chairs, alongside later chairs made by Morris. Further along, the **White Room** is a beautiful, light space dating from a 1660 extension, with Georgian panelling, a Morris *Millefleurs* tapestry woven in 1925 and, in the neighbouring closet, Rossetti's *Blue Silk Dress* (1868), a swoon-worthy portrait of Morris's wife, Jane. Highlights upstairs – among a delightful array of hanging textiles, portraits, original wallpaper and more – include **William Morris's Bedroom**, his four-poster bed bedecked with a pelmet painstakingly hand-woven with his "Verses for the Bed at Kelmscott" (1891):

The wind's on the wold
And the night is a-cold,
And Thames runs chill
Twixt mead and hill…

Beside is the lovely **Tapestry Room**, Rossetti's studio. Upstairs again, the simple **Attics** remain full of atmosphere; one displays a collection of Morris textiles. You return to the ground-floor **Old Kitchen** and out into the **gardens**. Despite the house's popularity – it's always busy – the charm and atmosphere of Morris's Arts and Crafts aesthetic come through loud and clear: this is a house to be happy in.

ACCOMMODATION AND EATING   KELMSCOTT

Plough Kelmscott ☎ 01367 253543, ⓦ theploughinn kelmscott.com. On the short walk through Kelmscott village between the car park and the house, you'll pass this attractive old pub that's handy for a pint and a decent enough lunch, though the clientele – nearly all manor visitors – are fairly captive, and the interior, with stuck-down willow branches arching across the flagstoned dining-room, speaks of designer aspirations not met. Mains £10–17. Eight guest rooms cover the basics. Daily 11am–11pm. **£85**

Bampton and around

A boggy stretch of the Upper Thames south of Burford and Witney could tempt you to explore. Aim first for **BAMPTON**, once important enough to merit its own castle. That was demolished in the eighteenth century, though the fine **church**, with a thirteenth-century spire and slightly later stone reredos, survives in what is a rather handsome village, with a Georgian air to its broad streets. Drop into **West Ox Arts** (Tues–Sat 10.30am–4.30pm, Sun 2–4pm; free; ⓦ westoxarts.com), a gallery displaying local art in the old town hall. If you're around on the last Monday in May, don't miss Bampton's **Day of Dance**, featuring live music and morris dancing, and look out for **Bampton Opera**

5

(ⓦbamptonopera.org) in July. "Bampton Footpaths", comprising maps and notes for walks in the area, is downloadable at ⓦwww.oxfordshirecotswolds.org.

RAF Brize Norton

Brize Norton • No public access

Unusually large aircraft flying unusually low over these fields is a giveaway: the skies over this part of Oxfordshire belong to the giant **RAF Brize Norton** airbase, which lies near **CARTERTON**, a mile or so north of Bampton. Detour onto the minor road between Bampton and Brize Norton village: this runs along the perimeter fence, giving rather extraordinary views of anonymous, super-sized military aircraft taxiing on the runway, yards away in plain sight.

Aston Pottery

Aston • Mon–Sat 9am–5pm, Sun 10.30am–4.30pm • ☎ 01993 852031, ⓦ astonpottery.co.uk

A mile east of Bampton near **ASTON**, the **Aston Pottery** has become a leading visitor attraction, with a showroom, café and gardens. The popularity of their comfortingly countrified ware, made on site and exported worldwide, means they remain a key village employer, keeping two dozen people in rural work.

Chimney Meadows Nature Reserve

Chimney • Always open • Free • ⓦ bbowt.org.uk

A minor road heads south to the Thames-side hamlet of **CHIMNEY**, where the **Chimney Meadows Nature Reserve** on the floodplain offers walks among flower meadows and wet woodlands, reclaimed in 2003 from intensive farming. From hides in the wetlands you can see kingfishers, egrets, cormorants and grebes.

Clanfield and Radcot Bridge

CLANFIELD is worth a look for the lancet windows of its thirteenth-century church, and for the access, one mile south, to **Radcot Bridge** – the oldest (some say second-oldest) crossing of the River Thames. It, too, is perhaps thirteenth-century, comprising three brief, humpback bridges in quick succession. This is a popular mooring-point for river boats, and just before the bridge, a turnoff leads west to **Kelmscott Manor** (see p.161). An easy circular **walk** entitled "Heaven on Earth in the Oxfordshire Cotswolds" (5 miles; 2hr; ⓦold.ruralways.org.uk) runs from Radcot across the water meadows to Kelmscott and back along the riverside Thames Path; pick up details at the Burford tourist office.

ACCOMMODATION AND EATING

★Plough Clanfield ☎ 01367 810222, ⓦ cotswolds ploughhotel.com. The building sets the scene, with its Jacobean gables and mullioned windows – a mood sustained inside, where the part-stone-flagged, part-parquet-floored bar is updated with modern sofas and rich red walls. Duck through to the dining room, laid with mix-and-match antique furniture; the menu has meat and veg options though concentrates on fish and seafood (mains £11–18). To stay, ask for one of the four traditionally styled bedrooms in the main house, rather than the newer options in the extension. Food served Mon–Thurs noon–2.15pm & 7–9pm, Fri & Sat noon–2.15pm & 7–9.30pm, Sun noon–3pm & 7–9pm. **£115**

BAMPTON AND AROUND

Trout Tadpole Bridge ☎ 01367 870382, ⓦ trout-inn .co.uk. A couple of miles south of Bampton, where Tadpole Bridge crosses the Thames, this lovely pub doubles as a rural restaurant and honest village local, with well-kept cask ales, including several Oxfordshire pints. It's a stand-out experience, from the warm welcome and superb setting to the courteous service. The food is classic English: rack of lamb, suckling pig, saddle of wild rabbit and the like. Mains £12–23. The pub is also a member of the Cotswolds Finest Hotels group, offering six spacious rooms, decorated in contemporary style. Mon–Thurs 11.30am–2pm & 6–9pm, Fri & Sat 11.30am–9pm, Sun noon–8.45pm. **£130**

Witney

5

A busy little town of about 25,000, located on the River Windrush twelve miles west of Oxford, **WITNEY** doesn't pay much attention to the tourism going on all around it. The town centre revolves around Corn Street, approaching from the west, and High Street, coming in from the north (where the A4095 is carried on the town's only bridge over the Windrush). Where they meet, by the Market Square, stands the **Buttercross**, an open-sided ex-dairy market building of about 1600. Witney's monthly **farmers' market** takes place here (see p.157). To the south, the long Church Green extends to **St Mary's Church**, with Norman elements surviving in what is chiefly early Gothic. In the other direction, past the seventeenth-century arcaded **Town Hall**, Witney's wonky **High Street** bustles away down the hill, lopsided (its west side higher than the east) and closely shaded by tree cover.

Witney Museum

75 High St • March–Oct Tues–Sat 10am–4pm, Sun 2–4pm • Free • ☎ 01993 775915, ⓦ witneyhistory.org

Strolling the High Street, past bits of Georgian and bits of Jacobean on either side, everybody occupied with cafés and commerce, brings you to the **Witney Museum**. This has a working loom, old photographs and displays on Witney's historic **blanket-making** industry, which sustained the town from the thirteenth century right through until the last mill closed in 2002.

Wychwood Brewery

The Crofts, behind Corn St • Tours: Fri 2pm, Sat 11am, 11.30am, 2pm, 2.30pm, 4pm & 4.30pm, Sun noon, 12.30pm, 2.30pm & 3pm • £7.50 • Booking essential ☎ 01993 890800, ⓦ wychwood.co.uk

After blankets, Witney's most famous claim to fame is as home town of the **Wychwood Brewery**, begun in the 1980s as an independent concern, but now – like its sister company on the same site Brakspear's – controlled by the national brewer Marston's. Nonetheless Wychwood flies the flag for Oxfordshire's grand old brewing tradition, with its best-selling "Hobgoblin" leading a range of highly acclaimed craft-brewed beers. It opens for **brewery tours**, which take 45 minutes to lead you through the brewing process before letting you loose to sample Hobgoblin and other beers.

ARRIVAL AND INFORMATION
WITNEY

By bus Buses stop on Market Square. The Witney Shuttle minibus (☎ 0800 043 4633, ⓦ witneyshuttle.com) runs several times a day between Heathrow Airport and Witney; advance booking essential.

Destinations Burford (Mon–Sat at least hourly, 5 on Sun; 20min); Charlbury (Mon–Sat hourly; 30min); Cheltenham (Mon–Sat 2–4 daily, 1 on Sun; 1hr); Chipping Norton (Mon–Sat hourly; 50min); Gloucester (Mon–Sat 2–4 daily, 1 on Sun; 1hr 20min); Kingham (Tues, Wed, 2 on Thurs; 50min); Minster Lovell (Mon–Sat every 30min, 1 on Sun; 5min); Northleach (Mon–Sat 2–4 daily, 1 on Sun; 30min); Oxford (every 15–20min; 35min); Stow-on-the-Wold (Tues & Wed; 1hr); Woodstock (Mon–Sat hourly; 30min).

Tourist office Partway along the High St, 3 Welch Way (Mon–Fri 9am–5pm, Sat 9.30am–5pm; ☎ 01993 775802, ⓦ www.oxfordshirecotswolds.org).

Walking tour Download a map and notes for the Witney Wool & Blanket Trail, a self-guided historical walk through the town, at ⓦ www.oxfordshirecotswolds.org.

ACCOMMODATION AND EATING

Corncroft 69 Corn St ☎ 01993 773298, ⓦ corncroft guesthousewitney.co.uk. Most of Witney's hotels are business-oriented: by contrast, this is a good central B&B, with eleven en-suite rooms done up in a mildly rustic countrified style. **£80**

★**Fleece** 11 Church Green ☎ 01993 892270, ⓦ fleece witney.co.uk. A step up from the in-town competition in both ambience – it's a lovely Georgian building near the church – and quality: go for a mix of cheeses, charcuterie, smoked fish and *crudités* as a starter, then try dishes such as roast lamb with a Moroccan salad or baked trout with almonds (mains £12–18). Also with ten stylish, individually decorated en-suite rooms. Food served Sun–Fri 8am–11pm, Sat 8am–midnight. **£90**

5

PAY THE T(R)OLL

A few miles east of Witney, to the south of **Eynsham** village, the B4044 road crosses the River Thames via **Swinford Bridge**, a beautiful Georgian structure opened in 1769. By a quirk of English law, the bridge is an investment opportunity: its own Act of Parliament states that the owner can charge a **toll** – fixed at 5p per vehicle – without paying any taxes on the income. Since the next bridge upstream is about twenty miles away, and the next bridge downstream is the Oxford ring road – not exactly renowned for free-flowing traffic – about four million vehicles use Swinford Bridge each year, generating a tidy £200,000 or so, tax-free.

Needless to say, the locals aren't happy. Every rush-hour, tailbacks of a mile or more build up through Eynsham as people pause on the bridge to hand over their 5p. In addition, the argument runs, why should people be paying extra on top of road tax for the privilege of driving to and from work? Nobody has a decent answer. In 2009, after the death of the previous owner, locals campaigned for Oxfordshire County Council to step in and abolish the toll. Instead, an anonymous buyer splashed out almost £1.1 million at auction to buy the bridge – and the tolls are still flowing in. The rich are getting richer, while the tailbacks (and pollution) grow. Track the protests at ⓦeynsham.org and ⓦscrapthetoll.blogspot.com.

Hollybush Inn 35 Corn St ☏ 01993 708073, ⓦ hollybush witney.co.uk. One of Witney's more congenial places to eat and drink, a renovated family-run pub in the town centre with a nice rear terrace and accomplished down-the-line pub grub (mains £11–16), as well as good beer and a lively atmosphere in the evenings. Sun–Thurs 11am–12.30am, Fri & Sat 11am–2am.

Lincoln Farm Park Standlake ☏ 01865 300239, ⓦ lincolnfarmpark.co.uk. Three miles south of Witney, this camping complex has been named the UK's Campsite of the Year by the AA. As well as five-star amenities, it has an on-site leisure centre with two indoor swimming pools and spa. Pitches **£28**

Ramsden and around

The most scenic road out of Witney is the B4022, a lovely drive climbing north up out of the Windrush Valley, over the tops and down again into the Evenlode Valley at Charlbury (see p.166). Past the turn for Poffley End, aim for **RAMSDEN**, a neat little village on the slopes. Once swamped by the Wychwood Forest, it was revealed when a path was cleared for Akeman Street, the Roman road linking St Albans with Cirencester. Download a map and notes at ⓦescapetothecotswolds.org.uk for "Step Into The Cotswolds: Walk 5", an easy **walk** through Ramsden and across rolling countryside in a circuit of a mile and three-quarters.

EATING AND DRINKING   RAMSDEN AND AROUND

Bird in Hand Whiteoak Green ☏ 01993 868321, ⓦ www.birdinhandinn.co.uk. A lovely old pub on the B4022 beside rolling fields. Newly renovated inside, with an excellent restaurant serving accomplished cuisine, from cajun chicken to crab fishcakes to bangers and mash, with plenty for vegetarians, served in a refined, warmly congenial setting. Mains £13–19; two-course lunch £11. They also have sixteen modern rooms, all en suite. Food served Mon–Fri noon–2pm & 6–9pm, Sat & Sun

noon–2.30pm & 6–9pm. **£100**

Royal Oak Ramsden ☏ 01993 868213, ⓦ royaloak ramsden.com/php. Just off the main road in Ramsden village, this old coaching inn has a reputation for culinary excellence, but in truth it may have been overtaken by its near-neighbour: things are looking a little tired these days, though it's congenial enough as a stop for thirsty walkers. Food served Mon–Fri noon–2pm & 7–10pm, Sat 11.30am–11pm, Sun noon–2pm.

Minster Lovell

Hooked into a corner of the River Windrush, a couple of miles upstream (west) of Witney, tiny, old **MINSTER LOVELL** will, sooner or later, take your breath away. There's no hurry, though: the village has been here since the Domesday Book (1086), which recorded it as Minster – its suffix came later in honour of the landowning Lovell family – and it may have been around much longer, since Akeman Street, the Roman road between St Albans and Cirencester, ran nearby. Either way, what survives is an alluringly rural cluster of thatched cottages, medieval inns and a strong sense of undisturbed history.

You approach down a slope off the main road (B4047) to an old, narrow bridge over the bubbling River Windrush; on the right stretches Wash Meadow, absurdly picturesque when a cricket match is going on. At a fork by the *Old Swan*, turn right and head along the village street between cottages.

St Kenelm's Church

Minster Lovell • Daylight hours • Free • ⓦ www.stkenelmschurch.co.uk

Towards the top of Minster Lovell village, bear right to reach **St Kenelm's Church**, a beautiful, still, resonant church rebuilt in 1450 by William Lovell, named for an eighth-century prince of Mercia who was also venerated at the now-destroyed abbey of Winchcombe (see p.127).

Minster Lovell Hall

Minster Lovell • Daylight hours • Free • ⓦ english-heritage.org.uk

The culmination of the village's charms lies immediately behind St Kenelm's Church, where William Lovell also built a large **hall** on a stretch of meadow beside the river. The house does not survive, largely dismantled in the 1740s, yet its **ruins**, open to the elements with crumbling towers and toothless windows, are picture perfect. A cobbled pathway leads to the entrance porch, vaulted inside, while beyond is the great hall, now roofless; by the river stand remnants of a tower, marking the far corner of what was a vast interior courtyard, giving an idea of the size of the house when complete. If you have any breath left after absorbing Minster Lovell's beauty, a first glimpse of these old stones in their riverside setting will banish it.

Minster Lovell Experience

130 Burford Rd • Mon–Fri 10am–1am & 2–5pm • £2 • ☎ 01993 775262, ⓦ minsterlovell.com & ⓦ minsterlovellexperience.com

For a vivid retelling of Minster Lovell's history, along with a dash of legend and perhaps a snatch of song, drop into the **Minster Lovell Experience**, run by Graham Kew out of his picture-framing business on the main B4047 Burford road above the village.

ARRIVAL AND DEPARTURE | MINSTER LOVELL

By bus Buses stop on the main road by the *White Hart* pub: Destinations Burford (Mon–Sat hourly, 1 on Sun; 15min); Cheltenham (Mon–Sat 2–4 daily, 1 on Sun; 50min); Gloucester (Mon–Sat 2–4 daily, 1 on Sun; 1hr 10min); Kingham (once on Thurs; 45min); Northleach (Mon–Sat 2–4 daily, once on Sun; 20min); Oxford (Mon–Sat every 30min; 35min); Witney (Mon–Sat every 30min, 1 on Sun; 5min); Woodstock (Mon–Sat hourly; 35min).

ACCOMMODATION AND EATING

Old Swan and Minster Mill Minster Lovell ☎ 01993 774441, ⓦ oldswanandminstermill.com. In the centre of the village, with the pub on one side of the road and the converted mill on the other, this place has been transformed in the last few years. The pub is now a gastropub, with different dining rooms, snugs and terraces dotted about, each serving refined modern British cuisine based on Slow Food principles (mains £10–17). Rooms upstairs have been superbly refitted, with luxury fabrics and classic country styling, while the 44 rooms across the way in the former mill have more chic about them, with contemporary design and a bolder colour palette. Food served Sun–Thurs 12.30–3pm & 6.30–9pm, Fri & Sat 12.30–3pm & 6.30–9.30pm. **£165**

The Evenlode Valley

Along with its southern neighbour the Windrush, which flows through Burford and Witney, the valley of the **River Evenlode** offers classic Cotswolds scenery. From its source near Moreton-in-Marsh, the river flows southeast through Oxfordshire, joining

5

the Thames above Oxford. Don't expect headline attractions or even very much to do: expect, rather, to lose yourself in the byways, stumble across a village pub or two, take in the views on a countryside walk. You could aim, if you like, for **Kingham** village, on the Oxfordshire-Gloucestershire border, where there's a little cluster of fine country inns, or perhaps **Charlbury**, a touch hillier but closer to the attractions of Woodstock.

North Leigh Roman villa

Always open • Free • Ⓦ english-heritage.org.uk

Parts of an early-fourth-century **Roman villa**, indicating impressive prosperity in what would have been dense, riverside forest, survives outside the village of **NORTH LEIGH**, off the A4095 Witney–Woodstock road. Before you reach the Oxford Bus Museum at Hanborough (see p.175), turn off left at the signs, drive through the outlying hamlet of **EAST END** and park in a marked layby. From here, the only approach is **on foot**, a third of a mile down a stony track into the valley of the River Evenlode. What survives is modest: a course or two of foundation stonework, with the remnants of a hypocaust system for underfloor heating. A panel explains the layout of the villa – which was substantial, with kitchens, baths and dozens of other rooms set around a courtyard. To one side, a **mosaic floor** in browns and reds lies protected by a modern shelter. What's just as evocative, though, are the sense of discovery, the setting – surrounded by hills echoing with bleats – and the occasional train passing on the Cotswold Line laid yards away, beside the Evenlode. As a mute counterpoint to Blenheim, another, younger, bolder, country palace barely two miles distant, it couldn't be more perfect.

Charlbury and around

Midway between Kingham and Woodstock, on the dipping and rising slopes above the Evenlode, the little market town of **CHARLBURY** makes for a modest halt on the Cotswold rail line. Cross the river from the **railway station** (built by Brunel) to reach the **church of St Mary**, part twelfth- and thirteenth-century though, unusually, with the internal layout reversed: since the 1990s, the congregation have chosen to turn their back on the dark chancel and pray westwards instead. From here climb into the narrow, close-set central streets, marked by many eighteenth-century buildings.

Stretching southwest from Charlbury is **Cornbury Park**, which encompasses the only substantial surviving part of the ancient Wychwood Forest. The Cornbury estate is privately owned, but go to Ⓦwww.oxfordshire.gov.uk/charlburywalk to download a map and notes for an eight-mile **circular walk** following the only public footpath through the forest.

Chadlington

Every road out of Charlbury offers great driving, especially the B4437 west to the Wychwoods, and the lovely B4022 (see p.164), climbing south into the Windrush Valley. The B4026 also climbs, north towards Chipping Norton; turn off left to reach **CHADLINGTON**, where the locals clubbed together in 2001 to save the village shop from closure, in the process turning it into one of the area's leading (and *very* un-fancy) **farm shops** (Ⓦchadlingtonqualityfoods.com).

ARRIVAL AND INFORMATION   **CHARLBURY AND AROUND**

By train Charlbury is served by trains on the London–Oxford–Worcester line.

Destinations Moreton-in-Marsh (hourly; 20min); Kingham (hourly; 10min); London Paddington (hourly; 1hr 15min); Oxford (hourly; 20min); Worcester (hourly; 1hr 5min).

By bus Buses stop in the village centre.

Destinations Burford (Mon–Fri 2 daily; 35min); Chipping Norton (Mon–Sat hourly; 20min); Oxford (Mon–Sat hourly; 55min); Witney (Mon–Sat hourly; 30min); Woodstock (Mon–Sat hourly; 25min).

Information Ⓦ charlbury.info and Ⓦ chadlington.com.

KELMSCOTT MANOR (P.161) >

5

ACCOMMODATION AND EATING

Bell Charlbury ☎01608 810278. Lovely eighteenth-century village inn, updated to serve as a decent restaurant serving seasonal British dishes (mains £12–18), and also with rather stylish, boldly decorated rooms. Food served Mon–Sat noon–2.30pm & 6–9pm, Sun noon–2.30pm. **£85**

Café de la Post Chadlington ☎01608 676461, ⓦcafedelapost.com. An exotic title for a general store doubling as a tearoom and simple restaurant, on a corner in Chadlington village. Grab a panini or carrot cake (around £5). Mon–Thurs 7.30am–5.30pm, Fri 7.30am–10.30pm, Sat 8am–9.30pm, Sun 9am–2pm.

Cotswold View Banbury Hill Farm, Enstone Rd ☎01608 810314, ⓦcotswoldview.co.uk. One mile north of Charlbury on the hilly B4022 Enstone road stands this popular caravan and camping park, with views stretching out over the Evenlode Valley and Wychwood Forest. They also have camping pods – insulated wooden huts that are an alternative to sleeping under canvas (from £42). The farm also has simple B&B. Closed Nov–March. **£72**; pitches **£25**

Rose and Crown Charlbury ☎01608 810103, ⓦrose andcrown.charlbury.com. A real drinkers' pub in the centre of the village, renowned for an ever-changing array of well-kept, properly poured local ales and for hosting occasional beer festivals and celebrations. Sun–Fri noon–midnight, Sat 11am–midnight.

The Wychwoods

North of Burford, the A361 climbs out of the Windrush valley, offering views towards the Evenlode before dropping down to a cluster of three neighbouring villages whose names recall the ancient forests of Wychwood which formerly covered this area (see p.176). Just west of the road is **MILTON-UNDER-WYCHWOOD** – of medieval foundation, like its siblings, and benefiting from a lovely six-mile circular walk through Fifield (download details at ⓦwww.oxfordshirecotswolds.org).

There's more interest in **SHIPTON-UNDER-WYCHWOOD**, directly on the A361. Here, overlooking the village green, the *Shaven Crown* is purportedly one of the ten oldest

---

THE COTSWOLD LINE RAILWAY

Kingham, Charlbury and a handful of other Evenlode villages are well served by regular trains on the **Cotswold Line**, which forms a link in the main line from London Paddington through Oxford to Evesham, Worcester and Hereford, now operated by First Great Western. It survived Beeching's Axe. Today, as well as giving urban visitors easy access to deepest Cotswold countryside, it forms a crucial axis of economic and cultural exchange, connecting small villages to big cities (for mutual benefit) and bringing money into the Cotswolds – not only tourism, but also in terms of rural businesses maintaining access to markets, and wealthy urban commuters being able to live in the country. Arguably, the proximity to London created by the railway has also helped Cotswold ideas, for instance about food quality or the value of rural lifestyles, gain currency nationwide.

Above all, it's beautiful. Other railways may have more natural drama, but few can match the evocative scenery of the forty-minute run beside the Evenlode from Oxford to Moreton. In June 1914, a week before the Great War erupted, poet **Edward Thomas** (1878–1917) was travelling this way when his train made an unscheduled stop at Adlestrop, a hamlet north of Kingham. His poem *Adlestrop* immortalized both the line and this part of the Cotswolds – though British Rail still closed Adlestrop station, regardless, in 1966.

Yes, I remember Adlestrop –
The name, because one afternoon
Of heat the express-train drew up there
Unwontedly. It was late June.

The steam hissed. Someone cleared his throat.
No one left and no one came
On the bare platform. What I saw
Was Adlestrop – only the name

And willows, willow-herb, and grass,
And meadowsweet, and haycocks dry,
No whit less still and lonely fair
Than the high cloudlets in the sky.

And for that minute a blackbird sang
Close by, and round him, mistier,
Farther and farther, all the birds
Of Oxfordshire and Gloucestershire.

5

pubs in Britain, in operation since at least the fourteenth century – perhaps earlier, since it was originally run by Cistercian monks from the now-demolished abbey at nearby Bruern, founded in 1147. The building is pure theatre, from its mullioned windows to its stone fireplaces and arching gateway.

Two miles east, **ASCOTT-UNDER-WYCHWOOD** is known for the "**Ascott Martyrs**", sixteen village women who, in 1873, spoke out in support of local labourers sacked for forming a trade union. The women's arrest and imprisonment in Oxford Castle led to rioting and, eventually, a royal pardon from Queen Victoria.

ACCOMMODATION AND EATING	THE WYCHWOODS

Shaven Crown Shipton-under-Wychwood ☎ 01993 830330, ⓦ theshavencrown.co.uk. Bought by new owners in late 2013, this famous old pub was under renovation at the time of writing. By the time you read this it should be open for business again – and worth checking out.

Kingham and around

When *Country Life* magazine calls you "England's favourite village", it could easily prompt a downward spiral. But for **KINGHAM**, set in the Evenlode Valley between Chipping Norton (the highest town in Oxfordshire) and Stow-on-the-Wold (the highest town in the entire Cotswolds), everything's looking up. Since that accolade – awarded on a range of criteria from architectural merit and natural setting to transport links, community spirit and quality of life – this cheery, noticeably upmarket village has gone from strength to strength. There's still nothing to do here, other than eat well, drink well, walk well and sleep well… but that's the point. The walk in from the railway station is lovely, marked by the Perpendicular tower of **St Andrew's Church**.

Daylesford Organic Farm

Daylesford · Mon Wed 9am–5pm, Thurs–Sat 9am–6pm, Sun 10am–4pm · ☎ 01608 731700, ⓦ daylesford.com

A mile or so north of Kingham, **DAYLESFORD** village, a few yards inside Gloucestershire, has won nationwide renown for **Daylesford Organic Farm**, founded in the 1980s when the local landowning Bamford family converted their farming estates to organic. Fashions caught up, and now Daylesford not only markets its own-brand produce but has a village **shop** – more like the smartest London food hall, vast, immaculate and expensive – stocking premium deli items of all kinds. It's a rather absorbing glimpse of Chelsea in the Cotswolds, even more so at weekends, with the car park lined by top-end 4WDs. On site, too, are a café-restaurant, day spa and cookery school.

Churchill and Sarsden Heritage Centre

Churchill · Sat & Sun 2–4.30pm · Free · ☎ 01608 658603, ⓦ churchillheritage.org.uk

A mile or so east of Kingham, along the B4450 Chipping Norton road in tiny **CHURCHILL**, is the **Churchill and Sarsden Heritage Centre**, a local history museum housed in the restored chancel of a now-destroyed medieval church, often with unusually engaging temporary exhibits on the area's past.

ARRIVAL AND DEPARTURE	KINGHAM AND AROUND

By train Kingham is served by trains on the London–Oxford–Worcester line. The station is a mile west of the village centre. Railbus #X8 (Mon–Sat hourly) meets arriving trains, running from the station to Kingham village green (5min) and Chipping Norton (15min).
Destinations Charlbury (hourly; 10min); London Paddington (hourly; 1hr 25min); Moreton-in-Marsh (hourly; 30min); Oxford (hourly; 30min); Worcester (hourly; 55min).
By bus Buses stop in the village centre.
Destinations Bourton-on-the-Water (Thurs & Sat; 40min); Burford (1 on Wed; 20min); Cheltenham (1 on Sat; 1hr 5min); Chipping Norton (Mon–Sat hourly; 10min); Stow-on-the-Wold (1 on Thurs; 15min).

5

WALKS AROUND KINGHAM

Kingham has loads of **walking** possibilities – not least within the **Foxholes Nature Reserve** (⊕ bbowt.org.uk), an ancient woodland famed for its spring bluebells. Longer routes abound: download maps and descriptions for many at ⊕ www.oxfordshirecotswolds.org. Walk 1 is a short **circular route** to/from Kingham Station (3.5 miles; 2hr 30min), exploring the fields around Bledington; a longer option is Walk 4 (9 miles; 5hr), also to/from the station but heading out past Foscot to Bruern, then skirting the Foxholes reserve to Idbury and back via Bledington. Several routes offer walks **from Kingham to Chipping Norton**: most straightforward is Walk 11 "Mills and Meadows" (5.5 miles; 3hr), along a stream to Swaleford Bridge and then across the meadows, or you could tackle the circuitous Walk 6 (9 miles; 5hr) which takes in woodland and fields around Adlestrop, Chastleton, Cornwell and Salford.

ACCOMMODATION AND EATING

With its high-profile gastropubs, Kingham has become a focus for food. Now lacking a farmers' market, the village instead hosts the **Cotswold Table** (⊕ thecotswoldtable.co.uk), billed as a "foodie's market", with dozens of artisan producers setting up alongside tableware makers and tea-party organisers. They run four times a year: check the website for details.

★**Daylesford Organic Farm** Daylesford ☎ 01608 731700, ⊕ daylesford.com. This super-sleek farm complex includes a spectacularly well-stocked deli and adjacent café, where light lunches – salads, risottos, grilled salmon and the like (£10–14) are filled out by cream teas and informal suppers (Fri & Sat only; booking essential). It's absurdly expensive, but very good – and rather fun to people-watch. Mon–Wed 9am–5pm, Thurs–Sat 9am–6pm, Sun 10am–4pm, also Fri & Sat 7–9pm.

★**Kingham Plough** Kingham ☎ 01608 658327, ⊕ thekinghamplough.co.uk. Book ahead for a meal to remember. The epitome of a Cotswold gastropub, this is one of the county's best restaurants, atmospherically housed in an old stone building by the large, open village green, with simple contemporary-country decor and a service ethic that perfectly blends efficiency and warm informality. Come here for local, seasonal produce of all kinds, expertly prepared (mains £16–25) and served off a short, daily-changing menu. They also have seven country-style rooms, both in the main house and a newer annexe. Food served Mon–Thurs noon–9pm, Fri & Sat noon–9.30pm, Sun noon–3pm & 6–8pm. **£95**

Kings Head Bledington ☎ 01608 658365, ⊕ thekingsheadinn.net. Just west of Kingham – yards into Gloucestershire – Bledington hosts another of the Cotswolds' most celebrated rural gastropub/hotels. This sixteenth-century inn overlooking the village green ticks every box, but quietly. With regulars supping pints at the bar, it doubles up as a restaurant of quality, serving local, ethically sourced food that taps directly into the English country mindset – think potted shrimps, steak-and-ale pie, venison and Cotswold lamb – alongside newer-fangled modern British fusion dishes (mains £13–15). The rooms, some floral, some designer-chic, are a snip. Food served Mon–Thurs noon–2pm & 6.30–9pm, Fri noon–2pm & 6.30–9.30pm, Sat noon–2.30pm & 6.30–9.30pm, Sun noon–2.30pm & 7–9pm. **£95**

Wild Rabbit Kingham ☎ 01608 658389, ⊕ thewildrabbit.co.uk. This eighteenth-century inn on Kingham's high street reopened recently under new ownership – Lady Bamford's, serving as an extension to her family's Daylesford empire. This is, in effect, London transplanted to the country – or, rather, a London retelling of an imagined country. Everything is picture-perfect, from the topiary to the immaculately styled contemporary rustic decor to the food on the plate, a knowingly smooth fusion of tradition and fashion. Mains £14–25. A clutch of sleekly modern rooms fills out the picture. Food served Tues–Sat noon–2.30pm & 7–9pm, Sun noon–3pm. **£120**

Chipping Norton

As "Gateway to the Cotswolds" Burford may have a touch of the Cinderellas about it, but it would be unfair to call its northern counterpart **CHIPPING NORTON** an ugly sister. This busy little market town, known locally as "Chippy", isn't the prettiest place in the Cotswolds, but it is flanked to the north and east by one of the least explored and most scenic corners of the region, where the limestone uplands are patterned by long dry-stone walls and sprinkled with tiny stone villages. King John granted a **wool fair** charter to the town in the twelfth century – "chipping" comes from *ceapen*,

Old English for market – but it reached its peak three hundred years later, when it acquired many of the stalwart stone buildings that now line up along the sloping **Market Square**, site of the monthly farmers' market (see p.157).

Chipping Norton Museum

4 High St • Easter–Oct Mon–Sat 2–4pm • £1.50 • 01608 641712, chippingnortonmuseum.org.uk

Opposite the steps of the Victorian **town hall** on the market square, **Chipping Norton Museum** has a modest but well-assembled collection covering the history of the town from Roman artefacts to World War II memorabilia, also taking in a huge postcard collection of local places and rural artefacts.

St Mary's Church

Church St • stmaryscnorton.com

St Mary's Church, just below the square – and beyond a handsome row of almshouses – looks every inch the Cotswold wool church, the modesty of its tower offset by the slender windows of its Perpendicular Gothic nave. The vaulted porch is equally striking, not least for the grinning devils and green men that peer down from the roof. By comparison, the interior is rather routine, though the nave is well lit and airy and the east window of the south aisle is a splendid affair, spiralling out from a central tulip; look out also for two superbly carved alabaster table-tombs commemorating sixteenth-century merchants and their wives.

Bliss Tweed Mill

No public access

Down in the valley just west of the town, the **Bliss Tweed Mill**, built in 1872 and now converted into apartments, recalls the textile mini-boom Chipping Norton enjoyed in the nineteenth century: it's a novel design, with a domed roof and towering, top-heavy chimneystack. Walk a few minutes out along the A44 for a grand view of it; if you drive into town from the west, the same vista opens on your right-hand side.

ARRIVAL AND INFORMATION
CHIPPING NORTON

By train At Kingham station (see p.169), five miles west of Chipping Norton, railbus #X8 meets arriving trains (Mon–Sat hourly; 15min).

By bus Buses stop on West St, the continuation of Market Sq.

Destinations Banbury (Mon–Sat hourly; 45min); Bourton-on-the-Water (Fri & Sat; 45min); Burford (Mon–Sat hourly; 30min); Charlbury (Mon–Sat hourly; 20min); Cheltenham (once on Sat; 1hr 15min); Hook Norton (Mon–Sat hourly; 20min); Kingham (Mon–Sat hourly; 10min); Oxford (hourly; 50min); Shipston-on-Stour (4 daily; 20min); Stratford-upon-Avon (4 daily; 45min); Witney (Mon–Sat hourly; 50min); Woodstock (hourly; 20min).

Information experiencechippingnorton.com.

Map

CHIPPING NORTON

Rollright Stones

0   100
yards

N

St Mary's

CHURCH LANE

CHURCH STREET

Theatre

GOODARDS LA.

MARKET STREET

MIDDLE ROW

HIGH STREET

SPRING STREET

HORSE FAIR

OVER NORTON ROAD

MARLBOROUGH ROAD

A361 BANBURY RD

A44 LONDON RD

ROCK HILL

ROWELL WAY

A44 NEW STREET

ALBION STREET

WARDS ROAD

Town Hall

CATTLE MARKET

Museum

WEST STREET

A351 BRAFORD RD

Banbury

Woodstock & Oxford

Moreton-in-March & Stow-on-the-Wold

Kingham

The Wychwoods, Burford & Charlbury

ACCOMMODATION
Cotswolds 39 1
Wild Thyme 2

EATING & DRINKING
Chequers 1
Jaffé & Neale 2
Wild Thyme 3

5

WALKS AROUND CHIPPING NORTON

Chippy's best **walks** include the **Glyme Valley Way** (ⓦ www.oxfordshire.gov.uk/glyme valleywalk), sixteen miles to Woodstock – chiefly downhill and walkable in a (long) day. See the website for full details, or you could split it in half (8 miles; 4hr): set out south then bear east to join the River Glyme near Lidstone, continuing through Enstone and across fields to end at Kiddington, from where bus #S3 returns you to Chipping Norton. The section from Kiddington into Woodstock is described separately (see p.176). Two **circular walks** to/from Chippy are also worthwhile (both at ⓦ www.oxfordshirecotswolds.org) – an easy one via Over Norton (2.5 miles) and a more taxing one (6.5 miles) across fields to Salford, Cornwell and back.

ACCOMMODATION AND EATING

Chequers Goddard Lane ☎ 01608 644717, ⓦ chequers -pub.com. Atmospheric pub just off the High St, behind the Jaffe & Neale bookshop and next door to the theatre – in the front it's an old-fashioned drinkers' local, but in the back it transmogrifies into a bright, airy, family-minded pub restaurant, serving brasserie favourites (mains £8–15) as well as lighter salads and sandwiches. Food served Mon–Sat noon–2.30pm & 6–9.30pm, Sun noon–4pm.

Cotswolds 39 39 New St ☎ 01608 430044, ⓦ cotswolds 39-bandb.co.uk. Quirky, rather charming little B&B in a modern house in the centre of Chipping Norton, with the tone set by the names of the two en-suite guest rooms: Chipping and – you guessed it – Norton. The beds are huge, the rooms are spotless: this is a lovely place to hole up. **£85**

★**Jaffe and Neale** 1 Middle Row ☎ 01608 641033,

ⓦ jaffeandneale.co.uk. This light, cheerful independent bookshop on the main square is a real Chippy institution, packed to the gunwales with books and plumb in the centre of the town's community life. One corner of the shop is taken up by a lovely little café – perfect for a cappuccino and a cake to re-energize your browsing. Mon–Fri 9.30am–5.30pm, Sat 9am–5.30pm, Sun 11am–5pm.

Wild Thyme 10 New St ☎ 01608 645060, ⓦ wildthyme restaurant.co.uk. Best restaurant in town, with a Cotswolds-wide reputation for innovative, perfectly show-cased modern British cooking displaying real panache – Tamworth pork in a prune jus, wild rabbit three ways, and so forth. Mains £14–19. They also have three stylish rooms, calming, grown-up and rather romantic. Tues 7–9pm, Wed–Sat noon–2pm & 7–9pm, Sun noon–2pm. **£75**

Great Tew

In a region which has beautiful villages and fine old pubs coming out of its ears, **GREAT TEW**, about five miles east of Chipping Norton via the A361 and B4022, takes the biscuit. Not strictly in the Cotswolds, it nonetheless has Cotswold character aplenty, its thatched cottages and honey-coloured stone houses weaving around grassy hillocks, flanked on all sides by rolling woodland.

ACCOMMODATION AND EATING   GREAT TEW

★**Falkland Arms** Great Tew ☎ 01608 683653, ⓦ falklandarms.co.uk. Idyllic, locally renowned country pub, which rotates guest beers in addition to its Wadworth cask ales, and sells a fine selection of single malts, herbal wines, snuff and clay pipes you can fill with tobacco for a smoke in the flower-filled garden. Little has changed

in the flagstone-floored bar since the sixteenth century, although the snug is now a small dining room serving home-made food (mains £9–17). It's also a charming place to stay: there are six rooms, sympathetically renovated and attractively furnished. Food served daily noon–2.30pm & 6–9.30pm. **£120**

Chastleton House

Chastleton • April–Sept Wed–Sun 1–5pm; March & Oct Wed–Sun 1–4pm • £8.50 • NT • Timed tickets, pre-bookable on ☎ 01494 755560, ⓦ nationaltrust.org.uk

Roughly four miles west of Chipping Norton – and the same distance east of Moreton-in-Marsh (see p.102) – stands **Chastleton House**. Built between 1607 and 1612 by Walter Jones, a wealthy wool merchant, this ranks among England's most splendid Jacobean houses, set amid ornamental gardens that include the country's first-ever croquet lawn (croquet's rules were codified here in 1865).

5

During the Civil War the Joneses were Royalist: they lost most of their wealth to the Cromwellian authorities and remained too poor thereafter to renovate or refurbish. Nothing was done to the house until 1800, when a few repairs were made – and then, virtually nothing since. From the day it was built until 1991, when it was put in the care of the National Trust, the house passed through family hands and was never sold.

Because of this, Chastleton has a special allure. Aside from the architecture, which is sublime, its interiors seem stuck in time, with unwashed upholstery, unpolished wood panelling and miscellaneous clutter clogging some of the corners. This dishevelled air is a credit to the National Trust, who wisely decided to stick to the "lived-in" look. Chastleton seems to have escaped history, claiming no connection to any major events or noteworthy people who might have been tempted to alter it. It feels less like a stately home than a time machine.

The tone is set by the first room, the **Great Hall**, entered through a carved oak screen: the soot marks above the fireplace remain unscrubbed, for a start. The hall's oak table is as old as the house. Other highlights include the **Great Chamber** upstairs, with an elaborate chimneypiece and moulded ceiling, and the hugely impressive **Long Gallery** at the top of the house, barrel-vaulted with an ornate plasterwork ceiling. Head down into the basement for the atmospheric **Old Kitchen** and adjacent **Beer Cellar**, featuring the longest ladder you're ever likely to see, 60ft in length and made in 1805 to facilitate gutter-clearing. Leave time to stroll the wonderful **topiary garden**.

The Rollright Stones

Always open • Free, but £1 donation in honesty box requested • ⓦ rollrightstones.co.uk

Driving west from Chipping Norton along the A44, it only takes a few minutes to reach the signed country lane that leads off to the right to the **Rollright Stones**, a scattering of megalithic monuments in the fields either side. The eerie array consists of large natural stones moved here – no one is sure why – plus several burial chambers and barrows. The largest is the **King's Men**, comprising over seventy irregularly spaced stones forming a circle about a hundred feet in diameter, one of the most important such monuments in the country. Signed just off the lane, it's also the easiest to find. The circle gets its name from a legend about a witch who turned a king and his army (of unknown identity) into these gnarled rocks to stop them invading England. Across the lane (which marks the Oxfordshire-Warwickshire border) stands the **King's Stone** monolith, offering pensive views across the countryside, while a third group – dubbed the **Whispering Knights** – lie a short walk southeast of the King's Men on the field margin. Roughly a mile east of the site, the **Wyatts Farm Shop** (☎01608 684835, ⓦ www.wyattsgardencentre.co.uk) has books and leaflets about the stones, as well as a café.

Woodstock

Eight miles northwest of Oxford, **WOODSTOCK** has royal associations going back to Saxon times, with a string of kings attracted by the excellent hunting in the Wychwood Forest, which formerly covered the area. Henry I built a royal lodge here and his successor, Henry II, enlarged it to create what is thought to have been a manor house-cum-palace, where Edward, the Black Prince, was born in 1330, where Henry VIII dallied with Catherine of Aragon and where the future Elizabeth I was imprisoned by her half-sister Mary in 1554. During the Civil War, Woodstock was a Royalist base: the manor house was badly damaged by Roundhead attacks in 1646 but Cromwell never got around to razing the ruins, which were only swept away by the Duke of Marlborough when work started on the construction of Blenheim Palace on the same site in 1704 (see p.177).

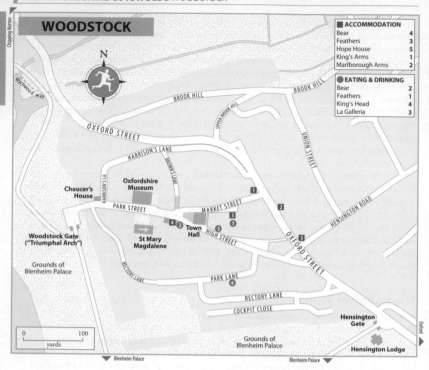

Long dependent on royal and then ducal patronage, Woodstock is now both a well-heeled commuter town for Oxford and a provider of food, drink and beds for visitors to Blenheim. Historic, dignified and attractive, it has Oxfordshire character in spades.

Oxford Street

An extremely pretty little place, Woodstock is characterized by handsome stone buildings gathered around a knot of streets beside the A44 Oxford–Evesham road, which here is **Oxford Street**, lined once with coaching inns and now with upscale fashion and crafts shops flanking the Woodstock Bookshop (ⓦwww.woodstock bookshop.co.uk). Opposite the corner with High Street, the elegant, bay-windowed **Hope House** is said to have been designed by Vanbrugh, architect of Blenheim; it now holds a boutique hotel.

Park Street

Gracious, tree-lined **Park Street** leads west from the Palladian **Town Hall**, site of the monthly farmers' market (see p.157). To one side is the famous *Bear Hotel*, whose origins go back to the 1250s, while opposite, reproduction stocks have been set up in front of an acacia-shaded Elizabethan building housing the Oxfordshire Museum (see opposite).

A step further along Park Street stands **Chaucer's House**, named for Thomas Chaucer, son of Geoffrey, who owned a house on this spot (the current building is seventeenth-century), while across the road, the **church of St Mary Magdalene** sports a Norman doorway with zigzag carving, an eighteenth-century square tower and an atmospheric yew-shaded churchyard – but a disappointingly bland Victorian interior.

5

Park Street continues to the end of the town, where a peremptory notice fixed to the wall warning fishermen to be quiet heralds a courtyard offering the exceptional sight of Nicholas Hawksmoor's Classical-style **Woodstock Gate** (sometimes known as the Triumphal Arch) into the grounds of **Blenheim Palace** (see p.177). If the officials in the ticket booth will let you, nip through to take a peek at the spectacular panorama just beyond: Blenheim Palace in the distance, Capability Brown's landscaped grounds, Vanbrugh's Grand Bridge over the lake – what Randolph Churchill termed "the finest view in England".

Oxfordshire Museum
Park St • Tues–Sat 10am–5pm, Sun 2–5pm • Free • ☎ 01993 811456, ⓦ www.tomocc.org.uk

Occupying an eighteenth-century house in the centre of Woodstock, the rather good **Oxfordshire Museum** offers an engaging take on the county's archeology, social history and industry. Part of the museum's lovely rear garden shelters original megalosaurus footprints, recovered from a local quarry and displayed amid a Jurassic garden of ferns, pines and redwoods.

ARRIVAL AND INFORMATION   WOODSTOCK

By bus Buses stop on Oxford St.
Destinations Burford (Mon–Sat hourly; 45min); Charlbury (hourly; 25min); Chipping Norton (hourly; 20min); Minster

Lovell (Mon–Sat hourly; 35min); Oxford (hourly; 30min); Witney (Mon–Sat hourly; 30min).
Information ⓦ wakeuptowoodstock.com.

ACCOMMODATION

HOTELS AND B&B

★ **Bear** Park St ☎ 01993 811124, ⓦ macdonaldhotels .co.uk. Behind the ivy-clad walls of this former coaching inn, whose history stretches back to the thirteenth century, lurks a stylish, modern chain hotel, packed with traditional features. From oak-carved four-poster beds to roaring log fires, bay windows to antique furniture – not to mention outstanding service – it ticks all the boxes. Plump, if you can, for the Marlborough Suite, where in the early 1960s Elizabeth Taylor and Richard Burton hid, away from their spouses (and the press). **£100**
Feathers Market St ☎ 01993 812291, ⓦ feathers.co.uk. A discreet, attractive little independent boutique hotel with 21 bedrooms, worked into seven adjacent seventeenth-century townhouses. Although traditional elements remain – a grandfather clock here, an oak bookcase there – the style is definitely upscale contemporary, with designer textiles, tastefully vivid wallpaper, modern lighting and

swanky bathrooms. Member of the Cotswolds Finest Hotels group. **£200**
Hope House Oxford St ☎ 01993 815990, ⓦ www .hopehousewoodstock.co.uk. Eighteenth-century townhouse with just three super-luxurious suites – all enormous and kitted out to the highest standards: antique furnishings, king-size four-poster beds, contemporary designer decor, and so forth. Service is attentive, while the breakfast (all local and organic) comes on Royal Doulton china. **£350**
King's Arms Market St ☎ 01993 813636, ⓦ www .kingshotelwoodstock.co.uk. Rather chic little hotel, with fifteen rooms done up in a fresh, appealing contemporary style – bowl sinks and Molton Brown in the bathroom, pale colours and light wood in the bedroom. Beware, though: the bar/restaurant area at ground level can remain busy until 11pm or later and traffic noise may also be an issue: if you want an early night, choose a room at the back. **£150**

OXFORD BUS MUSEUM

Three miles west of Woodstock, the **Oxford Bus Museum** (Wed & Sun 10.30am–4.30pm, May–Sept also Sat 10.30am–4.30pm; £4.50; ☎ 01993 883617, ⓦ oxfordbusmuseum.org.uk) comprises a giant warehouse crammed with vintage buses and coaches, many open for onboard exploration, along with memorabilia, models and ephemera – plus evocative whiffs of engine grease and waxed bodywork. On the first and third Sundays of the month (March–Oct) they do free rides on one of their old buses. Alongside is a separate exhibition on Morris Motors, the historic Oxford car maker. The museum is located on the A4095 Woodstock–Witney road beside **Hanborough** station: get there by train from Oxford (one stop), or on bus #233 (Mon–Sat hourly) between Woodstock (10min) and Witney (20min), which drops off outside.

5

WALKS AROUND WOODSTOCK

Woodstock lies at the heart of the former royal hunting forest of Wychwood, long since cleared for agriculture or settlement and now reduced to isolated woods here and there, most notably a stretch of forest at Cornbury Park, a private estate between Leafield and Charlbury. In an effort to preserve links with pre-industrial culture and encourage greater understanding of the landscape, rural activists and Oxfordshire council formed the Wychwood Project (☎01865 815423, ⓦwww.wychwoodproject.org), which has included the establishment of the 37-mile **Wychwood Way** circular trail. This forms a rough quadrilateral, waymarked from Woodstock and heading through Stonesfield, Chadlington, Ascott-under-Wychwood, Leafield, Ramsden, North Leigh, East End, Combe and back to Woodstock. The route bypasses Charlbury, but short-cuts connect to and from Charlbury railway station, facilitating half- and full-day walks: full details are in the Wychwood Way guidebook (£6), available online and at local tourist offices.

Another long-distance route worth tackling is the **Glyme Valley Way**, a full-day route running 16 miles from Chipping Norton to Woodstock; for more, see p.172. This is best tackled in a downhill (southerly) direction: if you're starting from Woodstock take the hourly bus #S3 to Kiddington, from where it's a gentle eight miles back, around farm buildings, past a medieval church at Glympton and then along the River Glyme past Wootton to end at the Woodstock museum. Full details, with maps and descriptions, at ⓦwww.oxfordshire.gov.uk.

Marlborough Arms 26 Oxford St ☎01993 811227, ⓦthemarlborougharms.co.uk. This ex-coaching inn now focuses exclusively on B&B, offering ten rather nice en-suite rooms that are light on the swankiness, heavy on the creature comforts. Go for Room 10, up under the sloping eaves – more like a mini-suite, with a kingsize bed, rolltop bath and walk-in shower. The public areas are a bit chilly – there's not much sense of life – but that's perfect if you just want to hole up in peace. **£120**

EATING AND DRINKING

With its long tradition of hospitality – a century and a half ago twelve stagecoaches a day were stopping here, served by dozens of inns – Woodstock still has plenty of places to eat and drink. However, with the quantity of holiday-makers passing through, quality at some of the tearooms can be patchy – and with Woodstock's ritzy aspirations, prices can also be uncomfortably high.

Bear Park St ☎01993 811124, ⓦmacdonaldhotels.co.uk. Traditional charm in the restaurant of this old coaching inn. Try to grab a table by the big bay window for classic, upscale, country-house hotel-style food – Gressingham duck, corn-fed chicken, Scottish beef and all. Two-course menu £32. Food served Mon–Thurs noon–2.30pm & 7–9.30pm, Fri & Sat noon–2.30pm & 6.45–10pm, Sun noon–2.30pm & 7–9pm.

Feathers Market St ☎01993 812291, ⓦfeathers.co.uk. Lovely restaurant in this boutique hotel. Expect minimalist portions, artfully presented, encompassing seasonal, organic ingredients – spring lamb or Cornish brill or mackerel, scallops in sherry or quail. Mains £17–22, or opt for the five-course Tasting Menu at £55 (plus £24 for wine pairings). Afterwards – or before – repair to the Gin Bar, which offers over fifty gins from around the world, as well as the Ultimate G&T (£13): Shetland dry gin from a numbered bottle, tonic made with hand-picked Peruvian quinine and ice cubes of Blenheim Palace's own spring water. Food served Sun–Thurs noon–9.30pm, Fri & Sat noon–10pm.

King's Head Park Lane ☎01993 812164, ⓦkingshead woodstock.co.uk. Purportedly Woodstock's oldest standing pub: above the door is a stone marked "1735". Tucked away slightly off the main drag, this is a more down-to-earth establishment than others in town, with decent, uncomplicated food: haddock fishcakes, chicken and mushroom pie, cheeseburgers and so on (mains £10–16, or three courses for £19) – plus local Cotswold ice cream and a board of all-Oxfordshire cheeses. Tues–Sat noon–11pm, Sun noon–6pm.

★**La Galleria** 2 Market Place ☎01993 813381, ⓦlagalleriawoodstock.com. Accomplished little Italian with an appealingly fresh interior of flowers set on white tablecloths, its terrace tables spilling out onto the cobbled "Shambles" – formerly the butchers' market – behind the Town Hall. Always popular, with a buzz of conversation inside and out. There are few surprises on the menu, but everything is cooked perfectly and served with grace: pastas are £9–11, mains – including grilled Dover sole (£24) – are mostly £14–19. Tues–Sat noon–2pm & 7–10pm, Sun noon–2.30pm & 7–10pm.

Blenheim Palace

5

Palace: mid-Feb to end Oct daily 10.30am–5.30pm; Nov to mid-Dec Wed–Sun same times; park daily 9am–6pm or dusk • Palace, park and gardens £22.50; park and gardens £13.50 • ☎ 01993 810530, ⓦ blenheimpalace.com

Nowadays, successful British commanders get medals and titles, but in 1704, as a thank-you for his victory over the French at the Battle of Blenheim (a small town in Bavaria, pronounced "blennim"), **Queen Anne** gave **John Churchill**, Duke of Marlborough (1650–1722), the royal estate of Woodstock, along with the promise of enough cash to build himself a palace. It is now designated as a World Heritage Site.

Work started promptly on **Blenheim Palace** under the guidance of **John Vanbrugh**, architect of Castle Howard in Yorkshire. However, Marlborough's formidable duchess wife, Sarah – who, it is said, had wanted Christopher Wren as architect – was soon at loggerheads with Vanbrugh, while the queen had second thoughts about the whole scheme. Treasury money dried up and, in 1712, construction work halted. The Marlboroughs went into self-imposed exile and only returned to Britain after Anne's death in 1714. With George I refusing to stump up any more cash, Marlborough decided to finish the house at his own expense, and reinstated Vanbrugh and his architectural assistant **Nicholas Hawksmoor**. Building work restarted in 1716 but creative differences persisted: Marlborough couldn't or wouldn't pay the going rate, meaning that skilled designers who had worked on the house previously, such as **Grinling Gibbons**, refused to return. Vanbrugh also departed in high dudgeon. Marlborough died in 1722, whereupon the Duchess brought Hawksmoor back. Within a couple of years the house was finished, though wrangling about interior fittings continued into the 1730s.

Equally as impressive is Blenheim's estate, through which passes the River Glyme. During the house's construction Vanbrugh had altered the river's flow and built his Grand Bridge, and the Duchess had had the Column of Victory (see p.180) installed in 1730 shortly after the 1st Duke's death, but it was only when the 4th Duke commissioned master landscaper **"Capability" Brown** in 1764 that the estate was

CHURCHILLS, SPENCERS AND VANDERBILTS

The history of the dukes of Marlborough is a complicated tale entwining three families. **John Churchill**, an English general, was made Earl of Marlborough by William III in 1689 – and then elevated to **Duke of Marlborough** by Queen Anne in 1702. He died in 1722 without surviving sons: it took a special Act of Parliament to allow his title to pass to his eldest daughter, **Henrietta**. On her death in 1733, the title reverted to the male line, passing to the 1st Duke's grandson, **Charles Spencer** (an ancestor of Lady Diana Spencer, Princess of Wales in the 1980s and 1990s). For two generations the dukes of Marlborough bore the Spencer surname, until the 5th Duke obtained the right in 1817 to reinstate "Churchill": to this day, the family is **Spencer-Churchill**. Winston Leonard Spencer-Churchill – who preferred to be known as **Winston Churchill** – was born in Blenheim Palace in 1874, grandson of the 7th Duke.

By the time the 9th Duke, **Charles**, inherited in 1892, the family was virtually bankrupt after decades of poor financial management. In a bid to inject new money into the estate, in 1895 Charles married the American railroad heiress **Consuelo Vanderbilt**. It was a loveless match of convenience: the Vanderbilts were simply paying for access to the British aristocracy, to the tune of, in today's money, several hundred million dollars – enough to ensure the survival of the Blenheim estate. Two sons were born in rapid succession, then Vanderbilt left her husband in 1906; they divorced in 1921.

The **11th Duke of Marlborough**, who lived in Blenheim Palace for much of his life, was John George Vanderbilt Spencer-Churchill (1926–2014). He effectively disowned his eldest son and direct heir, Charles (born 1955), who goes by the name Jamie Blandford, and who has twice been jailed, for forgery, criminal damage and dangerous driving. Blandford inherited the ducal title on his father's death in 2014, becoming the **12th Duke of Marlborough**, but ownership of Blenheim skipped over him to his son, George (born 1992).

5

transformed. Brown created the lake which exists today by damming the Glyme, and shaped the land with undulations and naturalistic tree-planting. Later dukes added follies and ornamental gardens.

The end result is England's grandest example of Baroque architecture, an Italianate palace of finely worked yellow stone, designed chiefly as a national monument to the military exploits of the 1st Duke and only secondarily as a home. Around it stretches some of the finest landscaping in the country. Everything is intended to wow.

East Gate

The main entrance to the palace complex is the massive, top-heavy **East Gate**, topped by a flagstaff. Walk through, across an enclosed courtyard past the **Orangery** on the left, and pass beneath the chunky, dense **Clock Tower Arch**, carved by Grinling Gibbons with English lions nonchalantly tearing chunks out of squawking French cockerels. You emerge into the **Great Court**, an expanse of stone paving and gravel paths: to the right opens a majestic vista over the park, centred on an arrow-straight axis climbing to the **Column of Victory** (see p.180), while to the left soars the imposing **north front** of the palace itself.

The facade

The palace's facade is designed to be daunting – and it is. A broad mass of pillars and stonework and towers and finials claws its way upwards, reaching a cluster of roofs topped with heroic Classical statues in the Renaissance style. Squat, spiky and utterly impenetrable, it encloses the courtyard on three sides. As you face the main entrance, its columns and pediment reminiscent of a Roman temple, the **private apartments** of the Duke of Marlborough's family are to the left (east). On the right a marked passageway beneath the colonnade leads through to the **café** and **Water Terraces** beyond. Dead ahead, climb the steps to the palace doors – but pause at the top to turn round and you'll see, perfectly aligned on the far horizon, the Column of Victory.

The interior
The Great Hall and Churchill Exhibition

As you enter the stunning **Great Hall**, staff will explain how to tour the interior (and whether the private apartments are open that day; see p.180).

To the left around the hall's perimeter, you could start upstairs with the "**Untold Story**", a forty-minute audiovisual trot through Blenheim's history, with interactive panels and video characterizations – or you could turn right for the self-guided Churchill Exhibition and to begin touring the palace's display rooms.

Before you do either, take in the hall itself – an extraordinary spectacle, with its vast marble floor, double rows of arches, high windows and carved Corinthian capitals. Opposite the door looms the main arch, topped by the arms of Queen Anne, with, behind, a bust of the 1st Duke above the entrance to the Saloon (which is visited later on the tour); on the ceiling some 70ft overhead, the 1st Duke kneels in victory before Britannia, in a heroic painting of 1716 by Sir James Thornhill.

The **Churchill Exhibition** comprises a half-dozen rooms in the west wing of the palace, housing fascinating displays on Winston's life, from the room where he was born in 1874 – admire his baby vest and a lock of his hair – to letters, paintings and the "US Honorary Citizen's Document" awarded by John F. Kennedy in 1963.

It returns you to a corridor of the Great Hall, alongside a cabinet with a collection of lead soldiers given to the 11th Duke in 1935. This is the spot from where the guided tours depart; you could pause here to join the next one – or just stroll onwards.

The drawing-rooms and writing-room

First comes the **China Anteroom**, lined with cabinets displaying Sèvres and Meissen porcelain including – at the far end on the right, bottom shelf – a soup tureen with handles made to look like sliced lemons and asparagus spears. At the back of the anteroom stands the Blenheim Bureau, designed by Viscount Linley to celebrate the millennium and set with a fine marquetry panel.

Alongside, the **Green Drawing-Room** sports a stunning ceiling in 24-carat gold leaf by Nicholas Hawksmoor. The furniture is Louis XV, while over the fireplace hangs a portrait of the 4th Duke; on the north wall, his wife, Caroline, dandles her baby in a painting by Joshua Reynolds. In the contrasting **Red Drawing-Room** – very English in style, with Chippendale chairs – two huge paintings face each other. On the right is the 4th Duke and family, by Reynolds (1778); on the left, the 9th Duke and family, by John Singer Sargent (1905). In the latter, Consuelo Vanderbilt wears a dress which deliberately echoes that worn by Lady Killigrew in a painting by Van Dyck which also hangs here.

The **Green Writing-Room** – with another Hawksmoor gilded ceiling – features the first of a series of Flemish tapestries in wool and silk commissioned while the palace was being built. Left of the fireplace is the victory scene from the Battle of Blenheim: the French commander Tallard is doffing his hat in surrender to the Duke of Marlborough, while, behind, mills blaze and French troops flee. To the right hangs a vigorous portrait of the duke at the age of 25, in black armour.

The Saloon and state rooms

Focal point of the palace and, in truth, the entire estate, is the **Saloon** or State Dining-Room, designed so that when the duke was seated in prime position, all the landscaping of the park – focused around the axis from the Column of Victory to this room – and all the architecture of the palace, also centred on this room, served to glorify his person. Around the walls are depictions of the peoples of the world, as if gazing into the room, by French artist Louis Laguerre (who left a self-portrait in the far right hand corner). The ceiling, showing the 1st Duke in victory, held back by the hand of Peace, is also by Laguerre. Today, the saloon is used by the family only once a year, on Christmas Day, when the table is extended to seat about forty.

Beside, three lavish state rooms house more tapestries. The **First State Room**, with a radiant portrait of Consuelo Vanderbilt at 17 over the fireplace, displays a copy of the Blenheim Dispatch, a note scribbled on the back of a tavern bill by the 1st Duke to inform Queen Anne of "a glorious victory". In the **Second State Room**, the tapestry on the left shows a rare artistic blunder: a dog with horse's hooves. The **Third State Room** was originally the duke's bedchamber, full of furniture from Versailles, including beautiful marquetry cabinets of ebony, overlaid with brass on tortoiseshell.

WINSTON CHURCHILL AND BLENHEIM

Winston Churchill, Britain's Prime Minister during most of World War II – and the "Greatest Briton of All Time" according to a public vote for a BBC TV show – once wrote: "At Blenheim I took two very important decisions: to be born and to marry. I am happily content with the decisions I took on both those occasions." The room where Churchill was born is preserved in the palace, along with memorabilia both personal and public: he often returned to Blenheim over his lifetime, proposing here, painting views of the house and gardens and researching the life of the 1st Duke for the biography *Marlborough, His Life and Times*, published in four volumes (1933–38). Churchill died in 1965 and, at his request, was buried in the family plot at St Martin's Church in **Bladon**, just outside the Blenheim estate. His grave can be visited today: narrow lanes climb steeply through Bladon village, on the south side of the A4095 road a mile or so outside Woodstock, to the modest little church, quiet and atmospheric. Perhaps coincidentally, the axis line which runs from the Column of Victory over Vanbrugh's bridge to Blenheim Palace can be extended to finish exactly at the Bladon churchyard.

5

The Long Library and Chapel

The palace's largest room, the **Long Library**, runs the length of the west wing. Originally planned by Vanbrugh to be a gallery, though for the most part executed by Hawksmoor (his stucco ceiling is exceptional), it is 184ft long and 33ft high. Ten thousand books line its walls, while at the far end looms an elaborate organ, installed in 1891. Stroll down the room, past family photos and a collection of ermine ceremonial robes, and exit behind the organ onto the honeystone colonnade above the Great Court. Signs lead down some stairs into the adjacent **Chapel**, a long, slender room with mostly Victorian furniture that is overwhelmed by a gigantic marble monument to the 1st Duke. Tellingly, the high altar is demoted to an inconsequential – and heterodox – position on the west wall to make space for it.

Tour of the private apartments

To allow you to enter the family's **private apartments**, a guide will open an anonymous door off the Great Court; this gives into what was the palace undercroft. Highlights include a billiard room and, alongside the kitchens, a functioning panel of Victorian bells – 47 of them – connected to rope-pulls in rooms all over the palace. Upstairs, you pass through a **Sitting Room**, hung with portraits by Lady Diana Spencer (1734–1808), daughter of the 3rd Duke, to the **Smoking Room**, which has views over the splendid **Italian garden** and a miniature painting of a packet of Marlboro cigarettes – a little pun on the family title. The twelve bedrooms upstairs and the servants' dorms in the attic (dubbed "Housemaids' Heights") are off-limits.

The gardens and park

Miniature train: March–Oct every 30min • 50p

Most people start their exploration of Blenheim's **formal gardens** by riding the narrow-gauge **miniature train** from the "Palace Station", located by the car parking area outside the main East Gate, on a short, looping journey to the **Pleasure Gardens** a few hundred yards to the east (also an easy walk). Here, as well as a café, you'll find a **butterfly house**, **lavender garden**, the **Marlborough Maze** – a huge hedge-maze – and other diversions.

Between the palace and the Pleasure Gardens, the **Secret Garden** – a twentieth-century creation – is a lovely place to sit, surrounded by bamboos, succulents, Japanese maples and more.

Otherwise, aim for the west side of the house, where fountains in the gorgeous **Water Terraces** spout beside the terrace of the palace café. Paths lead down to the lake on a long, circular route past the **Cascades** – part of Capability Brown's designs – the **Arboretum**, planted with cedar, beech and willow, and the vivid **Rose Garden** (with a picturesque **Temple of Diana**, where Winston Churchill proposed to his wife-to-be in 1908) and back to the palace: reckon on an hour or more in total.

Blenheim's open **park** is at least as enticing, with the path from the front of the house leading you down to Vanbrugh's **Grand Bridge** over the artificial lake – beside a strategically placed island of poplar trees – and up the other side to the hilltop **Column of Victory**, topped by a heroic statue of the 1st Duke. It's said that Capability Brown laid out the trees and avenues to represent the Blenheim battlefield.

ARRIVAL AND DEPARTURE   **BLENHEIM PALACE**

The Blenheim Palace estate has two **entrances**, both admitting cars, pedestrians and cyclists: the Hensington Gate lies just south of Woodstock on the A44 Oxford Rd, a few minutes' walk from the town centre, while the quieter Woodstock Gate (see p.175) is in the centre of Woodstock, at the far end of Park St.

By bus Bus #S3 (hourly) stops at the Hensington Gate, on its route to/from Chipping Norton (20min), Charlbury (25min) and Oxford (30min), as does bus #233 (Mon–Sat hourly) to/from Witney (30min), Minster Lovell (35min) and Burford (45min).

TOURS AND ACTIVITIES

Tours of the palace Free guided tours (35min) around the palace's display rooms depart about every quarter-hour or when enough people have gathered, though you're free to opt out and stroll at your own pace. On Sundays or when the palace is very busy, the tours are replaced by guides stationed in every room, who give details of the collections as you move through.

Tours of the private apartments On days when the family is absent, their private apartments in the east wing are sometimes opened for guided tours (£4.50 extra; 30min): to join, consult staff in the Great Hall.

Themed tours Check the website for details of occasional themed tours on – for instance – "The Unknown Winston" or "Ladies of Blenheim" (prices vary; book in advance).

Events Blenheim hosts many annual events, detailed on the website, including horse trials, jousting, charity bike rides and more, as well as a major literary festival every September.

Fishing Anglers can fish part of the lake for trout, under strict conditions (£28/day; booking essential).

Walking Several public rights of way pass through far-flung areas of the Blenheim estate, including stretches of the Wychwood Way and Oxfordshire Way near the Column of Victory. These are free to use; the easiest access is from a signed path opposite the *Black Prince* pub, down the hill from Woodstock town centre.

Banbury
and North
Oxfordshire

BROUGHTON CASTLE

Banbury and North Oxfordshire

North Oxfordshire offers a change of pace. Centred on the valley of the River Cherwell, flowing south from Banbury, and the Oxford Canal that was built alongside it in the eighteenth century, this is a lovely bit of the country for those who like to be at one remove from the hubbub. It has much of the Cotswolds' beauty, with rolling hills, honeystone villages, ancient churches and some of England's most romantic stately homes, but it stands well outside the Cotswolds proper, so consequently has nothing to live up to – prices are lower, restaurants less fancy, hotels trying less hard to wow. With the M40 motorway running through, and trains serving villages between Banbury and Oxford, you could do worse than base yourself here for a series of day-trips into more prestigious Cotswolds countryside further west.

The region revolves around the market town of **Banbury**, a down-to-earth place with a long history encompassing Civil War plotting and pre-Victorian industrial endeavour. Tangential to the Cotswolds, Banbury – perhaps surprisingly – also has little to do with Oxford, and prefers to think of itself standing alone, commanding a meadow-girt fiefdom that includes the sleepy dormitory town of **Bicester** and country villages around and about, including cosy **Deddington**. Nearby **Lower Heyford** gives access to walks and narrowboat holidays on the **Oxford Canal**.

On the Cotswold fringe west of Banbury, **Hook Norton** is a draw for its Victorian brewery – still turning out the best of Oxfordshire ales – while stately homes such as **Broughton Castle** and **Sulgrave Manor** offer evocative slices of historical interest. Further south towards Oxford, within spitting distance of grand Blenheim Palace (see p.177) on the edge of Woodstock (see p.173), you could put your feet up for a canalside pint in **Thrupp** – or aim for gentle **Islip**, on the edge of misty, desolate **Otmoor**.

Banbury

Although it officially plays the county's second fiddle to Oxford, **BANBURY** has never had much to do with its highfalutin neighbour. Indeed, for the last couple of centuries at least, this hardworking, unpretentious place has instead preferred to think of itself as the focus of "**Banburyshire**", an informal network of villages and rural farming communities in the town's immediate orbit which includes parts of the adjacent counties of Northamptonshire and Warwickshire but which pays little heed to the goings-on further south. Banbury is also unusually diverse, with significant populations of Poles – you'll see several Polish delis around town – and Pakistanis, almost all the latter originating from one small district of Kashmir. In mindset, preoccupations and accent, this is more of a Midlands town than a Cotswolds one.

Highlights

❶ Banbury Genial market town with a long history that serves as a gateway to the region, with access to road, rail and canal routes. **See p.184**

❷ Inn at Farnborough One of the best country restaurants in the area – a former village pub updated to take in top-rated modern British cuisine. **See p.191**

❸ Sulgrave Manor An Elizabethan farmhouse in the Northamptonshire countryside, with a unique link to both British and American history through the family of George Washington. **See p.192**

❹ Broughton Castle One of England's most romantic stately homes, its battlements and rose garden encircled by a moat. **See p.194**

❺ Hook Norton Brewery In a tiny Oxfordshire village, this unique Victorian tower brewery still turns out some of the best ale you'll ever sup. **See p.196**

❻ Deddington Farmers' Market This modest village midway between Banbury and Oxford is worth a special visit for its wonderful monthly farmers' market. **See p.196**

HIGHLIGHTS ARE MARKED ON THE MAP ON P.186

6

Brief history

Banbury has a long history: **Iron Age** and **Roman** settlements, exploiting a ford across the River Cherwell, were developed under a **Saxon** chieftain named Banna (thus "Banna's burgh"). The town appears in the **Domesday Book** (1086) as "Banesberie". In 1642, Banbury played a key role in the early stages of the **Civil War**, caught between Royalist and Parliamentary forces: it is said that Oliver Cromwell planned the Battle of Edgehill (see p.193) in the back room of the town's *Ye Olde Reinedeer* inn. Banbury's twelfth-century **castle** was demolished soon afterwards, the stones used to rebuild the town. Later prosperity arrived with the **canals** in the 1770s, the **railways** in the 1850s and the **motorway** in 1990, but in typically unsentimental fashion, for much of the last century Banbury was known best for hosting the largest cattle market in Europe, livestock being driven into town *en masse* – and often on the hoof – from as far afield as Scotland. The cattle market closed in 1998, though Banbury still thinks big: Britain's entire supply of Kenco originates here, from the **world's largest coffee factory**. As you drive into town,

BANBURY AND NORTH OXFORDSHIRE

HIGHLIGHTS

1. Banbury
2. Inn at Farnborough
3. Sulgrave Manor
4. Broughton Castle
5. Hook Norton Brewery
6. Deddington Farmers' Market

Cotswolds Area of Outstanding Natural Beauty (AONB)

0   5
miles

keep your windows open: you may sniff the aroma of roasting coffee, perhaps followed by the mouthwatering scents of fresh-baked bread (from the huge Fine Lady bakery) and melting chocolate (from the industrial chocolatiers Barry Callebaut) – a very continental combination of smells wreathing what is, in truth, a pretty ordinary market town.

Market Place and around

Ⓦ banburyoldtown.co.uk

6

With the site of Banbury's medieval castle now occupied by the **Castle Quay shopping mall**, start a stroll about town in the paved **Market Place** alongside, which has a couple of sixteenth- and seventeenth-century facades surviving in what is essentially still a Saxon layout, with one street entering (from the east) and two streets exiting (to the west). In the northern corner, the Neoclassical frontage of the old corn exchange, opened in 1857, now gives into the mall; just in front, a plaque set into the pavement marks the location of Banbury's original **High Cross**, demolished by order of the Puritan town authorities on July 26, 1600.

Banbury Museum

Castle Quay • Mon–Sat 10am–5pm • Free • Ⓦ banburymuseum.org

On the north bank of the Oxford Canal, but usually accessed through the tourist office hidden away inside the Castle Quay mall (Ⓦ castlequay.co.uk), the **Banbury Museum** forms a well-presented little collection showcasing the town's history, including a medieval cannon, Victorian textiles and diverting displays on Banbury cakes and the development of the canal network.

Tooley's Boatyard

Castle Quay • Guided tours: Easter–Oct Sat 2pm • £5.50 • Boat trips: Easter–Oct Sat 3pm (40min) • £5 • Booking essential • Ⓦ tooleysboatyard.co.uk

The Castle Quay mall backs onto the Oxford Canal, as it passes through town on the route between Oxford and Coventry. Tucked opposite the Banbury Museum, **Tooley's**

RIDE A COCK HORSE TO BANBURY CROSS

Banbury is well known in both Britain and America for a popular song or **nursery rhyme**:

Ride a cock horse
To Banbury Cross
To see a fine lady upon a white horse
With rings on her fingers
And bells on her toes
She shall have music wherever she goes.

The rhyme was first printed in 1744, but was almost certainly known long before that, probably in several different versions. Its meaning is hard to pin down. Some say "a fine lady" was in fact "a Fiennes lady" – that is, traveller **Celia Fiennes** (1662–1741), sister of the third Viscount Saye and Sele of Broughton Castle (see p.194), the first woman known to have visited every county of England; her memoirs recounting epic horse-rides from Newcastle to Cornwall in the 1680s and 1690s are still in print. Others link the "fine lady" to Lady Godiva, Elizabeth I or even pagan fertility festivals worshipping the goddess of the Earth.

As for "**cock horse**", Banbury Museum offers three explanations – first, that it was another name for a child's hobby horse (a good enough excuse for Banbury to stage a **Hobby Horse Festival** every July); or that it refers to riding a horse "a-cock", where a lady would ride side-saddle behind a gentleman on the same animal; or – most plausibly – that a "cock horse" was an extra horse that helped coaches tackle steep slopes: in the eighteenth century, as the London to Banbury coach stopped at the bottom of Stanmore Hill in Middlesex for a fifth horse to be attached, the local children would chorus "Ride a cock horse to Banbury Cross".

But it's all rather hazy. Marry this with the fact that the original Banbury Cross is no more (see above), and – as usual with folk rhymes – you're left with not much other than a pretty song.

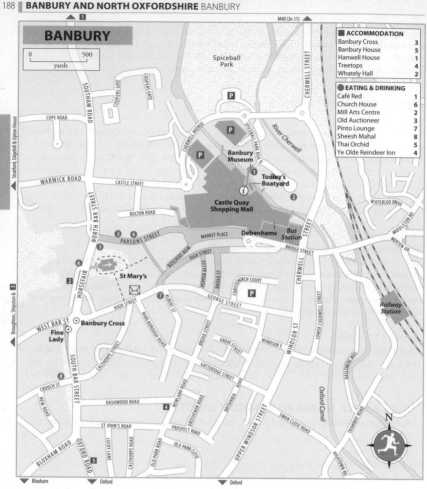

Boatyard is a narrowboat workshop and dry-dock on the canalside that has been in continuous use since 1790. It runs its own guided tours by prior arrangement, and also hires out the *Dancing Duck*, a 39ft narrowboat, for skippered or self-drive leisure cruises.

Ye Olde Reinedeer Inn

47 Parsons St • Mon–Sat 11am–11pm, Sun noon–10.30pm • Ⓦ ye-olde-reinedeer-inn-banbury.co.uk

Banbury's oldest pub stands halfway along pedestrianized Parsons Street, west out of the Market Place. **Ye Olde Reindeer Inn** still has its old wooden gates, marked with the date 1570. Legend has it that Oliver Cromwell held a council of war in the *Reinedeer*'s ornate **Globe Room** just before the Battle of Edgehill in 1642, and returned afterwards, possibly to try Royalist suspects, more plausibly to plan the two sieges of Royalist-held Banbury Castle (1644 and 1646). The room's oak panelling was sold in 1912, to local outrage, only returning in the 1960s after its chance discovery in a London warehouse. Pop in to have a look.

St Mary's Church

Horsefair • April–Oct Mon–Sat 10am–4pm; shorter hours in winter • ⓦ stmaryschurch-banbury.org.uk

Perched on a rise above the town centre, reached via lanes that dog-leg up behind Parsons Street, **St Mary's Church** was consecrated in 1797 on the site of a collapsed Gothic predecessor. It is reminiscent of Wren's London churches, with its pepperpot tower and Classical portico. The bright, painted interior and stained glass are Victorian, while a stone outside recalls *Gulliver's Travels* (1726), in which Jonathan Swift wrote of having "observed in the churchyard at Banbury several tombs and monuments of the Gullivers". The ones he saw have now gone, but Gulliver is an old Banbury name: to the left of the stone, for instance, you'll spot the grave of one Samuel Gulliver, died 1828.

6

Banbury Cross and around

St Mary's Church fronts **Horsefair**, an elegant street marked by the Jacobean facade of the *Whately Hall Hotel* opposite. Just to the south rises **Banbury Cross**, installed in 1859 to commemorate the wedding of Queen Victoria's eldest daughter to a Prussian prince. It's a dour slice of Neo-Gothic, yet stands in a significant location, where roads from Oxford, Warwick and the Cotswolds (Shipston-on-Stour) feed into Banbury's **High Street**. To one side stands a bronze statue of the "fine lady" from the nursery rhyme (see p.187), unveiled in 2005.

Follow the High Street back down into the town, passing on the right the sixteenth-century frontage of S.H. Jones, a local wine merchant. Just after you re-enter the pedestrianized shopping zone, on the left ironwork figures of livestock hang above the entrance to **Butcher's Row**, an alley which formerly held the town's meat market and now offers a whisper of atmosphere amid all the shops for the stroll back into the Market Place.

ARRIVAL AND GETTING AROUND   BANBURY

By car Banbury is two miles off the M40 at junction 11. Coming by car from Oxford, the A4260 via Kidlington and Deddington is a nicer, if slower, drive (roughly 22 miles). Other main routes are from Chipping Norton (A361) and Stratford-upon-Avon (A422).

By train The railway station, with frequent services from London Marylebone, Reading, Oxford and Birmingham (New St and Moor St) is five minutes' walk east of the town centre via Bridge St; the station has no bus links, so you have to walk or take a taxi.

Destinations Birmingham New St (hourly; 50min); London Marylebone (3 hourly; 55min); Oxford (every 30min; 20min); Stratford-upon-Avon (5 daily; 1hr).

By bus The bus station is behind Debenhams off Bridge St, served by local services as well as National Express coaches from Heathrow, Birmingham and further afield.

Destinations Chipping Norton (Mon–Sat hourly; 45min); Deddington (Mon–Sat hourly, 4 on Sun; 20min); Oxford (Mon–Sat hourly, 4 on Sun; 1hr 20min); Shipston-on-Stour (Mon–Sat every 2hr; 45min); Stratford-upon-Avon (Mon–Sat every 2hr; 1hr 10min).

By taxi There are taxi ranks at the railway station, Banbury Cross and opposite Debenhams. Otherwise try Castle Cars (ⓣ01295 270011, ⓦcastlecarsbanbury.co.uk) or Cherwell Cars (ⓣ01295 265555, ⓦcherwellcars.com).

BANBURY TO BATH: THE CROSS-COTSWOLD PATHWAY

Banbury is the starting point for the 86-mile **Cross-Cotswold Pathway**, part of the longer, coast-to-coast Macmillan Way (ⓦmacmillanway.org). The pathway runs more or less parallel to the Cotswold Way national trail (see p.32), but further east: starting in Banbury it heads west to Epwell, then turns southwest to Stow and onwards past Cirencester and Castle Combe to Box, from where a link heads into Bath. Full details are in a dedicated guidebook published by the Macmillan Way Association (£5), available on the website. If you're feeling fit, you could combine the Cross-Cotswold Pathway with a turn at Bath onto the Cotswold Way, for the week-long walk north along the ridge to Chipping Campden (see p.112), from where the 21-mile **Cotswold Link** returns you to Banbury – the whole circuit forms an epic 217-mile trek dubbed the **Cotswold Round**.

INFORMATION

Tourist office Banbury's tourist office (Mon, Tues, Thurs & Fri 8.45am–5.15pm, Wed 10am–5.15pm, Sat 10am–5pm; ☎ 01295 753752, ⓦ visitnorthoxfordshire.com) is inconveniently located inside the Castle Quay shopping mall. It's very well stocked with leaflets, maps and books, and staff can book accommodation for the whole region, as well as advise about the plentiful self-catering options nearby. ⓦ banburyshireinfo.co.uk is a good source of local information, while ⓦ banburyoldtown.co.uk covers aspects of the old town.

ACCOMMODATION

6

Banbury Cross 1 Broughton Rd ☎ 01295 266048, ⓦ banburycrossbandb.co.uk. Lovely B&B in a big old Victorian house three minutes' walk from Banbury Cross, offering a choice of sprucely presented singles, doubles, twins and family rooms, as well as the oak-panelled Broughton Suite. Breakfast is notably good, with locally sourced produce. **£60**

Banbury House Oxford Rd ☎ 01295 259361, ⓦ banbury house.co.uk. A Best Western hotel occupying a row of Georgian townhouses a short walk (uphill) from the centre. The style is fairly subdued, but it's a comfortable enough place to rest your head. They also run serviced apartments for rent nearby. **£99**

★**Hanwell House** 2 Lapsley Drive ☎ 01295 263001, ⓦ hanwellhouse.com. Friendly B&B on a new-build estate a mile north of the centre: it's a walk or bus ride into Banbury. Three rooms – an en-suite king, a twin and an en-suite double – are very neat and tasteful, with attention to detail (like home-made biscuits) lifting the place out of the ordinary. **£55**

Treetops 28 Dashwood Rd ☎ 01295 254444, ⓦ treetops banbury.co.uk. Decent, high-quality B&B in an Edwardian house on a hilly street just behind the town centre, run by a friendly local couple, with four en-suite doubles and a small single. **£80**

Whately Hall 17 Horsefair ☎ 01295 253261, ⓦ mercure.com. This hotel certainly looks the part – a fine seventeenth-century frontage in honeyed Cotswold stone stretching along a tree-shaded main street through the centre of town, right by Banbury Cross, and with its own resident ghost (Father Bernard, a Catholic priest who was the victim of a practical joke in 1687, died of fright and has restlessly roamed ever since). A good deal of character survives within, too, with plenty of oak panelling and a lovely enclosed rear garden, though the bedrooms lose the plot slightly, a sometimes uneasy mix of corporate chic and floral country house. **£109**

CAMPING

Anita's Mollington ☎ 01295 750731, ⓦ oxfordshire camping.co.uk. Decent caravan and camping site just off the A423 about three miles north of Banbury, within walking distance of the village pub and also offering self-catering accommodation. Pitches **£17**

Bo Peep Aynho Rd, Adderbury ☎ 01295 810605, ⓦ bo-peep.co.uk. Well-equipped four-star site a couple of miles south of Banbury near woodland off the A4260. Open March–Oct. Pitches **£18**

EATING AND DRINKING

Banbury's restaurants match its personality – unsentimental. The best-known delicacy is **Banbury cakes** (ⓦ banburycakes .co.uk), oval currant-filled pastries rather like Eccles cakes, but all the historic bakeries which once made and sold them have been pulled down. Only a handful of docile tearooms still oblige, notably *Banesberie* on Butcher's Row and *Café Red* (reviewed below). Otherwise, the town's strong Kashmiri community has given rise to unusually good **curry houses**: Parsons St, in particular, is shoulder-to-shoulder with them. But for real quality you'd do better to head out to one of the **villages**. We've listed three options below, or – within a fifteen-minute radius by car – consider the *Crown & Tuns* in Deddington, *Wykham Arms* in Sibford Gower or *Masons Arms* on the Chipping Norton road (for all, see p.196).

IN TOWN

Café Red Opposite Tooley's Boatyard ☎ 01295 270444, ⓦ cafered.co.uk. The only place in town where you can have a coffee and a bun on the waterside, with seating both indoors and on a canal-front terrace. Accessible from Banbury Museum as well as from the towpath. Mon–Sat 10am–3pm.

Church House 2 North Bar ☎ 01295 262292, ⓦ thechurchhousebanbury.co.uk. Lovely-looking old building in Cotswold stone opposite St Mary's Church, originally the church hall, now a pub and brasserie. The food is better than it was, with a decent choice of fish, risottos, steaks and salads – but come for the interior, a lofty space with a 45ft curved ceiling: it feels a tiny bit like sipping cocktails in a cathedral. Daily 11.30am–11pm.

Mill Arts Centre Spiceball Park ☎ 01295 252050, ⓦ www.themillartscentre.co.uk. Local theatre and music venue in a former mill beside the canal lock in the middle of town, whose café-bar is a relaxed and friendly spot for refreshments whether or not you're interested in a show. Mon–Fri 9.30am–11pm, Sat 10am–11pm.

Old Auctioneer 44 Parsons St ☎ 01295 270492, ⓦ theoldauctioneerbanbury.co.uk. Bright, quirky lounge-bar restaurant in a renovated seventeenth-century inn. Service can sometimes be a bit distracted but the food – fajitas, hand-thrown pizzas and specialities such as lamb and chorizo kebabs (£9–14) – is good. On the whole, great value. Mon–Fri 11am–midnight, Sat 10am–midnight, Sun 11am–10pm.

★**Pinto Lounge** 21 High St ☎01295 275467, ⓦthelounges.co.uk. The cheeriest welcome in town, in this popular wood-and-tiles pub and informal restaurant – pop in for coffee, a glass of wine or a full meal. They do brunches (fry-up or pancakes £6–8), posh fish and chips made with beer-battered pollock (£10), oddities such as falafel burger or hot dogs (£7) and a blackboard full of specials, with kids' meals and vegan or gluten-free menus too. Daily 9am–11pm.

Sheesh Mahal 43 South Bar ☎01295 266489, ⓦwww.sheeshmahalbanbury.co.uk. Best of Banbury's many Indian restaurants, occupying an old townhouse beside Banbury Cross and offering light, carefully spiced dishes and genial, courteous service. Mains £8–13. Sun–Thurs 6pm–midnight, Fri & Sat 4.30pm–midnight.

Thai Orchid 56 North Bar ☎01295 270833, ⓦthaigroup.co.uk. A Banbury institution for almost thirty years, with a cramped interior of extravagantly carved wood and its own fish-pond, serving exquisite Thai food at a lunchtime buffet and – better – à la carte in the evenings. All the classics are present on an encyclopedic menu, the spicing of the soups and curries is perfectly authentic and though service can be a bit perfunctory this is still a fine choice. Mains £9–15. Daily noon–2pm & 5.30–10.30pm.

★**Ye Olde Reinedeer Inn** 47 Parsons St ☎01295 270972, ⓦye-olde-reinedeer-inn-banbury.co.uk. Banbury's oldest and best pub – also signed as the *Old Reindeer*, the *Reindeer* and variations – a sixteenth-century gem that's full of history (see p.188) and offers well-cared-for local Hook Norton ales in a quiet, congenial ambience. Mon–Thurs 11am–11pm, Fri & Sat 11am–midnight, Sun noon–10.30pm.

OUT OF TOWN

★**Inn at Farnborough** Farnborough ☎01295 690615, ⓦwww.theinnfarnborough.co.uk. A rural restaurant of the highest quality, six miles north of Banbury just off the A423. The inn has kept its eighteenth-century looks outside, but has been transformed with a contemporary styled interior of rich colours and eye-catching decor, and truly outstanding food. Mains (£10–22) blend a modern British approach – shin of beef with spinach and carrots, venison or partridge in season – with innovative touches, such as char-grilled monkfish with saffron risotto. Set menus (£22–25 for three courses) are available; watch out, too, for special deals, such as half-price offers before 7pm. Mon–Sat 10am–3pm & 6–11pm, Sun 10am–midnight.

Fox at Farthinghoe Farthinghoe ☎01295 713965, ⓦfoxatfarthinghoe.co.uk. Bright and breezy renovated pub in a tiny Northamptonshire village five miles east of Banbury (also home to the excellent *Limes Farm* shop and tearoom ⓦlimesfarm.com). The menu – cullen skink soup, beer-battered haddock, lamb tagine – focuses on locally sourced produce, but the attraction is the locals-only feel, the busy, friendly ambience and the distinctly affordable prices. It's all rather fun. Mains £9–14. No food Sun eve. Mon–Thurs noon–2.30pm & 6–11pm, Fri & Sat noon–11pm, Sun noon–9pm.

Moon & Sixpence Hanwell ☎01295 730544, ⓦthemoonandsixpencehanwell.com. Pleasant old pub in this village a couple of miles out on Banbury's northwestern fringe, presenting classic British cuisine with an upmarket edge – for example, home-made venison, pork and chicken sausage, served as a starter with caramelized apples, or oven-roasted breast of guinea fowl stuffed with a herb mousse. Vegetarian dishes are available, best requested when booking (which is essential). À la carte mains cost £16–20, or a two-course set menu (Mon–Thurs) is £14 – and they also offer more affordable pub classics (Sun–Fri) such as fish and chips, steak and kidney pudding, and so on for £10–12 each. No food Sun eve. Mon–Sat noon–3pm & 6–11pm, Sun noon–6pm.

DIRECTORY

Bookshops Waterstones is in the Castle Quay mall – or have a browse at Books & Ink, an independent bookshop at 4 White Lion Walk (ⓦbooksandinkbookshop.com).
Hospital Horton Hospital, Oxford Rd ☎01295 275500.
Markets General market on Market Place (Thurs & Sat 9am–4.30pm; ⓦbanburymarket.co.uk). For farmers' markets, see below.

Pharmacy Boots in Castle Quay mall ☎01295 262015, ⓦboots.com (Mon–Sat 8.30am–5.30pm, Sun 10.30am–4.30pm).
Police station Warwick Rd ☎101, ⓦthamesvalley.police.uk (daily 8am–10pm).
Post office 57 High St (Mon–Sat 9am–5.30pm).

FARMERS' MARKETS

Dates may change around Christmas and New Year. See also ⓦlocalfoods.org.uk.
Banbury 1st Fri of month 8.30am–1.30pm ⓦtvfm.org.uk.
Bicester 2nd Sat of month 8.30am–1pm ⓦtvfm.org.uk.
Deddington 4th Sat of month 9am–12.30pm ⓦdeddingtonfarmersmarket.co.uk.

Around Banbury

Aside from the gloriously evocative manor house at **Sulgrave**, northeast of Banbury – built by the ancestors of George Washington, first president of the United States – we've kept our focus in this section on interesting diversions on routes towards Oxford, Stratford-upon-Avon or into the Cotswolds proper. Civil War history features strongly hereabouts, with battlefield walks at **Cropredy** and **Edgehill** and plotters' hideaways preserved at splendid Broughton Castle. Stately-home fans will also take to **Upton House**, while rural walkers have some interesting trails to tackle around the Oxford Canal village of **Heyford**.

Sulgrave Manor

Sulgrave • April–Oct Sat & Sun 11am–5pm; Aug Tues–Sun 11am–5pm; entry to house by guided tours only, at noon, 2pm & 4pm • £7.90 • ☎ 01295 760205, ⊛ sulgravemanor.org.uk

Eight miles northeast of Banbury in the Northamptonshire village of **SULGRAVE**, a successful wool merchant named **Lawrence Washington** – twice mayor of Northampton – built a manor house in the 1540s on land he had recently purchased from the Crown. A fine example of Elizabethan domestic architecture, the house slowly fell into disrepair over the centuries and would probably have been demolished but for the work of historians in the 1880s, who determined that Lawrence's great-great-grandson John had emigrated to Virginia in 1656 – and that John's great-grandson was none other than **George Washington** (1732–99), first president of the United States. By the turn of the twentieth century, with politicians and philanthropists on both sides of the Atlantic searching for ways to celebrate the centenary of the 1814 Treaty of Ghent, which had established peace between Britain and America, **Sulgrave Manor** was purchased to act as a focus for the "special relationship". The house was opened to the public in 1921 and is still held in trust for the peoples of both countries: the Union Jack and Stars and Stripes fly side-by-side, and this is one of the few places in the English countryside to stage a full-blown Fourth of July ceremonial party.

The manor is open for **guided tours** only. It's not a big house but the tours last an hour and a quarter: the guides are excellent, bringing the place alive with anecdotes, tales of family life and plenty of colourful context. Above the main door you'll see the Washington coat of arms – three stars and two stripes. (The family originated in County Durham: they adopted the name "De Wessyngton" in the twelfth century following their purchase of the Saxon-era estates around what is now Washington in Tyne and Wear.) Inside, you're led through the Great Hall, an oak-panelled music parlour, the fully-equipped kitchens, a lofty bedchamber, and more, amid plenty of Washingtoniana, including original portraits and memorabilia: the mix of Tudor architectural interest and American historical interest is very engaging. There's also a tearoom and pleasant, well-kept **gardens**.

To get here, follow the B4525 towards Northampton, then about four miles out of Banbury take a signed turn-off left towards Sulgrave.

ACCOMMODATION AND EATING   **SULGRAVE**

Star Sulgrave ☎ 01295 760389, ⊛ thestarinnsulgrave .com. An ancient Hook Norton pub just a short stroll down the road from the manor, with good beer, decent food (particularly strong on fish dishes) and it's a cosy option for B&B. Mon–Fri 11am–3pm & 6–11pm, Sat 11am–11pm, Sun 11am–5pm. **£69**

Cropredy

Four miles north of Banbury, peaceful **CROPREDY** was the scene of a major, if inconclusive, Civil War battle in 1644, when Roundheads prevented Royalist forces from crossing a bridge over the River Cherwell, but suffered significant losses in the

LLAMA TREKKING

For an unusual take on the Banburyshire countryside, **Catanger Llamas** (☎07875 136119, ⓦllamatrekking.co.uk), based at Weedon Lois near Sulgrave, can offer a variety of rides, including a two-hour stroll with llamas through fields and woods (£95 for two people). A pre-walk briefing on how to handle – and, if necessary, placate – your llama is, fortunately, included, and you also get the chance to visit the farm shop to buy llama-wool rugs and hats.

6

process. You can download a map and notes for the interesting **Battlefield Walk** around the village (4.5 miles) at ⓦwww.cherwell.gov.uk. Although the village gained a railway station in 1852 and lost it again in 1956, it has remained a landmark on the Oxford Canal for three hundred years: much of the walk follows the towpath.

The **Three Counties Ride** is an easy round-trip **cycle route** from Cropredy which passes through nearby Lower Boddington and Farnborough on quiet roads and country lanes: the full ride is seventeen miles (about 4hr), but several shortcuts are possible. See ⓦwww.cherwell.gov.uk or pick up a leaflet at Banbury tourist office. Beware that Cropredy and the surrounding area are swamped annually in mid-August by **Fairport's Cropredy Convention** (ⓦfairportconvention.com), a weekend music festival held near the village that always features 1970s rock/folk supremos Fairport Convention.

EATING AND DRINKING   CROPREDY

Red Lion Cropredy ☎01295 758680, ⓦtheredlion
cropredy.co.uk. A beautiful old thatched pub with a
roaring fire in winter, known locally for its ales and
family-friendly atmosphere. Phone ahead to check kitchen
times if you're after food. Mon–Sat noon–11pm, Sun
noon–10pm.

Wroxton and Edgehill

Driving on the A422 Stratford road from Banbury past **WROXTON**, whose handsome Jacobean abbey (ⓦwroxtonabbey.org) is now a college for American students, there suddenly comes a point where the road drops off a cliff. The 700ft scarp known, with good reason, as **EDGEHILL**, offers suddenly spectacular views out over the flatlands of Warwickshire – and was also the scene of the first pitched battle of the English Civil War, on October 23, 1642. Royalist armies, camped on top of the hill and threatening the garrison at Banbury, were confronted by Roundhead troops halted down below at Kineton on a relief march towards Banbury from Warwick. The battle, which took place in the fields south of Kineton, was inconclusive: much of the Parliamentarian infantry fled, but the Royalist cavalry broke ranks in pursuit and were driven back themselves. By nightfall, about a thousand men were dead, with more than twice that number wounded – and the war itself rumbled on for several more years. The battlefield is now mostly off-limits, part of a Ministry of Defence munitions depot, but there's a short **walk** around it (1.75 miles; 1hr), starting from the *Castle* pub (see below): download details from their website or ask at the bar.

ACCOMMODATION AND EATING   WROXTON AND EDGEHILL

★**Castle at Edgehill** Ratley ☎01295 670255, ⓦcastle
atedgehill.co.uk. Completely revamped in 2014, this old
Hook Norton pub incorporates a crenellated tower built on the
Edgehill ridge in 1742 to mark the centenary of the battle.
Enjoy a pint with the panoramic view from their garden, linger
for a meal (no food Sun eve) or stay overnight: their rooms
include four-poster beds in the tower. Mon–Thurs noon–
11pm, Fri & Sat noon–midnight, Sun noon–10pm. **£80**

★**Wroxton House** Wroxton ☎01295 730777,
ⓦwroxtonhousehotel.com. Part of the *Best Western*
group, this three-star village hotel occupies a seventeenth-
century thatched inn four miles west of Banbury. It's a
notably good choice, offering 32 rooms with simple,
modern decor, including some in thatched outbuildings,
and a genial brand of service that mixes efficiency with
informality. **£89**

Upton House

7 miles north of Banbury • March–Oct Mon–Wed & Fri–Sun 1–5pm; daily in July & Aug • £10.60 • NT • gardens open from 11am • 30min "taster" tours operate before formal opening (11.15am, 11.55am & 12.35pm; free) • ☎ 01295 670266, ⓦ nationaltrust.org.uk • Johnsons bus #269 between Banbury and Stratford stops nearby twice a day (not Sun)

Beside the A422 Banbury–Stratford road, a mile from Edgehill at the top of the slope, stands **Upton House**, built in 1695 and remarkable for the collection of **fine art** assembled by Walter Samuel, 2nd Viscount Bearsted (1882–1948), whose father founded the Shell oil company. It's an unusual experience, this far out in the country, to be taking in works by El Greco (his *El Espolio* is a highlight), Gainsborough, Reynolds, Stubbs and others – memorably, too, a pair of typically vivid London scenes by Hogarth, *Morning* and *Night*. Make time for the wonderful red and silver Art Deco bathroom, and the collection of Shell Oil memorabilia on the top floor. Don't miss a stroll in the splendid 1930s-style **gardens**. Compton Verney, another magnificent country-house art gallery, is a short drive away (see p.148).

ACCOMMODATION

NEAR UPTON HOUSE

Uplands House Upton ☎ 01295 678663, ⓦ cotswolds -uplands.co.uk. Charming rural guesthouse, rated five stars, in a lovely location six miles northwest of Banbury opposite Upton House, a few yards inside Warwickshire. The three en-suite double rooms are all done up in traditional style, though noticeably upscale – a four-poster bed in one, a Chinese-style mirror in another – with views over the beautiful rear gardens. __£50__

Broughton Castle

Broughton • May to mid-Sept Wed & Sun 2–5pm; July & Aug also Thurs • £9; gardens only £5 • ☎ 01295 276070, ⓦ broughtoncastle.com

Roughly three miles southwest of Banbury, just off the B4035 near the village of **BROUGHTON**, stands one of England's most photogenic stately homes. **Broughton Castle** isn't a castle at all – rather, it is a chiefly fourteenth-century manor house, in its own substantial grounds behind a battlemented gatehouse and surrounded by a broad moat. Built in golden Cotswold stone, embraced by lawns, water, topiary and a fragrant rose garden, and set amid its own wooded valley, it is nothing short of enchanting.

The house has been in the same family since being purchased by William of Wykeham in 1377: the current owners – Nathaniel Fiennes (born 1920) and his wife, the 21st **Lord and Lady Saye and Sele** – still occupy private apartments in the east wing. As well as public tours and other interests, the family makes good money from film producers: Broughton Castle has starred in, to name a couple of blockbusters, *Shakespeare in Love* and *The Madness of King George*, as well as numerous TV costume dramas. Lord Saye (he tends to drop the "and Sele") is second cousin to the explorer Sir Ranulph Fiennes and third cousin once removed to the actors Ralph and Joseph Fiennes.

Approaching the house is just about the most romantic part of all, making your way over the moat bridge and through the fourteenth-century fortified gatehouse to be confronted by the main facade, with its near-symmetrical sets of tall windows and chimney-stacks. Some of the windows on the west (right-hand) side are, in fact, false, filled in at some point and then repainted for effect.

The interior

You enter Broughton Castle at the **Great Hall**, a broad, light space of bare stone walls festooned with family portraits, suits of armour and medieval weaponry beneath a sixteenth-century plastered ceiling. Stout furniture in red plush has been drawn around the stone fireplace. As you stand by the door, on your right are some standing pikes: the hollow-sounding wall beside them was built by the set designers of *Shakespeare in Love* to conceal some pipework, and left as a memento. Less romantically, the orange carpet, with its vaguely heraldic design, is a relic of the Morecambe and Wise 1975 Christmas special, when Eric and Ernie filmed a song-and-dance number here with Diana Rigg.

Guides will direct you through the **Groined Passage**, its fourteenth-century vaulting in pristine condition, past a spiral staircase to the family's **Dining Room**, also vaulted, featuring beautiful sixteenth-century double-linenfold panelling in oak. You continue upstairs to the **Long Gallery**, remodelled in the 1760s, holding porcelain, marble busts and much portraiture. Rooms off it include the **King's Chamber**, its elegant oak bed, made by a local designer in 1992, suiting the lively French chimneypiece of 1554 rather well. Before you go back downstairs to the splendid Tudor **Oak Room** and out to the **gardens**, make your way upstairs again: as well as an exit onto the **roof**, offering breathtaking views over the moat and park, up here is perhaps the house's most interesting nook, the **Council Chamber**, a small, plain hideaway once described as "a room which hath no ears". From 1629 to 1640, a string of notable figures from the Roundhead opposition to Charles I plotted up here in secret, courtesy of their Puritan host, William Fiennes, 8th Baron Saye and Sele – nicknamed "Old Subtlety" for his political shrewdness. Little from that time survives, other than atmosphere.

The garden
In truth, the best of the house is outside: absorbing the views and the history over a quiet cup of tea on the lawns (the stables house a small **café**), and then exploring the dream-like **rose garden**, allows your imagination a free rein.

St Mary's Church
May to mid-Sept Wed & Sun 2–5pm; July & Aug also Thurs • Free

Beside Broughton Castle's gatehouse, tranquil fourteenth-century **St Mary's Church** appears lopsided inside at first glance, with only a nave and south aisle. It is known for its family monuments, which include ten **hatchments**, diamond-framed coats of arms common from the mid-seventeenth to mid-nineteenth centuries created to display the genealogy of a deceased nobleman. A leaflet by the door explains them in detail.

EATING AND DRINKING   **BROUGHTON**

Saye and Sele Arms Broughton ☎01295 263348, ⓦsayeandselearms.co.uk. This lovely old freehouse pub stands in Broughton village alongside the turnoff for the castle, in business since 1782. It's got bags of atmosphere, to go with well-kept beer and hearty English food (mains £12–16; no food Sun eve). Mon–Sat 11.30am–2.30pm & 7–11pm, Sun noon–5pm.

Bloxham
From Banbury Cross, the elegant, tree-lined South Bar road heads up the hill to become the Oxford road (A4260) running south towards Deddington. Partway up, turn off right to join the A361 towards Chipping Norton. Once free of Banbury, you'll pass a marked left turn for the **Wykham Park Farm Shop** (ⓦwykhampark.co.uk), one of the best in the area, before heading through **BLOXHAM**, a village dominated by, first, the Victorian buildings of Bloxham School and then reputedly the tallest church tower in the county, soaring 198ft above **St Mary's Church** at the top of the village and visible from miles around. The tower, like the church, is fourteenth-century, though St Mary's also has a Norman doorway and fragments of medieval wall-paintings above the chancel – as well as Victorian stained glass by William Morris and Edward Burne-Jones. Alongside is the village **museum** (Easter–Oct Sat & Sun 2.30–5pm; £1; ⓦbloxhammuseum.com), with changing exhibits on local themes.

Hook Norton
Signposted a few miles off the A361 Banbury–Chipping Norton road, **HOOK NORTON** is one of the prettier villages in the area, its high street flanked by thatched cottages. Aim first for the **church**, with an impressively tall Perpendicular tower;

inside, the early-Norman stone **font** features clear carvings of the pagan signs of the zodiac.

Hook Norton Brewery

Brewery Lane • Mon–Sat 9.30am–4.30pm • Tours Mon–Fri 11am & 2pm, Sat 10.30am & 1.30pm • £11.50 • ☎ 01608 730384, Ⓦ hooky.co.uk

At the west end of Hook Norton village looms the splendid Victorian **Hook Norton Brewery**, dating from 1849 and still fully-functioning – many say "Hooky" beers are Oxfordshire's best. There's an on-site shop and small **museum** but you'd do better to time your visit for a two-hour **brewery tour**, which shows the brewing process, explains more about the company and the village and ends with free samples. Advance booking is essential.

ARRIVAL AND DEPARTURE   HOOK NORTON

By bus Stagecoach bus #488 (not Sun) runs hourly to Hook Norton from Chipping Norton (25min) and Banbury (25min).

EATING AND DRINKING

IN THE VILLAGE

Pear Tree Hook Norton ☎ 01608 737482, Ⓦ hooky.co.uk. Charming eighteenth-century pub directly outside the brewery, a perfect pitstop on a thirsty summer's afternoon. Sun–Thurs noon–11pm, Fri & Sat noon–midnight.

Sun Inn Hook Norton ☎ 01608 737570, Ⓦ thesuninn-hooknorton.co.uk. Atmospheric village hostelry opposite the church, complete with inglenook fireplace, oak beams and stone flags. Also a good place for modern British pub cuisine (mains £11–15; no food Sun eve), with a few quiet, cosy double rooms, too (£80). Mon–Thurs 10am–11pm, Fri & Sat 10am–midnight, Sun noon–3pm & 7–10.30pm.

NEARBY

Gate Hangs High Whichford Rd ☎ 01608 737387, Ⓦ gatehangshigh.co.uk. This wonderfully named old inn stands alone at a quiet country crossroads just outside Hook Norton on the road towards Sibford. Come for the beer on a sunny day. Daily noon–11pm.

Masons Arms Swerford ☎ 01608 683212, Ⓦ masons-arms.com. Located plumb on the A361 Banbury–Chipping Norton road, this pleasant country pub emphasizes its ethically sourced food, a stylish, upmarket pub version of fine dining, especially strong on fish and seafood (mains around £12–16). No food Sun eve. Mon–Sat 11am–3pm & 6–11pm, Sun 11am–6pm.

★**Wykham Arms** Sibford Gower ☎ 01295 788808, Ⓦ wykhamarms.co.uk. In a peaceful village about three miles north of Hook Norton, this seventeenth-century inn has a flawless reputation across Banburyshire for its outstanding seasonal, local food, served in a distinctly upscale interior. Mains are £10–16, and the pub is renowned in particular for its Sunday roasts. No food Sun eve. Tues–Sat noon–3pm & 6–11pm, Sun noon–10.30pm.

Deddington

Around six miles south of Banbury on the A4260 Oxford road, **DEDDINGTON** is a graceful little town with a fine seventeenth-century church – look for the Gothic vaulting in the north porch. Supplementing the Market Place's clutch of rather nice delis and tearooms is one of Banburyshire's best (and best-loved) monthly **farmers' markets** (see p.191): try and time your visit to coincide with it.

ARRIVAL AND INFORMATION   DEDDINGTON

By bus Stagecoach bus #S4 stops hourly between Banbury (25min) and Oxford (55min).

Information Ⓦ www.deddington.org.uk.

EATING AND DRINKING

Crown and Tuns New St ☎ 01869 337371, Ⓦ puddingface.com. Deddington's gastronomic highlight. This cheery Hook Norton pub on the main road has been updated inside to double as a great local restaurant specializing in pies – huge ones, made fresh to order. The usual culprits are all present – beef and ale, pork and cider, chicken and mushroom – aided by less common options (venison with gin, salmon, pigeon) and veggie versions (potato and mushroom with tarragon, for instance). They cost around £11–14 and will keep you going for the rest of the day. Mon–Fri noon–3pm & 5.30–11pm, Sat & Sun noon–11pm.

BICESTER VILLAGE

Lying just east of the M40 junction 9 – easily reached from Banbury and Oxford – **Bicester Village** (Mon–Sat 9am–8pm, Sun 10am–7pm; ⓦ bicestervillage.com) isn't a village at all. A self-contained retail zone beside the humdrum little town of Bicester, this is, rather, an open-air, extremely swanky "outlet mall", packed with luxury fashion and homeware boutiques selling last season's stock at up to sixty percent off – think Polo Ralph Lauren, Versace, Gucci, Armani, Bulgari, D&G and so forth. Among the dining options on-site is a *Carluccio's*. Parking is plentiful but you could get there best by **train**: Bicester Town station is within walking distance, while a shuttle bus runs to the mall from Bicester North station.

6

Heyford and around

Shadowing the River Cherwell for most of the way between Banbury and Oxford, the **Oxford Canal** offers some pleasant walking, and benefits from **rail** access. Circular and station-to-station walks include the quiet route (4.5 miles) from **TACKLEY** station to **HEYFORD** station. The latter is located directly alongside **Lower Heyford wharf**, headquarters for Oxfordshire Narrowboats (see below). A **circular walk** (7 miles) is waymarked from Heyford station to Middle Aston and back along the towpath, and a shorter two-mile waymarked route covers both Lower and Upper Heyford, the latter located alongside what was once RAF Upper Heyford subsequently one of the US bases where nuclear-armed Cruise missiles were deployed in the 1980s. The base, now decommissioned, has become a business estate, though the missile bunkers are still visible.

Rousham House

Daily 10am–4.30pm • £5 • ⓦ rousham.org • 15min walk from Heyford station • hourly Stagecoach #S4 buses from Banbury (40min) and Oxford (35min)

In woodlands a mile west of Lower Heyford stands handsome **Rousham House**. The house itself – built in 1635 – is off-limits, but the gardens are the attraction, largely unaltered from their initial landscaping by William Kent early in the eighteenth century, featuring terraces, cascades, ponds, Gothic follies and a walled garden.

ARRIVAL AND DEPARTURE   HEYFORD AND AROUND

By bus Stagecoach bus #S4 stops in Tackley hourly between Banbury (45min) and Oxford (30min).
By train First Great Western trains run roughly every

two hours on the Oxford Canal Line between Banbury and Oxford, stopping midway at King's Sutton, Heyford and Tackley.

ACTIVITIES

Boat rental Oxfordshire Narrowboats (ⓣ 01869 340348, ⓦ oxfordshire-narrowboats.co.uk), based alongside Heyford station, can book holidays and short breaks on board traditional narrowboats, as well as offering one-day boat hire

(£150–225/day, depending on the season). You can pop in to nose around their boatyard (March–Oct daily 8.30am–5.30pm, Nov–Feb Mon–Fri 9am–4pm) or grab a tea and a bun at their café, *Kizzies* (see below).

ACCOMMODATION AND EATING

Canal Cottage Heyford Wharf ⓣ 01869 340348, ⓦ oxfordshire-narrowboats.co.uk. Three spruce B&B rooms alongside the Heyford boatyard – and, handily, 50yd from Heyford train station – in the former wharf manager's cottage, now renovated. Closed Nov–Feb. **£70**
Holt Hotel Hopcroft's Holt ⓣ 01869 340259, ⓦ holt hotel.co.uk. This coaching inn at a crossroads on the A4260 Banbury–Oxford road beside Lower Heyford began life in 1475. Rebuilt and augmented over the years, it is now an

86-room hotel, though purportedly is still haunted by the ghost of Claude Duvall, a seventeenth-century highwayman who used to hole up here. Rooms are comfortably old-fashioned, though good value. **£84**
Kizzies Bistro Heyford Wharf ⓣ 01869 340348, ⓦ oxfordshire-narrowboats.co.uk. Cheery little café on the canalside lawns beside Heyford station, serving teas and light lunches. Mid-July to end Aug daily 9am–5pm; May to mid-July and Sept Sat & Sun 9am–5pm.

A KIDLINGTON WALK

An easy **circular walk** of about four miles starts at the church in Kidlington, crosses the fields past Hampton Poyle to a ruined Elizabethan manor house at Hampton Gay, heads along the River Cherwell and then back from Thrupp through riverside woods to Kidlington again. Download a full route description and map at ⓦ www.oxfordshire.gov.uk/kidlingtonwalk.

Kidlington and Thrupp

Once famed for its apricots, **KIDLINGTON**, five miles north of central Oxford – and even closer to Woodstock (see p.173) – is now renowned for sternly insisting that it is still a village, despite having a population topping seventeen thousand. It has resisted all attempts at redefinition and thus currently qualifies as pretty much the largest village in Britain, though, in truth, Kidlington looks like a town, walks like a town and quacks like a town – a pretty mundane one, at that. Some character persists in the streets around the thirteenth-century **St Mary's Church**, located about half a mile east of the main A4260 road via High Street, where many Georgian townhouses also survive, but otherwise aim instead for **THRUPP**, one mile north – an end-of-the-road hamlet beside the Oxford Canal that deserves a lazy afternoon. Pretty cottages aside, Thrupp's standout feature is the *Boat Inn* (see below). From here, it's a canalside **walk** of about seven miles into central Oxford – especially scenic as you cross Port Meadow (see p.240) in front of the "dreaming spires".

ARRIVAL AND DEPARTURE   KIDLINGTON AND THRUPP

By bus Kidlington High St and the turnoff for Thrupp on the A4260 are both served by Stagecoach bus #S4 hourly between Banbury (hourly; 1hr) and Oxford (20min), and by Heyfordian bus #203 to/from Woodstock (every 2hrs; 15–20min). Kidlington is also linked to central Oxford by city bus #2/2A/2B (every 5min; 20min).

ACTIVITIES

Boat rental Oxfordshire Narrowboats (☎ 01869 340348, ⓦ oxfordshire-narrowboats.co.uk) has an office in Thrupp for narrowboat hire (£150–225/day, depending on season).
Canoe and kayak rental Thrupp Canoe and Kayak Hire (☎ 01865 842708, ⓦ tckh.co.uk), located by *Annie's Tearoom* at the canal bridge in Thrupp, rents by the hour or day (canoes £15/£60; kayaks £10/£35), and can provide maps and route suggestions.

ACCOMMODATION AND EATING

Bell at Hampton Poyle Hampton Poyle ☎ 01865 376242 ⓦ thebellathamptonpoyle.co.uk. An independent nine-room boutique hotel worked into an old village pub just northeast of Kidlington. The style is tasteful and retrained; the restaurant serves wood-fired pizza, salads, honey-glazed pork belly, seafood grills and so on (mains £12–18). **£120**
Boat Inn Thrupp ☎ 01865 374279, ⓦ theboatinn thrupp.co.uk. Family-run pub occupying a sixteenth-century canalside farmhouse: great atmosphere, great beer and unusually good food (mains £9–14) – modern British in style with fresh, seasonal ingredients and a pride taken in careful presentation. Sit back on the terrace and gaze over the canal, often fringed with wildflowers and spanned just to the east by an elegant lift bridge. Daily 11am–11pm.
Diamond Caravan Park Bletchingdon ☎ 01869 350909, ⓦ diamondpark.co.uk. Small site north of Kidlington that takes caravans, motorhomes and tents, also with a swimming pool and kids' play area. Closed Nov–Feb. Pitches **£18**

Islip

ⓦ islip.org.uk

A couple of miles east of Kidlington, and linked to Oxford by bus and train, **ISLIP** (pronounced "eye-slip") makes for a lovely counterpoint to the urban pace of its bigger neighbours. There's not much here – a couple of pubs, a handful of streets lined by seventeenth- and eighteenth-century cottages (most of them updated to suit the monied lifestyles of their twenty-first-century residents) – but the calm and sense of timelessness are rather alluring. The poet and novelist Robert Graves lived in Islip in the early 1920s; his meetings here with Siegfried Sassoon fuelled his World War I memoir *Goodbye to All That*, published in 1929. But it is Islip's status as the birthplace of **Edward the Confessor** – England's last Anglo-Saxon king, bar Harold – in around 1004, which has most resonance.

St Nicholas' Church

Church Lane • ⓦ stnicholasislip.wordpress.com

Although Edward's church is no more, the arcade that separates the nave from the north aisle within Islip's current **St Nicholas' Church** dates from just after, in the twelfth century. As you walk into this wonderfully atmospheric building, behind the fifteenth-century font ahead of you – and flanking a modern portrait of Edward – admire a stone-carved lion and hunting dog, gifts from Westminster Abbey in London, itself founded by Edward in 1065.

The Confessor's Way

The **Confessor's Way** is a short path waymarked around Islip village: from the church it heads down to the *Swan* (ⓞ 01865 379751, ⓦ swan-islip.co.uk), a fine eighteenth-century inn (with space to park a car), across the bridge over the leafy River Ray – scene of a Roundhead victory in April 1645 – and between the fields to cross the River Cherwell, re-enter the village and end at the church. The whole thing is only a mile, but it encapsulates both the beauty of Oxford's countryside and the mood of Islip's long history. The village hall-cum-shop (Mon–Fri 10am–noon & 3–6pm, Sat 10am–noon, Sun 3.30–5pm; closed Wed am) opposite the church, sells a booklet on the walk, or there's a map of the route on the wall outside.

Otmoor

Some four thousand acres of fenland stretching from Oxford to Bicester, **Otmoor** is a world apart – misty, boggy and largely uninhabited. It is thought that Lewis Carroll visited: Otmoor's patchwork appearance, divided by ditches and hedges, made its way into *Through the Looking Glass*, described by Alice as a landscape "marked out like a large chessboard". This sliver of fame helped when, in 1980, the government proposed building the new M40 motorway across the moor: environmental campaigners bought a nondescript field, renamed it "**Alice's Meadow**", divided it up into three thousand tiny parcels of land and sold each one off to its supporters. This was effectively sabotage: it meant the government would have been forced to fight each new "landowner" in the courts over compulsory purchase orders. The motorway was built on an alternative route, skirting the moor to the east – and the laws on land purchase were changed to ensure such a thing could never happen again. **Walking** isn't easy here, partly because of the boggy ground and partly because a chunk of the moor is taken up by a Ministry of Defence rifle range – seek advice before venturing onto open ground, or check with the RSPB (ⓦ rspb.org.uk), who administer a wetland reserve on the moor.

A narrow road strikes east from Islip for a few miles to **CHARLTON-ON-OTMOOR**, which has a fine medieval church with a characteristic square tower and sixteenth-century carved rood screen.

EATING AND DRINKING   **OTMOOR**

★ **Nut Tree Inn** Murcott ⓞ 01865 331253, ⓦ nuttree inn.co.uk. This fifteenth-century pub doubles as one of Oxfordshire's finest rural restaurants. Located alongside the village duck-pond – the ducks will greet you when you arrive – the low-beamed thatched building has been lovingly spruced up: there's a contemporary feel to the dining area. The owners (awarded a Michelin star) keep Gloucester Old Spot pigs and also grow their own vegetables: expect seasonal, local, ethically sourced food. Mains (£17–30) might include slow-roasted belly of pork or pan-fried Cornish pollock – or you could opt for the eight-course tasting menu (£55 plus £48 for wine; vegetarian and vegan menus available), or the £18 two-course set menu (Tues–Thurs plus Fri lunch). Service is warm and relaxed, to suit the ambience. Tues–Sat noon–2.30pm & 7–9pm, Sun noon–3pm.

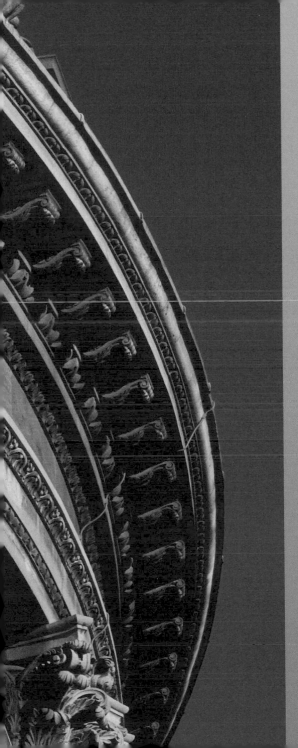

Oxford

RADCLIFFE CAMERA

Oxford

When visitors think of Oxford, they almost always imagine its university, revered as one of the world's great academic institutions, inhabiting honey-coloured stone buildings set around ivy-clad quadrangles. The image is accurate enough, but although the university dominates central Oxford both physically and spiritually – also preserving access to riverside parkland, unexpectedly peaceful amid the clamour – the wider city has an entirely different character, its economy built chiefly on heavy industry.

7

This small city of just 150,000 presents as impressive a collection of Gothic, Classical and Revival **architecture** as anywhere in Europe, set amid a vivid, engaging urban environment that is both compact and easily navigable. The leading colleges – **Christ Church**, **Merton**, **Magdalen**, **St John's** – are fascinating to explore; marry them with the dozen or more others which pack the city centre, plus the university's showpiece buildings such as the **Bodleian Library**, **Sheldonian Theatre**, **Radcliffe Camera** and extraordinary **Ashmolean Museum**, and few national capitals can keep pace.

Losing yourself in the splendid architecture and evocative isolation of the colleges is seductively easy. It takes something of an effort to subvert Oxford's obvious narrative and instead access the equally rich, and often quite separate, history and outlook of the surrounding city, represented most tangibly for visitors by the fine **Museum of Oxford**, the **castle** remains, the commercial *joie-de-vivre* of the **Covered Market** and outlying community neighbourhoods such as **Jericho**. Oxford was where Britain's first mass-produced cars were manufactured in the 1920s and, although there have been more downs than ups in recent years, the plants at **Cowley**, southeast of the centre, are still vitally important to the area. The fact that the **Mini** – a national icon – is still produced in Oxford to this day is a source of huge local pride.

It's that to-and-fro between what's known as "**town**" and "**gown**" (that is, the city and the university) which makes a stay here unique – that, and the fact that more than half of the city's population is under thirty. The shopping streets are buzzing, pubs – many of them historical curiosities – are packed, restaurateurs and hoteliers search for innovative, creative ways to make their mark... it's quite a whirl. Yet **Magdalen Bridge** still represents something of a border. To the west is the city centre, dominated by college grandness in both architecture and mindset, while to the east – notably in **Headington** and along the **Cowley Road** out towards the **Blackbird Leys** estate – lies ordinary, working Oxford, unusually ethnically diverse and harbouring pockets of poverty and deprivation which entirely counter the Oxford stereotype. As throughout the city's history, those "dreaming spires" stand for only part of the story.

PUNTING ON THE RIVER

Highlights

❶ Bodleian Library One of the world's great libraries, notable for its history, its architecture and the stunning interior of its Divinity School. **See p.213**

❷ New College Seclusion, medieval architecture and a magnificent chapel make this one of the most rewarding colleges to visit. **See p.215**

❸ Punting Take to the water in a traditional flat-bottomed boat on either of Oxford's rivers and indulge in a lazy riverbank picnic to boot. **See p.217**

❹ Covered Market A blast of commercial reality in the city centre, with old-fashioned

butchers, bakers and fishmongers laying out their wares. **See p.222**

❺ Christ Church College Take in the splendour of Oxford's biggest, grandest college, with magnificent architecture – and plenty of Harry Potter associations. **See p.225**

❻ Ashmolean Museum World-class art and historical collections in Britain's longest-established museum. **See p.229**

❼ Jericho A village within the city, perfect for aimless strolling along narrow canalside streets just northwest of the centre. **See p.231**

HIGHLIGHTS ARE MARKED ON THE MAP ON PP.206–207

Brief history

Although some tales date the establishment of a settlement near the confluence of the Thames and Cherwell rivers as early as 1000 BC, it seems more likely that Oxford was founded after the Romans had departed, probably during the **Saxon** era in the eighth century AD. One legend has it that the oxen ford which gave the town its name may have been the work of Offa, king of Mercia from 757 to 796, though the town's foundation is most persuasively linked with **St Frideswide**, an Anglo-Saxon princess who miraculously restored the sight of a blinded suitor with water from a holy well. The priory she founded, located on a tongue of land near where the Cherwell meets the Thames, was destroyed by fire – along with its records – in 1002 but was refounded 120 years later under the **Normans** to house her relics, subsequently becoming a focus for pilgrimage. (Frideswide's well survives today in the grounds of St Margaret's Church in Binsey, roughly a mile northwest of Oxford, while the site of her priory now falls within the walls of Christ Church College.)

Clerical scholarship and the rise of academia

Around this time **Henry I** (1069–1135) chose Oxford as the royal residence: both Richard the Lionheart and King John were born in the palace of **Beaumont**, located

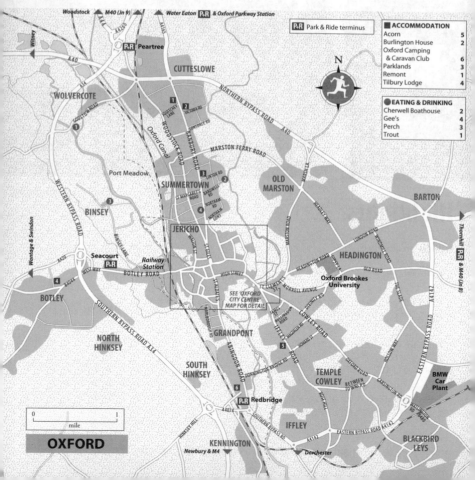

7

near where the Ashmolean Museum stands today. Henry, known as "Beauclerc" ("Good Scholar"), also hosted formal study at Beaumont during his reign – augmented in the decades following when English clerical scholars, expelled *en masse* from the University of Paris in 1167, returned home. They gravitated towards Oxford, pursuing a form of academic monasticism: their custom of living, dining, praying and studying together under the guidance of a master, in halls founded mostly by wealthy bishops, was the forerunner of college life. As the number of halls and colleges grew, a committee developed to administer them – and Oxford's **university** was born.

Aided by royal patronage, and the development of the wool trade across the Cotswolds during the thirteenth century, Oxford's prosperity grew alongside its academic reputation, sparking the first conflicts between the city and the university – "**Town**" and "**Gown**". In 1209, two scholars were executed for the murder of a local woman. Many students subsequently departed, some heading east to found a new university in Cambridge. The notorious **St Scholastica Day Riot**, of February 10, 1355, saw an argument about beer escalate to armed conflict between students and townsfolk, in which more than ninety people died. Yet, mutual resentment notwithstanding, town and gown had become co-dependent, with a host of trades from weaving and shoemaking to stone-masonry supporting academic life. Money continued to pour into the university (and thus the town) from the Church and the aristocracy, both of which were equally keen to foster the creation of an educated elite for, respectively, holy orders and royal service.

The sixteenth to nineteenth centuries

Henry VIII's dissolution of the monasteries in 1536 briefly threatened the university – then still, chiefly, an ecclesiastical entity. Monastic orders were expelled and their property taken over by the colleges, but Henry had a personal stake in the university's survival: four years earlier he had taken over Cardinal College, founded by Wolsey in 1525 on the site of St Frideswide's Priory, and renamed it Henry VIII's College. (As part of the reorganization within the Church of England it was shortly afterwards refounded as Christ Church College.)

Oxford survived, but maintained a reputation for religious turbulence. In 1555 Henry's daughter, **Mary**, chose the city for the heresy trial of three influential Protestant clerics. Bishops Hugh Latimer and Nicholas Ridley and archbishop Thomas Cranmer – the "**Oxford Martyrs**" – were all found guilty and burnt at the stake on what is now Broad Street, Latimer famously remarking, "Be of good comfort, Master Ridley: we shall this day light such a candle in England as I trust shall never be put out." At his trial Cranmer, who had previously confessed to heresy, rounded on his accusers and reconfirmed his Protestant faith, an action which stunned Mary and gave new heart to her religious opponents.

Pear Tree Park & Ride, Witney, Woodstock & M40 North

Water Eaton Park & Ride, Kidlington & Banbury

St Sepulchre's Cemetery

ADELAIDE ST

Observatory St

Green Templeton

RADCLIFFE OBSERVATORY QUARTER

Radcliffe Infirmary

WOODSTOCK ROAD

BANBURY ROAD

PARKS ROAD

JUXON STREET

CRANHAM TERRACE

VENABLES CL

BLOMFIELD PL

KING ST

WALTON STREET

Somerville

St Giles'

KEBLE ROAD

Keble

MOUNT ST

ALLAM ST

CRANHAM ST

JERICHO STREET

HART STREET

JERICHO

BLACKHALL ROAD

CANTERBURY ST

VICTOR ST

ALBERT STREET

GREAT CLARENDON STREET

Oxford University Press

LITTLE CLARENDON STREET

St Giles'

LAMB & FLAG PASSAGE

MUSEUM ROAD

St Barnabas

WELLINGTON ST

ALBERT ST

WALTON CRESCENT

WALTON LANE

WELLINGTON SQUARE

WELLINGTON PLACE

St John's

NELSON STREET

RICHMOND ROAD

WALTON STREET

ST JOHN STREET

PUSEY STREET

St Cross

WORCESTER PLACE

BEAUMONT BLDGS

PUSEY LANE

Ruskin College

Oxford Canal

PUSEY PL

Ashmolean Museum

Trinity

BEAUMONT STREET

Oxford Playhouse

MAGDALEN ST EAST

Balliol

Worcester

GLOUCESTER STREET

FRIARS ENTRY

BROAD STREET

BEWLEY ROAD

Bus Station

GLOUCESTER GREEN

GEORGE STREET

SHIP STREET

Jesus

CORNMARKET

Said Business School

HYTHE BRIDGE STREET

WORCESTER STREET

NEW INN HALL STREET

Oxford Union

MARKET STREET

Covered Market

Railway Station

BOTLEY ROAD

PARK END STREET

Nuffield

St Peter's

BULWARKS LANE

ST MICHAEL'S STREET

Clarendon Centre

CARFAX

HOLLYBUSH ROW

ST THOMAS STREET

NEW ROAD

BONN SQ.

QUEEN ST

Town Hall

BECKET STREET

Oxford Castle

CASTLE STREET

BLUE

OSNEY LANE

OSNEY LANE

PARADISE STREET

PARADISE SQ.

Westgate Shopping Centre

St Ebbe's

ST EBBE'S STREET

PEMBROKE STREET

ST ALDATE'S

OXPENS ROAD

River Thames

NORFOLK STREET

OLD GREYFRIARS STREET

Pembroke

BREWER STREET

ROSE PLACE

PIKE TERR

LITTLEGATE ST

ALBION PLACE

Ice Rink

THAMES STREET

SPEEDWELL STREET

Alice's Shop

CROMWELL ST

ST ALDATE'S

TRINITY STREET

BLACKFRIARS RD

GREEK LANE

CHARLES ST

DALE CLOSE

TRINITY STREET

FRIARS WHARF

BALTIC WHARF

MARLBOROUGH RD

LAKE CL

Punts

River Thames

0   100
yards

⊠ Public entrance to college

OXFORD CITY CENTRE

Redbridge Park & Ride & Abingdon

7

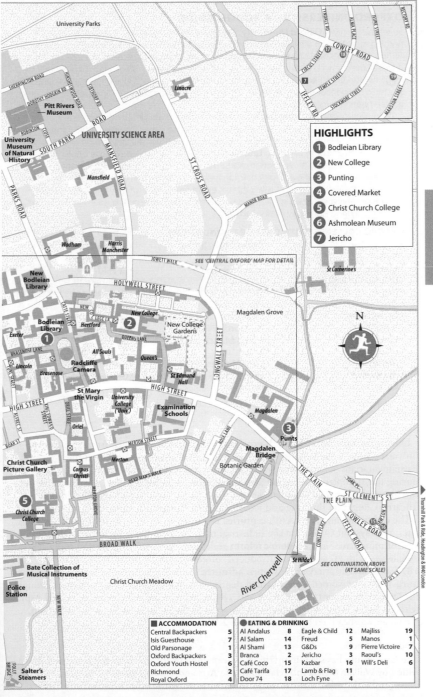

HIGHLIGHTS

1. Bodleian Library
2. New College
3. Punting
4. Covered Market
5. Christ Church College
6. Ashmolean Museum
7. Jericho

University Parks

Pitt Rivers Museum

University Museum of Natural History

UNIVERSITY SCIENCE AREA

Linacre

Mansfield

Wadham

Harris Manchester

New Bodleian Library

Bodleian Library

Hertford

New College

New College Gardens

Magdalen Grove

St Catherine's

HOLYWELL STREET

JOWETT WALK   SEE 'CENTRAL OXFORD' MAP FOR DETAIL

Exeter

Lincoln

Radcliffe Camera

All Souls

Queen's

Brasenose

St Mary the Virgin

University College ('Univ')

Examination Schools

St Edmund Hall

Magdalen

HIGH STREET

Orlel

Punts

Christ Church Picture Gallery

Corpus Christi

Merton

MERTON STREET

DEAD MAN'S WALK

Magdalen Bridge

Botanic Garden

THE PLAIN

ST CLEMENT'S ST

Christ Church College

THE PLAIN

COWLEY ROAD

IFFLEY ROAD

BROAD WALK

St Hilda's

SEE CONTINUATION ABOVE (AT SAME SCALE)

Bate Collection of Musical Instruments

Police Station

Christ Church Meadow

River Cherwell

Salter's Steamers

N

Thornhill Park & Ride, Headington & MAO London

COWLEY ROAD

JEFFLEY RD

■ ACCOMMODATION		● EATING & DRINKING					
Central Backpackers	5	Al Andalus	8	Eagle & Child	12	Majliss	19
Isis Guesthouse	7	Al Salam	14	Freud	5	Manos	1
Old Parsonage	1	Al Shami	13	G&Ds	9	Pierre Victoire	7
Oxford Backpackers	3	Branca	2	Jericho	3	Raoul's	10
Oxford Youth Hostel	6	Café Coco	15	Kazbar	16	Will's Deli	6
Richmond	2	Café Tarifa	17	Lamb & Flag	11		
Royal Oxford	4	Door 74	18	Loch Fyne	4		

OXFORD UNIVERSITY – A ROUGH GUIDE

So where, exactly, is **Oxford University**? Everywhere – and nowhere. The university itself is nothing more than an administrative body, setting examinations and awarding degrees. Although it has its own offices (on Wellington Square), they are of no particular interest. What draws all the attention are the university's constituent **colleges** – 38 of them (plus another six religious foundations known as Permanent Private Halls), most occupying historic buildings scattered throughout the city centre. It is they which hold the 800-year-old history of the university, and exemplify its spirit.

The university operates a **federal** system: all the colleges are independent and self-governing, in most cases selecting their own students and remaining responsible for them throughout their time in Oxford. It's the colleges that teach, not the university, mainly through weekly one-to-one or small-group **tutorials**. Students keep the same college tutor for the duration of their course (three years in most instances), live in college accommodation, use the college library, meet in the college "common room" and compete in college sports teams. Their only contact with the university, other than at **exam** time, may be if they choose to attend lectures or seminars – which students from different colleges attend together – or if they use facilities in a university library or laboratory.

OXFORD COLLEGES (WITH DATE OF FOUNDATION)

- **University** 1249
- **Balliol** 1263
- **Merton** 1264
- **St Edmund Hall** c.1278
- **Exeter** 1314
- **Oriel** 1326
- **Queen's** 1341
- **New** 1379
- **Lincoln** 1427
- **All Souls*** 1438
- **Magdalen** 1458
- **Brasenose** 1509
- **Corpus Christi** 1517
- **Christ Church** 1546
- **Trinity** 1555
- **St John's** 1555
- **Jesus** 1571
- **Wadham** 1610
- **Pembroke** 1624
- **Worcester** 1714
- **Hertford** 1740
- **Harris Manchester** 1786
- **Keble** 1870
- **Lady Margaret Hall** 1878
- **Somerville** 1879
- **Mansfield** 1886
- **St Hugh's** 1886
- **St Anne's** 1893
- **St Hilda's** 1893
- **St Peter's** 1929
- **Nuffield**** 1937
- **St Antony's**** 1950
- **Linacre**** 1962
- **St Catherine's** 1963
- **St Cross**** 1965
- **Wolfson**** 1966
- **Kellogg**** 1990
- **Green Templeton**** 2008

*Admits fellows only. **Admits graduate students only.

During the **Civil War**, Charles I, expelled from London, set up court in Oxford: the university backed the Royalist cause, while much of the town supported the Parliamentarians. Charles remained for almost five years, slinking out in disguise during the 1646 Parliamentarian **Siege of Oxford** – following which, the restoration of the monarchy heralded a golden age of university expansion, with the Sheldonian Theatre, Clarendon Building and iconic **Radcliffe Camera** all going up.

The eighteenth and nineteenth centuries saw progress on two fronts. **Canals** and, later, **railways** put Oxford on the industrial map as a commercial hub between London and Birmingham – and **academic reform** sealed the university's reputation for excellence, with examinations introduced, professors finally permitted to marry in 1877 and, shortly afterwards, women admitted as undergraduates (though it was not until 1920 that women were awarded degrees). Religious controversy persisted, though: the **Oxford Movement** of the 1830s and 1840s, led by Cardinal Newman, caused a split within High Church Anglicanism which spurred the creation of Anglo-Catholicism. Newman was beatified by Pope Benedict XVI in 2010.

Modern Oxford

The last century has seen, if anything, a deepening of the gulf between town and gown. Aided by **William Morris** (no relation to the Arts and Crafts pioneer) who launched mass production of cars at his works in Cowley, as well as other Oxford industries

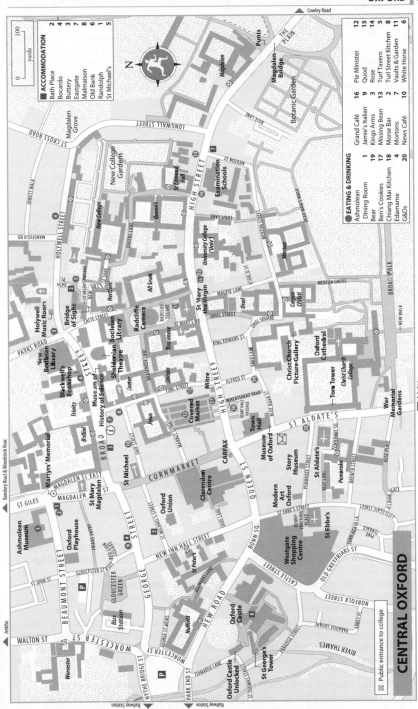

CENTRAL OXFORD

⊠ Public entrance to college

■ ACCOMMODATION

Bath Place	2
Bocardo	4
Buttery	3
Eastgate	7
Malmaison	8
Old Bank	6
Randolph	1
St Michael's	5

● EATING & DRINKING

Ashmolean Dining Room	1	Grand Café	12
Bear	19	Jamie's Italian	15
Ben's Cookies	17	Kings Arms	14
Chiang Mai Kitchen	18	Missing Bean	5
Edamame	4	Morse Bar	8
G&Ds	20	Mortons	7
		News Café	6
		Pie Minister	16
		Quod	9
		Rose	14
		Turf Tavern	13
		Turf Street Kitchen	2
		Vaults & Garden	11
		White Horse	10

(notably printing and brewing), town prosperity grew exponentially in the first half of the twentieth century, even while Edwardian attitudes at the university – portrayed in Evelyn Waugh's 1945 novel *Brideshead Revisited* – ossified into **elitism**. Postwar civic development, as well as student disaffection and reform after 1968 (and the success of a new, more egalitarian university, **Oxford Brookes**), helped restore some balance, but attitudes remain entrenched on both sides. Eight hundred years of mutual resentment is unlikely to dissipate overnight.

Broad Street

Marking what was the town ditch, just beyond the now-vanished northern walls, **Broad Street** is one of Oxford's most handsome thoroughfares, a quiet, spacious street festooned with parked bicycles. On one side rise Balliol College and gates shielding views to the lawns of Trinity College; on the other jostles a line of higgledy-piggledy shop facades which include the **tourist office**, at number 15. Just outside the tourist office, a cross set into the road marks the spot where the "**Oxford Martyrs**" (see p.205) were burnt at the stake for their Catholicism – Hugh Latimer and Nicholas Ridley in October 1555, Thomas Cranmer five months later. The event is also commemorated by the **Martyrs' Memorial**, a Victorian monument round the corner in Magdalen Street.

Two doors down, 17 Broad Street houses what was the first-ever **Oxfam** charity shop when it opened in 1948: the "Oxford Committee for Famine Relief", founded during World War II, continues its work today from head offices in Cowley. Nearby, grab an espresso or a sandwich at *Morton's* café (see p.237), at number 22, to view a section of the city wall – dating from the early thirteenth century – which survives overlooking their rear terrace. At the corner of Turl Street, look up: gazing out from a vantage point atop the roof of Exeter College (see p.217) stands the 2009 **Antony Gormley sculpture** *Another Time* – a 7ft figure in iron of a naked man.

Balliol College

Broad St • No set hours, usually daily 10am–5pm • £2 • ☎ 01865 277777, ⓦ www.balliol.ox.ac.uk

Sporting a fine Victorian Gothic frontage opposite the tourist office, designed in 1868 by Alfred Waterhouse, **Balliol College** (pronounced bay-lee-yul) is one of the university's oldest, founded around 1263 by Scottish noble John de Balliol as penance for insulting the bishop of Durham. Despite its antiquity, Balliol has little to offer architecturally: remodelled and rebuilt in the nineteenth century, it presents an unexceptional assembly of buildings, haphazardly gathered around two quads – pleasant for a stroll, regardless.

Trinity College

Broad St • No set hours, usually Mon–Fri 9am–12.15pm & 1.30–4pm, Sat & Sun 1–4pm • £2 • ☎ 01865 279900, ⓦ www.trinity.ox.ac.uk

Beside Balliol, wrought-iron gates reveal the splendid Front Quad of **Trinity College**. Entry is alongside, beside three seventeenth-century lodge-cottages. Behind them the manicured lawns stretch back to the richly decorated **chapel**, awash with Baroque stuccowork. Its high altar is flanked by an exquisite example of the work of master wood-carver Grinling Gibbons – a distinctive performance, with cherubs' heads peering out from delicate foliage. The chapel and stone-flagged **hall** are entered from amid an attractive ensemble of late seventeenth-century buildings around **Durham Quad**: Trinity was originally named Durham College, founded in 1286, purchased by Oxfordshire landowner Sir Thomas Pope during the dissolution of the monasteries and refounded in 1555.

Located next door to each other, Trinity and Balliol are, as you might expect, arch-rivals, living out a grudge which goes back 750 years to John de Balliol's dispute

WHY VISIT AN OXFORD COLLEGE?

• For the **architecture**. Each college has its own atmosphere, characterized by Gothic, Classical, Victorian, even contemporary architecture: to find examples of such original styles so well maintained, and rubbing shoulders with each other so harmoniously, is very rare.

• For the **sense of discovery**. Colleges do not advertise: there are no signs on the street indicating which college is which. You make your own enquiries, follow your own path, and are free to discover what you will.

• For a slice of **real life**. Colleges are not tourist attractions: despite their somewhat rarefied atmosphere and appearance, they are places of work, offering a glimpse into the daily lives of people of diverse backgrounds from all over Britain and the world.

In short, colleges are the repository of the city's history and character. In Florence, visit churches. In Istanbul, visit bazaars. In Oxford, visit colleges.

WHAT DOES A COLLEGE LOOK LIKE?

There's no standard ground-plan, but most Oxford colleges – and all the most interesting historic examples – look similar, and are generally shielded from the street behind high stone walls: it's impossible to tell the character of the place from outside. The college **porter**, sitting in a **lodge** (an office beside the main entrance gate), controls access. Beyond, college buildings are arranged around a quadrangle, or **"quad"**. Doorways from the quad access numbered **staircases** within each building, off which lie the residential rooms of tutors and other teaching staff (known as **"dons"**) and students. Passageways may lead through to other quads beyond.

Two buildings are normally open to visitors. The **hall** is where students and academics eat breakfast, lunch and dinner. Generally a grand, high-ceilinged chamber, often with wood panelling, vaulting and perhaps a stone fireplace, it is invariably hung with portraits of notable **alumni** (past students) or prominent figures associated with the college. Students take their food from a self-service buffet and sit communally at long tables, often on wooden benches, while staff are served separately at **"high table"**, raised on a dais at the back of the hall beneath a portrait of the college founder or benefactor. The other building usually open is the **chapel**: every college has one and they are all – unusually – T-shaped: there is no nave, and instead transepts serve as an antechapel leading into the choir, where stalls face each other across an aisle. Behind the altar often rises a wall of statues in ornate niches, known as a reredos.

HOW TO VISIT

Colleges operate restricted public **opening hours** – often just a couple of hours in mid-afternoon, and sometimes less than that during the exam season (late April to early June). Some impose an **admission charge**. For details check the "Visitors" pages of the university website (Ⓦox.ac.uk), or phone the relevant college.

However, regardless of published hours, it's always worth trying your luck and asking at the **porter's lodge**, located beside the main college entrance: porters have ultimate discretion and if you ask they may let you wander in. On the other hand, they may tell you that the college is closed that day for a function or conference – and if you're *very* unlucky, you might pay for admission only to discover during your visit that, say, the college chapel is closed for choir practice or the dining hall is off-limits because of an event that evening. You're unlikely to get your money back in these situations.

WHICH COLLEGES ARE BEST?

We've described many of the colleges in the pages following, but you'd need Olympic stamina and dedication to visit all 38. If there is a single "must-see" it would be Christ Church, for its cathedral and magnificent dining hall; otherwise, dropping into more or less any college can make for an atmospheric quarter-hour. A speculative, subjective checklist, in no particular order, might run as follows:

• **Five should-sees**: Christ Church, Merton, New, All Souls, Magdalen
• **Five could-sees**: Brasenose, St John's, Queen's, Lincoln, Jesus
• **Five might-sees**: Exeter, University, Pembroke, Trinity, Keble

with Durham's bishop. This has become ritualized with the singing of the *Gordouli*, a scatological verse yelled over the wall by Balliol students at their adversaries, usually at unsociable hours of the night. It includes the lines: "I'd rather be a bastard than a bloody Trinity man / Bloody Trinity! / Trinity's burning, pour on petrol / Bloody Trinity!"

Blackwell's bookshop

48 Broad St • Mon–Sat 9am–6.30pm, Sun 11am–5pm • ☎ 01865 792792, ⓦ blackwell.co.uk

Broad Street is perhaps best known as the home of **Blackwell's**, Oxford's leading bookshop, founded by Benjamin Blackwell in 1879 and now a global concern. The original outlet, at number 50, still forms part of the main shop, a creaky, lopsided warren which now spreads from 48 to 53 (flanking the old *White Horse* pub; see p.241) and reaches both above and below ground: its immense, subterranean Norrington Room, extending beneath the adjacent quadrangle of Trinity College, has three miles of shelving. Across the road, Blackwell's has a separate art and poster shop at number 27.

7

Museum of the History of Science

Broad St • Tues–Fri noon–5pm, Sat 10am–5pm, Sun 2–5pm • Free • ⓦ www.mhs.ox.ac.uk

The east end of Broad Street showcases much of Oxford's most monumental architecture, not least the fine seventeenth-century building opposite Blackwell's bookshop. Originally home to the Ashmolean collection (see p.229), it now houses the fascinating **Museum of the History of Science**. Start on the entrance level, which features cases crammed with antique microscopes and astrolabes, as well as a diverting collection of early spectacles. Against the back wall stands one of the world's oldest pendulum clocks, an elegant piece made in the early 1660s by one Ahasuerus Fromanteel. As you make your way up the creaky staircase, don't dismiss the huge, intricately detailed depiction of the moon as a recent NASA image: it is, in fact, a pastel by English artist John Russell dating from 1795. This extraordinary work was rehung in 2007 when a visiting astronomer noticed that it was upside down – whereupon Russell's signature, lurking unnoticed for decades in the top left corner, was rediscovered at bottom right.

The upper gallery has more cases packed with dizzyingly complex mathematical instruments, from a Roman sundial and an "equatorium", used to establish the position of the planets, to a surveying sextant used by Isambard Kingdom Brunel and Elizabeth I's astrolabe. Venture down to the basement for Lewis Carroll's photography kit and, amazingly, a blackboard used by Albert Einstein during a lecture in Oxford on May 16, 1931: it remains as he left it, scrawled with a series of equations in chalk that – apparently – show the density, radius and age of the universe.

The "Emperors"

The Museum of the History of Science is fronted by four glum, pop-eyed Classical-style busts, all curly locks and togas, with thirteen more adorning pillars between a grand curve of railings to the left. These are usually known as the "**Emperors**", and they've been here in one form or other for almost 350 years – the current crop were unveiled in 1976 after a Victorian set had worn smooth – though nobody knows who they represent or what the point of them might be. Some maintain, plausibly, that they depict the history of beards.

Sheldonian Theatre

Broad St • Feb–Nov Mon–Sat 10am–4.30pm, July & Aug also Sun 10.30am–4pm; Dec & Jan Mon–Fri 10am–3.30pm • £3.50 • ⓦ www .sheldon.ox.ac.uk

At the eastern end of Broad Street, a curving set of railings with stone steps leading up mark an enclave of buildings connected with the university, rather than with individual

NAME YOUR RIVER

Two rivers embrace Oxford, meeting at a point just south of the city centre. To the west is the **Thames**, en route from its Cotswolds source to London. Most maps rename the stretch of the river within Oxford as the "Thames or **Isis**" – the latter is an affectation stemming from disdain for the river's old Celtic name *tamesas* (meaning "dark water"). Sixteenth-century scholars thought to instil more lofty Classical associations by adapting part of the old name to evoke the Greco-Roman goddess Isis; it was also about this time that someone decided to stick a Greek-looking "h" into the Celtic name for the river, thus creating "Thames". The machinations stuck, though in truth few Oxford locals today, other than university types, use the term Isis; it's become a cartographer's fancy.

The city's other river, to the east, is the **Cherwell**, whose name is pronounced by a certain sector of Oxford society as "charwell".

colleges. First comes the **Sheldonian Theatre**. One of the first buildings designed by Sir Christopher Wren, in 1663, it was intended to be a reworking of the Theatre of Marcellus in Rome, though Wren – then a 31-year-old professor of astronomy – had not visited Italy at the time and his design is timid in comparison. The exterior of the D-shaped building, particularly the magnificent southern facade, is the best of it; inside, though the column-less space, spanning more than 70ft, is impressive, there's not much sense of drama. The theatre sometimes stages lectures and concerts but it was designed principally for university ceremonies – notably matriculation, graduation and the June event *Encaenia*, where honorary degrees are awarded. You can make your way up to the cupola, an 1838 replacement of Wren's original, for some striking views over Oxford's rooftops.

7

Bodleian Library

Broad St • Closed to the public; some rooms accessible on tours (see p.214) • ① 01865 287400, Ⓦ www.bodley.ox.ac.uk

Christopher Wren's pupil Nicholas Hawksmoor designed the **Clarendon Building**, a domineering, solidly symmetrical edifice topped by allegorical figures that lies immediately east of the Sheldonian Theatre, completed in 1713 to house the Oxford University Press. It now forms part of the **Bodleian Library**. Founded by scholar Sir Thomas Bodley in 1602, the Bodleian is now the UK's largest library after the British Library in London, with an estimated 117 miles of shelving. It includes the rather refreshingly modernist 1930s **New Bodleian** (now known as the **Weston Library** after extensive renovation) directly opposite the Clarendon, designed by Sir Giles Gilbert Scott and linked to the main building by tunnels beneath Broad Street. Yet despite its nine libraries spread across Oxford, plus a host of off-site storage facilities from a Swindon warehouse to a Cheshire salt mine, space remains tight. As one of the UK and Ireland's six copyright libraries, the Bodleian must find room for a copy of every book, pamphlet, magazine and newspaper published in Britain.

Old Schools Quadrangle

Mon–Fri 9am–5pm, Sat 9am–4.30pm, Sun 11am–5pm • Free

Behind the Clarendon and across a gravel courtyard – note the diagonal line in the paving by the Clarendon's south facade, which shows the former line of Oxford's medieval city wall – you enter the Bodleian's beautifully proportioned **Old Schools Quadrangle**, completed in 1619 in an ornate Jacobean-Gothic style and offering access to all of the university's academic faculties, or schools: the name of each is lettered in gold above the doorways which ring the quad. On the east side rises the handsome **Tower of the Five Orders**, which gives a lesson in architectural design, its tiers of columns built according to the five classical styles – in ascending order Tuscan, Doric, Ionic, Corinthian and Composite.

The Divinity School

Mon–Fri 9am–5pm, Sat 9am–4.30pm, Sun 11am–5pm • £1

In the quad, a statue of William Herbert, 3rd Earl of Pembroke, stands before the elegant facade of the **Divinity School**, highlight of a visit to the Bodleian. Begun in 1424, and sixty years in the making, this exceptional room, reached via a vestibule known as the Proscholium, is a masterpiece of late Gothic architecture, featuring an extravagant vaulted ceiling adorned with a riot of pendants and 455 decorative bosses. Built to house the university's theology faculty, it was, until the nineteenth century, also where degree candidates were questioned in detail about their subject by two interlocutors, with a professor acting as umpire. Few interiors in Oxford are as impressive.

Duke Humfrey's Library

Only accessible on guided tours

On the floor above the Divinity School stands the atmospheric **Duke Humfrey's Library**, in working use as a reading room from its completion in 1487 right through to 2014, when its collections were transferred to the new Weston Library building. The room, extensively added to during the early seventeenth century, is distinguished by its superb beamed ceiling and carved corbels.

Convocation House

Only accessible on guided tours

Alongside the Divinity School is the **Convocation House**, a sombre wood-panelled chamber where parliament sat during the Civil War, which now sports a fancy fan-vaulted ceiling completed in 1759.

Gladstone Link

Only accessible on guided tours

Beneath the Old Schools quad, tunnels link the Bodleian with the Radcliffe Camera a hundred yards or so south. Formerly a storage area dating from 1912, featuring iron bookshelves hanging on rollers that were first proposed by Victorian prime minister William Gladstone, this subterranean zone was renovated and reopened in 2011 as the **Gladstone Link** reading room.

TOURS   **BODLEIAN LIBRARY**

An **audio-guide** is available for self-guided tours of the quad and Divinity School (40min; £2.50) – or there's a host of **guided tours** to those few areas of the Bodleian open to the public. It's always advisable to **book in advance** with the tours office (Mon–Sat 9am–4pm, Sun 11am–4pm; ☎ 01865 287400, ⊛ www.bodley.ox.ac.uk), located inside the Great Gate on Catte St.

Mini tour 30min; £5. Divinity School and Duke Humfrey's Library. Mon–Sat 3.30pm, 4pm & 4.40pm, Sun 12.45pm, 2.15pm, 3.15pm, 4pm & 4.40pm.

Standard tour 1hr; £7. Divinity School, Duke Humfrey's Library and Convocation House. Mon–Sat 10.30am, 11.30am, 1pm & 2pm, Sun 11.30am, 2pm & 3pm.

Extended tour "Upstairs Downstairs" 1hr 30min; £13. Divinity School, Duke Humfrey's Library, Convocation House, Gladstone Link, Radcliffe Camera. Wed & Sat 9.15am; booking essential.

Extended tour "Reading rooms" 1hr 30min; £13. Divinity School, Duke Humfrey's Library, Convocation House, Upper Reading Room. Sun 11.15am & 1.15pm; booking essential.

Catte Street

Beside the buttery stonework and mullioned windows of Hertford College, **Catte Street**, running along the side of the Bodleian, was once known as Mousecatcher's Lane, then Cat Street, before Victorian gentrification as Catherine Street; it reclaimed its feline origins last century, though with the affectation of medieval spelling. A short walk south brings you to the Radcliffe Camera (see p.216).

Bridge of Sighs

Spanning **New College Lane** just off Catte Street, the iconic **Bridge of Sighs** is an archway completed in 1914 to link two buildings of Hertford College. In truth it bears little resemblance to its Venetian namesake but nonetheless has a certain Italianate elegance. It was designed, so the story goes, to give residents of Hertford's older buildings to the south a way to reach the newfangled flushing toilets being installed across the road without having to venture out of doors.

New College Lane

Under the Bridge of Sighs, atmospheric, traffic-free **New College Lane**, a favourite cyclists' rat-run, extends east, flanked for the most part by high, medieval stone walls. Squeeze down narrow **St Helen's Passage** – decorously renamed from its original title, Hell's Passage – on the left to reach the famed *Turf Tavern* (see p.241) and the seventeenth-century cottages on Bath Place, insinuated into kinks of the medieval city walls. Just past St Helen's Passage, the modest house on the left, topped by a mini-observatory, was the home of astronomer Edmund Halley (1656–1742), discoverer of the comet which bears his name.

New College

New College Lane • Daily: Easter–Oct 11am–5pm, rest of year 2–4pm • Easter–Oct £3, rest of year free • ☎ 01865 279555, Ⓦ new.ox.ac.uk

New College Lane jinks between blank walls before reaching the tall, rather sinister gate-tower of **New College**. (Note that access in winter is usually via the gate in Holywell Street instead.) Founded in 1379, New College was built rapidly under the guidance of founder William of Wykeham, bishop of Winchester, whose statue adorns the gatehouse beside that of the Virgin Mary. The buildings surrounding the attractive **Front Quad** date mostly from the last quarter of the fourteenth century, though their splendid Perpendicular Gothic architecture was somewhat tempered by the addition of an extra storey in 1674.

The cloisters and chapel

On the left side of Front Quad a passage leads through to the tranquil **cloisters**, home to an ancient holm oak, while nearby a door gives access to the **chapel**, one of the finest in Oxford, for its contents as much as its design. The antechapel contains some superb fourteenth-century stained glass and the west window – of 1778 – holds an intriguing (if somewhat unsuccessful) nativity scene based on a design by Sir Joshua Reynolds. Beneath it stands the 1951 sculpture *Lazarus* by Jacob Epstein; Khrushchev, after a visit here, claimed that the memory of this haunting work kept him awake at night. The chapel itself, with a hammerbeam ceiling by George Gilbert Scott, is dominated by a magnificent nineteenth-century floor-to-ceiling stone **reredos**, consisting of about fifty canopied figures, mostly saints and apostles, with Christ Crucified as the centrepiece. A dim portrait of St James, on the north wall, is by El Greco.

The hall and garden

Across the Front Quad, 21 stone steps lead up to the **hall**, a beautiful room featuring sixteenth-century linenfold panelling. An archway nearby leads through to the modest **Garden Quad**, flanked by Palladian architecture, with the flowerbeds of the **College Garden** beckoning beyond tall wrought-iron gates. Wedged into the northeast corner of the city walls (which survive in plain view), the garden was a cemetery during the Black Death, revamped in later centuries with the addition of a conspicuous grassed **mound** to afford views over the grounds.

Radcliffe Square

Radcliffe Square, encircled by the most splendid of "gown" architecture, is Oxford's great theatrical set-piece. Standing with your back to the Decorated Gothic steeple of the great university church of St Mary the Virgin, the view across the square is exceptional, taking in the Perpendicular facade of All Souls College chapel on the right, the Gothic frontage of the Bodleian Library ahead, the mixed Gothic and Renaissance architecture of Brasenose College to the left and, dominating the centre of the square, the Radcliffe Camera.

Radcliffe Camera

Closed to the public; accessible only on Bodleian Library's extended tour: Wed & Sat 9.15am • £13 • booking essential • ☎ 01865 287400, ⓦ www.bodley.ox.ac.uk.

The mighty rotunda of the **Radcliffe Camera**, built between 1737 and 1748 by James Gibbs, architect of London's St Martin-in-the-Fields church, displays no false modesty. Dr John Radcliffe, royal physician (to William III), was, according to a contemporary diarist, "very ambitious of glory": when he died in 1714 he bequeathed a mountain of money for the construction of a library. Gibbs was one of the few British architects of the period to have been trained in Rome and his design is thoroughly Italian in style, its limestone columns ascending to a delicate balustrade, decorated with pin-prick urns and encircling a lead-sheathed dome. Taken over by the Bodleian Library in 1860, it now houses a reading-room, accessible to the public only on the Bodleian's "extended tour" (see p.214).

Brasenose College

Radcliffe Sq • No set hours, usually Mon–Fri 2–4.30pm, Sat & Sun 9.30–10.30am & 2–4.30pm • £2 • ☎ 01865 277830, ⓦ www.bnc.ox.ac.uk

Reached directly from Radcliffe Square, **Brasenose College** offers something of a haven: its elegant Tudor **Old Quad**, dating from 1516, remains more or less untouched, bar the addition of dormer windows in the seventeenth century. Look in the hall porch for a panel describing how to decipher the large **sundial** of 1719, which adorns the quad's north wall. In the **hall**, hanging over the high table, you'll spot a bronze door-knocker in the shape of a nose, from which the college got its name. Made sometime in the twelfth century – or perhaps earlier – the brazen nose was stolen in 1330 by a group of students, who took it to Stamford in Lincolnshire with the aim of founding a new university. Their caper fizzled out, but the knocker stayed in Stamford until the building with the door to which it had been attached came up for sale in 1890. Brasenose bought the entire building in order to reclaim their emblem. Stroll through to the **Chapel Quad** to climb the stairs of a barrel-vaulted porch into the college **chapel**, designed in the 1650s in a striking blend of Gothic and Renaissance styles, and housing an eye-popping painted plaster ceiling of fan vaulting. Emerging onto Radcliffe Square, turn right and you'll spot, flanking the wooden door of a side entrance, two wonderful **gilded fauns**; C.S. Lewis noticed them, too, and used them as the inspiration for Mr Tumnus in his *Narnia* books.

All Souls College

High St • Mon–Fri 2–4pm, closed Aug • Free • ☎ 01865 279379, ⓦ www.all-souls.ox.ac.uk

Running the entire east side of Radcliffe Square, its immense chapel windows the epitome of the Perpendicular Gothic style, **All Souls College** is one of the quietest places in central Oxford: it has no undergraduates. Uniquely, it admits only "fellows" – that is, distinguished scholars – either by election of existing fellows, or by an exam reputed to be the hardest in the world. Each year two graduates, at most, are awarded fellowships. There is no teaching: fellows may pursue their research in Oxford or elsewhere, the only requirement being occasional attendance at formal weekend dinners. The result is that All Souls is generally silent. Sightseers gather at the elaborate gates on Radcliffe Square, wondering how to gain access to the lovely quad beyond: turn right and walk around the corner onto High Street to reach the **college entrance**. This gives onto the modest Front Quad, location of the spectacular fifteenth-century **chapel**, with its gilded hammerbeam roof and neck-cricking reredos (though all its figures are Victorian replacements). Move through to the spacious **North Quad**, the object of all that admiration: Hawksmoor's soaring Gothic twin towers face the Radcliffe Square gates, while ahead, the Codrington Library – also Hawksmoor – sports a conspicuous, brightly decorated sundial designed by Wren.

Turl Street

Leading south between Broad Street and High Street, modest **Turl Street** – named for a long-demolished twirling turnstile gate at its northern end, designed to keep cattle out of the town – is one of Oxford's most atmospheric streets. Narrow and pedestrianized, shaded at its northern end by a huge chestnut tree, it nonetheless hums with activity, straddling as it does "town" and "gown" – shoppers at the Covered Market mixing with students and dons passing between the street's three colleges: Exeter, Jesus and Lincoln.

Exeter College

Turl St • Daily 2–5pm • Free • ☎ 01865 279600, ⓦ www.exeter.ox.ac.uk

In medieval **Exeter College** aim for the elaborate Gothic Revival chapel, conceived by Gilbert Scott in the 1850s. It contains a fine set of **stained-glass windows** illustrating biblical stories – St Paul on the road to Damascus, Samson bringing down the pillars of the Philistine temple – as well as a superb Pre-Raphaelite tapestry, the *Adoration of the Magi*, a collaboration between William Morris and Edward Burne-Jones, both former students.

TAKING TO THE WATER

Punting is a favourite summer pastime among both students and visitors, but handling a **punt** – a flat-bottomed boat ideal for the shallow waters of the Thames and Cherwell – requires some practice. The punt is propelled and steered with a long pole, which beginners inevitably get stuck in riverbed mud: if this happens, let go of it and paddle back, otherwise you're likely to be dragged overboard. The Cherwell, though narrower than the Thames and therefore trickier to navigate, provides more opportunities for pulling to the bank for a picnic, an essential part of the punting experience.

There are two central **boat rental** places: Magdalen Bridge Boathouse (☎ 01865 202643, ⓦ oxfordpunting.co.uk), beside the Cherwell at the east end of the High Street; and Salter's Steamers (☎ 01865 243421, ⓦ salterssteamers.co.uk) at Folly Bridge, south of Christ Church. Opening times vary: call for details, or try and arrive early (around 10am) to avoid the queues which build up on sunny summer afternoons. At either expect to **pay** £20 per hour plus a deposit of about £50; ID is required. Punts can take a maximum of five people: four sitting and one punting. Both boathouses also rent out **chauffeured punts** (£50–60/hr) and cheaper **pedaloes**. Another option is the Cherwell Boathouse (☎ 01865 515978, ⓦ cherwellboathouse .co.uk), a bit further out – north of the centre on Bardwell Road – but in a lovely location and also slightly cheaper.

Alternatively, Salters Steamers runs **passenger boats** along the Thames from Folly Bridge downstream to Abingdon, about eight miles south, between late May and mid-September. There are two boats daily in each direction; the return trip takes four hours and costs £20. Oxford River Cruises (☎ 01865 987147, ⓦ oxfordrivercruises.com) also sets sail from Folly Bridge (April–Oct): prices and schedules for their half-dozen cruises – including a "lunchtime picnic" trip – are given online.

Jesus College

Turl St • Daily 2–4.30pm • £2 • ☎ 01865 279700, ⓦ www.jesus.ox.ac.uk

On the west side of Turl Street, **Jesus College** makes for an attractive stop: its two small, sixteenth-century quads are gentle on the eye and the atmospheric hall sports portraits of Elizabeth I – founder of the college in 1571 – and T.E. Lawrence ("of Arabia"), Jesus's most famous alumnus.

Lincoln College

Turl St • Mon–Fri 2–5pm, Sat & Sun 11am–5pm • Free • ☎ 01865 279800, ⓦ www.linc.ox.ac.uk

Above Turl Street rises the distinctive circular spired tower of All Saints Church, rebuilt after the original collapsed in 1700. The church, now deconsecrated, serves as the library for **Lincoln College**, founded in 1427 and presenting a charming, ivy-clad Front Quad that has remained largely untouched since then. Its chapel sports unusual enamelled – rather than stained – glass and a host of richly carved woodwork.

Lincoln backs directly onto Brasenose; the single door between the two colleges is opened only once a year, at noon on Ascension Day, when members of Brasenose are invited through to sup free beer at Lincoln's expense, in commemoration of some half-remembered inter-collegiate slight. Long ago, Lincoln took to tainting the ale with ivy, Brasenose say in order to discourage excessive consumption, but Lincoln maintain merely as continuance of a brewing tradition – before hops arrived in England – which used herbs such as ground ivy as a flavouring agent. Brasenose partakes regardless.

High Street

Oxford's **High Street** – universally abbreviated to "The High" – runs in a graceful curve west from Magdalen Bridge to Carfax, lined with buildings of interest all the way along, and marking a transition from "gown", at its eastern end, to "town" around Carfax.

Magdalen College

High St • Daily: July–Sept noon–7pm, rest of year 1–6pm or dusk • £5 • ☎ 01865 276000, ⓦ www.magd.ox.ac.uk

Its stone buildings clustering together on the north side of the High Street, and its chunky sixteenth-century bell tower dominating the views over this part of town, **Magdalen College** (pronounced *mawdlin*) sprawls across a large site, also taking in a swathe of riverside meadow. Founded in 1458 by William Waynflete, bishop of Winchester, it served during the Civil War as a fortified redoubt for Royalist troops. At the college's boundary, Longwall Street marks where Oxford's eastern gate stood until its demolition in 1772.

Magdalen is the focus for Oxford's **May Day** festivities: choristers sing Latin hymns from the top of the bell tower at 6am every May 1, to the accompaniment down below of Morris dancing, much revelry and, once Magdalen Bridge reopens to traffic, the occasional splash as reckless types pursue the tradition of jumping off – a 30ft drop into just a few feet of water. Hospitalizations are common.

The college

From Magdalen's High Street entrance, you emerge into **St John's Quad**, named for the twelfth-century hospital of St John the Baptist which occupied the site: high on the right-hand wall is a pulpit from which a sermon is preached every June 24, John's feast day. Below it, a narrow arch gives into the triangular **Chaplain's Quad**, at the base of the soaring bell tower. Back in St John's Quad, turn right and right again to discover the door into the **chapel**, which has a handsome reredos, though you have to admire it through the windows of an ungainly stone screen. The adjacent fifteenth-century **cloisters**, perhaps the finest in Oxford, are adorned by standing figures, some biblical and others folkloric, most notably a tribe of grotesques. At the southeastern corner, stairs rise to the **hall**, where two Magdalen alumni confront each other in silence: a bust of Lord Denning above the fireplace, directly opposite another of Oscar Wilde.

The Grove and Addison's Walk

Passages on the northern side of the cloisters face the Neoclassical **New Building**, completed in 1733 to be part of a grand new quad which never materialized. To the left, a fence bars access to the **Grove**, Magdalen's own deer park – you might spot the sixty-strong herd roaming – while to the right a little bridge over the River Cherwell connects with **Addison's Walk**, a lovely footpath which encircles a water meadow; rare wild snake's-head fritillaries flower here in spring and the deer often graze this way during the summer and autumn. In the far (northeastern) corner, cross two wooden bridges to reach the secluded **Fellow's Garden**.

Botanic Garden

Rose Lane • Daily 9am–6pm; March, April, Sept & Oct closes 5pm; Nov–Feb closes 4pm • £4.50 • Ⓦ www.botanic-garden.ox.ac.uk

Bounded by a graceful curve of the River Cherwell, the university's **Botanic Garden** is the oldest of its kind in England, established in 1621. Reached along Rose Lane from opposite Magdalen College entrance, and still enclosed by its original high wall, it comprises several different zones, from a lily pond, a bog garden and a rock garden through to borders of bearded irises and variegated plants. There are also six large **glasshouses** housing tropical and carnivorous species.

St Edmund Hall

Queen's Lane • No set hours, usually daily 10am–4pm • Free • Ⓣ 01865 279000, Ⓦ www.seh.ox.ac.uk

Leading north off the High Street, Queen's Lane makes for an attractive detour: a short way up on the right is the entrance to **St Edmund Hall**. Though a fully-fledged college only since 1957, "Teddy Hall" can trace its history back to the thirteenth century: it's the only survivor of the medieval halls which predated the formation of colleges. Its attractive sixteenth-century Front Quad, centred on an ancient well, leads through to **St Peter-in-the-East**, originally Saxon, now deconsecrated to serve as the college library. The only part open to the public is its vast **crypt** (ask about access at the porter's lodge), but the yew-shaded churchyard is one of the loveliest hideaways in central Oxford. It backs onto the gardens of New College (see p.215).

Queen's College

High St • No set hours • Free • Ⓣ 01865 279120, Ⓦ www.queens.ox.ac.uk

Beside Queen's Lane, and entered from the High Street, stands **Queen's College**, whose handsome Baroque buildings cut an impressive dash. Erected in a single period (1682–1765), Queen's benefited from the skills of several talented architects, most notably Wren

---

FIRST FOR COFFEE

By the ornate **Examination Schools** building towards the eastern end of the High Street – especially busy in June, when students sit their exams here dressed in the obligatory "subfusc" garb of dark suit, white shirt and gown – two cafés face each other across the street, both claiming to be **England's oldest coffee house**. To the south, the *Grand Café* (see p.237) occupies the site of a coffee house opened by a Lebanese Jew named Jacob in or just after 1650. Opposite, the *Queen's Lane Coffee House* stands where a Syrian Jew named Cirques Jobson launched a competing enterprise at roughly the same time. Whichever was first, Oxford's gentlefolk were drinking coffee – and also hot chocolate – several years ahead of London.

and Hawksmoor. Crossing straight across its expansive, cloistered **Front Quad** leads to the entrance of the most diverting building, the unusually spacious **chapel**, designed – or at least influenced – by Wren, with a ceiling filled by cherubs amid dense foliage.

University College

High St • No set hours • Free • ☎ 01865 276602, ⊕ www.univ.ox.ac.uk

The long facade and twin gateway towers of **University College** rise above the south side of the High. "Univ" spuriously claims Alfred the Great as its founder, but – that aside – it is still Oxford's oldest college, endowed in 1249. Nothing, though, remains from that period. The attractive Jacobean-Gothic buildings around the **Main Quad** conceal, in the northeastern corner, a shrine-like domed chamber housing a white marble sculpture of Shelley, who was expelled from Univ in 1811 for writing a pamphlet entitled *The Necessity of Atheism*. Guilt later induced the college to accept a memorial: Edward Onslow Ford's sculpture of the limp body of the poet (who drowned in Italy in 1822), borne by winged lions and mourned by the Muse of Poetry shows pathos or melodrama, depending on your taste.

Church of St Mary the Virgin

High St • Daily 9am–5pm, July & Aug until 6pm • Free; tower £3 • ⊕ www.university-church.ox.ac.uk

Midway along the High Street just behind Radcliffe Square, **St Mary the Virgin** is a hotchpotch of architectural styles, but mostly dates from the fifteenth century. Its distinctive Baroque **porch**, flanked by chunky corkscrewed pillars, was installed in 1637 with the approval of William Laud, Archbishop of Canterbury and religious adviser to Charles I. Shortly afterwards, when Parliament tried Laud for high treason, this porch was cited as evidence of excessive Catholicism. Laud was finally executed at the height of the Civil War in 1644.

The church's **interior** is disappointingly mundane, though the carved poppy heads on the choir stalls are of some historical interest: the tips were brusquely squared off when a platform was installed here in 1555 to stage the heresy trial of Cranmer, Latimer and Ridley, the "Oxford Martyrs" (see p.205). The church's other diversion is its **tower**: as recompense for climbing 127 steps, you gain stupendous views over Radcliffe Square, the spires of All Souls and much of central Oxford.

Rhodes Building

High St • No public access

The hulking presence of the **Rhodes Building**, a 1911 bequest to Oriel College by diamond tycoon Cecil Rhodes (1853–1902), overshadows the High Street across from St Mary's. Under renovation at the time of writing, it marks a transition point: west from here – and from the splendid Victorian frontage of Brasenose College opposite, with its gables, oriel windows, gate-tower and battlements – "gown" fades into "town", as shops, restaurants and cafés take over the High Street.

The Mitre

17 High St • Mon–Sat 11.30am–11pm, Sun noon–10.30pm

On the High Street at the corner with Turl Street, the *Mitre* is one of Oxford's oldest inns, in existence for more than 700 years, chiefly as a coaching inn owned by nearby Lincoln College. The current incarnation dates from around 1630, but is now, sadly, run by an unimaginative restaurant chain: step into the old bar for a swift half, but step out again before you get hungry.

FROM TOP VIOLINS IN ASHMOLEAN MUSEUM (P.229); BRIDGE OF SIGHS (P.215) >

Covered Market

High St • Mon–Sat 9am–5.30pm, Sun 10am–4pm • Ⓦ oxford-coveredmarket.co.uk

For refreshment on the hoof – as well as a fascinating glimpse into the everyday life of Oxford away from all the pomp and history of the colleges – drop into the **Covered Market**, wedged between the High Street and Market Street. Opened in 1774, it remains full of atmosphere, home to butchers, bakers, fishmongers, greengrocers and cheese sellers as well as a welter of excellent cafés, patisseries and even some clothes boutiques and shoe shops. Whatever you do, don't miss the *Ben's Cookies* stall (see p.237), where sensational cookies are baked continuously throughout the day and sold by weight.

Carfax tower

Carfax • Daily 10am–5.30pm, Oct closes 4.30pm, March closes 4pm, Nov–Feb closes 3pm • £2.20

The busy **Carfax** crossroads is a fulcrum, where chiefly "gown" architecture along the High Street to the east is balanced by the distinctly "town" atmosphere of Cornmarket and Queen Street to the west. This has been a crossroads for more than a thousand years: roads met here in Saxon times, and the name "Carfax" derives from the Latin *quadrifurcus* ("four-forked"). The junction is overlooked by a square thirteenth-century **tower**, adorned by a pair of clocktower jacks, which is all that remains of St Martin's Church, demolished in 1896 to ease traffic access. You can **climb** it for wide views over the centre, though other vantage points – principally St Mary's (see p.220) – have the edge.

Queen Street

From the base of Carfax tower, shop-heavy **Queen Street** bustles westwards past the bland, paved **Bonn Square**, named for Oxford's twin city in Germany. This was once the graveyard of the medieval St Peter-le-Bailey Church and much controversy surrounded its 2008 redevelopment, which saw trees felled and skeletons reburied. Opposite looms the 1970s-vintage **Westgate shopping centre**, a none-too-pretty lump.

Cornmarket

Storming north of Carfax, **Cornmarket** is now a busy pedestrianized shopping strip lined with familiar high-street stores. There's precious little here to fire the imagination – the *Crown Tavern*, once at 3 Cornmarket (not to be confused with the current *Crown* across the road, beside *McDonald's*), was where William Shakespeare lodged on his regular visits to Oxford, but it has long since vanished. Further north on the left, pleasant **St Michael's Street** is the location of the **Oxford Union** (see Ⓦoxfordunion.org for access info), the university debating society, where scores of budding politicians have flexed their oratorical muscles, while directly opposite on the corner of **Ship Street** is a splendid old wood-framed building, probably fifteenth-century; once the *Ship Inn* it is now occupied by ordinary shops.

The top of Cornmarket is central Oxford's busiest corner, crowded with buses and shoppers. To the east is **Broad Street** (see p.210), a short walk north is **St Giles** (see p.229), while to the west **George Street** fights a path through to **Gloucester Green**, a paved square which hosts open-air markets (see p.241) and the main bus station.

St Michael-at-the-Northgate

Cornmarket • Daily 10.30am–5pm, Nov–March closes 4pm • Church free; tower £2.50 • Ⓦ www.smng.org.uk

Towards the north end of Cornmarket stands **St Michael-at-the-Northgate**, a church recorded in the Domesday Book, with a late fourteenth-century font where

Shakespeare's godson was baptized in 1606. The church's Saxon **tower**, built in 1050, is Oxford's oldest surviving building; as well as rooftop views you can see the door of the cell in which Latimer, Ridley and Cranmer were imprisoned (see p.205) and a modest treasury, including an eleventh-century sheela-na-gig.

Merton Street

South of the High Street, a succession of lanes and alleyways cut through to some of the finest of Oxford's college architecture, ranged along medieval **Merton Street**, still cobbled and offering some of Oxford's most picturesque urban views. Alongside the medieval Postmasters' Hall on Merton Street, gates on the left give access to Merton College's **Real Tennis Court**, an indoor space for playing this ancestor of lawn tennis – still with racquets and a net, but using a solid ball and featuring squash-like rebounds off the interior walls. You might be lucky and catch a game in progress. Past Merton and Corpus Christi, the street ends at gates giving access to the Christ Church Picture Gallery (see p.227).

7

Merton College

Merton St • Mon–Fri 2–5pm, Sat & Sun 10am–5pm • £3 • ☎ 01865 276310, ⦿ www.merton.ox.ac.uk

Merton College is historically the city's most important. Balliol and University colleges may have been founded earlier, but it was Merton – established in 1264 by Thomas de Merton, Lord Chancellor and the bishop of Rochester – which set the model for colleges in both Oxford and Cambridge, being the first to gather its students and tutors together in one place. Merton retains a good deal of its original medieval architecture.

Entry is via the fifteenth-century **gatehouse**, above which a stone-carved panel shows Walter de Merton kneeling before the "Book with Seven Seals" of Revelation, observed by a lamb, unicorn, woodland animals and John the Baptist. The cobbled **Front Quad** feels rather disordered; opposite stands the **hall**, rebuilt by George Gilbert Scott but retaining its ornate thirteenth-century door.

Mob Quad and the library

Merton's compact but charming **Mob Quad** is Oxford's oldest (completed in 1378), still ringed by mullioned windows and Gothic doorways: the quad layout is now familiar to us, but it developed here organically, with buildings added over the course of a century to form an enclosed space.

The atmospheric **library**, on the south side of Mob Quad, uniquely permits public access (usually on guided tours only). Completed in the 1370s, it was the first library in England to store books upright on shelves, rather than in piles. Much of the woodwork, including the panelling, screens and bookcases, dates from the Tudor period, but some fittings are original.

The chapel and Fellows' Quad

On the north side of Mob Quad, an archway leads through to the **chapel**, which dates from 1290. Walter de Merton's intention was that this hugely grand space would form merely the choir and transepts for a much larger, naved church; standing here today, the scale of that imagined building boggles the mind. Funds ran out before his vision could be realised, and the truncated T-shaped form which survives served as the model for all future college chapels. The antechapels house numerous monuments to benefactors, including Thomas Bodley, founder of the Bodleian, whose funerary plaque shows him surrounded, oddly, by ungainly-looking allegorical ladies. The chapel's stained glass is largely original thirteenth-century work; the stunning east window, with seven lancets and a rose, is especially beautiful.

MEADOW WALKS

A pleasant walk begins at the wrought-iron gates on the south side of Merton Street, just past Merton's chapel tower: these give access (daylight hours only) to **Merton Grove**, a footpath – punctuated by a turnstile – which opens onto expansive views across Christ Church Meadow to the tree-lined riverbanks beyond.

From here, turn left (east) to follow **Dead Man's Walk** beside the walls of Merton College, with broad views on your right across the lawns of Merton Field; this was originally the funerary route to Oxford's Jewish cemetery, which fell into disrepair after the expulsion of the Jews from England in 1290 and was refounded in the seventeenth century as a botanic garden (see p.219). Alternatively, head straight on (south) to meet the grand **Broad Walk**, which gives access left to the banks of the River Cherwell and right to the lovely, tree-shaded **New Walk**, progressing further south to the Thames. In summer, a walk along the banks of Cherwell here is lovely, with punts passing and friends picnicking.

7

From the Front Quad, wander south into the seventeenth-century **Fellows' Quad**, venue for the self-consciously weird **Merton Time Ceremony**. On the last Sunday in October, at exactly 2am – the moment when the clocks go back one hour, marking the end of British Summer Time – college members, in full gowned regalia, link arms and walk backwards around the quad, drinking port and toasting "good old times". The ceremony ends after an hour, at 2am Greenwich Mean Time.

Corpus Christi College

Merton St • Daily 1.30–4.30pm • Free • ☎ 01865 276700, ⓦ www.ccc.ox.ac.uk

Along Merton Street is a gateway leading into **Corpus Christi College**. Founded in 1517 with what was acclaimed at that time as one of the finest libraries in Europe, it today has one of Oxford's smallest student populations. Pop in to see its paved Front Quad, focused on a pillared sundial of 1581 topped by a gilded pelican.

Oriel College

Oriel Sq • No set hours, sometimes daily 2–5pm • £2 • ☎ 01865 276555, ⓦ www.oriel.ox.ac.uk

Entered via gates on Oriel Square, just off Merton Street's western end, **Oriel College** has a beautiful seventeenth-century Jacobean-Gothic Front Quad. Don't miss its small, narrow chapel, which includes some contemporary stained glass and an oratory dedicated to Cardinal Newman (1801–1890), a leading figure in the Oxford Movement (see p.208).

The Bear

6 Alfred St • Mon–Thurs 11am–11pm, Fri & Sat 11am–midnight, Sun 11.30am–10.30pm • ☎ 01865 728164, ⓦ bearoxford.co.uk

Two medieval alleys, Bear Lane and Blue Boar Street, meet at what is often claimed as **Oxford's oldest pub**, *The Bear*. It is recorded here as early as 1242, though the current building dates from the seventeenth century. It's posher than it used to be (see p.241), but remains famous for its collection of ties.

St Aldate's

Buses negotiating the busy Carfax crossroads turn constantly in and out of **St Aldate's**, the main road heading south, which drops down towards the squat Tom Tower of Christ Church College (see p.225) and onwards to Folly Bridge over the Thames. Spreading down the street by the crossroads, Oxford's ostentatious Victorian **Town Hall** reflects a municipal determination not to be overwhelmed by the university.

Museum of Oxford

St Aldate's • Mon–Sat 10am–5pm • Free • ☎ 01865 252334, ⓦ museumofoxford.org.uk

At the Town Hall's south side, a staircase gives access to the fine **Museum of Oxford** – often ignored, though it does a great job of telling the history of the city. Start downstairs with displays on prehistory and the Roman and Saxon eras, including a grave slab tentatively identified as that of St Frideswide and the city's 1191 charter. Reconstructions of period interiors, such as the parlour of a sixteenth-century inn, are particularly absorbing. The ground-level galleries cover intricate exhibits on Victorian Oxford, including a reconstruction of a Jericho kitchen of the 1880s, and take the story through to the rise of twentieth-century industry, from cars to marmalade. Well worth an hour or two.

Modern Art Oxford

30 Pembroke St • Tues–Sat 11am–6pm, Sun noon–5pm • Free • ☎ 01865 722733, ⓦ modernartoxford.org.uk

Almost under Tom Tower, narrow Pembroke Street branches west to the outstanding **Modern Art Oxford** gallery, founded in 1965 and hosting an excellent changing programme of temporary exhibitions. It's worth stopping by, whatever happens to be showing.

7

Story Museum

42 Pembroke St • Hours vary • Admission varies • ☎ 01865 790050, ⓦ storymuseum.org.uk

With patrons that include literary superstars Philip Pullman, Michael Morpurgo, Jacqueline Wilson and Michael Rosen, Oxford's **Story Museum** was conceived to preserve and evoke the city's long tradition of storytelling. It remains a work in progress, housed in three old buildings on Pembroke Street that were fully opened in 2014 with a changing programme of playful, quirky exhibitions alongside talks, readings and one-off events. Plans include a studio theatre, more gallery space and – one day – a rooftop walkway among the dreaming spires. Drop in, whether or not you have kids in tow.

Pembroke College

Pembroke Sq • No set hours • Free • ☎ 01865 276444, ⓦ www.pmb.ox.ac.uk

Accessed from tree-shaded Pembroke Square, alongside the Victorian church of St Aldate's, **Pembroke College** is little-visited, but was eulogized by John Betjeman in his verse autobiography *Summoned by Bells* (1960) as "so polite and shy", yet with more character than its better-known neighbours. If Betjeman's words appeal, you'll enjoy the atmosphere of Pembroke's seventeenth- and eighteenth-century buildings. Make your way through a passage from the "second quad" (Chapel Quad) into the New Quad, formed in 1962 when adjacent Beef Lane was closed off and a row of houses incorporated into the college grounds.

Christ Church College

St Aldate's • Mon–Sat 10am–4.30pm, Sun 2–4.30pm • July & Aug £8.50, rest of year £7–8; discounts when the hall and/or cathedral are closed • Tour times vary (check online); around £13 • ☎ 01865 276492, ⓦ www.chch.ox.ac.uk

The Tom Tower of **Christ Church College** dominates views along St Aldate's, lording it over the facade and main entrance of what is Oxford's largest and most prestigious college. Visitor access is further south, a signed five-minute walk away: continue down St Aldate's, turn left through the tiny War Memorial Gardens and onto **Broad Walk**, a tree-lined path which leads across **Christ Church Meadow** (see p.227). You'll see the college entrance on the left.

Albert Einstein and no fewer than thirteen British prime ministers were educated at Christ Church and the college also claims the distinction of having been founded three times, first by Cardinal Wolsey in 1525, then by Henry VIII after the cardinal's fall

OXFORD TIME

One of the oddest of Oxford's many idiosyncrasies is that it keeps its own **time**. Before the railways most British towns followed their own local time, but the adoption of London time as the national standard in the 1840s and 1850s erased the differences – barring Oxford. Located just over one degree of longitude west of the Greenwich Meridian, the city is officially five minutes and two seconds behind London time. To this day, Christ Church College's "Great Tom" bell rings out every night at 9.05pm (it tolls 101 times, to mark the number of students at the college's foundation), and all services in the Christ Church cathedral begin five minutes after the advertised time. Lewis Carroll adopted the oddity into his *Alice* books: the White Rabbit (who was modelled on the contemporary Dean of Christ Church) was perpetually late despite always checking his pocket-watch – presumably because it was set to Oxford time.

7

from favour and finally, after the Reformation – when the second college was suppressed – in 1545, when it assumed its present name. Overlooking the confluence of the Thames and the Cherwell, Christ Church occupies the site of the eighth-century priory founded by St Frideswide, which was destroyed by Danish invaders in 1002 and refounded by the Augustinians. The college chapel, uniquely, is also the cathedral for the Oxford diocese.

In addition to the standard self-guided itinerary described below, you could book ahead with the college for a "**Behind the Scenes Tour**", taking in areas normally off-limits to visitors.

The cloister and hall staircase

As you enter Christ Church from the south, through the Victorian Gothic **Meadow Building**, passages lead through to the tranquil, fifteenth-century **cloister**, part-demolished by Wolsey to clear space for his grand new quad (see below). Move on to one of Oxford's most impressive spaces, the hall **staircase**, laid out in the 1820s beneath a stupendous fan-vaulted ceiling installed in 1640. A door on the right has the words "No Peel" studded into it – student political graffiti from 1829, objecting to the plans of Home Secretary (and Christ Church alumnus) Sir Robert Peel for reform of anti-Catholic laws.

The Hall

Often closed to visitors 11.40am–2.30pm

Head up to the **Hall**, Oxford's largest and grandest college refectory – famously featuring as Hogwarts Hall in the *Harry Potter* films – its three long tables, seating about 250, surrounded by dark wood panelling beneath a superb hammerbeam roof. Charles I held court here when the Parliamentarians were in control of London. It's a hugely atmospheric space, hung with portraits of past scholars by a roll-call of well-known artists, including Reynolds, Gainsborough and Millais. Lewis Carroll, author of *Alice's Adventures in Wonderland* (who, under his real name **Charles Dodgson**, was a mathematics tutor at Christ Church), is commemorated with a portrait by the door; images of characters from his books are set into the fifth stained-glass window on the left, and as you pass the fireplaces you'll see long-necked figures flanking the grates, looking remarkably similar to how Alice ended up after she sampled the hookah-smoking caterpillar's mushroom.

Tom Quad

At some 260ft square **Tom Quad** is the largest in Oxford, so large in fact that the Royalists penned up their mobile larder of cattle here during the Civil War. The quad's soft, honey-coloured stone makes a harmonious whole, but it was actually built in two main phases, with the southern side dating back to Wolsey, the north finally finished in the 1660s. Rising above is **Tom Tower**, added by Christopher Wren in 1681 to house the seven-ton "Great Tom" bell, named for Thomas Becket, which was recovered from Osney Abbey near Oxford during the Dissolution.

Oxford Cathedral

Last admission 4 or 4.15pm

Christ Church's college chapel is otherwise known as **Oxford Cathedral**. The Saxon priory of St Frideswide, located on this site, was rebuilt in the twelfth century but suppressed in 1524; its church survived and was granted cathedral status soon afterwards by Henry VIII, during his ecclesiastical reforms following the break with Rome.

Architecturally, it's unusually discordant, with all sorts of bits and bobs from different periods – not helped by the fact that Wolsey demolished the west end to make space for Tom Quad. The dominant feature is the sturdy circular columns and rounded arches of the Normans, but there are also early Gothic pointed arches and the chancel ceiling is a particularly fine example of fifteenth-century stone vaulting. The battered **shrine of St Frideswide**, in the Latin Chapel – to the far left (northeast) of the entrance – was destroyed during the Dissolution, but the pieces were found down an old well and gamely assembled by the Victorians. Today, it exhibits some of the earliest natural foliage in English sculpture, a splendid filigree of leaves dating from around 1290. The shrine is overlooked by an equally rare, two-storey, stone and timber **watching loft**, from where custodians would keep a close eye on the tomb of the saint. Also here is a deeply coloured **stained-glass window** by Edward Burne-Jones, crammed with biblical bodies; it was completed in 1858, long before Jones got into his Pre-Raphaelite stride, but there are three examples from his later period along the rest of the back of the chancel, with the **St Catherine Window**, in the right-hand corner of the church, being the finest. A stained-glass image of the martyrdom of Thomas Becket survives nearby, created in 1320 and defaced during the Reformation, though still discernible: the saint kneels while his four knightly killers lurk behind.

7

Christ Church Picture Gallery

Canterbury Quad, Christ Church • July–Sept Mon–Sat 10.30am–5pm, Sun 2–5pm; June same times but closed Tues; Oct–May Mon & Wed–Sat 10.30am–1pm & 2–4.30pm, Sun 2–4.30pm • £4, or £2 with a Christ Church admission ticket • Free tour Mon 2.30pm • ☎ 01865 276172, ⓦ www.chch.ox.ac.uk/gallery

Beyond Peckwater Quad, dominated by the whopping Neoclassical library, is the cobbled, pocket-sized Canterbury Quad, where stands the **Christ Church Picture Gallery**. Designed in 1968 behind the original frontage, it displays an impressive array of works by many of Italy's finest artists from the fifteenth to eighteenth centuries, including Veronese and Filippino Lippi. There's also a good showing by the Flemish and Dutch – Van Dyck, Frans Hals and so forth. The gallery's collection of Old Master drawings is world-class, taking in examples by Leonardo, Michelangelo, Raphael and Rubens, displayed in temporary, themed exhibitions.

A gateway off Canterbury Quad exits to Oriel Square, or you could return through the Christ Church grounds to exit onto St Aldate's.

Christ Church Meadow

From the St Aldate's entrance to Christ Church College, the **Broad Walk** footpath runs east and west along the edge of **Christ Church Meadow**. Popular with strollers, the meadow fills in the tapering gap between the rivers Cherwell and Thames and offers lovely views over the sports pitch of Merton Field and back to the towers of both Christ Church and Merton colleges. Head east along Broad Walk towards the

---

ALICE'S DAY

If you happen to be in Oxford in early July, look out for events around **Alice's Day** – an innovation created by the nascent Story Museum (ⓦ storymuseum.org.uk/alice). Celebrations take in music, exhibitions and lectures around town – past themes include "The Dodo: from extinction to icon" and "Lewis Carroll and Surrealism" – as well as shows for children, costumed processions, hunting the snark in the botanic gardens and, of course, a Mad Hatter's Tea Party. Full details online.

Cherwell, or cut south along the similarly tree-lined (and perhaps prettier) **New Walk** to reach the Thames. Partway along Broad Walk, **Merton Grove** (see p.224) heads north to reach Merton Street, Dead Man's Walk and the Botanic Garden.

Alice's Shop

83 St Aldate's • Daily 9.30am–6.30pm; Sept–June 10.30am–5pm • ☎ 01865 723793, ⓦ aliceinwonderlandshop.co.uk

On St Aldate's south of Tom Tower, more or less opposite the War Memorial Gardens stands the quaint little **Alice's Shop**, now crammed full of Alice souvenirs but in Victorian times a sweet-shop, known to Lewis Carroll. It makes an appearance in *Through the Looking-Glass*, staffed by a spectacled sheep, and described by Alice as "the queerest shop I ever saw!"

Bate Collection of Musical Instruments

St Aldate's • Mon–Fri 2–5pm, May & June also Sat 10am–noon • Free • ☎ 01865 276139, ⓦ www.bate.ox.ac.uk

Signposted off St Aldate's, within the university's Faculty of Music, you'll find the **Bate Collection of Musical Instruments**, displaying over a thousand instruments of all kinds and styles, including the earliest surviving double-keyboard harpsichord, made in 1700, and a Javanese gamelan.

Folly Bridge

At the lower, southern end of St Aldate's stands **Folly Bridge** over the Thames, likely location for the Saxon-era oxen ford which gave the city its name. The current bridge, busy with traffic, is nineteenth-century; just to one side stand the famous *Head of the River* pub and a boat-rental station. This stretch of river is where many college **rowing** teams train (ⓦ ourcs.org.uk): the college boathouses are a short way south at the confluence of the Thames and Cherwell, venue for both the Torpids races in February or March and the more prestigious Summer Eights in late May.

Oxford Castle

Looming above New Road, west of Carfax, is the site of what was **Oxford Castle**, a motte-and-bailey fortress built in 1071. In December 1142 it was besieged by King Stephen, who had usurped the throne after the death of Henry I; Henry's daughter Matilda only escaped by dressing in white as camouflage against the snow and fleeing over the frozen river. The motte (mound) survives, though the buildings atop it were demolished after the Civil War.

In later centuries a cluster of stern Victorian edifices beside the mound served chiefly as Oxford's prison. The prison was decommissioned in 1996 – it now houses the luxurious *Malmaison* hotel (see p.235), serving as the focus for the shops, lounge bars and restaurants of the rather over-gentrified "Oxford Castle Quarter" (ⓦ oxfordcastlequarter.com).

Oxford Castle Unlocked

Castle Yard • Daily 10am–5pm; tours every 20min, last at 4.20pm • £9.95; discount for booking online • ☎ 01865 260666, ⓦ oxfordcastleunlocked.co.uk

To one side of the *Malmaison* hotel, the excellent heritage centre **Oxford Castle Unlocked** offers memorable forty-minute **guided tours**, during which costumed warders lead you up the Saxon-era **St George's Tower**, show you medieval prison cells and take you down into the Romanesque crypt beneath **St George's Chapel**, telling tales of wars, executions and hauntings along the way.

St Giles and around

Beyond the north end of Cornmarket, beside Oxford's grandest hotel, the *Randolph*, the Martyrs' Memorial (see p.205) gazes north up **St Giles**, a broad, graceful tree-lined boulevard. On the left, look out for the seventeenth-century *Eagle & Child* pub, favoured haunt of the "Inklings" literary group which included C.S. Lewis and J.R.R. Tolkien; they met here from the 1940s until Lewis's death in 1963. You can pop in to see the old front rooms of the pub (see p.241), which include the fireplace nook where the writers sat to share ideas and discuss their work, now hung with memorabilia.

On the east side of St Giles, a passage beside the *Lamb & Flag* pub cuts east to Keble College and the Natural History and Pitt Rivers museums (see p.230).

Ashmolean Museum

Beaumont St • Tues–Sun 10am–5pm • Free • ☎ 01865 278000, ⓦ www.ashmolean.org

Occupying a mammoth Neoclassical building on the corner of St Giles and Beaumont Street, opposite the *Randolph Hotel*, the **Ashmolean Museum** grew from the collections of the magpie-like **John Tradescant**, gardener to Charles I and an energetic traveller. During his wanderings, Tradescant built up a huge assortment of artefacts and natural specimens, which became known as Tradescant's Ark. He bequeathed everything to his friend and sponsor, the lawyer Elias Ashmole, who in turn gave it to the university. Today the Ashmolean possesses a vast and far-reaching collection, second in the country only to the British Museum in London, and showcased to superb effect in bright, uncluttered contemporary galleries. Allow half a day to scratch the surface, a full day (or more) to dig a little deeper.

Ancient art

The **Egyptian** rooms are not to be missed: in addition to well-preserved mummies and sarcophagi, there are unusual frescoes, rare textiles from the Roman and Byzantine periods and several fine examples of relief carving, such as those on the Taharqa shrine. Look out, too, for the superb Islamic ceramics in the **Islamic art** collection, while the **Chinese art** section boasts some remarkable early Chinese pottery with the simple monochrome pots of the Sung dynasty (960–1279) looking surprisingly modern. The archeologist Arthur Evans had close ties with the museum and he gifted it a stunning collection of **Minoan** finds from his years working at Knossos in Crete (1900–06): pride of place goes to the storage jars, sumptuously decorated with sea creatures and marine plants. A further highlight is the extraordinary **Alfred Jewel**, a tiny gold, enamel and rock crystal piece of uncertain purpose. The inscription translates as "Alfred ordered me to be made" – almost certainly a reference to King Alfred the Great.

European art

The museum is very strong on **European art**. Amongst the **Italian** works, watch out for Piero di Cosimo's *Forest Fire* and Paolo Uccello's *Hunt in the Forest*, though Tintoretto, Veronese and Bellini feature prominently as well. **French paintings** make a strong showing too, with works by Pissarro, Monet, Manet and Renoir hanging alongside Cézanne and Bonnard, and there's a representative selection of eighteenth- and nineteenth-century **British artists**: Samuel Palmer's visionary paintings run rings around the rest, though there are lashings of Pre-Raphaelite stuff from Rossetti and Holman Hunt to assorted cohorts.

Tradescant's Ark

Don't miss the basement display of treasures from **Tradescant's Ark**. A particular highlight is **Powhatan's mantle**, a handsome deerskin wall-hanging which belonged to the father of Pocahontas. Other items down here with the wow factor include Guy Fawkes' lantern, Elizabeth I's gloves and the death mask of Oliver Cromwell.

St John's College

St Giles • Daily 1–5pm or dusk • Free • ☎ 01865 277300, ⓦ sjc.ox.ac.uk

Occupying splendid buildings on the east side of St Giles, **St John's College** is reputedly the richest in Oxford: it is said that one could walk from St John's College Oxford to St John's College Cambridge – perhaps eighty miles – and remain on St John's-owned land the whole distance. The college was founded in 1555 on the site of a pre-existing Cistercian monastery; the statue of St Bernard above the gatehouse and much of the splendid **Front Quad** date from the earlier, fifteenth-century foundation. The hall, on the left of Front Quad, is not open to visitors, and the chapel, alongside, was ruined with Victorian "improvements", but through the passage between them lies **North Quad**, overlooked by the intriguing, Modernist **Beehive Building** of 1960, named for its hexagonal bedrooms. From Front Quad, a fan-vaulted passage opposite the gatehouse leads to the Italianate Renaissance architecture of **Canterbury Quad**, featuring scalloped niches holding bronze statues of Charles I and, opposite, his wife Henrietta Maria. Straight ahead, another passage ducks through to the extensive college **gardens**.

Oxford University Museum of Natural History

Parks Rd • Daily 10am–5pm • Free • ☎ 01865 272950, ⓦ www.oum.ox.ac.uk

From the Ashmolean, it's a brief walk north up St Giles to the *Lamb & Flag* pub, beside which an alley cuts east through to the **Oxford University Museum of Natural History**. The building, constructed under the guidance of John Ruskin, looks like a cross between a railway station and a church – and the same applies inside, where a High Victorian-Gothic fusion of cast iron and glass features soaring columns and capitals decorated with animal and plant motifs. Exhibits include some impressive dinosaur skeletons, models of exotic beasties, a four-billion-year-old meteorite, and so on.

Pitt Rivers Museum

Parks Rd • Mon noon–4.30pm, Tues–Sun 10am–4.30pm • Free • ☎ 01865 270927, ⓦ www.prm.ox.ac.uk

Oxford's eye-popping **Pitt Rivers Museum** is housed in the same building as the University Museum of Natural History: it is accessed via a door at the rear of the ground-floor level. Founded in 1884 from the bequest of Grenadier Guard-turned-archeologist Augustus Henry Lane Fox Pitt Rivers, this is one of the world's finest ethnographic museums and an extraordinary relic of the Victorian age, arranged like an exotic junk shop with each intricately crammed cabinet labelled meticulously by hand. The exhibits – brought to England by, among others, Captain Cook – range from totem poles and mummified crocodiles to African fetishes and gruesome shrunken heads. Don't miss their "after hours" events, including spooky candlelit tours.

Keble College

Parks Rd • Daily 2–5pm • Free • ☎ 01865 272727, ⓦ www.keble.ox.ac.uk

At the northern end of Parks Road you can't miss **Keble College** (pronounced *keeble*) – it looks like an overgrown gingerbread house. The college was founded in 1870, in memory of Tractarian cleric John Keble. Its architect, William Butterfield, has bequeathed a *tour de force* of Gothic Revival, complete with turrets, pinnacles, ornamental chimney clusters, steeply pitched gables – the whole nine yards, done not in gentle Oxford stone but in vivid red brick, interspersed with polychromatic patterning in decorative white and blue brick. Its appearance tends to evoke strong reactions. Venture through to the main **Liddon Quad**; on the right looms the gigantic **chapel**, covered rather exhaustingly with ornament both inside and out, and hosting in a side-chapel Holman Hunt's Pre-Raphaelite masterpiece *The Light of the World*.

Jericho

For a pleasant stroll away from the dreaming spires – and a flavour of workaday residential Oxford to boot – aim for **JERICHO**, just northwest of the centre.

This was Oxford's first suburb, originally little more than a cluster of cottages around a travellers' inn: the origin of the name is uncertain, perhaps deriving from the biblical idea of Jericho as a place outside, on the fringes. As Oxford grew in the nineteenth century, workers arrived to service industries including the canal and a local iron foundry, but it was the **Oxford University Press**, which moved into grand Neoclassical premises on **Great Clarendon Street** in 1830, that spurred development. Hardy characterized the area as a cholera-ridden slum in *Jude the Obscure*.

Today, Jericho retains a quite different feel from the city centre – quiet, almost village-like, with a strong community atmosphere, its ragtag population of students and young professionals mixing with local families and old-timers who've been here all their lives. We outline a walking tour in the box below.

ARRIVAL AND DEPARTURE   OXFORD

Oxford is not the easiest city for new arrivals to negotiate. Public transport drops off in locations that are either inconvenient – the railway station – or unpredictable: buses and coaches have a variety of termini around the central area, depending on the operator and route. Driving in the centre can be difficult: you'd do better to use the "park-and-ride" options around the city perimeter. Wherever you arrive, an efficient – and very green – option for getting you and/or your bags to your hotel is to book **Oxon Carts** (☎ 07747 024600, ⓦ oxoncarts.com; see p.233), a cycle-rickshaw firm charging around £10 for a trip across the city centre.

BY PLANE
Oxford's tiny airport (☎ 01865 290600, ⓦ oxfordairport .co.uk), six miles north of the centre in Kidlington – and ambitiously retitled "London Oxford Airport" – mainly handles private jets, plus a few short-hop scheduled flights. To reach Oxford city centre, either take bus #2/2A/2B, book ahead for the shuttle (£10; ☎ 0845 644 7099, ⓦ oxfordairportshuttle.com), or grab a taxi (about £15). From the airport Woodstock (see p.173) is nearer than Oxford – only a couple of miles west.

BY TRAIN
Trains come into Oxford from around the UK (for major routes see p.21). The railway station is at the western edge

---

A JERICHO WALKING TOUR

Walton Street is where Jericho's daily dramas are played out, a long, curving thoroughfare of some character, still largely residential. Just past **Ruskin College**, an adult-education centre known for its social activism, Richmond Road on the left leads to the modest **synagogue**. Oxford's Jewish community is unique in Britain for its independence, remaining unaffiliated with any of the national Jewish organizations – and for conducting both conservative Orthodox and liberal Progressive services at the same time in the same building. They publish an excellent online history of the Jews in Oxford, and occasionally run Jewish tours of the city; ⓦ oxfordjewishheritage.co.uk has details.

Continue along Nelson Street and turn right on Canal Street to dig into the heart of Jericho. Above looms the white campanile of **St Barnabas**, a large church built in 1868 on canalside land newly drained for development. Modern housing here breaks the atmosphere, and the old **Castle Mill boatyard** – which was forcibly closed in 2005, in the face of local protests – has stood derelict since plans to build luxury flats on the site were quashed. Follow lanes back onto Walton Street; the *Jericho Tavern*, on the corner of Jericho Street, stands on the site of the district's original inn. A stroll north leads to an alley on the left giving into **St Sepulchre's Cemetery**, opened in 1850 on the site of an abandoned farm as overflow to handle victims of the cholera epidemic. Full since 1945, and now without a chapel, the semi-overgrown graveyard makes for an atmospheric interlude before a return to the buzz of city life – or extend your walk out onto Port Meadow and beyond (see p.240). Otherwise stroll back down Walton Street and turn left along **Little Clarendon Street**, one of Oxford's liveliest restaurant strips, which meets Woodstock Road just north of St Giles.

BETWEEN OXFORD AND THE M40

Although much of Oxford's hinterland to the east and south of the city lies beyond the remit of this book, if you're driving to or from the M40 motorway you could plan a diversion or two. Dominating the picturesque Thames-side village of **Dorchester**, eight miles south of Oxford, **Dorchester Abbey** (daily 8am–6pm; free; ⓦ dorchester-abbey.org.uk) was built in the twelfth century to replace earlier Saxon foundations; it is magnificent, sporting exquisite stained glass. A shade further south, over Shillingford Bridge, drop in for tastings and sales at the **Brightwell Vineyard** (Fri–Sun noon–6pm; ☏ 01491 832354, ⓦ brightwellvineyard.co.uk).

Southeast of Cowley off the B480, the *Mole Inn* (☏ 01865 340001, ⓦ moleinn.com) in tiny **Toot Baldon** is a fine rural gastropub – or drop into the well-stocked farm shop of the wacky *Crazy Bear* hotel/restaurant (daily 9am–6pm; ☏ 01865 890714, ⓦ crazybeargroup.co.uk) at nearby **Stadhampton**.

Top billing goes to *Le Manoir aux Quat'Saisons* (☏ 01844 278881, ⓦ manoir.com), the five-star country restaurant and hotel of renowned chef Raymond Blanc, on the edge of **Great Milton** village, eight miles southeast of Oxford. It's everything you might wish for: a sixteenth- and seventeenth-century manor house, beautifully preserved outside and tastefully updated inside, set in seven acres of lavish, naturalistic gardens. We couldn't possibly do justice to the food here; suffice it to say that it's world-class. À la carte mains cost around £50, set menus start from £120 or a daily three-course lunch menu is £80. Book at least two months in advance. Rooms from around £550.

7

of the city centre: exit the station forecourt onto traffic-heavy Frideswide Square, and then it's an unromantic ten-minute walk left past the Said Business School and along busy Hythe Bridge St (and its continuation George St) into the centre. Taxis wait outside the station, or you could take the frequent buses #1, #3, #4 or #5 – they stop near Carfax (either Queen St or St Aldate's) and on the High St by Queen's College. The new Oxford Parkway station is at the northern edge of the city, served by direct buses into the centre.
Destinations Banbury (every 30min; 20min); Birmingham New St (hourly; 1hr 10min); Charlbury (hourly; 20min); Kingham (hourly; 30min); London Paddington (every 30min; 1hr); Moreton-in-Marsh (hourly; 35min).

BY BUS AND COACH

Two companies operate most buses: Stagecoach (☏ 01865 772250, ⓦ www.stagecoachbus.com/oxfordshire) and Oxford Bus (☏ 01865 785400, ⓦ oxfordbus.co.uk) – though there are several smaller firms as well. A few routes terminate at the railway station, but most end up in the centre. The bus station on Gloucester Green, off George St, is the terminus for many, including Oxford Tube and #X90 coaches from London (see p.21), Airline coaches from Heathrow and Gatwick airports (see p.22) and National Express coaches from around the UK. Other buses arrive on one or other of the main streets, most commonly Magdalen St, George St, St Aldate's or St Giles.

BY CAR

Driving towards Oxford you'll be cajoled into joining the ring road, a dual carriageway punctuated by too many roundabouts that is notorious for peak-hours jams. Negotiating the ring road is made doubly confusing by its lack of consistent numbering. Coming from London via M40

junction 8, ring road signs will bring you onto either the A40 around the north of Oxford or the A4142 around the south of the city. Coming from Birmingham via M40 junction 9, the A34 leads you to the confusing Pear Tree interchange in North Oxford, to either head on around the western ring road or branch off into the city centre. Coming from Newbury via A34, you arrive at the Hinksey Hill roundabout on the ring road, near the southern end of Abingdon Rd.

PARKING IN OXFORD

Central Oxford is not car-friendly and the council is deliberately giving traffic the squeeze: many streets are pedestrianized and parking in the city centre (see p.234) is both limited and expensive.

PARK AND RIDE (P+R)

Oxford has five large park-and-ride car parks (ⓦ parkandride .net), clearly signposted at strategic points around the ring road. All offer cheap parking (around £2 a day) as well as frequent buses into the city centre (usually every 8–15min: Mon–Sat from 6am, Sun from 8am; £2.70 return). Up to three children under 16 travel free. All five sites stay open 24hrs, but if you're only in Oxford for the day, take note of the last bus times back to each site from the city centre (Mon–Sat around 11pm, Sun around 7pm). Water Eaton has no buses on Sundays, but expect that timetable to change with the opening of the Oxford Parkway train station alongside it. Thornhill and Water Eaton impose a 72hr maximum stay; the others have no maximum (7 days £10). Caravans and motor-homes have secure parking zones at Redbridge (☏ 01865 252489) and Water Eaton (☏ 0845 337 1138) – but they're usually kept locked, so check with staff onsite or phone ahead to confirm access details.

Pear Tree P+R North of Oxford at A34/A44. Bus #300.
Redbridge P+R South of Oxford at A34/A423. Bus #300.
Seacourt P+R West of Oxford at A34/A420. Bus #400.

Thornhill P+R East of Oxford on A40. Bus #400.
Water Eaton P+R North of Oxford, beside Oxford Parkway train station. Bus #500.

INFORMATION

Tourist office Oxford's well-equipped tourist office is plumb in the centre of town at 15 Broad St (Mon–Sat 9.30am–5.30pm, Sun 10am–4pm; Oct–March closes 30 minutes earlier; ☎01865 252200, ⓦvisitoxfordand oxfordshire.com). Staff can offer a wealth of information – though very little is free: expect to pay for a map or a Visitor's

OXFORD TOURS

WALKING TOURS

The tourist office runs dozens of excellent guided **walking tours**, starting from their premises on Broad Street. Check in person or online for details of dozens more private tours – both tailor-made walks with a personal guide and more unusual options.

The best bet for an introduction to the city centre and colleges is the **University and City Tour** (daily 10.45am & 2pm; also 11am & 1pm if there's sufficient demand; 2hr; £8.50, or £9 if the Divinity School is included) – but you could pick from more than a dozen other specialist themed walks which run regularly, including Alice in Wonderland, the English Civil War, Science at Oxford, Gargoyles and Grotesques, Tolkien and C.S. Lewis, and more. The most popular are the **Inspector Morse tour** (Sat 1.30pm; also some Mon & Fri same time; 2hr; £10) and the **Harry Potter tour** (July & Aug about every 2 weeks Fri 1.45pm; rest of year monthly; 2hr; £15). Everything is detailed on the website, which also includes an option to **book in advance** – advisable for all tours.

Blackwell's bookshop (see p.212) also runs guided walks (April–Oct only; all 1hr 30min): a **Literary Tour** (Tues 2pm, Thurs 11am; £8), an "**Inklings**" **Tour** focused on C.S. Lewis and Tolkien (Wed 11.45am; £8) and **Historic Oxford Tour** (Fri 2pm; £8).

Many smaller outfits tout for business on Broad Street. From outside Trinity College gates, **Oxford Walking Tours** (☎07790 734387, ⓦoxfordwalkingtours.com) has introductory tours of the city and colleges (March–Oct daily every hour 11am–4pm; rest of year usually 2–4 times daily; 1hr 30min; £9.50) as well as evening **ghost tours** (June–Sept daily 7.30pm; rest of year Fri & Sat 7.30pm; 1hr 30min; £9.50).

Bill Spectre's Oxford Ghost Trail (☎07941 041811, ⓦghosttrail.org) is an entertaining walk around the city centre led by a guide dressed as a top-hatted Victorian undertaker. It starts from outside the gift shop at Oxford Castle Unlocked (Fri & Sat 6.30pm; additional tours in July & Aug; 1hr 45min; £8). For a shorter walk, you can join at 7pm outside the tourist office, as the tour passes by.

RICKSHAW TOURS

Oxon Carts (☎07747 024600, ⓦoxoncarts.com) – half a dozen students who've set up a firm offering **cycle rickshaw** transport – has a great itinerary through the medieval lanes of the city centre, covering more ground than most walks. The rickshaws can seat one or two people only. Book in advance: tours run on demand (1hr; £25).

CYCLING TOURS

The Carter Company (☎01296 631671, ⓦthe-carter-company.com) offers a one-day **cycling tour** through Oxford and nearby countryside – either self-guided (£40) or on a guided itinerary that goes out to Blenheim (June–Aug daily 10am; from £90). The price includes rental of a bike and helmet. Book at least three days ahead. See also the many guided and self-guided tour options at Bainton Bikes (☎01865 311610, ⓦbaintonbikes.com).

BUS TOURS

City Sightseeing (☎01865 790522, ⓦcitysightseeingoxford.com) runs an open-top **bus tour** around the edges of the medieval city centre (every 10–15min daily 9.30am–6pm; Oct–April ends 1hr earlier; £14). Tickets are valid all day: you can board at any of twenty pick-up/drop-off points (including Broad Street opposite the tourist office) and then hop on or off as you like. Also available are two-day tickets, family discounts and good-value combo deals with Oxford Castle, walking tours and other attractions.

7

7

Guide. They also sell discounted tickets for a range of nearby attractions, including Blenheim Palace and the Cotswold Wildlife Park, as well as tickets for coaches to London.

Listings and websites *Daily Info* (ⓦ dailyinfo.co.uk) is the continually updated online version of Oxford's student newssheet. You'll spot the paper version (printed twice a week) pinned up in colleges and cafés around town. Otherwise, pick up a copy of *The Guide*, the Thursday entertainment pullout in the daily *Oxford Mail* (ⓦ oxford mail.co.uk) or have a look at ⓦ inoxford.com or ⓦ oxford cityguide.com. Oxford's concert season of classical music is outlined at ⓦ musicatoxford.com.

GETTING AROUND

ON FOOT

The easiest way to get around central Oxford – indeed, the only way to get under the skin of the place – is to walk. For an idea of distance, just about the longest walk you're likely to do in one go might be from the rail station to Magdalen Bridge; this is roughly a mile and a quarter, and you would pass almost everything of interest in the city centre on the way.

BY BIKE

Oxford is full of bikes, and two wheels will get you to outlying districts more easily and often more quickly than a bus. Ask at the tourist office for the very useful, free Oxford Cycle Map, also downloadable at ⓦ www.oxfordshire.gov .uk/cycling.

Bike rental Several of Oxford's many bike shops offer bike rental and repairs, including Bainton Bikes, who operate out of Walton St Cycles, 78 Walton St (ⓣ 01865 311610, ⓦ baintonbikes.com). They charge £10 for a day or £18 for three days. Always book ahead. Others, with slightly higher prices, include Bike Zone, 28 St Michael St (ⓣ 01865 728877, ⓦ bike-zone.co.uk) and the mobile back-of-a-van service Back on Trax (ⓣ 07773 325552, ⓦ backontrax .co.uk).

BY BUS

As a short-stay visitor you're unlikely to use buses. The exception might be if you're staying at a hotel or B&B on one of the approach roads (Banbury Rd or Woodstock Rd in the north, Botley Rd in the west, Abingdon Rd or Iffley Rd in the south, or Headington Rd in the east), in which case you may need to use buses to get to and from the city centre. Stagecoach and Oxford Bus (see p.232) operate most city buses; a citywide one-day pass is £4 – or £8 for two adults and up to three children.

BY CAR

As gridlock on Beaumont St and Hythe Bridge St can testify – not to mention peak-hour jams at other pinch-points around the city – driving in Oxford is often frustrating and time-consuming. Most of the city-centre streets are pedestrianized; those that aren't have time restrictions or deliberately obstructive one-way rules. Four "bus gates" ring the central area, monitored by cameras: drive through the ones on Magdalen St, George St or Castle St at any time, or the one on the High St between 7.30am and 6.30pm daily, and you'll get a £60 fine. If you have a reservation at a city-centre hotel and want to drive in to unload, check with hotel staff beforehand about access restrictions. Several central hotels offer parking for guests (generally £10–20 a night; always book ahead).

Park and ride Instead of driving in, you'd do much better to take advantage of Oxford's excellent park and ride facilities (see p.232).

Car parks If you have to drive in, aim for the largest car park in town (see ⓦ oxford.gov.uk/parking), alongside the Westgate shopping mall, accessed off Thames St. Expect to pay £12–15 for half a day, or £23–29 for up to 24hrs.

On-street parking On-street parking (locations specified at ⓦ oxfordshire.gov.uk/parking) is limited to two hours maximum during the day (Mon–Sat 8am–6.30pm; about £3–4 for 2hrs), with unlimited parking at other times (about £2–3). On some streets the two-hour limit applies on Sundays as well.

BY TAXI

There are taxi ranks at Carfax, Gloucester Green, St Giles and the railway station. Otherwise try ABC Radio Taxi Oxford (ⓣ 01865 242424, ⓦ abcradiotaxis.co.uk) or Royal Cars (ⓣ 01865 777333, ⓦ www.royal-cars.com).

ACCOMMODATION

With supply struggling to keep pace with demand, Oxford's central **hotels** can be expensive. There are a few more affordable hotels in or near the centre, but at the budget end of the market you're better off choosing a **guest house** or **B&B**, which are plentiful if usually some distance out. As usual, though, the divisions between these are fuzzy: in terms of price, facilities and service a good B&B can easily trump a mediocre hotel – and staying in a B&B doesn't automatically expose you to swirly carpets and lopsided pelmets. Oxford's demanding clientele (and their high rate of repeat bookings) means that standards are, on the whole, satisfyingly high. Ask at the tourist office for details of **self-catering** options, including serviced apartments in the city centre for two or three nights – even check with them in the summer, when most places impose a one-week minimum stay. Wherever you stay, book ahead – either direct or (for a small fee) through the tourist office.

HOTELS

★**Bath Place** 4 Bath Place ☎01865 791812, ⓦwww .bathplace.co.uk; map p.209. This unusual hotel comprises a handful of higgledy-piggledy medieval cottages around a tiny cobbled courtyard off Holywell St. There are sixteen creaky rooms, each individually decorated in antique style – canopied beds, exposed beams and so forth. Some rooms feel a touch compact; the hotel labels these "smaller doubles" and prices them lower. By contrast, steep spiral stairs lead to room 11 ("superior king"), with rooftop views and a huge carpeted bathroom. The central location is excellent, though the famous *Turf Tavern* is round the corner: the courtyard does see foot traffic to and from the pub. Secure parking nearby (£15/night). **£120**

Bocardo 24 George St ☎01865 591234, ⓦthebocardo .co.uk; map p.209. Friendly boutique hotel occupying the upper floors above the *Jamie's Italian* restaurant. Rooms are small and quirkily designed, with bright colours, though the ones facing George St's clubs and bars may stay noisy late into the evenings. Breakfast not served (but there are cafés on the doorstep). **£130**

Eastgate 73 High St ☎01865 248332, ⓦmercure.com; map p.209. Modern four-star chain hotel insinuated into an ex-coaching inn. Public areas feature sleek, contemporary styling and the hotel's *High Table* brasserie has developed a good reputation. Rooms are blandly modern, but this is still a reliable choice with warm service and a very central location. **£150**

★**Malmaison** Oxford Castle, New Rd ☎01865 268400, ⓦmalmaison.com; map p.209. Classy and atmospheric designer hotel occupying what was a Victorian prison, part of the Oxford Castle complex. Rooms – which take up three cells, knocked through – are nothing short of glamorous, featuring contemporary bathrooms and hi-tech gadgets: being walked along the (now carpeted) catwalks through the prison hall is quite an eye-opener. Head through to C wing for bigger mezzanine suites. Parking £28/night. **£210**

Old Bank 91 High St ☎01865 799599, ⓦoldbank -hotel.co.uk; map p.209. Great location for a slick and sleek boutique hotel in a Georgian edifice plumb on the High St, converted from (you guessed it) an old bank. All 42 bedrooms are decorated in crisp, modern style – pastel shades and whites – and some have great views over All Souls College opposite. Look out for "stay and dine" deals with *Quod* restaurant (see p.239) or *Gee's* (see p.238), both part of the same group. Free parking. **£220**

Old Parsonage 1 Banbury Rd ☎01865 310210, ⓦoldparsonage-hotel.co.uk; map pp.206–207. Completely refurbished in 2014, this lovely upmarket hotel occupies a charming, wisteria-clad stone building dating from 1660 near the church at the top of St Giles. The 35 rooms are tastefully furnished in a bright modern manner and the location is nigh-on perfect, across the road from the parks but only a stroll from the hustle and bustle of Jericho and/or the city centre. Free parking, and free walking tours for guests on request. **£235**

Randolph 1 Beaumont St ☎01865 256400, ⓦrandolph-hotel.com; map p.209. Oxford's most famous hotel, long the favoured choice of the well-heeled visitor, occupying a well-proportioned neo-Gothic brick building opposite the Ashmolean Museum with a distinctive, nineteenth century interior – the carpeted staircase is especially handsome. Now part of the Macdonald chain, still with traditional service, well-appointed bedrooms and a distinguished club atmosphere. Top-floor rooms are quietest. Limited parking (£28/night). **£224**

Royal Oxford Park End St ☎01865 248432, ⓦwww .royaloxfordhotel.co.uk; map pp.206–207. Convenient three-star, occupying a posh-looking building facing onto Frideswide Sq, 2mins walk from the railway station and right by a stop for buses from Thornhill and Seacourt park-and-ride car parks. Chiefly a business hotel – the 26 bedrooms are clean and functional, service is smooth and efficient – but the location and modest prices make it worth considering. Some traffic noise. Limited parking (£5/night). **£150**

B&B AND GUESTHOUSES

CENTRAL

Buttery 11 Broad St ☎01865 811950, ⓦthebuttery hotel.co.uk; map p.209. Slap-bang central location for this friendly sixteen-room guest house-cum-hotel, with modest rooms (including one single), mostly on the large

7

YOUR IVORY TOWER AWAITS

For an overnight stay that is light on service but rich in atmosphere – and *very* Oxford – check ⓦoxfordrooms.co.uk for details about staying in a **college room** on a B&B basis. Expect little (or no) hotel-style service, but you may score with a view over a historic quad, and are free to soak up the college ambience and roam the grounds at will. Breakfast is generally served in the wood-panelled college dining-hall. This is also a great option if you're **travelling solo**: although there are some twins and doubles, the vast majority of rooms are singles (not all of them en suite). Historic colleges in the scheme – which runs mainly during the summer months (mid-June to mid-Oct), with some availability at Easter and Christmas – include Christ Church, Jesus, Keble, Lincoln and Magdalen. Depending on dates, rates for single rooms hover either side of £50 (some as low as £30); doubles or twins from roughly £70.

side, plainly but decently decorated. You're paying slightly over the odds for the location – but choose a back room to avoid the noise of carousing students on Broad St late at night. Stairs are narrow and steep. **£115**

★ Richmond 25 Walton Crescent ☎ 01865 311777, ⓦ the-richmond-oxford.co.uk; map pp.206–207. Quiet B&B attached to the excellent *Al-Shami* Lebanese restaurant (see p.239) in Jericho. Expect few frills – rooms are simple and unrenovated – but prices are remarkably low, the welcome is warm and you get a choice of breakfasts: English or – uniquely for Oxford – Lebanese (hummus, olives, white cheese, pitta bread and more). **£65**

FURTHER OUT

Acorn 260 Iffley Rd ☎ 01865 247998, ⓦ oxford-acorn .co.uk; map p.204. Huge Edwardian house a couple of miles southeast of the centre offering a friendly, efficient welcome and a well-kept interior. The fourteen guest rooms are fresh and pretty, all en suite (bar a single and small twin), with quiet ones overlooking the rear garden. Good value. **£76**

Burlington House 374 Banbury Rd ☎ 01865 513513, ⓦ burlington-house-oxford.co.uk; map p.204. Excellent, very high quality boutique-style B&B in the upmarket North Oxford suburb of Summertown. Twelve large bedrooms fill a Victorian house, built in 1889, now rejuvenated with a thoroughly modern ambience and superb attention to detail – luxurious fabrics, feature walls, bright designs. Sumptuous breakfasts and generous service exemplify the approach. **£110**

Isis Guesthouse 45 Iffley Rd ☎ 01865 613700, ⓦ isisguesthouse.com; map pp.206–207. Ten minutes' walk southeast of the centre – and a short stroll from both Magdalen Bridge and the bars of Cowley Rd – this big old Victorian house serves most of the year as lodgings for students at St Edmund Hall, but over the summer months morphs into a congenial, well-run B&B, with 37 en-suite and shared-bath rooms. For the location, and the quality, it's a bargain. July–Sept only. **£90**

Parklands 100 Banbury Rd ☎ 01865 554374, ⓦ parklandsoxford.co.uk; map p.204. Pleasant fifteen-room B&B in a large Victorian house with a garden and bar. It's a cheerful choice, with parking and good attention to detail, though lots of stairs may put some people off. **£105**

Remont 367 Banbury Rd ☎ 01865 311020, ⓦ remont

-oxford.co.uk; map p.204. Very classy hotel-style B&B in Summertown, a couple of miles north of the centre. The approach throughout is of a chic boutique hotel, with black leather, dark wood, vivid fabrics, contemporary eco-friendly bathrooms and speedy wi-fi. Service is warm and accommodating, and breakfast is fantastic, in terms of both the food and the airy, modern buffet-style dining area. **£120**

Tilbury Lodge 5 Tilbury Lane ☎ 01865 862138, ⓦ tilbury lodge.com; map p.204. Unpretentiously modern guest house in Botley, well west of the centre, that offers unusually good value for money. The rooms are tasteful and uncluttered, enhanced by home-made cakes and other treats, mighty breakfasts and the genuinely outgoing, friendly owners, for whom nothing seems too much trouble. A great find. **£90**

HOSTELS

Central Backpackers 13 Park End St ☎ 01865 242288, ⓦ centralbackpackers.co.uk; map pp.206–207. Award-winning hostel, independently owned and operated, with fifty beds in dorms (sleeping 4, 6, 8 and 12, including female-only), 24-hour access, a good range of facilities and a friendly can-do attitude. Located on a lively street midway between the railway and bus stations: expect late-night noise from nearby bars and clubs. Dorm (including breakfast) **£22**

Oxford Backpackers 9a Hythe Bridge St ☎ 01865 721761, ⓦ hostels.co.uk; map pp.206–207. Independent hostel with 120 beds in dorms (sleeping 4, 8, 10, 14 and 18, including female-only) and 24-hour access – but a touch scruffier and more make-do than its near-neighbour. Central location. Dorm (including breakfast) **£20**

Oxford Youth Hostel 2a Botley Rd ☎ 0845 371 9131, ⓦ yha.org.uk; map pp.206–207. In a clumpy modern block behind the railway station, with 24-hour access, this popular YHA hostel has 187 beds in four- and six-bedded dorms plus nine double rooms, with good facilities and a decent café and restaurant. Dorm (including breakfast; £3 supplement for non-members) **£18**

CAMPING

Oxford Camping & Caravan Club 426 Abingdon Rd ☎ 01865 244088, ⓦ campingandcaravanningclub.co.uk; map p.204. Fully equipped site in a convenient location a mile or so south of the centre beside a busy road, with tent pitches and hookups for caravans and motorhomes. Pitches **£18**

EATING

With so many students and tourists to cater for, Oxford has a wide choice of places to eat. Lunchtimes tend to be very busy, especially during the week, though there's no shortage of options – we've listed some of the better **cafés** and delis, but you'll have no difficulty finding somewhere for a midday bite, including at the Covered Market (see p.222). Oxford's **restaurant** scene now takes in fine-dining restaurants to match those in London (on both quality and price), as well as a diverse range of more affordable outlets for high-quality, seasonal cooking. A diverse palette of ethnic restaurants also helps to keep interest levels high. For the best choice, avoid the city centre and instead stroll either northwest to the engaging district of Jericho, where Walton St and Little Clarendon St offer a string of pleasant restaurants, or southeast to the Cowley Rd, buzzing with after-work lounge bars and restaurants of all kinds.

CAFÉS

★**Ben's Cookies** 108 Covered Market ☎01865 247407, ⓦbenscookies.com; map p.209. This hole in the wall – the first outlet in the Ben's Cookies chain – has been churning out the best cookies in Oxford, perhaps England (and some say the world) since 1984, from ginger to peanut butter to triple chocolate chunk. They bake different varieties constantly: it's pot luck what's hot when you turn up. Mon–Sat 9.15am–5.30pm, Sun 10am–4pm.

★**G&Ds** 94 St Aldate's ☎01865 245952, ⓦgdcafe .com; map p.209. Buzzy local café just down from Carfax offering everything from (delicious) ice cream to bagels and full breakfasts. The cow murals are good fun too. Also try the other two *G&Ds* around town, at 55 Little Clarendon St and 104 Cowley Rd. Daily 8am–midnight.

Grand Café 84 High St ☎01865 204463, ⓦthegrand cafe.co.uk; map p.209. Vies with the *Queen's Lane Coffee House*, directly over the road, for which is older – both opened around 1650. This is the more glamorous of the two, with marble pillars, gold leaf and an Art Deco style mirrored interior. The food is posh, and not cheap – smoked salmon and scrambled eggs £8.50, cream tea £8. Pop in to be seduced by the surroundings. Daily 9am–6.30pm, also Thurs–Sat 7–11pm for cocktails.

Missing Bean 14 Turl St ☎01865 794886, ⓦthemissingbean.co.uk; map p.209. Plate-glass windows look out onto this pleasant old street, as conversation swirls and reputedly the best coffee in Oxford goes down. A fine, friendly spot. Mon–Fri 8am–6.30pm, Sat 9am–6.30pm, Sun 10am–5.30pm.

Mortons 22 Broad St ☎01865 200860, ⓦwww .mortonsatwork.co.uk; map p.209. Long-standing Oxford café and sandwich bar, easily missed from the street but with upstairs seating (well, a room lined with stools) and a rear garden. All their coffee is Fairtrade, and all their milk is organic. Also at 22 New Inn Hall St, 39 Little Clarendon St and 103 Covered Market. Daily 8.30am–5pm.

News Café 1 Ship St ☎01865 242317; map p.209. Breakfasts, bagels and daily specials, plus beer and wine in this brisk and efficient café. Plenty of local and international newspapers are on hand too. Sun–Thurs 9am–5pm, Fri & Sat 9am–6pm.

Rose 51 High St ☎01865 244429, ⓦthe-rose.biz; map p.209. Lovely independent tearoom with an ethical bent: free-range eggs, organic flour and meat, locally sourced clotted cream. Sociable, lively and pleasant, with the added bonus of fresh-baked scones daily. Mon–Sat 9am–7pm, Sun 10am–6pm.

★**Vaults & Garden** Radcliffe Sq ☎01865 279112, ⓦthevaultsandgarden.com; map p.209. Occupying the atmospheric stone vaulted chambers of the university's old congregation house, built in 1320 beside the church of St Mary the Virgin, this always-busy café serves up good-quality organic, locally sourced wholefood, as well as coffee and cake. A small outside terrace area gazes up at the Radcliffe Camera. Cash only. Daily 8.30am–6pm.

Will's Deli 15 Woodstock Rd ☎01865 316228, ⓦwills deli.co.uk; map pp.206–207. A stroll north along St Giles lies this fabulous little locals' deli and café, with a wide range of delicious veggie and vegan salads and mains – all organic, prepared daily. Daily 8am–5pm.

A WEEKEND IN OXFORD

FRIDAY NIGHT
Toast your weekend with a **champagne cocktail** in the Randolph's *Morse Bar* and a slap-up **dinner** at, say, *Al Shami*, *Gee's* or *Jamie's Italian*.

SATURDAY
Start the day with a visit to the **Covered Market**, to relax with a coffee while getting a flavour of town life and watch the butchers and fishmongers lay out the new day's wares. Extend the theme by dropping into the **Museum of Oxford**, or join one of the introductory **walking tours** offered by the tourist office. Grab lunch on the hoof and then devote the afternoon to "gown" life: choose two or three of the **colleges** (Christ Church, Merton and New would make a fine hat-trick) and pick up the atmosphere of the old city-centre streets (Broad, Merton, Turl) – or the water meadows behind Christ Church – as you go. End the day with a **punt**, before setting off down the **Cowley Road** to sample Oxford's lounge bars and ethnic restaurants, and perhaps find some live music.

SUNDAY
Begin with a lazy brunch in one of **Jericho**'s taverns and cafés – or, if you prefer, a genteel 11.15am "coffee concert" at the Holywell Music Room – before tackling the wonder that is the **Ashmolean Museum**. Sample more history at **Oxford Castle Unlocked**, or opt for a country walk in the deer park of **Magdalen College** – then settle in at *Quod* for early-evening jazz followed by dinner.

7

RESTAURANTS

BRITISH

Cherwell Boathouse Bardwell Rd ☎01865 552746, ⓦcherwellboathouse.co.uk; map p.204. Popular rustic restaurant in an Edwardian boathouse on the banks of the River Cherwell, just north of central Oxford, serving classic British cuisine – rack of lamb with spring vegetables, fillet of trout with rainbow chard, and so forth – alongside an especially highly regarded wine list. Mains £16–24 – or midweek two-course set lunch £14. Book well ahead. Daily noon–2.30pm & 6–9.30pm.

Door 74 74 Cowley Rd ☎01865 203374, ⓦdoor74.co.uk; map pp.206–207. Relaxed little bistro in the heart of the Cowley Rd bustle, serving outstanding seasonal contemporary British cuisine to an appreciative, foodie clientele. The signature dish is their organic beef burger with onion marmalade (£10), or you could try dishes such as whole sea bream, or linguine tossed with clams. Mains £10–14. Tues–Sat noon–11pm, Sun 11am–4pm.

Gee's 61 Banbury Rd ☎01865 553540, ⓦgees-restaurant.co.uk; map p.204. A well-established formal restaurant occupying chic Victorian conservatory premises in North Oxford. The inventive menu takes in British seasonal dishes such as asparagus and locally reared spring lamb, aided by steaks, fish dishes and more Continental cuisine – lobster linguine, bouillabaisse, duck confit. Mains £14–24; two-course early supper menu (Mon–Fri until 6pm) £13. Book ahead. Sun–Thurs 10am–10.30pm, Fri & Sat 10am–11pm.

Loch Fyne 55 Walton St ☎01865 292510, ⓦlochfyneseafoodandgrill.co.uk; map pp.206–207. Jericho outlet for this highly regarded nationwide chain of fish and seafood restaurants, serving a range of ethically sourced dishes from poached Scottish haddock to Cromer crab. Steaks and veggie options (such as goat's cheese with roasted beetroot) add variety. The interior stretches far back – airy and spacious, with skylights and smart contemporary styling – and the bar area is perfect for a light lunch on the go. Mains £12–17; two-course set menu £10.50. Mon–Thurs 11.30am–10.30pm, Fri 10.30am–11pm, Sat 9am–11pm, Sun 9am–10.30pm.

★**Pie Minister** 56 Covered Market ☎01865 241613, ⓦpieminister.co.uk; map p.209. Your nose will lead you to this fantastic little pie shop inside the Covered Market, with a counter for take-aways and a sit-down restaurant section. The wide choice includes deerstalker pie (venison and red wine), moo pie (beef and ale), heidi pie (goat's cheese and spinach), and so on, all substantial items accompanied by creamy mashed potato, gravy and minty peas for around £5–6. Unmissable. Mon–Sat 10am–5pm, Sun 11am–4pm.

★**Turl Street Kitchen** 16 Turl St ☎01865 264171, ⓦturlstreetkitchen.co.uk; map p.209. Much-loved hideaway on one of Oxford's most charming back streets, closely linked with both "town" and "gown". Food is seasonal and hearty – parsnip soup, braised free-range chicken with chickpeas, fennel and wild garlic gratin – served cheerfully in a cosy setting of sofas and grained wood. Mains £8–14. All profits support a local charity. Sun–Thurs 8am–midnight, Fri & Sat 8am–1am.

EUROPEAN

Al Andalus 10 Little Clarendon St ☎01865 516688, ⓦtapasoxford.co.uk; map pp.206–207. Congenial tapas bar with fresh, contemporary decor, a good selection of Spanish wines, great tapas (around £5, with plenty for vegetarians) and live flamenco on weekend nights adding to the buzz. Mon–Thurs noon–3pm & 5–11pm, Fri–Sun noon–midnight.

Branca 111 Walton St ☎01865 556111, ⓦbranca-restaurants.com; map pp.206–207. Large and informal brasserie-restaurant offering a wide-ranging menu, though Italian dishes predominate. Much-loved spot for those seeking a casual, buzzy get-together or a romantic tête-à-tête, with atmosphere for both and amiable service. Mains £10–16. Daily noon–11pm.

Jamie's Italian 24 George St ☎01865 838383, ⓦjamiesitalian.com; map p.209. Italian restaurant under the Jamie Oliver banner – always busy, featuring a laid-back interior of exposed bricks, graffitied walls and hams hanging above the salad station. The rustic-style food is marked by trademark informality: mixed antipasti arrive on a plank of wood, the pasta menu runs from

---

FARMERS' MARKETS

Oxford's main **farmers' market** is held at Gloucester Green on the first and third Thursdays of every month (9am–3pm; ⓦlsdpromotions.com), featuring local produce from all over the Cotswolds. If you can't make that, try the smaller farmers' markets – hosting many of the same stallholders – around town. Nearest to the centre is North Parade market (4th Sat 9am–2pm; ⓦnorthparademarket.com), while other options are: Cowley Road/East Oxford (every Sat 10am–1pm; ⓦeastoxfordmarket.org.uk), Wolvercote/North Oxford (every Sun 10am–1pm; ⓦwolvercotefarmersmarket.co.uk), Abingdon Road/South Oxford (every Sun 9.30am–noon; ⓦsouthoxfordfarmersmarket.org.uk), Summertown (every Sun 10am–2pm; ⓦyourevent organisers.co.uk) or Headington (2nd & 4th Fri 8am–1.30pm; ⓦheadington.org.uk). More information at ⓦlocalfoods.org.uk.

seafood *bucatini* to *penne pomodoro*, while mains include "lamb chop lollipops". Mains £11–18. Mon–Sat noon–11pm, Sun noon–10.30pm.

★ **Manos** 105 Walton St ☎ 01865 311782, ⓦ manosfoodbar.com; map pp.206–207. Family-run Greek deli and café-bistro on a sunny Jericho corner, offering budget meals of salads and wraps (£5 or less) alongside delicious Mediterranean mains such as butter beans in tomato sauce, spinach and feta tart or wine-and-pork sausages (£7–9) and, of course, coffee and pastries. Mon–Wed 9.30am–9pm, Thurs–Sat 9.30am–10pm, Sun 11.30am–8pm.

Pierre Victoire 9 Little Clarendon St ☎ 01865 316616, ⓦ pierrevictoire.co.uk; map pp.206–207. Independently owned French brasserie on this popular restaurant street that consistently comes up trumps in both food and service. Start with snails, roquefort soufflé or black pudding and move on to rib-eye steak, chicken with goat's cheese, roast rabbit or Cornish mussels – or dip your way through a Savoyard-style cheese fondue. Mains are £11–18, but take advantage of £10–12 set menus at lunch and dinner. Mon–Sat noon–2.30pm & 6–11pm, Sun noon–10pm.

INDIAN AND EAST ASIAN

Chiang Mai Kitchen 130a High St ☎ 01865 202233, ⓦ chiangmaikitchen.co.uk; map p.209. Oxford's best Thai restaurant, a smart little place in a seventeenth-century timber-framed house off the High St. All the classics are served – and then some – and it's particularly strong on vegetarian dishes. Mains around £9. Mon–Sat noon–10.30pm, Sun noon–10pm.

Edamame 15 Holywell St ☎ 01865 246916, ⓦ edamame.co.uk; map p.209. Voted as one of the best Japanese restaurants in Britain, this tiny canteen-style place enjoys a flawless reputation for authenticity, food and welcome. No bookings are taken, so you may have to queue (and then share a table) – but it's worth it. Tuck into ramen noodle soup with pork, chicken or tofu, for instance, or salmon teriyaki. There's plenty for vegetarians. Thursday night is sushi night – hugely popular, so turn up early. Mains £6–9. Beware odd hours: Wed 11.30am–2.30pm, Thurs–Sat 11.30am–2.30pm & 5–8.30pm, Sun noon–3.30pm. Cards not accepted at lunchtime.

Majliss 110 Cowley Rd ☎ 01865 726728, ⓦ majliss.co.uk; map pp.206–207. Although the acclaim for Oxford's best curry has long been directed at *Aziz*, further down the Cowley Rd, *Majliss* has won plaudits for its fresh outlook, super-efficient service and delicious cooking. There's an impressive buzz about the place: the interior is tasteful, with contemporary decor, and the menu takes in a range of unusual Bangladeshi fish and seafood curries and South Indian *dosa* (savoury pancakes), in among more familiar biryanis and kormas. Booking recommended at the weekend. Mains £6–13. Mon–Thurs noon–2.30pm & 5.30pm–midnight, Fri–Sun noon–midnight.

INTERNATIONAL

Ashmolean Dining Room At Ashmolean Museum, Beaumont St ☎ 01865 553823, ⓦ ashmoleandiningroom.com; map p.209. Contemporary, open-plan restaurant occupying a stunning space on the museum's rooftop level, with an outside terrace. Cuisine runs from chorizo, crêpes and squid to lamb and sea bream, alongside a range of cheeses and charcuterie. Mains £11–17. Also a fine spot for posh afternoon tea (£15). Has its own opening hours, independent of the museum. Tues–Thurs 10am–4.30pm, Fri & Sat 10am–10pm, Sun 10am–4.30pm.

Café Coco 23 Cowley Rd ☎ 01865 200232, ⓦ cafecoco.co.uk; map pp.206–207. Pleasantly informal bar-cum-restaurant plumb on the Cowley Rd – something of an Oxford institution, serving pizzas and vaguely Continental-style dishes, plus comforting American desserts like pecan pie and waffles, to a frequently packed house. The volume goes up as the beers (and cocktails) go down. Mains £8–11. Mon–Sat 10am–midnight, Sun 10am–6pm.

Quod 92 High St ☎ 01865 202505, ⓦ quod.co.uk; map p.209. Landmark brasserie in a central location. Once the solemn hall of a bank, the spacious, stone-flagged interior now offers picture windows onto the High St and colourful contemporary art. Plump for the bargain two-course set lunch (£13) – think devilled kidneys on toast or minty courgette soup, followed by steak *béarnaise* or mushroom tagliatelle. À la carte mains are £12–17. There's a nice bar to one side, and live jazz on Sunday (5–7pm). Mon–Sat 7am–11pm, Sun 7am–10.30pm.

MIDDLE EASTERN

Al Salam 6 Park End St ☎ 01865 245710; map pp.206–207. Informal Lebanese restaurant on an always-buzzing street. The food includes a long choice of authentic hot and cold mezze (£3–4) and good variety of expertly prepared kebabs and grills (£8–9). The difference comes in the atmosphere: this is a great place for a mid-budget romantic dinner, or a fun night out – service is unfailingly outgoing. They sometimes lay on the Oriental kitsch a bit thick, what with the occasional bellydancer, but it's all part of the fun. Daily noon–11pm.

★ **Al Shami** 25 Walton Crescent ☎ 01865 310066, ⓦ al-shami.co.uk; map pp.206–207. Splendid family-run Lebanese restaurant opposite Oxford's synagogue on a placid Jericho back street, serving authentic mezze, grills and kebabs to a knowledgeable local clientele. Its undramatic interior, which features windows spanning the curve of the building, also includes a magnificent back room sporting Syrian-style inlaid wood panelling. Mezze cost £3–5, mains £7–9 – or go for the extensive set menu from £15 per person. There's plenty for veggies and vegans. Wash it down with a Lebanese wine – and make sure you sample their high-quality Lebanese arak (aniseed-flavoured spirit). Daily noon–midnight.

7

DRINKING AND ENTERTAINMENT

Oxford has plenty of **pubs** and **bars** – not all of them student dives. The ones we pick out are notable for their atmosphere and/or their beer, and many also host **live music**. Devotees of **classical music** are also well catered for, with halls and some college chapels offering concerts and recitals. Live **theatre** is another option, with high-quality productions supplemented by more casual open-air Shakespeare in summer. For **listings** guidance, see p.234.

BARS

Café Tarifa 56 Cowley Rd ☎01865 256091, ⓦfacebook.com/cafetarifaoxford; map pp.206–207. Atmospheric lounge bar on the happening Cowley Rd decked out in Moorish/Arabian style, with cocktails and cushions, also hosting a variety of generally chilled live music and DJ nights and cult movie screenings. Mon–Thurs 5pm–midnight, Fri 5pm–12.30am, Sat noon–12.30am, Sun 5–11pm.

Freud 119 Walton St ☎01865 311171, ⓦfreud.eu; map pp.206–207. Occupying a nineteenth-century former church, this fashionable café-bar is an upmarket spot for cocktails and chit-chat, along with good Italian/Mediterranean food (mains from £8). Live music some nights too – but the architecture and the interiors are the main attraction. Mon–Thurs 4.30pm–midnight, Fri 4.30pm–2am, Sat 11am–2am, Sun noon–midnight.

★**Kazbar** 27 Cowley Rd ☎01865 202920, ⓦkazbar .co.uk; map pp.206–207. Eye-poppingly beautiful lounge bar-cum-restaurant in a hippyish/Moorish style – adobe, incense, lanterns, bar stools in cracked tan leather and bartenders in embroidered jackets. Food and cocktails are great, and there's always a buzz. Mon–Thurs 5pm–midnight, Fri 5pm–12.30am, Sat noon–12.30am, Sun noon–11pm.

Morse Bar At Randolph Hotel, Beaumont St ☎01865 256400, ⓦrandolph-hotel.com; map p.209. Traditional hotel bar – roaring fire, club armchairs, wood panelling – which featured so often in *Inspector Morse* that the hotel renamed it to match. Specializes in whisky and champagne cocktails. Daily 10.30am–midnight.

Raoul's 32 Walton St ☎01865 553732, ⓦraoulsbar .com; map pp.206–207. Famed Jericho cocktail bar, with a retro 70s theme, great tunes and a devoted clientele who know (and love) their drinks. Navigate the mammoth

A RIVERSIDE WALK: FROM TROUT TO PERCH

This leisurely half-day **walk** leads from the city centre to two of Oxford's best-loved pubs and back again. Start on Walton Street in Jericho (see p.231): just past the alley for St Sepulchre's cemetery, Walton Well Road leads left over the railway tracks onto **Port Meadow**, a large stretch of common parkland between the Thames and the canal which has had free and open access for at least a thousand years. Follow paths (and the river) northwards for roughly an hour's ramble to the village of **Wolvercote** – also accessible on bus #6 (every 15–20min; £2) from Magdalen Street in central Oxford.

In Wolvercote village, the Godstow Road heads left (west) across a stream before bumping into the legendary **Trout** pub (☎01865 510930, ⓦthetroutoxford.co.uk; see map p.204). Made famous by *Inspector Morse* – though an Oxford favourite long before television – this rambling, seventeenth-century riverside inn, bedecked in ivy, enjoys a picture-perfect location alongside the old Godstow Bridge, with its own wooden footbridge just downstream and a broad, south-facing terrace overlooking the water. The interiors have been done up: beer is the main draw, but this now doubles as a decent restaurant for good Modern British cooking (honeyed gammon, calves' liver and onions, rack of lamb, and so on, as well as stone-baked pizzas and more, including veggie options), though it can get phenomenally busy, especially on sunny weekends, when service can suffer. Mains £8–17. If you intend to eat, book in advance.

From the *Trout*, cross the river and follow the Thames Path southwards along the western bank for about half an hour to reach a little path leading right (west) to the **Perch** (☎01865 728891, ⓦthe-perch.co.uk; see map p.204), set 100yd back from the riverbank in **Binsey** village. Another historic, thatched pub dating from the seventeenth century (though with its origins going back another five hundred years or so), this was a favourite of Lewis Carroll and C.S. Lewis, and still offers a peaceful, well-pulled pint, as well as a lovely beer garden and upmarket French cuisine in its restaurant (mains £13–18). Around half a mile north on Binsey Lane stands St Margaret's Church, location of St Frideswide's well (see p.204).

From the *Perch*, you can follow the Thames Path south into the city centre – or take Binsey Lane, which joins the main Botley Road about half a mile west of Oxford rail station. Both the *Trout* and *Perch* are accessible by road, though to drive between them you'd have to go the long way round via the western bypass.

menu of cocktails to choose a fave or three. Sun–Tues 4pm–midnight, Wed–Sat 4pm–1am.

PUBS

Bear 6 Alfred St ☎ 01865 728164, ⓦ bearoxford.co.uk; map p.209. Tucked away down a narrow side street in the centre of town, this tiny old pub (the oldest in Oxford, founded roughly 800 years ago) has not been themed up – and a good job too. Offers a wide range of beers amid its traditional decor, which includes a collection of ties, framed on the wall. Mon–Thurs 11am–11pm, Fri & Sat 11am–midnight, Sun 11.30am–10.30pm.

Eagle & Child 49 St Giles ☎ 01865 302925, ⓦ nicholsons pubs.co.uk; map pp.206–207. Dubbed the "Bird & Baby", this was once the haunt of J.R.R. Tolkien and C.S. Lewis. The beer is still good and the old wood-panelled rooms at the front are great, but the pub is no longer independently owned – and feels it. The food (and atmosphere) are corporate, and the modern rear extension is a travesty. Pop over to the road to the *Lamb & Flag* (see below) to compare. Mon–Thurs 11am–11pm, Fri & Sat 11am–midnight, Sun noon–10.30pm.

★Jericho 56 Walton St ☎ 01865 311775, ⓦ www .thejerichooxford.co.uk; map pp.206–207. Much-loved tavern in the heart of Jericho, outside the city centre, which doubles up as a leading indie music venue, hosting Oxford's renowned Famous Monday Blues session every Monday night from 8pm (see ⓦ famousmondayblues.co.uk). Sun–Fri noon–midnight, Sat 11am–midnight.

Kings Arms 40 Holywell St ☎ 01865 242369, ⓦ kings armsoxford.co.uk; map p.209. Pleasant seventeenth-century city-centre pub on the crossroads with Broad St, Catte St and Parks Rd, offering great people-watching from its front terrace. Snug rooms at the back and a decent choice of ales aid the congenial atmosphere – though beware: it's also one of Oxford's most popular student pubs. Daily 10.30am–midnight.

★Lamb & Flag 12 St Giles ☎ 01865 515787; map pp.206–207. Generations of university types have relished this quiet old tavern, which comes complete with low-beamed ceilings and a series of cramped but cosy rooms in which to enjoy hand-drawn ale and genuine pork scratchings. Cash only. Mon–Sat noon–11pm, Sun noon–10.30pm.

Turf Tavern 4 Bath Place ☎ 01865 243235, ⓦ theturf tavern.co.uk; map p.209. Small, atmospheric medieval pub, reached via narrow passageways off Holywell St or New College Lane, with a fine range of beers, and mulled wine in winter. Abundant seating outside. Typical pub grub on offer includes Sunday roast from £9. Mon–Sat 11am–11.15pm, Sun 11am–10.30pm.

White Horse 52 Broad St ☎ 01865 204801, ⓦ white horseoxford.co.uk; map p.209. A tiny old pub beside Blackwell's bookshop in the town centre with snug rooms, pictures of old university sports teams on the walls, real ales and good food (fish and chips £10). Daily 11am–11pm.

THEATRE AND CLASSICAL MUSIC

Creation Theatre ☎ 01865 766266, ⓦ creationtheatre .co.uk. Unattached troupe, best known for its regular summer season of Shakespeare at unusual venues around town – Headington Hill Park, the roof of the Said Business School, on the factory floor of BMW's Mini production plant, and so on.

Holywell Music Room 32 Holywell St ☎ 01865 766266, ⓦ www.music.ox.ac.uk; map p.209. This small, plain, Georgian building was opened in 1748 as the first public music hall in England. It offers a varied programme, from straight classical to experimental, with occasional bouts of jazz. Popular Sunday morning "coffee concerts" (ⓦ coffeeconcerts.co.uk) run year-round.

New Theatre George St ☎ 01865 320760, ⓦ new theatreoxford.org.uk. The city's main commercial venue hosts a popular programme of theatre, dance, pop music, musicals and opera.

North Wall South Parade ☎ 01865 319450, ⓦ thenorth wall.com. This much-loved arts centre located in posh Summertown, a mile or so north of the centre, hosts small-scale theatre, comedy and workshops.

Oxford Playhouse 11 Beaumont St ☎ 01865 305305, ⓦ oxfordplayhouse.com; map p.209. Professional touring companies perform a mixture of plays, opera and concerts at the city's leading theatre.

Sheldonian Theatre Broad St ☎ 01865 277299, ⓦ www .sheldon.ox.ac.uk; map p.209. Seventeenth-century edifice in the city centre that is Oxford's top concert hall, despite rather dodgy acoustics, with the Oxford Philomusica symphony orchestra in residence (ⓦ oxfordphil.com).

7

DIRECTORY

Bookshops The leading university bookshop is Blackwell's (see p.212). Be sure to drop into the relaxed Albion Beatnik Bookstore in Jericho (34a Walton St; ☎ 07737 876213, ⓦ albionbeatnikbookstore.blogspot.com), for "interesting twentieth-century books", as well as readings, events and jazz evenings.

Hospital John Radcliffe Hospital, Headley Way ☎ 01865 741166, ⓦ ouh.nhs.uk. See p.35.

Markets Every week, Gloucester Green hosts a food

market (Wed 9am–5pm) and an arts and crafts market (Thurs 9am–5pm). Farmers' markets, see p.238. Covered Market, see p.222.

Pharmacy Boots, 6 Cornmarket ☎ 01865 247461, ⓦ boots.com (Mon–Sat 8am–8pm, Sun 11am–5pm).

Police station St Aldate's ☎ 101, ⓦ thamesvalley.police.uk (daily 24hr).

Post office 102 St Aldate's (Mon–Sat 9am–5.30pm).

CORINIUM MUSEUM, CIRENCESTER

Contexts

History

The earliest settlers in the area now known as the Cotswolds arrived in Mesolithic times, about seven or eight thousand years ago. The evidence for this shows in the form of flint implements that have been discovered scattered in modern arable fields at many sites in the Cotswolds. Mesolithic tribes cleared small patches of primeval forest, but clearance on a large scale did not take place until Neolithic times, roughly 4200–2000 BC.

Prehistoric times

During the **Neolithic period**, human society moved from nomadic hunting and gathering to a more settled agrarian existence, which included the introduction of domesticated sheep and goats as well as barley and einkorn wheat (one of the earliest cultivated forms of wild wheat). This pioneer farming comprised no more than garden plots but spread rapidly.

The Neolithic people also left their mark on the landscape in the form of long barrows such as **Hetty Pegler's Tump** and **Belas Knap**, among many that can be seen in the Cotswolds today. It's thought that these Neolithic tombs expressed not only respect for dead ancestors but also functioned as territorial markers overlooking communities in the valleys below. With plentiful local stone suitable for building readily available, many outstanding monuments from the period have survived across the region.

Woodland clearances greatly accelerated during the **Bronze Age** (around 2500 BC to 750 BC) and began to permanently change the landscape. During this time, the culture of one particular group of people later dubbed the "Beaker Folk" was characterized by worship at stone circles. The **Rollright Stones** near Chipping Norton are a relic of this period.

Iron-working was one of a series of new technologies introduced to Britain from the European mainland during the **Iron Age**, after 750 BC. Population growth led to competition for land and the development of a more territorial society where tribes were organized into larger, more cohesive groups.

The most readily identifiable features of the Iron Age landscape are the large **hillforts**, many of which can still be seen in the Cotswolds today: at least seventeen can be found along the Cotswold escarpment, with Bredon Hill Fort and Meon Hill Fort in the northern Cotswolds among the most impressive examples. Bagendon, north of Cirencester, is believed to have been an Iron Age tribal capital – the site, interestingly, contained a coin mint and must therefore have been an important local centre. Iron Age people were probably also responsible for the prehistoric ridgeways, green tracks which can still be seen today. Hillforts of various sizes have also been identified at Uley, Painswick, Leckhampton Hill, Sodbury, Crickley and Shenberrow.

4200–2000 BC	2500–750 BC	1st century AD
Large-scale clearance of forest by early tribes, beginnings of agriculture and livestock domestication.	Continued clearance of forest and woodland during the Bronze Age: approximate era of construction of the Rollright Stones.	Development of road network through the Cotswolds, including Fosse Way, Ermin Way and Akeman Street.

The Roman era

In the Cotswolds, as was the case for much of England, the **Roman invasion** in the first century AD was followed by rapid development of towns and villas, supported by a network of forts.

The lasting legacy of the era is **Roman roads** like the Fosse Way, which clearly define the landscape of the modern Cotswolds. Before the Romans arrived there were just trackways and informal routes. Initially Roman roads were probably built for military movement, but commerce followed shortly thereafter.

The Fosse Way (now the A433 and A429) intersects Cirencester on its cross-country route from Exeter to Lincoln: it runs the whole length of the Cotswolds between Bath, Stow-on-the-Wold and Moreton-in-Marsh. Another Roman road, the Ermin Way, runs northwest to Gloucester (following the modern A417) and south towards Silchester and London (following the A419). A third example, Akeman Street, heads east into what is now Oxfordshire, following the modern B4425.

Under its Roman name Corinium, **Cirencester**, on the edge of the Cotswolds, was the second-largest city in Roman Britain and capital of the late-Roman province of Britannia Prima. Gloucester (Glevum) was built on the site of an earlier legionary fortress. To the south (and outside the scope of this book), **Bath** (Aquae Sulis) grew up around the naturally hot sacred springs as a religious leisure town: its baths were one of the great architectural complexes of the Roman Empire.

The peace and stability offered by the centralized Roman administration ensured great prosperity for the Cotswolds; luxurious **villas** such as that at Chedworth were built all around the area. These varied in size and opulence from farmhouse-style properties to large and impressive country houses. **Estates** and land holdings surrounding these residences were organized to provide food for the inhabitants of the villa and their workers. Wool and corn production were the principal activities, and enabled the owners of these vast rural estates to generate great wealth. This was displayed in the construction of imposing temples and civic buildings in the towns and ever more elaborate mosaics, formal gardens and impressive buildings on their rural estates.

The Saxon period

As Roman control waned in the fifth and sixth centuries AD, the Angles, Jutes and Saxons – peoples from the area of modern Germany and Denmark – began to invade and settle in England. After gradual incursions into British territories, the Battle of Dyrham in 577 ensured the **West Saxons** gained control over the townships of Bath, Cirencester and Gloucester, extending their power shortly afterwards to the Cotswolds and the Severn Vale.

The Saxons took over a region of extensive farmland, with villages and farmsteads. It was the **Saxon kings** who created the basis of today's Cotswold landscape by reorganizing **towns** and countryside during the ninth and tenth centuries.

Perhaps the most notable landscape features to arise from the Saxon period were the **churches** and **monastic sites** that were being founded from the end of the seventh century onwards. Saxon ministers and monasteries are known to have been established at numerous locations including Bath, Gloucester, Tetbury, Withington, Bibury and Hawkesbury.

4th century AD	577 AD	678 or 679 AD
Peak of Roman wealth and power, exemplified by the huge villa at Chedworth.	Battle of Dyrham won by Saxons, ensuring their control over Cirencester, Gloucester and Bath: end of Roman influence.	Origins of Gloucester Cathedral, as churches and monastic communities develop under the Saxons.

By the time of the **Domesday Book** in 1086, most of the Cotswolds' present-day villages were already in existence. Domesday shows that large areas were under agriculture, with sheep grazing and arable crops the main fields of activity.

The rise of the wool trade

The origins of the Cotswolds' distinctive breed of sheep aren't fully known, though many historians believe they were introduced by the Romans. Traditionally known as "**Cotswold Lions**", these shaggy beasts thrived on the limestone banks and grasses, producing excellent wool that was long and lustrous.

After the Romans left, **monasteries and abbeys** such as Hailes, Tewkesbury and Llanthony took over vast tracts of land and ran large flocks of Cotswold sheep. They processed some of the wool into cloth for their own use but they also exported it. In the Golden Age of the **medieval wool trade** some 500,000 Cotswold Lions grazed the hillsides.

This growth in the wool trade across the Cotswolds created a legacy of fine houses and churches in market towns. The very name "Cotswolds" – "sheep shelters" (cots) in 'rolling hills' (wolds) – traditionally conjures a picture of sheep-dotted grasslands, and the late medieval era was the heyday of the local wool trade, the area's thin-soiled slopes making ideal sheep-farming country.

The wealth generated by merchants and landowners from the wool and the cloth trade have had a profound and lasting influence on the Cotswold landscape. Many impressive **manor houses** went up on the proceeds, but perhaps the most enduring symbols of this trade are the region's "**wool churches**", imposing, richly detailed structures built at this time in the main wool-trading towns throughout the Cotswolds. Notable examples survive at Northleach, Burford and Chipping Campden.

The region's wool trade supported the national economy. One symbol of this is the Woolsack, the well-padded official seat of the Lord Chancellor, speaker of the House of Lords in London, which was introduced in the reign of Edward III (1327–77) as a marker of the importance of the Cotswold wool trade.

Dissolution, Civil War and enclosure

The **Dissolution of the Monasteries** in the sixteenth century had a profound impact on the society and landscape of the Cotswolds. While the end of monastic life undoubtedly destabilized the rural economy, it also brought with it many opportunities for landowners and wealthy wool merchants, who were able to acquire land previously owned by monasteries and build great **mansions** surrounded by large areas of parkland. Striking examples in the region include Stanway House, Sherborne Park, Dyrham Park and Cirencester Park.

The **Thirty Years War** (1618–48) also had a major impact on the Cotswolds wool trade, leaving many spinners and weavers facing unemployment. It was not until new products, colours and techniques imported from Europe were assimilated that trade revived.

The **English Civil War** tore the Cotswolds apart, as it did much of the rest of the country. The Cotswold hills were of vital strategic importance and Edgehill, Lansdown Hill and Stow-on-the-Wold witnessed three encounters between Royalists and

1086	c.15th century	18th century
The Domesday Book – a survey of England – shows the Cotswolds is largely agricultural, mainly sheep and arable farming.	Peak in construction of 'wool churches', built with the proceeds of trade in textiles, including fine examples at Chipping Campden and Northleach.	Growth of textile industry in the Stroud valleys, with dozens of mills taking advantage of water power from fast-flowing streams.

Parliamentarians. **Edgehill**, in 1642, was the first major battle following Charles I's rift with Parliament: it was intended to be decisive, but in reality ended up as a stalemate. **Lansdown Hill**, the following year, was also inconclusive. Three years later the situation was rather different, as Roundheads chased Cavaliers into **Stow-on-the-Wold** in 1646. There was a pitched battle in the town square; two hundred people were killed and around 1500 imprisoned in the church overnight.

After the Civil War, **textile mills** became an ever more significant feature of the Cotswold landscape. The evolution of weaving and woollen cloth manufacture in the Cotswolds may be traced in the valleys around Stroud, Dursley, Nailsworth and Painswick, which were shaped by the growing cloth industry. Fast-flowing streams to provide power to fulling mills, the availability of **fuller's earth** – a clay-like material – to cleanse the wool and Cotswold Lion sheep to supply the fleece gave competitive advantage to such locations. By the 1700s there were around 170 active mills dotted throughout the Stroud valleys.

As the population of England rapidly grew, increasing demand for food, the **parliamentary enclosures** of the late eighteenth and early nineteenth centuries allowed farmers to consolidate their land into larger, single holdings and build farmhouses, often surrounded by trees to provide shelter and beautify their setting.

While wealthy landowners stood to gain from enclosure, some local people, whose forebears had enjoyed a range of rights to work the land under the old subsistence strip farm system, lost out. Many were thrown into poverty.

Industrialization and the modern era

After 1760 the pace of enclosure accelerated, effectively creating the patchwork landscape of fields bounded by hedgerows and dry stone walls that we see today. The Napoleonic Wars and growing urban populations in the expanding industrial cities increased the demand for food, leading to more land being enclosed.

It was during this period that canals emerged as an economic and reliable way to transport goods. The **Cotswold Canals** – the **Stroudwater Navigation**, completed in 1779, and the **Thames & Severn Canal** of 1789 – together linked the River Severn at Framilode to the River Thames near Lechlade, enabling goods (mainly coal) to be transported between the two great rivers. Meanwhile, in the southern Cotswolds, the **Kennet & Avon Canal**, completed in 1810, boasted its busiest wharf at Bradford-on-Avon, handling coal from the Somerset coalfields as well as other bulky goods like local cheeses.

By 1800 **cloth-making** had so expanded that large multi-storey stone buildings were erected to house the looms. Unpretentious terraced houses were built along the hillsides, while the mill-owners erected Georgian and Palladian townhouses.

By 1850 the industry was in decline, partly due to competition from the new steam-powered mills of northern England. The remainder of the nineteenth century was a period of serious rural decline, the result of which in the Cotswolds was a partly depopulated landscape, bypassed by the Industrial Revolution. It was this underdevelopment that so enchanted artists and designers such as William Morris and Ernest Gimson, forerunners of the **Arts and Crafts movement** that came to enrich the area with new skills and sensibilities.

1850s	1880s–1910s	1930s
Decline of Cotswolds manufacturing, as rural mills superseded by urban factories of northern England, and the region largely bypassed by railway-building.	Zenith of the Arts and Crafts movement, led by William Morris, which valued design and craft skills originating from rural traditions.	Emergence of motor cars spurs tourism growth across the Cotswolds, notably at Bourton-on-the-Water.

Agriculture was again revived by **World War I** as the nation turned to its own resources, no longer able to rely on imports. Mills that had once produced cloth were transformed into engineering works manufacturing agricultural equipment. Industry thrived as mechanization came to farming. Roads were surfaced, and with the coming of the motor coach came the first tourists. By the 1930s places like Bourton-on-the-Water were extremely popular tourism destinations, bringing much needed income to the Cotswolds.

World War II saw another awakening of the land, as agriculture was again asked to fill the national larder. Since that time the Cotswolds has continued to see many changes, reflecting national trends in population growth, further mechanization, greater personal affluence and increased mobility and leisure time.

This history section was researched and written by the Cotswolds Conservation Board (⦾ cotswoldsaonb.org.uk), with contributions by Sian Ellis.

1959	1998	2004
Publication of *Cider With Rosie* by Laurie Lee helps establish the image of a Cotswolds idyll.	Development of the long-standing Cotswold Way into a National Trail.	Establishment of the Cotswolds Conservation Board to oversee sustainable development in the Cotswolds Area of Outstanding Natural Beauty.

Books

The Cotswolds are awash with opportunities for further reading – indeed, in a region so famous for its beauty, it can be a relief to exercise a different set of muscles by reading about the place rather than relying solely on appearances. The few choices below are not intended to form a comprehensive bibliography. Rather, they are a selection of some easily accessible, broadly representative titles; those with the ★ symbol are particularly recommended.

Cotswold **memoirs** from the early and middle years of the last century abound, but most are now out of print. We haven't touched on the many widely known titles that mention the Cotswolds within a larger frame of reference, such as Bill Bryson's *Notes from a Small Island* or Simon Jenkins' *England's Thousand Best Churches*. Of the dozens of **walking guides** – both commercially produced books and smaller, often self-published pamphlets (which you'll find for sale in local tourist offices) – we've picked out a noteworthy handful. We've also included a small selection of books which could serve as an introduction to **Oxford**.

A word about purchasing: we've tried, here and there throughout the guide, to draw attention to **independent bookshops** that survive in towns and – sometimes – villages across the region. Although it's easy to buy books and maps online, or at chain bookstores in larger towns, try to hunt down a locally owned bookshop instead: these places offer a degree of expertise and local knowledge that can far outstrip the competition – not to mention stock that may include titles of local interest that are difficult or impossible to find elsewhere. See ⓦlocalbookshops.co.uk for listings.

OXFORD

James Attlee *Isolarion: a Different Oxford Journey.* Intriguing sidelong glance at Oxford constructed around a route along the busy, unpretentious Cowley Road: rather than medieval architecture and dreaming spires, this is more about pubs and street culture, woven around a meditation on the meaning of place.

Colin Dexter The *Inspector Morse* series. Traditional crime writing which brilliantly evokes the atmosphere and daily life of Oxford. Any of the thirteen novels in the series – from *Last Bus to Woodstock* (1975) through to *The Remorseful Day* (1999) – alongside a handful of short stories published separately, offers identifiable Oxford settings, as Dexter constructs superb plots centred on his famously prickly detective. The TV series (1987–2000), starring John Thaw, ran for 33 episodes, not all of which were based on Dexter's work.

★**Jan Morris** *Oxford.* A classic account of the city by one of Britain's most distinguished travel writers, first published in 1965. Also seek out her anthology of almost a thousand years of writing on the university, published as *The Oxford Book of Oxford*.

★**Philip Pullman** *Northern Lights; The Subtle Knife; The Amber Spyglass.* Hugely entertaining and thought-provoking novels, set partly in Oxford – though an Oxford from a slightly other world. Brought together as a trilogy under the title *His Dark Materials*.

Geoffrey Tyack *Oxford: an Architectural Guide.* Accomplished, broad-brush approach to understanding the city's architecture, in a chronological format from the eleventh century to the present day.

Jenny Woolf *The Mystery of Lewis Carroll: Understanding the Author of Alice in Wonderland.* Detailed biography of Carroll, delving deep into his private life in Oxford – and notably unearthing his previously undiscovered bank accounts. Fascinating stuff.

THE COTSWOLDS

FICTION

Jane Bailey *Tommy Glover's Sketch of Heaven.* Beautifully written evocation of Cotswold village life during World War II, as Kitty, an eight-year-old London evacuee, tries to adjust. Follow this with Bailey's *Mad Joy*, another wartime Cotswold yarn.

Jilly Cooper *Riders*. The first – and most famous – of the *Rutshire Chronicles* series of racy blockbuster paperbacks, partly set in the Cotswolds countryside (Cooper lives in Bisley, near Stroud). The plot is constructed around a feud between two showjumpers, but it doesn't really matter: as one reviewer neatly put it, "Sex and horses – who could ask for more?".

Katie Fforde *Flora's Lot*. One of the best-known novelists at work in the Cotswolds today, Fforde frequently draws on rural life to inform and enrich her unique brand of comic romantic fiction – not least in this light, charming tale of a townie who tries to rejuvenate a country antiques business.

HISTORY AND BACKGROUND

★**Jane Bingham** *The Cotswolds: A Cultural History*. Inspiring, fascinating analysis of what the Cotswolds has meant to insiders and outsiders alike over centuries, using analysis of literary and artistic sources – and a deep understanding of the place – to shed unusually clear light.

William Fiennes *The Music Room*. Beautifully written memoir, placing the author's childhood, growing up at the moated Jacobean mansion Broughton Castle near Banbury, alongside the family drama of his epileptic, increasingly violent brother. A moving, memorable read.

★**Laurie Lee** *Cider with Rosie*. The archetypal Cotswold tale, a memoir of the author's childhood in Slad, just north of Stroud, in the years after World War I – vivid, lyrical and utterly absorbing. Essential reading.

J.B. Priestley *English Journey*. Minor gem of early travel writing, as Priestley travels around England in 1933, beautifully describing Burford, the Slaughters, Bourton-on-the-Water and elsewhere and – even then – decrying the tide of tearooms and urban day-trippers.

★**Rob Rees** *The Cotswold Chef: a Year in Recipes and Landscapes*. Slim volume packed with seasonal recipes by Rees (see also p.28), a chef and tireless advocate for Cotswold food producers.

Ivor Smith *Memoirs of a Cotswold Vet*. Herriot-style account of life in a small veterinary practice over the

years 1972 to 2001, laced with humour, insight and colourful characters.

Ian Walthew *A Place in My Country: In Search of a Rural Dream*. An urban writer ups sticks to a Cotswold village. It's a familiar format, but this is a book which breaks the mould: the author not only deftly describes the country characters around him, but begins to empathize with them, as an image emerges of a rural economy decimated by wealthy outsiders and a rural culture relentlessly undermined by a national preoccupation with all things urban.

Rev. F.E. Witts *The Diary of a Cotswold Parson*. The day-to-day doings of Reverend Witts of Upper Slaughter covering the period 1820 to 1852, as he commutes daily to Gloucester and observes the building boom in Cheltenham.

NATURE AND WALKING GUIDES

Anthony Burton *Cotswold Way*. The official National Trail guide for the Cotswold Way, complete with Ordnance Survey mapping. Of the many other books on the path, the most diverting is Mark Richards' *The Cotswold Way*, the first-ever guide (published in 1973, when Richards was a full-time Cotswold farmer, and subsequently updated): its route descriptions are supplemented with a wealth of local knowledge and Wainwright-style pen-and-ink drawings.

Iain Main, Dave Pearce & Tim Hutton *Birds of the Cotswolds: a New Breeding Atlas*. Updated guide to the region's bird life, taking into account habitat changes since the 1980s and featuring maps and photos.

Nicholas Mander *Country Houses of the Cotswolds*. A lavishly illustrated account of more than thirty of the region's grandest houses, drawn from the archives of *Country Life* magazine.

Helen Peacocke *Paws Under the Table: 40 Dog-Friendly Pubs and Walks from Oxford to the Cotswolds*. Does what it says on the tin.

Tony Russell *The Cotswolds' Finest Gardens*. The former head forester at Westonbirt Arboretum – now a BBC gardening regular – describes sixty of the region's best publicly accessible gardens, alongside an array of colour photos.

Small print and index

Rough Guide credits

Editor: Tim Locke
Layout: Nikhil Agarwal
Cartography: Rajesh Chhibber
Picture editor: Michelle Bhatia
Proofreader: Stewart Wild
Managing editors: Mani Ramaswamy, Andy Turner
Assistant editor: Payal Sharotri
Production: Nicole Landau

Cover design: Nicole Newman, Rhiannon Furbear-Williams, Nikhil Agarwal
Photographer: Chloë Roberts
Editorial assistant: Rebecca Hallett
Senior pre-press designer: Dan May
Programme manager: Gareth Lowe
Publisher: Joanna Kirby
Publishing director: Georgina Dee

Publishing information

This second edition published June 2015 by
Rough Guides Ltd,
80 Strand, London WC2R 0RL
11, Community Centre, Panchsheel Park,
New Delhi 110017, India
Distributed by Penguin Random House
Penguin Books Ltd,
80 Strand, London WC2R 0RL
Penguin Group (USA)
345 Hudson Street, NY 10014, USA
Penguin Group (Australia)
250 Camberwell Road, Camberwell,
Victoria 3124, Australia
Penguin Group (NZ)
67 Apollo Drive, Mairangi Bay, Auckland 1310,
New Zealand
Penguin Group (South Africa)
Block D, Rosebank Office Park, 181 Jan Smuts Avenue,
Parktown North, Gauteng, South Africa 2193
Rough Guides is represented in Canada by Tourmaline
Editions Inc. 662 King Street West, Suite 304, Toronto,
Ontario M5V 1M7
Printed in Singapore
© Matthew Teller 2015

Maps © Rough Guides
Contains Ordnance Survey data © Crown copyright and
database rights 2014
No part of this book may be reproduced in any form
without permission from the publisher except for the
quotation of brief passages in reviews.
264pp includes index
A catalogue record for this book is available from the
British Library
ISBN: 978-1-40935-664-6
The publishers and authors have done their best to
ensure the accuracy and currency of all the information
in The Rough Guide to the Cotswolds, however, they
can accept no responsibility for any loss, injury, or
inconvenience sustained by any traveller as a result of
information or advice contained in the guide.
1 3 5 7 9 8 6 4 2

MIX
Paper from
responsible sources
FSC
www.fsc.org FSC™ C018179

Help us update

We've gone to a lot of effort to ensure that the second edition of **The Rough Guide to the Cotswolds** is accurate and up-to-date. However, things change – places get "discovered", opening hours are notoriously fickle, restaurants and rooms raise prices or lower standards. If you feel we've got it wrong or left something out, we'd like to know, and if you can remember the address, the price, the hours, the phone number, so much the better.

Please send your comments with the subject line "**Rough Guide the Cotswolds Update**" to mail@uk.roughguides.com. We'll credit all contributions and send a copy of the next edition (or any other Rough Guide if you prefer) for the very best emails.

Find more travel information, connect with fellow travellers and plan your trip on ⓦ roughguides.com.

ABOUT THE AUTHOR

Matthew Teller (⊕matthewteller.com) is a writer and journalist living on the Cotswold fringes. He writes for the BBC as well as newspapers and magazines in Britain and around the world, is a regular on Radio 4's From Our Own Correspondent and has written or contributed to many Rough Guides over the years. He blogs at QuiteAlone.com and tweets @matthewteller.

Acknowledgements

The **author** would like to thank all those throughout the Cotswolds who offered support and guidance with such generosity – PRs, press officers and visitor relations teams at museums, attractions, hotels and restaurants all round the region (forgive the general approach!); staff at TICs and VICs, who do a magnificent frontline job every day helping people make the most of this wonderful part of the world; and in particular, Nicola Greaves at the Cotswolds Conservation Board, Anne Bartlett, Charlie Hammond at Giffords, the wonder that is Tim Tarby-Donald of Visit Banbury, and Ian Weightman for helping to spread the news. At **Rough Guides**, huge thanks to my patient, knowledgeable editor Tim Locke for a splendid job tracking the details while never losing sight of the big picture, and to Natasha Foges and Mani Ramaswamy for getting the ball rolling.

Photo credits

All photos © Rough Guides except the following:
(Key: t-top; c-centre; b-bottom; l-left; r-right)

p.1 Robert Harding Picture Library/Adam Burton
p.2 Robert Harding Picture Library/Jose Moya
p.4 Robert Harding Picture Library/Adam Woolfitt (tr)
p.5 SuperStock/Jon Bower/Loop Images
p.9 Alamy Images/Andrew Baskott (tl); 4Corners/Richard Taylor (tr)
p.11 SFL Travel (t); Alamy Images/Heritage Image Partnership Ltd (b)
p.12 Robert Harding Picture Library/Ellen Rooney
p.13 Alamy Images/nagelestock.com (t); Corbis/Mike Kemp (c); Robert Harding Picture Library/Stuart Black (b)
p.14 Alamy Images/Bruce Cairns (t); travelibUK (c); Robert Harding Picture Library/Andrew Michael (b)
p.15 Getty Images/Ivan Vdovin/AWL Images (t); Corbis/Stephen Dorey (br)
p.16 Corbis/LatitudeStock (t); Dorling Kindersley/Tony Souter (b)
p.17 Alamy Images/eye35.pix (c); Dreamstime.com/Whiskybottle (b)
p.18 Alamy Images/David Stares (tr)
p.20 Alamy Images/David Gilbert (t)
pp.40–41 SuperStock/Cindy Stern/Loop Images
p.43 Corbis/Clive Nichols
p.59 Corbis/Alan Copson (t); Alamy Images/Adrian Sherratt (b)

pp.76–77 Corbis/Aflo
p.79 SuperStock/Travel Pictures Ltd
p.111 Dreamstime.com/Rose444
pp.118–119 Robert Harding Picture Library/Stuart Black
p.121 Robert Harding Picture Library/Eurasia (t); Alamy Images/foto-zone (b)
pp.134–135 Alamy Images/Les Ladbury
p.137 Heritage Motor Centre
pp.152–153 Corbis/2/Peter Adams/Ocean
p.155 Getty Images/Christopher Gallagher
p.167 Society of Antiquaries/Kelmscott Manor
pp.182–183 Alamy Images/Ian Mcilgorm
p.185 Alamy Images/Neil McAllister
pp.200–201 SuperStock/Jon Bower/Loop Images
p.203 Corbis/Jon Bower/Loop Images
p.221 SuperStock/Steve Vidler (t); Robert Harding Picture Library/Ian Dagnall (b)
p.243 Alamy Images/Holmes Garden Photos

Front cover & spine Arlington Row, Bibury © Getty Images/Fuste Raga
Back cover Gloucestershire countryside © AWL Images/Peter Adams (t); Sezincote House and Gardens © Joe Wainwright (bl); The Lygon Arms, Chipping Campden © Alamy Images/imageBROKER (br)

Index

Maps are marked in **grey**

Map symbols

The symbols below are used on maps throughout the book

▬▬▪	International boundary	@	Internet café/access	🏛	Abbey
▬▪	Province boundary	⊠	Post office	✂	Battle site
▬ ▬ ▬	Chapter division boundary	ⓘ	Information office	☆	Viewpoint
	Major road	♦	Museum	⊠	Public college access
	Minor road	⊞	Hospital	⸸	Church (regional maps)
	Motorway road	◆	Place of interest	⊤	Gardens
	Pedestrian road	⚓	Ferry/boat stop	▲	Mountain peak
	Railway	⌣	Bridge		Cliffs
	Ferry route	⊙	Statue		Wall
	Footpath	🝔	Waterfall		Church (town maps)
	River	🏛	Stately home		Building
✈	Airport	♯	Castle		Park
★	Bus/taxi	∴	Ruin		Area of Outstanding Natural Beauty (AONB)
P	Parking	🗼	Lighthouse		

Contains Ordnance Survey data
© Crown copyright and database right 2014

Listings key

■ Accommodation

● Restaurants/cafés

A ROUGH GUIDE TO
ROUGH GUIDES

Published in 1982, the first Rough Guide – to Greece – was a student scheme that became a publishing phenomenon. Mark Ellingham, a recent graduate in English from Bristol University, had been travelling in Greece the previous summer and couldn't find the right guidebook. With a small group of friends he wrote his own guide, combining a highly contemporary, journalistic style with a thoroughly practical approach to travellers' needs.

The immediate success of the book spawned a series that rapidly covered dozens of destinations. And, in addition to impecunious backpackers, Rough Guides soon acquired a much broader and older readership that relished the guides' wit and inquisitiveness as much as their enthusiastic, critical approach and value-for-money ethos.

These days, Rough Guides feature recommendations from shoestring to luxury and cover more than 120 destinations around the globe. Our ever-growing team of authors and photographers is spread all over the world, particularly in Europe, the US and Australia.

Rough Guides now number around 200 titles, including Pocket city guides, inspirational coffee-table books and comprehensive country and regional titles, plus technology guides from iPods to Android. As well as print books, we publish groundbreaking ebooks for every major digital device.

Visit ⓦ roughguides.com to see our latest publications.